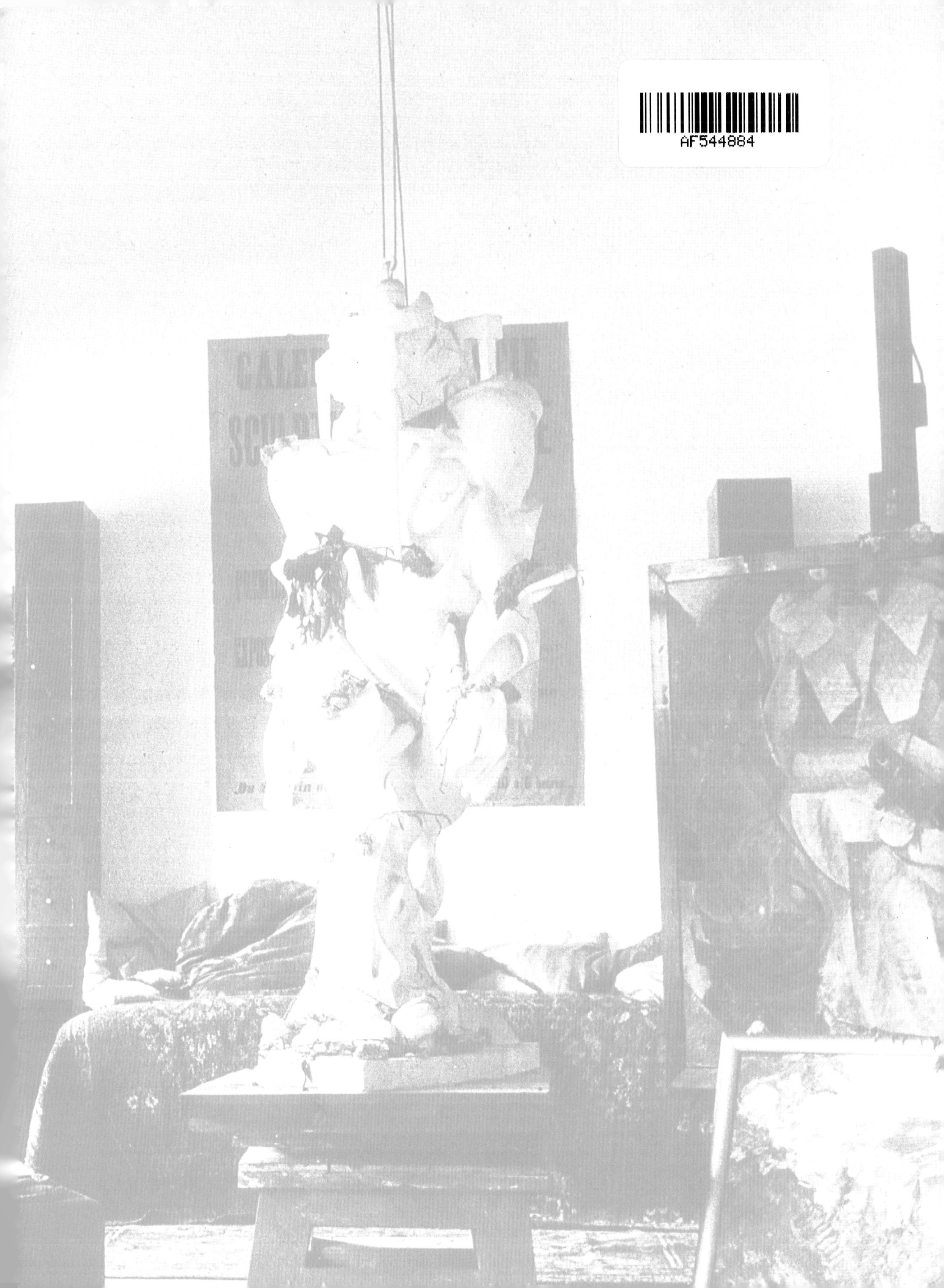

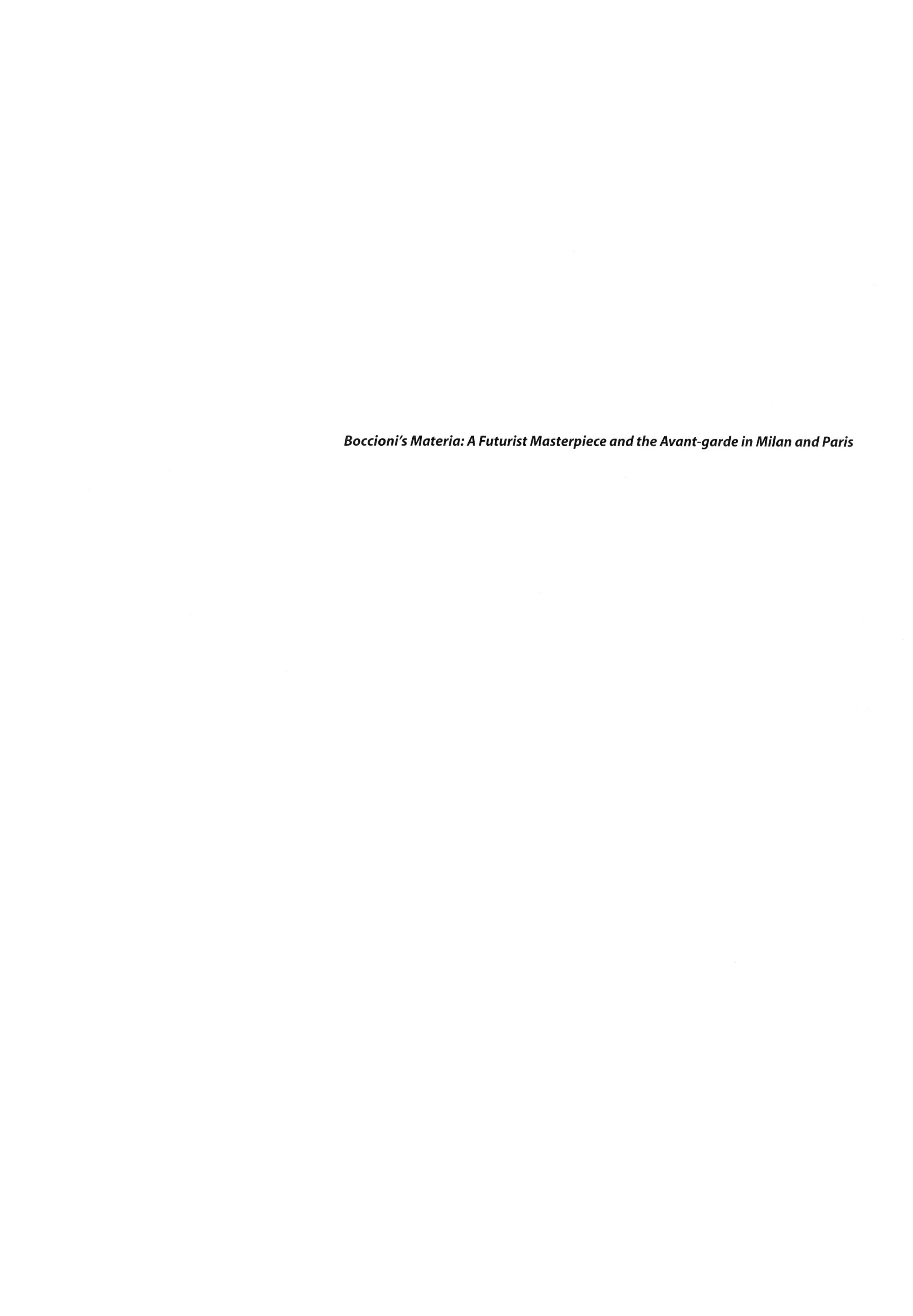

Boccioni's Materia: A Futurist Masterpiece and the Avant-garde in Milan and Paris

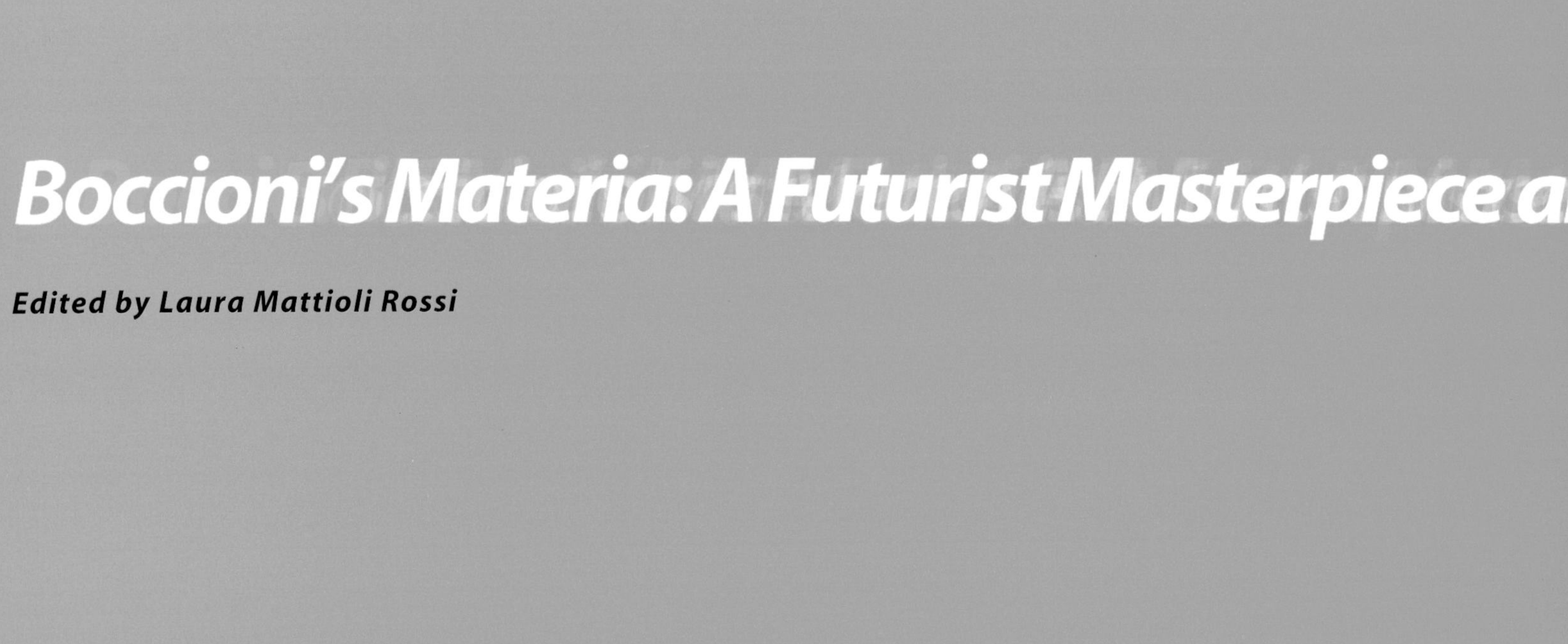

Boccioni's Materia: A Futurist Masterpiece ar

Edited by Laura Mattioli Rossi

Guggenheim MUSEUM

the Avant-garde in Milan and Paris

Published on the occasion of the exhibition
Boccioni's Materia: A Futurist Masterpiece and the Avant-garde in Milan and Paris

Organized by Laura Mattioli Rossi
with Vivien Greene

Solomon R. Guggenheim Museum, New York
February 6–May 9, 2004

ISBN 0-89207-303-9 (hardcover)
ISBN 0-89207-304-7 (softcover)

Guggenheim Museum Publications
1071 Fifth Avenue
New York, New York 10128

Hardcover edition available through
D.A.P./Distributed Art Publishers
155 Sixth Avenue, 2nd floor
New York, New York 10013
Tel: (212) 627-1999; Fax: (212) 627-9484

Distributed outside the United States and Canada by Thames & Hudson, Ltd., London

Design: Eileen Boxer / BoxerDesign
Production: Tracy Hennige, Melissa Secondino
Editorial: Meghan Dailey, Stephen Hoban, Edward Weisberger

Printed in England by Balding + Mansell

Cover: Self-portrait of Umberto Boccioni, seated in front of *Materia*, 1913 (detail of fig. 59.7)

Contents

This exhibition is supported by

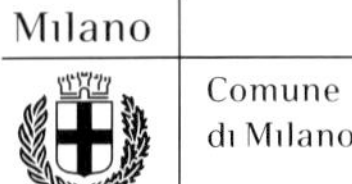

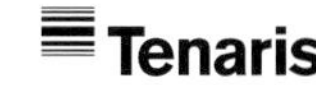

Additional support is provided by the Leadership Committee for *Materia*, Maurice Kanbar, and the Italian Cultural Institute.

The museum thanks the Italian Ministry of Foreign Affairs for its patronage and support.

Transportation assistance provided by

Alitalia

Leadership Committee for *Materia*

His Excellency Sergio Vento,
The Ambassador of the Republic of Italy to the United States, *Honorary Chair*

Paolo and Betsy Bianco

Patti Cadby Birch

Daniele D. Bodini

Princess Giulia Borghese

Nicola Bulgari

Tomaso Cenci and Isabella Ferretti Cenci

Andrea and Claire Danese

Isabella Del Frate Rayburn

Mario Draghi

Peter and Maria Wirth

The Comune di Milano is honored to be involved in this important cultural event at the Solomon R. Guggenheim Museum.

The works of art exhibited in *Boccioni's Materia: A Futurist Masterpiece and the Avant-garde in Milan and Paris* testify to a historically unique artistic period in our country and our city, and to the important influences on the principal European cultural movements of those years. They speak of the relationship between Umberto Boccioni's work and the city of Milan during a time of profound political and economic change in Italy and Europe. Of no lesser importance were those social and urban transformations that came to define the identity of Milan as a twentieth-century modern capital and leading industrial center in Italy.

This exhibition retraces the development of Boccioni's creativity and is enriched by important artworks that he was able to study in Paris. For the first time since 1916, it will be possible to view together three portraits of the artist's mother painted in 1912.

Today, the Civiche Raccolte d'Arte of Milan own many of the best works by Boccioni, and they are delighted to introduce several of the most important examples to an American audience. The exhibition presents these masterpieces in a new and original way that enhances interpretations.

In addition, one of the main goals of our administration is the opening of a major museum dedicated to twentieth-century art, to be established in the Arengario building, one of Milan's most significant twentieth-century architectural landmarks.

The Comune di Milano would like to thank all those who have collaborated on this exhibition, which will certainly be critical toward the knowledge of Milanese Futurism and its links to other avant-gardes. It is further hoped that this will signal the beginning of a relationship between the Guggenheim and Milanese institutions, in the wake of a renewed and solid history of cultural and economic exchanges between the cities of Milan and New York.

SALVATORE CARRUBBA
Commissioner for Culture, Museums
and International Relations

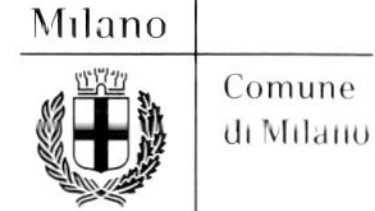

GABRIELE ALBERTINI
Mayor of Milan

SALVATORE CARRUBBA
Commissioner for Culture, Museums
and International Relations

ALESSANDRA MOTTOLA MOLFINO
General Director for Culture

ERMANNO A. ARSLAN
Director, Civiche Raccolte d'Arte of Milan

ANDREA VENTO
Director of International Relations

Preface

The Guggenheim Museum has long been dedicated to the study and presentation of twentieth-century Italian art. While our particular bond with Italy is no doubt fostered by the Solomon R. Guggenheim Foundation's presence in Venice with the Peggy Guggenheim Collection, even on our own shores Italian art has played a prominent role in the museum's programming, which in past decades has included exhibitions ranging from Futurism to postwar Italian culture to contemporary video installations. Indeed, the Guggenheim held its first exhibition on Italian Futurism in New York in 1973–74 with *Futurism: A Modern Focus, The Lydia and Harry Lewis Winston Collection*, organized at a time when Futurism was little recognized outside of Italy and a small circle of specialists. With *Boccioni's Materia: A Futurist Masterpiece and the Avant-garde in Milan and Paris*, scholarly investigations begun then are taken further, as Futurism is considered within the greater context of European modernism.

The exhibition traces the evolution of a single artist, Umberto Boccioni, through the creation of his pivotal Futurist masterpiece, *Materia*, painted in 1912 in Milan, at a time when the Lombardy capital was quickly transforming into a dynamic and modern city. It further examines the important Futurist activities that took place in Milan and underscores Boccioni's development of key Futurist thematics in his art. Through his exploration of color, the sculptural qualities of form, the multidimensionality of space, and the problematics pertaining to movement, he crystallized his ideas regarding the dynamism of matter and the fusion of interior and exterior spaces—notions integral to the Futurists' synthetic conceptualization of motion, simultaneity, and spatial relationships. But, rather than simply present the artist's production as an independent occurrence, *Boccioni's Materia* examines it in relation to works by his European contemporaries—Georges Braque, Robert Delaunay, Marcel Duchamp, Albert Gleizes, Juan Gris, Fernand Léger, and Pablo Picasso—whose Cubism was at the center of the art debate to which Boccioni especially responded. Many of these artists are well represented in the Guggenheim's core collection, and we have had the fortuitous privilege to include seminal paintings from our holdings on this occasion. The exhibition allows for a view of Boccioni's dynamic representations vis-à-vis related paintings created in the same period. Such juxtapositions permit a singular look at the synchronicities and differences between some of the most influential artistic figures of the early twentieth century.

Usually, the painting *Materia* resides at the Peggy Guggenheim Collection in Venice, where it is on long-term loan to that institution as part of the Gianni Mattioli Collection. And, indeed, the discussions that took place in front of this complex work with Dr. Laura Mattioli Rossi, a noted art historian and the daughter of the collector, led to the inception of this project. I extend our deepest thanks to Laura Mattioli Rossi for her unstinting dedication to this exhibition and the ambitious publication accompanying it, which are the result of years of intensive research. We also thank Vivien Greene, Associate Curator, for her crucial role in bringing the project successfully to fruition. The publication would not have been possible without the ground-breaking contributions of the authors, to each of whom I extend our gratitude.

Boccioni's Materia encompasses a small but tremendously elite group of works. Loans of paintings, sculptures, and drawings of such high quality are only possible with the cooperation and collaboration of lenders both public and private. I must acknowledge here our profound thanks for their generosity.

We are grateful to the Italian Ministry of Foreign Affairs for its patronage and support of this project from its nascent stages. At the Ministry, I extend our thanks to Ambassador Giuseppe Baldocci, Secretary General, and to the Department of Cultural Promotion and Cooperation, in particular to Ambassador Francesco Aloisi de Larderel, Director General; Lucio Alberto Savoia, Vice Director General; Elisabetta Kelescian, Coordinator; and Francesco De Luigi, Capo Ufficio II. In addition, we are deeply appreciative of His Excellency Sergio Vento, Ambassador of the Republic of Italy to the United States, whose counsel and input have been critical to the project's realization. I also thank Giuliano Urbani, the Italian Minister of Culture, and Alain Elkann, advisor to the Minister, for their friendship and support of the Guggenheim's Italian programs.

The realization of *Boccioni's Materia*, ultimately, is due to the philanthropic support of our sponsors. We are extremely grateful to the Comune di Milano, and in particular to Gabriele Albertini, Mayor of Milan; Salvatore Carrubba, Commissioner for Culture, Museums and International Relations; Alessandra Mottola Molfino, General Director for Culture; Ermanno A. Arslan, Director, Civiche Raccolte d'Arte of Milan; and Andrea Vento, Director of International Relations. They immediately understood the importance of this exhibition and assisted us not only financially but also by granting many key loans from Milan's important civic collections and museums, one of the main repositories of the works of the city's adoptive son. We are also grateful to Tenaris for their generous and enthusiastic support of this exhibition and extend our special thanks to Paolo Rocca, Chairman and CEO. We also thank Maurice Kanbar and the Italian Cultural Institute, particularly its newly appointed Director, Claudio Angelini, for their help. Our gratitude goes as well to Alitalia for the essential transport services they provided. Furthermore, I salute and thank all the members of our Leadership Committee for *Materia*, whose vision in supporting this exhibition was pivotal for its presentation to the Guggenheim's international public.

THOMAS KRENS
Director, The Solomon R. Guggenheim Foundation

Acknowledgments

Every exhibition, great or small, comes to fruition due to the efforts, enthusiasm, and support of an extensive number of remarkable people, many of whom work together as a team, even across oceans. We are deeply indebted to everyone who contributed in some way to realize *Boccioni's Materia: A Futurist Masterpiece and the Avant-garde in Milan and Paris*.

This exhibition emerged pursuant to conversations with Thomas Krens, Director, Lisa Dennison, Chief Curator and Deputy Director, and Philip Rylands, Director of the Peggy Guggenheim Collection, Venice. We are grateful to them for their faith in this project and for the support they have given us over the past four years.

Boccioni's Materia could not have been realized were it not for the instrumental role played by Karole Vail, Assistant Curator. We must express our deepest thanks for her unflagging dedication to the successful realization of all aspects of this exhibition, from the grace and diplomacy she demonstrated in the negotiation of loans to the care she took with the numerous and multifaceted issues associated with the completion of this catalogue. We are also thankful to Beatriz Zengotitabengoa, former Curatorial Assistant, who did much important groundwork in the early stages of the exhibition, and to Nat Trotman, Curatorial Assistant, who came in at a crucial time to assist with the final stages of this exhibition. In Milan, we gratefully recognize the support of Barbara Geremia, Assistant Curator to the Mattioli Collection. Pepi Marchetti Franchi, Executive Associate to the Director, deserves a very special acknowledgment for her commitment to this project and for her tireless efforts to secure funding at a difficult time.

The loans we have been granted for this exhibition are extraordinary and we are profoundly appreciative to all of our lenders, without whom we could not have achieved our goals. We wish to thank Luca Barilla; Prof. Dr. Reinhold Baumstark, General Director, Dr. Carla Schulz-Hoffmann, Curator, and Dr. Bernhart Schwenk, Curator of Contemporary Art, Bayerische Staatsgemäldesammlungen, Munich; Ernst Beyeler and Dr. Markus Bruderlin, Chief Curator, Fondation Beyeler, Riehen/Basel; Malcolm Rogers, Ann and Graham Gund Director, Frederick Ilchman, Assistant Curator of Paintings, and Marietta Cambareri, Curator of Decorative Arts and Sculpture, Art of Europe, Boston Museum of Fine Arts; James N. Wood, Director, and Daniel Schulman, Associate Curator of Modern and Contemporary Art, The Art Institute of Chicago; Dr. Maria Teresa Fiorio, Superintendent for the Historical, Artistic, and Demo-ethno-anthropological Heritage of Milan and Western Lombardy; Dr. Salvatore Carrubba, Commissioner for Culture, Museums and International Relations, and Dr. Alessandra Mottola Molfino, General Director for Culture, Comune di Milan; Dr. Ermanno A. Arslan, Director, Dr. Arnalda Dallaj, Curator, Gabinetto dei Disegni, and Dr. Marina Pugliese, Curator, Museo d'Arte Contemporanea, Civiche Raccolte d'Arte of Milan; Roberta Cremoncini, Director, Alexandra Noble, Curator, Christopher Adams, Assistant Curator, and Lucy Bestwick, Exhibitions Assistant, Estorick Collection, London; Dr. Gabriele Mazzotta, President, Raffaella Resch, and Anna Chiara Ferrero, Fondazione Antonio Mazzotta; Massimo Di Carlo, Director, and Laura Lorenzoni, Galleria dello Scudo, Verona; Dr. Bianca Alessandra Pinto, Director, Galleria Nazionale d'Arte Moderna; Dr. Mario Serio, Director General for Historical, Artistic, and Demo-ethno-anthropological Heritage of Rome; Danila Marsure Rosso, Museo Medardo Rosso, Barzio, Italy; Glenn Lowry, Director, Kirk Varnedoe, the late Chief Curator, John Elderfield, Chief Curator, Gary Garrels, Chief Curator of Drawings, and Cora Rosevear, Associate Curator, The Museum of Modern Art, New York; Anne d'Harnoncourt, The George D. Widener Director and CEO, Ann Temkin, former Muriel and Philip Curator of Twentieth-Century Art, and Michael R. Taylor, Associate Curator of Modern and Contemporary Art, Philadelphia Museum of Art; the late Gabriella Targetti Russoli and Sandra Russoli, Milan; Dr. Ulrich Krempel, Director, Dr. Dietmar Elger, Dr. Norbert Nobls, and Francesca Talpo, Assistant Curator, Sprengel Museum Hannover; Prof. Peter-Klaus Schuster, Director, and Dr. Roland März, Curator, Neue Nationalgalerie, Staatliche Museen zu Berlin; Sir Nicholas Serota, Director, and Susan Liddell, Senior Curator, Collections Division, Tate Modern, London; Dr. Sabine Fehlemann, Director, and Brigitte Müller, Registrar, Von der Heydt-Museum, Wuppertal, Germany; Dr. Antonello Manuli, Milan; and Dr. Francesco Micheli, Milan. Their ongoing collaboration was essential to the realization of this exhibition, and we are grateful to them for their commitment on our behalf. We thank those collectors who wish to remain anonymous.

For all their efforts, special thanks are owed to Giuliano Urbani, Minister of Culture; His Excellency Sergio Vento, the Ambassador of the Republic of Italy to the United States; Gabriele Albertini, Mayor of the Comune di Milano; Andrea Vento, Director of International Relations, Comune di Milano; Maurizia Garzia and Alessandra Bognetti, International Relations Department, Comune di Milano; Claudio Angelini and Tina Cervone, Italian Cultural Institute, New York; Eugenio Magnani, Director, Italian Government Tourist Board; and Pasquale Ferrara, Cultural Attaché, and Armando Varricchio, Commercial Attaché, at the Italian Embassy in Washington, D.C. We are also most grateful to Giulio Libutti, Vice President for North America, and Marta Marie Lotti, Director, Press and Public Relations, Alitalia; as well as to Danilo Maitti, Managing Director, Arteria.

In addition, colleagues at institutions, universities, archives, and libraries in the United States and Europe provided important support and precious assistance during the extensive research that went into this exhibition. We wish to thank Wim de Wit, Head, Special Collections and Visual Resources, and Curator of Architectural Drawings, Lora Chin, Assistant Registrar, Beverly Faison, Staff Assistant, and Ted Walbye, Special Collections Assistant, Research Library, The Getty Research Institute; Dr. Gabriella Belli, Director, Paola Pettenella, Twentieth-Century Archivist, Francesca Velardita, Curator of Historical Archives, Museo di Arte Moderna e Contemporanea di Trento e Rovereto; Robert Rosenblum, Stephen and Nan Swid Curator of Twentieth-Century Art, Carmen Gimenez, Curator of Twentieth-Century Art, Susan Davidson, Curator, and Tracey Bashkoff, Associate Curator, Solomon R. Guggenheim Museum; Silvana Pasquin, MöbelTransport Chiasso; Sandra Botti; Alberta Margutti; Zaira Fallacara; Alessandra Montana; Dr. Riccardo Cebulli; Professor Marisa Dalai Emiliani, President of the Scientific-Historical-Artistic Studies, University of Rome, for her studies on the spatial and perspective aspects of *Materia*; Dr. Sergio Rebora, Giuseppe Dal Pian, Licia Dal Pian Boccioni, Fiorenzo Mancini, Dr. Angelo, and Silvia Calmarini; and Professor Antonello Negri and Dr. Leonardo Capano, Accademia Albertina Turin.

We do indeed feel privileged to have this elegant catalogue designed by Eileen Boxer. Her sensitivity to the material is manifest in her aesthetic conception. We are indebted to the authors who contributed to this catalogue. Each has brought to light new and significant material that will certainly expand the current perspective on Boccioni and Futurism. It is with great pleasure that we thank Dr. Emily Braun for her astute contextualization of Boccioni's oeuvre within the Parisian avant-garde; Dr. Giovanna Ginex for her careful study of Boccioni and photography, the result of an arduous search to recuperate and, for the first time, properly identify and date the multitude of prints relating to Boccioni's artistic production; Dr. Flavio Fergonzi, for his insightful examination of Boccioni and Bergson; Dr. Fausto Petrella for expanding the discourse on Boccioni and psychology; and Dr. Gianluca Poldi for his expert study of Boccioni's pigment application, which has shed new light on this artist's technique. Anna Schultz, an exceptional intern, contributed significant support not only to the organization and research surrounding this exhibition, but also compiled the selected bibliography herein. Emily Braun deserves an additional note of recognition for her precious advice during the entire course of our research and her careful and patient editorial reading of the translations.

In our admirable Publications Department we must acknowledge Edward Weisberger, Editor, for his attention to and patience with myriad issues and to Melissa Secondino, Assistant Production Manager, for tending to all matters related to the ideal reproduction of the illustrations included herein. Moreover, the translations so thoughtfully executed by Stephen Sartarelli are to be commended. The production of an ambitious book requires the masterful skills of many people. Thus, we extend our thanks to Anthony Calnek, Deputy Director of Publications and Communications, Elizabeth Levy, Director of Publications, Elizabeth Franzen, Managing Editor, Meghan Dailey, Associate Editor, Stephen Hoban, Editorial Assistant, and Tracy Hennige, Production Assistant, for expertly seeing the catalogue through to fruition. David M. Heald, Director of Photographic Services and Chief Photographer, Ellen Labenski, former Assistant Photographer, and Kim Bush, Manager of Photography and Permissions, deserve praise for resolving reproduction problems. We also thank Vittorio Calore and Luciano Pollini for the generous use of their photographs and personal archives, as well as Jacopo Cima, who provided many photographs.

An exhibition of such eminent, but also fragile, paintings, sculptures, and works on paper could only arrive safely at its destination and be shown to its best advantage because of the care taken by the various registrarial, conservation, art services, and preparation staffs. We have been lucky to have the constant vigilance of several Guggenheim Museum registrars, who arranged for the safe transport of this exhibition: Rosa Berland, Registar, admirably handled the complexities surrounding each loan and maintained a calm demeanor in the face of many a challenge. We must also acknowledge Meryl Cohen, Director of Registration and Art Services, Elissa Myerowitz, former Registrar, Jody Myers, Associate Registrar for Outgoing Loans, and Ted Mann, Assistant Registrar for Collections and Outgoing Loans, who all had a hand in the often convoluted process of securing our loans. Paul Schwartzbaum, Chief Conservator; Gillian McMillan, Senior Conservator; Nora Nagy, Sculpture Conservator; Julie Barten, Conservator, Exhibitions and Administration; and Mara Guglielmi, Paper Conservator, all assisted in the careful review of each piece's condition and we are grateful for their input.

The physical appearance of an exhibition is dependent on appropriate design and expert installation. *Boccioni's Materia* benefits from a thoughtful plan, subtly implemented by an incredible group of colleagues. For this beautiful presentation, we wish to thank Ana Luisa Leite, Manager of Exhibition Design, Barry Hylton, Senior Exhibition Technician, Michael Sarff, Construction Manager, Peter Read, Manager of Exhibition and Fabrication Design, MaryAnn Hoag, Chief Lighting Designer, Jeff Clemens, Associate Preparator, and Liz Jaff, Associate Preparator for Paper. We also gratefully acknowledge the fine graphic treatment realized by Marcia Fardella, Chief Graphic Designer, and Concetta Pereira, Production Coordinator. We are indebted to the special expertise of Paul Kuranko, Media Arts Specialist, who was responsible for the design and realization of the touchscreen component of the exhibition.

Naturally, many more were instrumental to *Boccioni's Materia* success, and we offer our heartfelt appreciation to Kendall Hubert, Director of Corporate Development; Hillary Strong, Manager of Corporate Sponsorship; Scott Wixon, Manager of Art Services and Preparations; Lynn Underwood, Director of Information Integration and Management; Marc Steglitz, Deputy Director of Finance and Operations; Marion Kahan, Exhibition Program Manager, who expertly intervened at key moments to help with contractual matters; Gail Scovell, General Counsel; Brendan Connell, Assistant Legal Counsel; Stefanie Roth, Assistant General Counsel; and Christina Kallergis, Financial Analyst. In addition, we must thank our colleagues at the Peggy Guggenheim Collection, who were an important link to Italy and patiently helped navigate many situations across the Atlantic. We were fortunate to also have the support of a wonderful group of curatorial interns over the past years, whose role on such a project cannot be underestimated. We thank Ilaria Dupré, who worked tirelessly on this exhibition for an extensive time and made herself an invaluable member of our curatorial team. We are also appreciative of the efforts of Veronique Colaprete, Francesca Grassi, Lauren Rosebush, and Catharina Van Mossevelde.

LAURA MATTIOLI ROSSI
Guest Curator

VIVIEN GREENE
Associate Curator

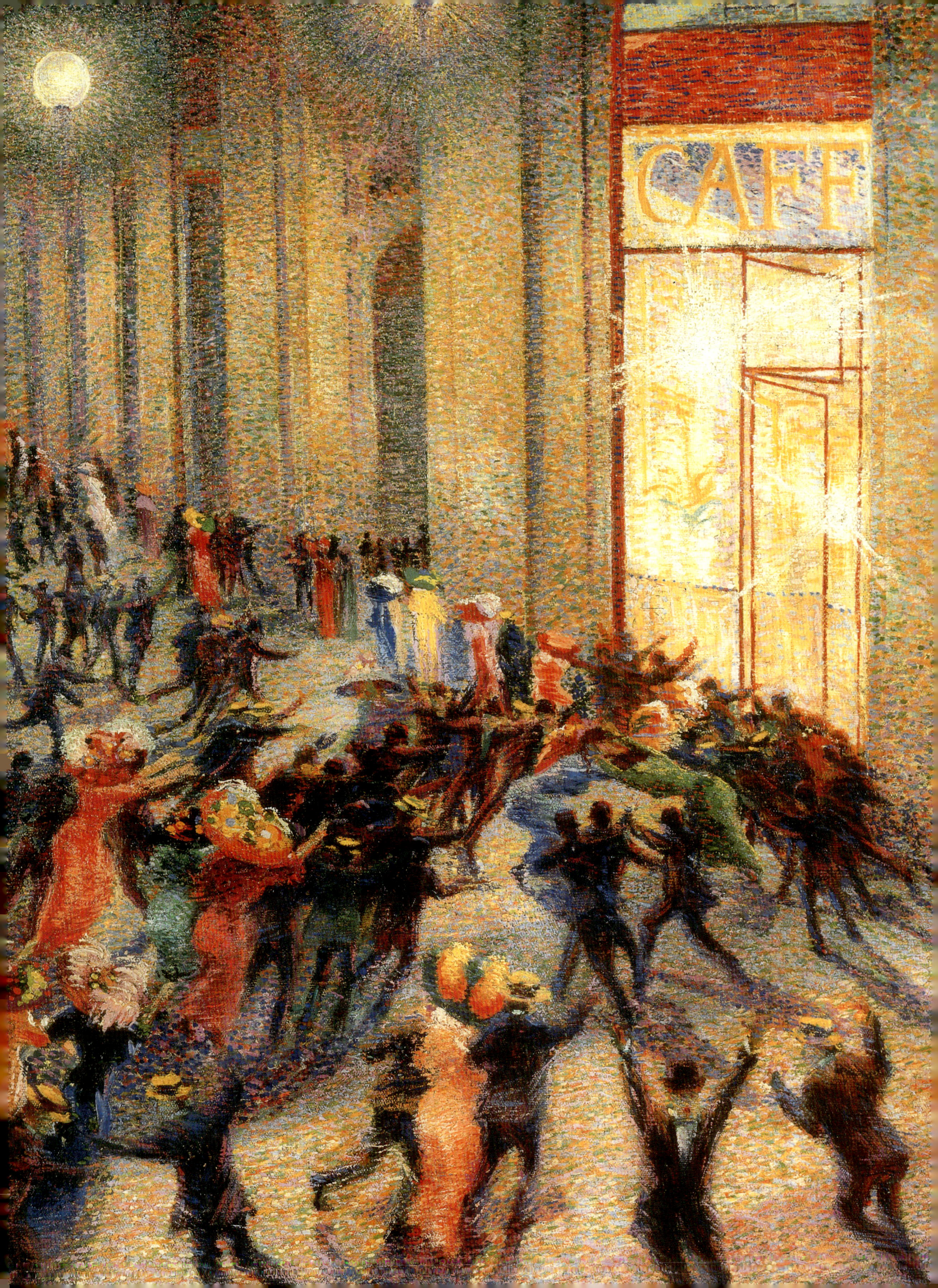
CAFF

Vulgarians at the Gate

EMILY BRAUN

They call the Futurists madmen, charlatans, clowns, rascals, bluffeurs, obfuscators, and even worse.

But why, they ask, why do they go on stage to impose their ideas about art on everyone else? Here again the puritans forget many things. The theater is not a bordello, a casino or a place of infamy. . . . In many different ways the theater has taken the place of the church of old. Modern men who want to be in touch with the multitude do well to avail themselves of the modern temple.

—GIOVANNI PAPINI[1]

In traditional art histories, Italian Futurism has been perceived as a poor second cousin of French Cubism, a minor if scrappy player in the development of modernist abstraction. To be sure, several of the key Futurists, led by Umberto Boccioni, derived their mature style from the Cubist decomposition of form and materialization of space. The Parisian champions of Cubism were quick to point out the Futurists' indebtedness, while also denigrating their efforts as a "popular, flashy art."[2] Much of the public sparring between sides came down to a matter of national pride and chauvinism. But as T. S. Eliot observed, bad poets imitate, good poets steal. The Futurists usurped the Cubist vocabulary of form and used it to entirely different ends, as reflected in the names of the movements themselves: "Cubism" stood for a revolutionary style in art; "Futurism" proclaimed a revolutionary style of life. More exactly, much to the chagrin of the Parisian art world, Futurism signaled a new means of packaging and promoting the creative endeavor, one that blurred the lines between avant-gardism and public relations. It was precisely the extrapictorial interests of Futurism—its embrace of commodity culture, in contrast to the "pure painting" of the Cubist enterprise—that led to consternation on both sides of the critical discourse. The stand-off between Cubism and Futurism had as much to do with accusations of plagiarism as it did with differing conceptions of modernism/modernity. What was the public role of art? How was the artist to engage with modern life and with a new audience, that of the masses? The Cubists flirted with these questions but remained on the side of fine art when they formulated the production and reception of their works. The Futurists crossed the line into spectacle, not only in their behavior but also within the frame of their images.

Any account of the relationship between the two movements is fraught with problems of definition: whose Cubism and whose Futurism? By 1910, a strict division was established between Georges Braque and Pablo Picasso (the so-called private Cubists) on one side and the Salon Cubists (public Cubists) on the other. The history of Cubism has been written according to a hierarchy of taste reinforced by dealers as well as scholars: Picasso and Braque are followed by Fernand Léger, Juan Gris, and Robert Delaunay (notably, their work is closest to that of the Futurists), while Albert Gleizes, Jean Metzinger, and Henri Le Fauconnier come across as pale imitations of the real thing, "jackdaws in peacocks' feathers," as Guillaume Apollinaire initially snubbed them.[3] Significantly, scholarship on the "lesser" Cubists has focused on ideological content, as if to fill in for the lack of pictorial achievements that was already recognized in their own time. A qualitative difference also separates Braque from Picasso despite their "unique creative dialogue."[4] In the race toward Cubism, the slow and steady Braque occasionally pulls ahead, but in this fable the hare wins anyway. The historiography of Cubism is first and foremost a study of Picasso's inventions and intentions, whether the approaches are biographical, formalist, sociocultural, or semiotic. Recent studies claim that the true achievements of Cubism lie in collage, where the heterogeneity of means and refusal of traditional trompe-l'oeil illusionism make plain the conventions of representation. Picasso's position becomes even more privileged since it is his work alone that fully realizes the linguistic dimension of visual signs.[5] The Futurists were keenly aware of the distinctions, idolizing Picasso even as they pursued an agenda that placed them, like all the rest, among the "vulgarizers" of Cubism, those whom Gertrude Stein dubbed "the earthquake school."[6]

For its part, Futurism was not a monolithic entity; dominated by the authoritative figure of F. T. Marinetti, it was a literary and

Facing page
Detail of Umberto Boccioni, *Riot in the Galleria*, 1910 (fig. 5)

political movement first and secondarily a style in art. Marinetti gave birth to Futurism on February 20, 1909, in a feat of autogenesis witnessed publicly on the front cultural page of the Parisian daily *Le Figaro*. In "The Founding and Manifesto of Futurism," he disavowed his enervated past as an ivory-tower Symbolist poet and announced the creation of a new aesthetic, based—like the manifesto itself—on provocation and performance. It is fair to say that Marinetti *is* Futurism and, despite periodic internal rebellions, the movement remained his concept and under his directive until his death in 1944. The challenge led by the Florentine Futurists Giovanni Papini and Ardengo Soffici in the years 1913–15, for example, was less an alternate program than a rebellion against the personal style and hucksterism of the Milanese impresario. All the more shocking that not one English-language biography of Marinetti exists. Fashioning himself as a human dynamo or the "caffeine of Europe," he directed the Futurists' energies into music, theater, architecture, the applied arts, graphic design, fashion, cinema, and radio. With dozens of individual practitioners in a variety of fields, Futurism can only be taken whole as an interdisciplinary movement united by a radical nationalist program. By contrast, Cubism never articulated an activist sociopolitical agenda and was notably lacking in theoretical texts by its main protagonists, Braque and Picasso. And whereas the identity of Cubism as a dominant avant-garde practice waned with World War I, Futurism continued through the 1920s and 1930s, transformed but still innovative and activist.

Within the fine arts, Futurism was characterized by diverse approaches to the representation of modernity. Soffici was one of Cubism's most prescient critics on either side of the Alps, and his insistence on the autonomous constructive laws of painting was far removed from the narrative interests and mimetic style pursued by his compatriots. Boccioni, Carlo Carrà, and Gino Severini were directly influenced by Cubism, but Giacomo Balla and Luigi Russolo looked to a completely different model: the chronophotography of Etienne-Jules Marey. Registering the diagrammatic trajectory of objects in motion, Marey's photographs also eliminated traditional chiaroscuro and perspective, resulting in a radically flattened pictorial space that had little to do with Cubist scaffolding. (Contemporaneous with Balla, Marcel Duchamp used Marey's photographs to distance himself from Cubism, and from painting for that matter.)[7] Balla did not accompany the younger Futurists, Boccioni and Carrà, on their studio visits to Paris in October 1911 and was conspicuously absent from the debut Futurist exhibition, *Les Peintres futuristes italiens*, that took place February 5–24, 1912, at Galerie Bernheim-Jeune.[8] The French critics' rebuffs to Futurism and the ensuing blood feuds between French and Italian avant-gardes did not embroil him. Categorizing Futurist painting wholly as an offshoot of Cubism does a double disservice, given that Boccioni, Carrà, and Severini—the three "Cubist" Futurists—were no longer part of Futurism by 1916. Boccioni had died, and Carrà and Severini, as well as Soffici, had broken ranks with Futurism, leading a wartime "return to order" by promoting a classicizing figurative style. It was left to Balla to develop a Futurist language of pure abstraction and realize the "Futurist reconstruction of the universe" (to borrow the title of a manifesto he wrote with Fortunato Depero) in fashion, decorative arts, and interior design.[9] In the period between World Wars I and II, Balla and his protégés Depero and Enrico Prampolini joined Marinetti in leading the second national and international phase of Futurism.

The extrapictorial interests of Futurism imbued the imagery and style of its painting and sculpture, relegating the Italians to the sidelines of art history written according to a formalist modernist narrative.[10] Although the Museum of Modern Art in New York owns more important Futurist paintings than any other public institution in the world, it has organized only one Futurist exhibition and that was over forty years ago. With the exceptions of Boccioni and Severini, no Futurists have been the subject of monographic exhibitions organized by American institutions, and the lack of a Balla retrospective has reinforced the standard interpretation of Futurism as having been a mere derivative of Cubism.[11] In any event, the interpretative templates used for museum shows are inadequate to represent the Futurist movement in its varied dimensions. That the second phase of Futurism, with its numerous artists and activities, remains virtually unknown outside Italy is a result of the erroneous perception that Italy was a cultural backwater under Benito Mussolini.[12] It is no coincidence that the revisionist studies of Futurism over the last decade have taken place, with few exceptions, outside of art history and from an interdisciplinary approach. In the fields of comparative literature, political and cultural history, and gender studies, Futurism has come into its own as the first modernist avant-garde, if by avant-garde we mean a deliberate attack on high culture as an autonomous sphere removed from everyday life.[13]

In his infamous *Mafarka le futuriste* (1909)—an epic novel of abjection, replete with homoeroticism and misogyny—Marinetti articulated his most public fantasy of a man giving birth to a mechanical offspring. This work, which led to charges of obscenity and a well-publicized trial, served as a larger metaphor for Futurism's unholy parturition from fin-de-siècle Symbolist culture. Undoubtedly, Futurism denatured the art profession, begetting a new tradition. At far remove from the Cubists' studio enterprise, Futurists turned the making of art into cultural strategy and political action, setting the stage literally and figuratively for the antiart polemics of Dada and Happenings of Fluxus and Neo-Dada. Futurism also prefigured Pop art's transactions with mass-media celebrity and its vernacular glance. The legacy of Futurism as the "ur" avant-garde was ignored for decades in the critical literature, however, due to its infelicitous marriage with Italy's Fascist regime.[14]

The Mother of the Avant-Garde

Marinetti intuited that the mass media and capitalist enterprise would revolutionize the venues and reception of high art. He harangued against the museum and academy insofar as they represented traditional models of didacticism and edification; no longer wanting enlightenment, contemporary humanity desired entertainment based on the constantly new and the unrelentingly sensational. Like a stage manager for variety theater (his preferred form of popular entertainment), Marinetti choreographed the performance of Futurism as a series of improvised acts and shocking exploits.[15] Violence was the operative metaphor for Futurist activism, not in a fracas of fisticuffs—though that was often the result—but in belligerent words and a barrage of publicity. The Futurists were the first to articulate the avant-garde project of destroying the paradigm of fine art as a sphere apart from mundane reality. In their attack on aesthetic autonomy, they assaulted the boundaries between elite and popular, private and public, unique contemplative object and mesmerizing collective event. The Futurists did not merely incorporate images of commodity culture; they immersed their art in the circulation of goods. Even paintings and sculptures were subject to widespread distribution, direct engagement with a large audience, and rapid consumption through a circus of exhibitions, reviews, manifestos, and pamphleteering. In at least one instance, artists' canvases were performed as theater, brought on stage during a Futurist happening. For Futurists, modernity was inseparable from speed. As a temporal condition, modernity was at the greatest distance from the past; as a condition of artistic production, it was based on a new concept of originality driven by the creation of market expectation and demand.

"The Founding and Manifesto of Futurism" was the first Futurist artwork, creating buzz about a movement that had as yet no adherents or much substance beyond its own incendiary statements. The actual text was but one part of the operation; Marinetti sent out advance copies and placed it simultaneously in several publications and languages to insure a huge critical response. Fusing the political and literary manifesto with the audacious sell of advertising, he grabbed attention with a series of rapid-fire declamations, one more outrageous than the next. As Marjorie Perloff has shown, the dizzying array of rhetorical devices—repetition, hyperbole, parody—drew the reader in while expelling the possibility of sustained analysis.[16] One manifesto was immediately followed by another (some fifty between 1909 and 1914) in a variety of print media from daily press and cultural journal to flyer and exhibition catalogue. Like the daily news, the content of the manifestos was readily consumed, if maldigested, and soon outmoded by the next preposterous pronouncement. Marinetti's substantial personal wealth allowed him to anticipate strategies of editorial marketing in the publication of his journal *Poesia* from 1905 to 1909 and in later Futurist tomes. He sent complimentary copies to leading critics, planted reviews, paid prestigious authors to write for these publications, and devoted pages to editorial opinions by outside contributors.[17]

Futurist manifestos engendered a new reactive relationship with the reader, one that was further developed in visual layouts of boldfaced and directional print, columns of text, and gaps on the page. In 1912, from similar modernist principles of fragmentation and rupture, Marinetti invented *parole in libertà* (words-in-freedom): strings of nouns without cohesive syntax, whose emphatic aural and visual presence forced mental leaps, what he termed a "chain of analogies" between "seemingly diverse and hostile things." As the manifesto blurred literary genres, so too did words-in-freedom force the viewing of text as image, with words deliberately scattered over the page in the making of diagrams and other iconic signs. In his "Technical Manifesto of Futurist Literature" (1912), Marinetti claimed that his new poetics were inspired by the mechanical muse of a whirling propeller. Flying high in a biplane above Milan, he "looked at objects from a new point of view, no longer head on or behind, but straight down and foreshortened."[18]

Marinetti's first programmatic exposition of words-in-freedom was *Zang Tumb Tuuum* (1912–14), based on the account of a Bulgarian-Turkish conflict he had written as a war correspondent for the French daily *Gil Blas* (in whose pages, ironically, the Futurist movement was repeatedly maligned).[19] With the reportage of battle, he performed his aim "to redouble the expressive force of words," since it linked the factual style of journalistic immediacy with the literal bombardment of the senses. Indeed, on an ideological level Marinetti intended to shape the audience into an activated mass prepared for

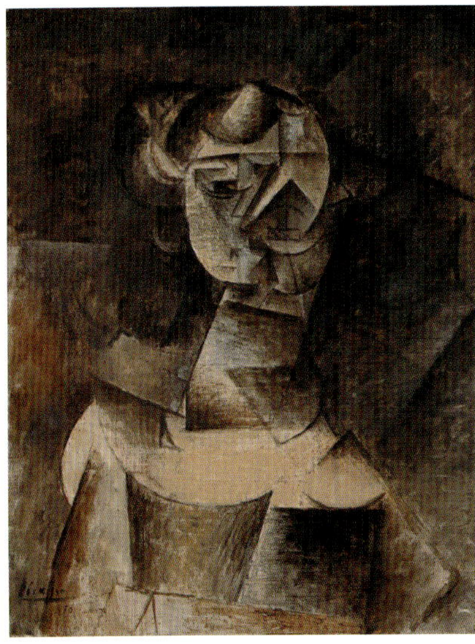

Fig. 1 Pablo Picasso
Mademoiselle Léonie, 1910
Oil on canvas, 25⁹⁄₁₆ × 19¹¹⁄₁₆ inches (65 × 50 cm)
Private collection, Switzerland

revolution or war. He dubbed his liberated language the "wireless imagination," that is, a means of communicating "telegraphically" at high velocity with the greatest economy of means. Marinetti's verbal-visual revolution was a pointed refutation of Symbolist refinement and interiority, which he associated, above all, with the writing of Stéphane Mallarmé. Instead of a hermetic language closed onto itself in a "static ideal," Futurist poetics emphasized speed and directness, a jarring rush of pure sensation and "violent onomatopoeias."[20]

Once transformed in the live acts of utterance and gesticulation, Marinetti's words-in-freedom realized their full mimetic potential. They were unleashed upon the audience in a hailstorm of primitive sounds and speech, the verbal equivalent of brute matter. He introduced a new physical energy to the act of performing, akin to the "swift actuality," the "contortions and grimaces," of theatrical revues.[21] By performing their manifestos and words-in-freedom on the stage and in the streets, the Futurists created a new form of audience participation that evolved into *serate*, or happenings. They baited the public with advance publicity, low-cost or free tickets, and stunts and improvisation guaranteed to incite a free-for-all, not to mention eager takers for the next performance.[22]

In June 1913, when Marinetti, the "Italian cyclone," first performed his words-in-freedom (what one local critic called "nuttiness on the loose") before a Parisian audience, the press eagerly reported the ensuing brouhaha: "The recitation unleashed the tumult. The conference ended amid clamor, overwhelming the orator who, now, shouted out of breath, finally had to admit defeat."[23] In his manifesto "The Variety Theatre," dated September 29 of that year, Marinetti made clear the analogies between avant-garde activism and popular forms of amusement. Both destroyed the coherence of a unified work of art and, with it, the traditional relationship between artist and public. "It doesn't remain static like a stupid voyeur," wrote Marinetti of the new audience, "but joins noisily in the action, in the singing, accompanying the orchestra, communicating with the actors in surprising actions and bizarre dialogues."[24] No wonder Parisian critics glibly described them in equally theatrical terms as the Futurist "troupe."

As planned, the Futurists' blatant, if creative, use of publicity resulted in an unprecedented number of attacks and parodies in the press, both at home and abroad. In Paris, Marinetti's "The Founding and Manifesto of Futurism" was a resounding success, as determined by the attention — mostly negative — it garnered. The affiliation of art with advertising techniques proved the most offensive. Reviewers argued that the enormous energy devoted to American-style publicity could only be in reverse proportion to the genuine quality of the work involved. The Futurists' exaggerated claims to novelty served the huckster's practice of duping the public to buy worthless goods. For the popular press — whose hostility toward modernism as a hoax projected the public's general incomprehension — Futurism was synonymous with avant-gardism. Indeed, as Jeffrey Weiss has argued, the use of the suffix "-ism" as a pejorative denoting excess and insincerity came into common currency only after Marinetti's manifesto.[25] Even the term "Cubism," used for the first time in spring 1909, came about after the appearance of Futurism on the Parisian scene.

It was one thing, however, for Futurism to be derided by art world "outsiders" — to whom it was, as we have seen, synonymous with the charlatanism of avant-gardism — but quite another for it to be spurned by the very champions of new art. The Futurists bore the brunt of art-market politics from 1911 on, when the Salon Cubists emerged to challenge Braque and Picasso. While Apollinaire lent his promiscuous critical support to Delaunay, Gleizes, Metzinger, and others, he continued to sideline Futurist painters as *pompiers*—as imitators — more interested in depicting the "subject" than the "plastic problems" inherent to painting itself. In a sleight of hand, Apollinaire then co-opted the term "simultaneity" in championing the French *l'esprit nouveau* of a vernacular modernity. The Futurists "would deserve a lot of credit, if the boastfulness of their declarations and the insolence of their manifestos did not dispel any indulgence we might be tempted to feel toward them," he admonished in a 1912 review of their first Paris show.[26] Other Parisian critics concurred that the art of making manifestos did disservice to the reputation of the Futurist enterprise in painting and sculpture. Racing to press with their own embattled declarations of superiority and brilliant new theories, the Futurists hardly had time, it would seem, to devote themselves to the real task at hand. Futurism was but a religion of speed for *arrivistes*, a means of making careers in a hurry. Not only the Salon Cubists but even Picasso and Braque were influenced by the Futurist spirit in the air.

For art dealer Daniel-Henry Kahnweiler, the public uproar over the modernist avant-garde and its association with the burlesque and the bluff threatened the reputations of Braque and Picasso, artists with whom he had exclusive contracts. Kahnweiler isolated his artists from the pack and the public by exhibiting them only in his gallery or in select venues abroad, placing their work with discerning collectors, and avoiding, rather than courting, sensationalist press. "What's the use of a scandal if one wants to work?" he repeatedly asserted.[27] By contrast to Marinetti, Kahnweiler drew a cordon sanitaire between the high-end art market and the common

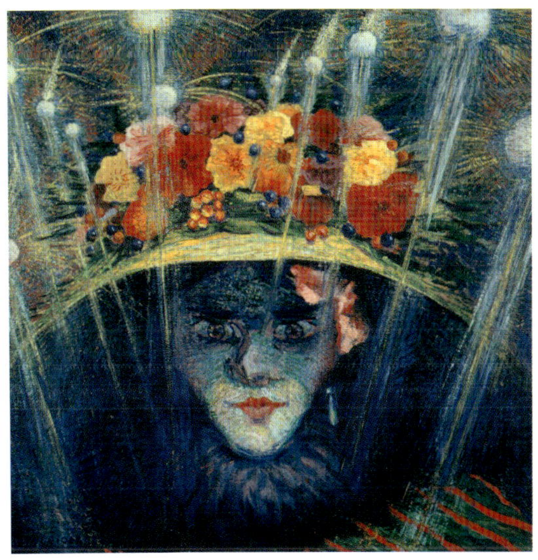

Fig. 2 Umberto Boccioni
The Modern Idol (*Idolo moderno*), 1911
Oil on canvas, 23½ × 23 inches (59.7 × 58.4 cm)
Estorick Collection, London

marketplace in an effort to insure artistic purity and integrity.[28] Long after the Futurists' marketing strategies were acknowledged as an authentic form of aesthetic transgression, used to *épater le bourgeois*, French critics still resisted the possibility of Futurist masterpieces in art.[29] That Futurist avant-gardism made problematic the concept of masterpiece in the age of masterful marketing was another matter. The Futurist aestheticization of everyday life proved too threatening to the insular practices of aesthetic modernism.

Facets and Flux

In summer 1911, Soffici was preparing his article "Picasso e Braque," the first critical treatment of the new art in Italy. But he met with resistance from his editor at *La Voce*, Giuseppe Prezzolini (himself no provincial hack), who claimed the Italian public would be angry and horrified, like himself, by the photographs of the "incomprehensible" Cubist works. Replied Soffici, "Italy is in such a hole of ignorance with regard to art, that it will be serious if we don't do something to dig it out. . . . When I talk about Picasso, I know I am talking about a master, not only of the future, but of today, and if Italy must understand one day just what is art, we will have the honor of being the first to point out the best artists of our time." Soffici's text was published in August but without illustrations; subsequently appearing in the December issue, Picasso's *The Oil Mill* (1909, cat. no. 17) and *Mademoiselle Léonie* (1910, fig. 1) and Braque's *Glass, Plate, and Knife* (1910) were the first Cubist images to be reproduced in Italy.[30]

Young Italian artists were at a particular disadvantage in the development of European modernism, given the geographical distance from Paris, the lack of a marketing infrastructure of galleries and salons, and the aesthetic burden of their cultural patrimony. They had neither familiarity with Paul Cézanne's work nor contact with tribal art, the sources that triggered the new spatial and linguistic conventions of Cubism. When Futurist artists joined Marinetti's bandwagon with their own manifestos in 1910, they were painting in a Divisionist style, a distinctly Italian variant of Neo-Impressionism, with overlays of Symbolist notions of synesthesia: equivalents for nonvisual sensations such as sound and smell. The works of 1909–11 are frequently categorized as "pre-Futurist," implying a degree of inadequacy by comparison to the theoretical content of the manifestos, in which the ideas of Henri Bergson and Paul Souriau are already evident.[31] Yet Boccioni's *The Modern Idol* (1911, fig. 2) or Carrà's *Leaving the Theater* (1909) are advanced in their interpretation of heterogeneous flux, in the depiction of disintegrating mass and fluid contours generated by a pictorial continuum of light and color. Because the Futurists aimed at rendering "the *dynamic sensation* itself," they needed to impart the tactile values as well as the purely optical effects of perception.[32] The intense, high-keyed chromatic vibrations and scintillating brushwork of their Divisionist style were forcefully integrated into a Cubist division of mass and volume. The Futurists were precocious within Italy for seeking out Cubism's influence. To be up-to-date and competitive abroad was also to counter the European view of Italian culture as "a land of the dead."[33] That no other Italian painters or sculptors did so testifies to the degree of the Futurists' actual rupture with the past.

Soffici's position among Italian artists (and French critics) was exceptional. He had known Picasso since the days when the artist lived at the Bateau Lavoir in Montmartre; no mere hanger-on, he witnessed the unfolding pictorial drama of *Les Demoiselles d'Avignon* (1907) and earned Picasso's approbation for his perspicacious commentary. His essay "Picasso e Braque" deserves examination in some length because he was privy to step-by-step developments and because it was published just a few months before Boccioni and Carrà's trip to Paris in mid-October 1911, where they saw Cubist works for the first time.[34] Soffici posited Cubism as a reaction to Impressionism, noting the seminal role of Cézanne and African art in privileging conceptual over naturalistic modes of representation. Though Soffici did not label the distinct phases or refer to specific pictures by name, his essay follows the evolution of Cubism from what he termed the deep "wefted" space of 1909, to the shallower, abstract scaffolding of spring 1911, where Picasso wove "a melodious fabric of lines and tones," interspersed with "hieroglyphs" or visual cues that "work on the beholder."

Impressionism, Soffici began, was an art of rendering pure optical sensation, one that ignored our desire for the "concrete" and the "corporeality" of things. Well-versed in contemporary theories of vision, he argued that "the visual perception of the real has as much to do with sight as with sense of touch" or tactile values remembered from previous experience.[35] The merit of Picasso was to "defeat" Impressionism through the intuitive application of "seeing" what we "know." When looking at a violin, Soffici explained, we not only consider the plane in front of our eyes but also remember aspects of the physiognomy hidden from view. Picasso's further achievement was the projection of this known, three dimensional reality on a flat surface, through the purely pictorial means of "lines, foreshortenings, and tonal modulations." Soffici showed that Picasso liberated drawing from the burden of describing; it became a means for deformation and a sign alluding to things. Here, Soffici anticipated Kahnweiler's famous explanation that Cubism was a form of script, while confirming its debt to Symbolist theories of signs, or "equivalents."[36] For Picasso, line "now simply has the value of a hieroglyph through which a lyrically intuited truth is written, for whomever can decipher it." With comparison to the "elliptical syntax" of Mallarmé, Soffici claimed Picasso's drawing to be a "ductile instrument," capable of "thousands of nuances" and "fluctuating meanings."

Most important, for our purposes, are Soffici's conclusions on the audience for this "complex, difficult and disconcerting art," which penetrated the innate laws of painting. The Cubist painter fixed objects in space as "invariable types," which were broken apart in an intuition of their "multiple characteristics and appearances." These contemplative mysteries—the intellectual and poetic pleasures—may risk moments of obscurity, as Soffici readily admitted. But this was an art for the elect, so far ahead of its time that "today it can only be loved and understood by a few. Only later, much later—and maybe never—will it please the multitude," which prefers "pastiche" in any event. Soffici's prophecy rings true, given the decades of art-historical interpretation that have yet to exhaust the meanings of Cubism. In the context of his own time, he inadvertently rehearsed the self-constructed elitism of the new art and its private circle of dealers and collectors, who sought to distinguish themselves—through the most advanced of aesthetic tastes—from mere followers, the philistine bourgeoisie, and the working class.[37] The deliberate hermeticism and ironic play of Cubism in its means of production and intended reception was the cardinal point of difference with Futurist art. "I oppose the decorative, precious aesthetic of Mallarmé and his search for the rare word," Marinetti announced. "I do not want to suggest an idea or a sensation with passéist airs and graces. Instead I want to grasp them brutally and hurl them in the reader's face."[38]

Soffici's overall view of Italy as a stagnant backwater was a common lament among his generation of Italian intellectuals (the same ones who bristled when the accusation of provincialism came from the French). An identical desire for renewal motivated the radicalism of the Futurist project and led to Soffici's rapprochement with the group even after he had initially disparaged its art as hopelessly behind the times. In the pages of *Lacerba*, the journal that Papini and Soffici ran from 1913 to 1915, Boccioni and Carrà published their theoretical challenges to Cubist painting, convinced as they were of Marinetti's dictums, especially the need to represent what the Futurists referred to as the "tangible miracles of contemporary life."[39] As a sure-footed interlocutor, Soffici made plain the differences between the "pure painting" of Braque and Picasso's pictures and the activist agenda of his Italian peers, but he eventually justified Futurist dynamism, a "plastic" style adapted to the movement of modern life.[40] Through purely pictorial means, the Futurist depiction of motion achieved a superior synthesis, according to Soffici, since it combined Impressionist light effects with Cubist tactile form, brilliant color with tonal modeling. Rendering multifold sensations was key to a sensationalist art, to a spectacle of images that unfolded before the viewer's eye.

The when and how of the Futurists' exposure to Cubism has been well documented in the literature. In addition to Soffici's essay, there were accounts by Severini, who had lived in Paris since 1906. Severini's detailed letters revealed him as a useful in-camera informer, despite his actual mortification over the Futurists' gaucheries and antics in Paris. His observations on the latest developments, however, were less informed than Soffici's, as well as being biased by a projection of Futurist interests onto Cubist practice. The real impact came in mid-October 1911, when the neophytes Boccioni and Carrà toured galleries, viewed the public Cubists at the Salon d'Automne, and met Apollinaire and Picasso (though not Braque, who was then in Céret). Unlike Soffici, their understanding of Cubism was necessarily a synchronic one, an overlay of developments from *Les Demoiselles d'Avignon* in 1907 to the introduction of painted letters and numbers in the near abstractions of autumn 1911. The works done by Boccioni immediately upon his return to Italy through the 1912 series of paintings and sculptures with *Materia* (1912, cat. no. 27) at its center show the influence most clearly. Yet the specifics of borrowed motifs reveal less about the Futurist debt to Cubism than the ingenuity of their integration into an audacious art of "the punch and the slap."[41]

Foremost among the shock of the new was the Futurists' encounter with *Les Demoiselles d'Avignon*, which they could have seen in Picasso's studio, where it was occasionally unveiled. Related canvases and studies were owned by Gertrude Stein, whose salon at 27, rue de Fleurus the Futurists would visit the following year, during their February–March 1912 sojourn in Paris. Although today it is no longer considered the first Cubist picture, *Demoiselles* represented a radical assault on traditional pictorial unity and decorum.[42] The full colonialist and misogynist content of Picasso's savage distortions were likely lost on the Futurists, as they were on other contemporaries. Nonetheless, after his exposure to "central-African fetishes in the atelier of our Montmartre friends," Boccioni heralded the role of "barbaric races" in the "violent" rejuvenation of Western art.[43] The almond shaped, blackened-out eyes and the twisted wedge of the nose from the masklike faces of *Demoiselles* became recurrent features in portraits such as *Materia,* while several sketches by Boccioni (e.g., *Figure*, 1912,

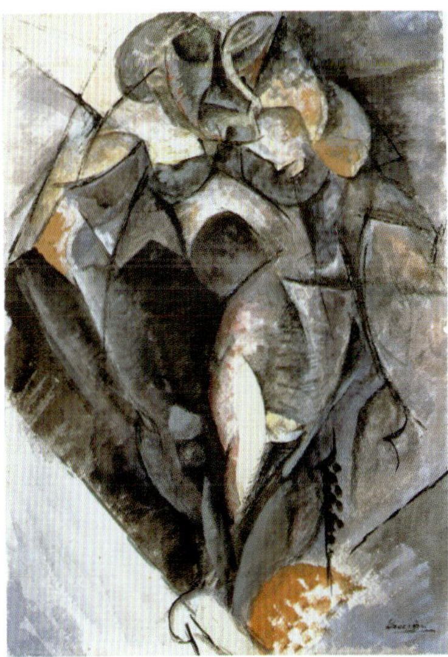

Fig. 3 Umberto Boccioni
Figure (Figura), 1912
Watercolor and tempera on paper,
22 3/16 × 15 1/4 inches (56.3 × 38.7 cm)
Civiche Raccolte d'Arte, Gabinetto dei Disegni, Milan

fig. 3) incorporate the body type of Picasso's standing *gisante* figure.

More important, the influence of *Les Demoiselles d'Avignon* lay in the Futurist trope of the *antigrazioso* (antigracious, antigraceful), the deliberate breaking with the conventions of bourgeois good taste and "feminine indolence." "We must fell, smash and destroy our tradition of harmony," abjured Boccioni, "since it makes us succumb to a 'graciousness,' comprised of a bashful, sentimental pandering."[44] *Antigrazioso* was the Futurist interpretation of French modernist primitivism. Italy had no colonial empire in Africa or Oceania, nor did its retardataire industrial development allow the luxury of projecting a paradise lost of creative succor onto the cultural "other."[45] Rather than exorcising the ills of Western civilization through the "soft" primitivism of Paul Gauguin or the "savage" primitivism of Picasso, the Futurists embraced a punk sensibility of alienated modernity.[46] "They shout at us, 'Your literature won't be beautiful!'" vaunted Marinetti. "And how lucky! We make use, instead, of every ugly sound, every expressive cry from the violent life that surrounds us."[47]

Gendered masculine, the term *antigrazioso* was applied exclusively by Boccioni to portraits of women—notably, his mother and the intellectually formidable critic Margherita Sarfatti—onto whose images Boccioni grafted the distinctive masklike features of Picasso's works. The transfer of prostitutes' faces to represent women who were anything but underlines Boccioni's concept of *antigrazioso* as intrinsic to the artwork's process itself, the physically aggressive, even brutal handling of form. Of course, the sense of violence done is even more forceful when enacted on the female body—the allegorical embodiment of beauty and the classical tradition—as Picasso's original transgression had shown. Out of secrecy or fear, Picasso reputedly hid *Les Demoiselles d'Avignon* and its studies from view; it is all the more impressive that Boccioni left himself open to incredulity and derision when he showed his works in the most public terms. The superficial distortions of Metzinger's *Tea Time* (1911), the dainty hit of the 1911 Salon d'Automne, pale by comparison to the eviscerated flesh and ungainly facial grimaces of the *Antigrazioso* series, *Materia* included. Boccioni's use of caricatural deformation differs conceptually, however, from Picasso's synecdochic use of line in his 1910 portraits such as *Daniel-Henry Kahnweiler* (cat. no. 11). Calling themselves "primitives of a new and completely transformed sensibility," the Futurists broke violently, even comically, with the decorum of naturalistic representation, yet they never reconfigured the fragments into a new metalanguage of the visual, as did Braque and Picasso.[48] Masters of hyperbole and bombast, Futurists were the rhetoricians, versus the Cubist grammarians, of modern art.

Concurrent with the tribal-inspired works, Boccioni could have seen Picasso's Analytic Cubist canvases, absorbing from them a new formal vocabulary of accentuated volumes and shifting *passage*. Paintings such as *The Oil Mill* of 1909 provided models for a stacked, if differentiated, space between foreground and background. Boccioni's actual treatment of bodies owed much to Picasso's portraits of 1910, in which contours were broken open and line dispersed, resulting in an ever shallower, latticework space. Yet the Futurists modified Cubist facets, never reducing them to hovering crystalline planes; Boccioni, for example, insisted on full-bodied masses, ellipses, and extended contour lines to create the illusion of physical impact between things. In sum, he developed a sculptural painting for his faceted portraits, underlined by his appropriation of Picasso's *Head (Fernande)* (1909, cat. no. 30) as their prototype.[49] In that Analytic Cubist sculpture, Picasso cleaved the surface into geometric parts, rendering the physiognomy from different points of view, but retained a traditional modeled mass. Boccioni embarked on a similar dialogue between painting and sculpture, wherein the illusion of pierced, three-dimensional solids in *Those Who Go* (1911) through *Materia* leads directly to his first plasters and the plastic deformations of the modeled *Antigrazioso* (1912–13, cat. no. 31).

In most general terms, Cubists deconstructed the devices of trompe l'oeil illusionism in painting—perspective and chiaroscuro—and in doing so asserted the actuality of a painting as flat and literal object. Unlike Cubists, the Futurists never shattered the metaphor of a painting as a window through which we look into deep space. They needed depth of plane in order to project an object's expansive trajectory in a narrative of motion. Boccioni retained the window in numerous images like *Simultaneous Visions* (1911, cat. no. 8) and *Materia,* where it is implied by the illusionistic motif of a balcony or balustrade. This device signals a point of entry for the eye opening onto the scene outside, as well as its simultaneous rebound into the space of the viewer, where the "street enters the house" (Boccioni's wording of a title for a 1911 painting; see cat. no. 7). Broken fragments of railing illustrate the sheer force of interpenetrating objects and also symbolize the overcoming of divisions between the inside and outside of material bodies or between private and public spheres. The dissolution of boundaries is the key to the Futurist imagination, predicated on the projection of the self onto the world and the dispersion of dynamic energy from inert matter. It informs fusions of bodies and space and painterly evocations of the indeterminate flow that defines reality

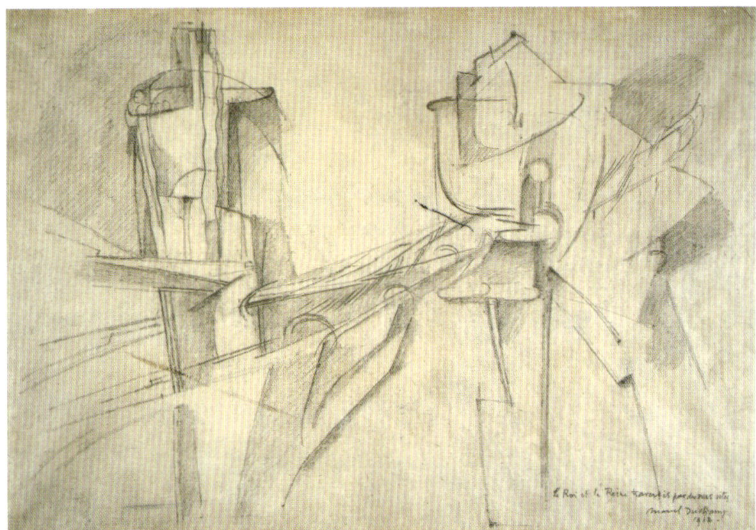

Fig. 4 Marcel Duchamp
The King and Queen Traversed by Swift Nudes
(Le Roi et la Reine traversés par des nus vites), 1912
Graphite on Japanese laid paper,
10¾ × 15⅜ inches (27.3 × 39.1 cm)
Philadelphia Museum of Art, Louise and Walter Arensberg Collection, 1950

beyond what the naked eye can see. It also justifies bombardment of the viewer with optical and tactile sensations bound together in hyperactivity, as if to extend the perceptual experience of the picture beyond the frame into the space of the beholder.

The subject of Boccioni's art is not the nature of representation, as it is with Cubism, but the representation of perception as an indivisible flow of sensory-motor movements and dynamic "states of mind." Boccioni drew heavily from the writings of Bergson to legitimize Futurist activist aesthetics and provide a philosophical underpinning for an art of physical force and objects in motion. Bergson posited the act of perception as physiological and psychological extension, an overlay of tactile and visual sensations with memory images. As in *Materia*, Boccioni's most Bergsonian canvas, matter is both churning energy and an ever expanding "aggregate of images," transformed by reciprocal actions of force and resistance.[50] Bergson defined reality as heterogeneous flux or duration, and this dynamic process of being and becoming can only be intuited, not quantified; it is opposed, in its indivisible essence, to intellectual analyses that divide space and time into static intervals or units. Cubist facets broke open form and knit the surface into a fluctuating fabric of materialized space. They enabled a visual dialectic between the inviolability of form and the indivisibility of matter, and hence provided the pictorial means to illustrate Bergson's *durée*.

Despite his overly intellectualized writings and misappropriations of Bergson's amorphous ideas, Boccioni's paintings and sculptures remain elementary — and as a result, visually powerful — in the representation of a violent, primitive reality. Boccioni depicted the collision and interpenetration of bodies and space, the attraction and repulsion of molecular activity, the simultaneous overlay of narrative action and disparate images. "Matter is neither sad nor gay," affirmed Marinetti, dispensing with the emotive resonance of the fin-de-siècle poetic sign. "Its essence is courage, will power, and absolute force." Theatrical effect, more than the artistic or scientific divination of underlying truths, served the Futurist agenda. As Marinetti insisted, "I want to introduce the infinite molecular life into poetry not as a scientific document but as an intuitive element. It should mix, in the work of art, with the infinitely great spectacles and dramas, because this fusion constitutes the integral synthesis of life."[51]

In his essay "What Divides Us from Cubism" (1914), Boccioni focused on the issue of dramatic action. Cubists were "analyzers of fixity" who "killed unity, fervor and emotion" in art; by isolating the object and suppressing movement, Cubism became a "lifeless" exercise in decomposing and enumerating the parts of things. By contrast, Futurist painting created an ever-accelerating narrative of motion, of "the gravitation, displacement, reciprocal attractions of forms, masses and colors."[52] In such works as *Materia* and *Forces of a Street* (1911), Boccioni jump-started the immobile Cubist model into a spiraling or radiating mass, violently impacted by sharp and cutting planes that "scythe through space."[53] Using "lines of force," he further inscribed the "absolute" and "relative" movements of an object, that is, its unimpeded internal dynamic and its transformation by interpenetrating objects and ambience. Futurist forms "have a life outside of intelligence," wrote Boccioni, since they expand beyond the limited faculties of empirical analysis and "project themselves into the infinite."[54] Cubists obstinately continued to paint "frozen aspects of nature" and in doing so revealed their stubborn attachment to the past, to classical values, which the Futurists in their celebrated gesture of cultural patricide, completely disavowed. In both their heated prose and high-pitched art, Futurists deliberately debunked the value of cerebral faculties in art. Inevitably, the critical discourse, then as now, established a qualitative difference between the intellectual, nonmimetic content of Braque and Picasso and the literal-minded expressionism of the Futurists.[55]

The Futurists aimed at another kind of reciprocal movement, that between artist and viewer. Boccioni's writings are littered with claims on how motor sensation and mental "states of mind" will be imparted through pictorial means. They also reveal his attempt, under Marinetti's influence, to move beyond contemplative Symbolist aesthetics to a "mechanical" sensibility of shock, diversion, and chaotic excitement.[56] Zigzagging planes, compelling arabesques, and flickering strokes portended the artist's intuition of ceaseless flux, which was then absorbed by the viewer in an analogous process of emphatic immersion in the pictorial flow. The resulting effect, however, was not Symbolist ennui or interiority but the extroverted, hard-hitting forces of the street. As the Futurists intended, "These force-lines must draw in and entangle the spectator, who will then also be obliged to struggle, in some way, with the protagonists in the picture."[57] They expected their images to arouse and provoke, and they did. Two of Boccioni's paintings were vandalized while on public exhibition — dynamic encounters without parallel in the contemporary history of Cubist painting.[58] To incite, amuse, and overwhelm reason with sensory diversions, these were the qualities of twentieth-century spectacle cultivated by Futurist art.

For Boccioni, "dynamic heat, violence, and incidental variety" created the emotive content of painting. Initially, his images burst with realistic details: passing trams, rattling carriages, electric lights, buildings on the rise. These were temporary if necessary "bridges"

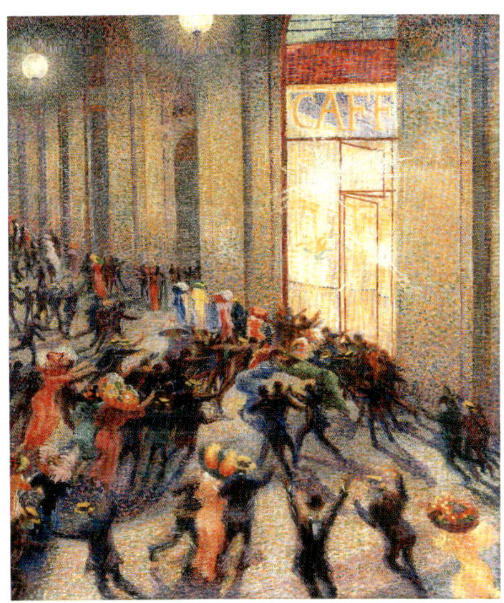

Fig. 5 Umberto Boccioni
Riot in the Galleria (Rissa in Galleria), 1910
Oil on canvas, 29 15/16 × 25 3/16 inches (76 × 64 cm)
Pinacoteca di Brera, Milan

of communication with the "crowd," whose eyes were otherwise "warped by routine."[59] After contact with Cubism, anecdotal details were subsumed in the configuration of centripetal and centrifugal motion—for example, the rotating shoulder blades of the woman in *Simultaneous Visions*, or the spinning disks of a halo in *Horizontal Construction* (1912, cat. no. 28). Painted numbers (inspired by Cubist paintings of 1911) momentarily stop the action as they identify a train engine or the hypothetical distance between things. In *Materia,* a galloping horse with multiple limbs and a striding figure, broken down into overlapping planes, depart and distract from the central image of the mother. Oddly disjunctive in the context of the overall composition, they show Boccioni's absorption with yet another visual model of movement: Marey's chronophotographs. The cyborg on the right, with its ghostlike trail, is a reverse of the central figure in Duchamp's *The King and Queen Traversed by Swift Nudes* (1912, fig. 4), which Boccioni could have seen in Paris during his visits there in February–March and November 1912 and which was similarly inspired by Marey's photographic prints.[60] As the basis for a cinematic depiction that artificially divides space and time into quantitative units, Marey's model was ultimately rejected by Boccioni as a mechanical medium and hence unartistic.[61] Moreover, movement spread over the surface plane did not have the same desired effect as the three-dimensional projection of forms spiraling into deep space—what Boccioni called the style of "plastic dynamism."

In *Materia*, the early Analytic Cubist model of sculptural painting served Boccioni well. The eye of the spectator is propelled inward around eviscerated masses in a muscular action of expanding and contracting space; it ricochets off illuminated trajectories like the action of a pinball machine, whirling through a succession of overlapping images. By combining this effect with their use of diaphanous webs of atomized light in riveting colors, the Futurists succeeded in their much-vaunted aim of placing "the spectator in the center of the picture."[62] In Futurist art, this concept—though indebted to Symbolist notions of aesthetic empathy—was married to the actual physical and visual experience of the street, to the thoroughly modern experience of being jostled amid moving traffic and negotiating passersby. The eye is made conscious of aggressive manipulation, of being pushed and interrupted, as it careens from one visual stimulus to another. In Analytic Cubist painting, by contrast, the separation of optical and tactile sensations results in a disembodied relationship with the spectator, who slowly penetrates the monochrome scrim and grid of hovering fragments, losing his or her sense of time in the purely conceptual space of pictorial signs.

Bergson's theories provided common ground between the Futurists and the Salon Cubists, whose works were on view at the 1911 Salon d'Automne and 1912 Salon des Indépendants when the Italian artists visited Paris. Both groups aimed at a qualitative (intuitive), as opposed to quantitative (analytic), representation of time and space, as is evident in Gleizes's *Portrait of Jacques Nayral* (1911, cat. no. 13), in which multiple perspectives and coalescing planes provide visual analogues to subjective states of prolongation and discontinuity. But the respective interpretations of Cubist facets and Bergsonian flux were applied to profoundly different attitudes toward modernity and the experience of the picture. The fragmented surface and decorative overlays of such paintings as Gleizes's *Harvester Threshing* and Metzinger's *The Bathers*, both 1912, belie the traditional Salon subject matter underneath—epic sweeps of French countryside and allegories of national fecundity—and the academicism of their burnished hues. Their Cubist *passage*—the interconnected, fluid planes of space—is used to illustrate Bergson's notion that the past is prolonged into the present. The duration of collective memory and biological regeneration symbolizes the organic continuity of the French people and its spiritual *élan vital*.[63] This reactionary modernism upheld classical values of harmony, stability, and permanence, represented by the retrograde iconography of the toiling peasant and the arcadian nude and by a rather prosaic pictorial equilibrium. Futurists ruthlessly expunged these subjects; they repudiated tradition and the past, basing their art on radical rupture, on a forward projection that never looked back.

Instead, the Futurists bear closer comparison with Delaunay and Léger, with whom they had in common an urban iconography, vibrant colors, a greater degree of rhythmic abstraction, and emphatic sensory-motor effects. Their interest in expressing movement and the psychological dynamism of modern life shared roots in Bergson, as well as in the unanimism of Jules Romain and other writers of the group Abbaye de Créteil.[64] Paintings in Delaunay's *Eiffel Tower* series of 1909–12 (one of which was exhibited in the 1911 Salon des Indépendants) evince a direct response to the first Futurist manifestos, even as he developed a unified pictorial style that the Futurist painters had not yet achieved (e.g., *Eiffel Tower*, 1911, cat. no. 19). In 1913, Apollinaire's championship of Delaunay and Léger as "Orphic" painters—who were using purely pictorial means to represent the "simultaneity" of "life itself"—prompted Boccioni, who was undoubtedly right, to accuse them of artistic plagiarism.[65] In Delaunay's case, simultaneity was used with specific reference to the optical effects of scintillating color contrasts—in short, the same Neo-Impressionist

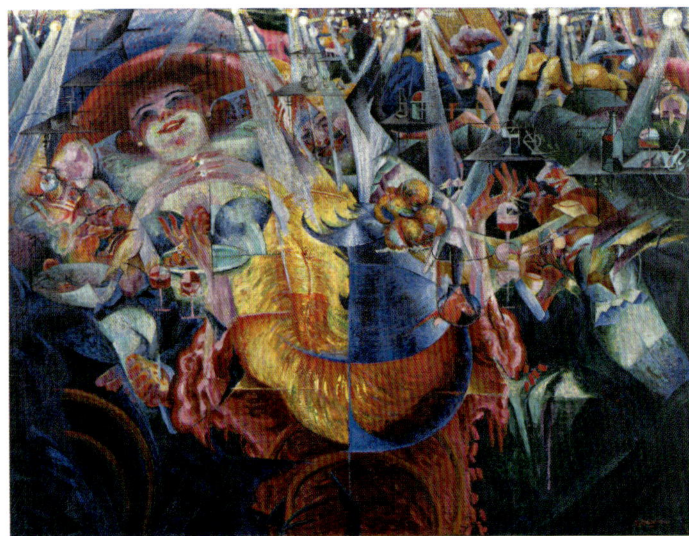

Fig. 6 Umberto Boccioni
The Laugh (*La risata*), 1911
Oil on canvas, 43⅜ × 57³⁄₁₆ inches (110.2 × 145.2 cm)
The Museum of Modern Art, New York, Gift of Herbert and Nannette Rothschild

theory of innate complementaries that inspired the Futurists. Although more abstract than the Futurists' anecdotal narratives of motion, Delaunay's *Windows* series of 1912–14 often includes realistic details of modern city life interjected amid surging color fields.[66] More to the point, the spiritualism contained in Delaunay's soaring spires and celestial disks betrays a latent traditionalism that was anathema to the Futurists, with their insistence on a modern vernacular based, above all, on the machine.

The Futurists engaged in a more compelling dialogue with Léger; the muscular volumes depicted by the French artist (initially inspired by Braque's 1908 cubistic landscapes) provided a direct model for a dynamic, sculptural style of painting.[67] In such works as *Study for Three Portraits* (1910–11) and *Nude Model in the Studio* (1912–13, cat. no. 16), Léger contrasted three-dimensional bulk with flat, *passage* planes to project the sensation of indivisible *durée*. Human limbs, similar to the arms in *Materia*, are fashioned like churning cylinders; volumetric drums and cubes converge with a fluctuating surface energized by rhythmic lines. Léger, in turn, was influenced by the Futurists' depictions of successive movement and emotive "states of mind," as well as by their infatuation with modern technology.[68] And like them, he combined realistic details with pictorial abstraction to register rapid and disjunctive change on the viewer's eye. In paintings of 1912, however, the Futurists delivered more narrative diversions and visual punches than Léger's imminent *Contrast of Forms* series of 1913. And the comic force of the Futurists' modernity—the exaggerated grimaces, the incongruous rapid-fire juxtapositions of streetcars and hairdos—was lost on their more serious-minded French contemporaries.[69]

The Parisian Cubists distanced themselves from the Futurists, whom they considered noisy hawkers of wares, but they may well have been referring to the loudness of the canvases themselves, which were unnaturally garish in color, like the painted faces of ladies of the night. Gaudy hues, combined with a luminous surface of individuated brushstrokes, gave rise to the spectacle of a fleeting modernity, of "everything solid melting into air."[70] These are neither Delaunay's sunlit prismatics (obvious allusions to stained-glass windows) nor the rational primary colors of Léger's standardized forms. Boccioni's *Riot in the Galleria* (1910, fig. 5), *The Roundup* (1910), *The Laugh* (1911, fig. 6), and *The Modern Idol* are unique in depicting the artificial illumination of sites of commodity—the shopping arcade, the popular theater, the prostitute—and their electrifying appeal. Three of these Divisionist canvases were included in the 1912 exhibition at Galerie Bernheim-Jeune, demonstrating the continuity of Boccioni's first Futurist style with recent Cubist-inflected canvases of surging street life. "Our life, redoubled by noctambulism, has multiplied our perceptions as colourists," the Futurists declared. "The time has passed for our sensations in painting to be whispered."[71]

Much has been made of the obvious difference between the glitter of Futurism and the subtle monochromes of Braque and Picasso's Analytic Cubism, but the significance goes far beyond the surface. As a sign, color acts as the emotive and uncontrollable element in painting, and this connotation reinforced the view of Cubism as highly refined, inaccessible art and Futurism as its vulgar profligate. Colors "shine forth and dance upon our flesh with untold charms, voluptuous and caressing," proffers "Futurist Painting: Technical Manifesto." "The public must utterly forget its intellectual culture, in order not to take possession of a work of art, but abandon itself to it."[72] Drawing out the metaphor, the particularly brash quality of Futurist canvases seduced through brash display, gave heightened pleasure to the senses, and, in its performative aspects, drew attention to the selling of art. That Marinetti prostituted high culture was opined in the French press; the link between professions was made clearly, however facetiously, in the pages of *Lacerba*: "We must put whores and artists on the same level. Whores as much as artists use their gifts and their talents to give others delight and gratification, and they do it, as a rule, only for pay. . . . Every art works the senses. And a great artist knows how to excite them in the most pleasurable way."[73]

In its celebration of the culture of the street and music hall, Futurism bore less connection to the studio enterprise of Cubism (with its debt to Mallarmé's self-reflexive poetics) than to the earlier model of modernity envisioned by Charles Baudelaire, with whose work Marinetti, a "gallicized Italian," was well versed.[74] Baudelaire was the first to identify transient spectacle as the subject for the painter of modern life, and to see the commodity fetish in the figure of the prostitute. However ambivalently, he also recognized that the purity of creative genius would inevitably be contaminated by market forces and mass taste.[75] "If you can't beat them, join them," was Marinetti's up-to-date attitude to the threat of the fine artist's professional obsolescence in an age of mechanical reproduction and rampant consumerism. The Futurist poet-artist no longer viewed the "fleeting forms of beauty" with the detachment of Baudelaire's flaneur or of an Impressionist painter; instead, he immersed himself in the masses to render the crowd into a work of art.[76]

The Futurist Wo(mb)man

In the eyes of French critics, the Futurists were vulgar because they imitated Cubism, because they were popularizers, and because

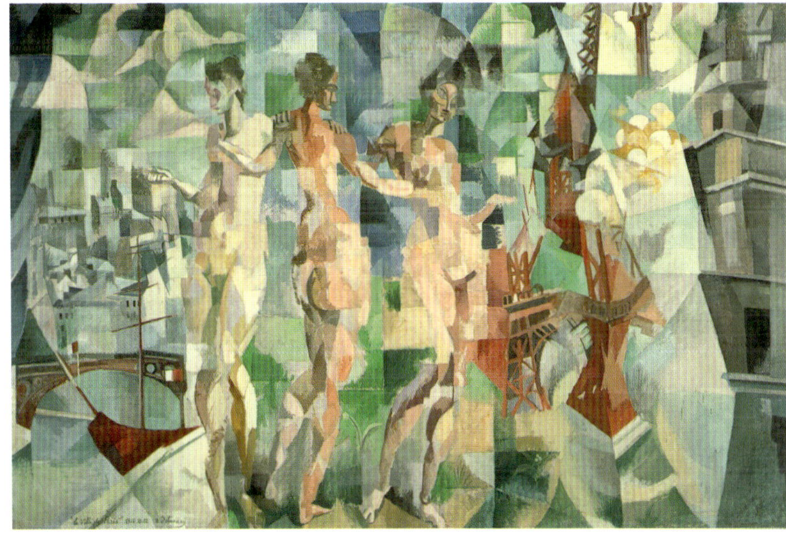

Fig. 7 Robert Delaunay
The City of Paris (*La Ville de Paris*), 1912
Oil on canvas, 105⅛ × 159¹³⁄₁₆ inches (267 × 406 cm)
Musée National d'Art Moderne, Centre Georges Pompidou, Paris

their conduct was coarse and their materials were common. In short, the Futurists' overt embrace of "feminine" mass culture was antithetical to the purity and autonomy of "masculine" high art.[77] Woman as mass culture was inseparable from Boccioni's definition of modern life, predicated as it was on display and seduction. During his first trip to Paris in 1906, he wrote home about the motorized vehicles, plethora of advertisements, and seething public life of the café, but nothing mesmerized him more than the sight of the new woman, whose personal appearance clearly complemented his artistic goals:

> *I have seen women as I have never imagined could exist! They are entirely painted: hair, lashes, eyes, cheeks, lips, ears, neck, shoulders, bosom, hands and arms! But painted in a manner so marvelous, so skillful, so refined, as to become works of art. And note that this is even done by women of low station. They are not painted to compensate for nature; they are painted for style, and with the liveliest colors.*[78]

How to account for this exhilarating vision in the context of Marinetti's infamous "contempt for women" proclaimed in "The Founding and Manifesto of Futurism"? His shocking statements and the repulsive imagery of his earlier Symbolist misogynist poetry were of their time, but the manifesto had the merit of igniting a heated debate on sexual difference and the social constitution of gender. Within the Italian context, the ferocity of his assault partook of the Futurists' radical efforts to modernize a country far behind the rest of Europe. Woman was a rhetorical figure for the passive and weak, a Decadent stereotype of a seductive and sentimental femininity. Informed by contemporary theories of biological essentialism, Marinetti perceived the predatory nature of woman as a threat to a newly resistant and impenetrable masculinity. The imagery of a soft and swelling feminine morass was obliterated, in theory, by one of streamlined, infinitely reproducible nonorganic forms.[79] In a self-conscious gendering of prose, Marinetti described the evolution from art to "action-art, that is, energy of will, aggression, possession, penetration, joy, brutal reality in art . . . , geometric splendor of forces, forward projection."[80]

Marinetti's ideal of a steely warrior, impervious to both feminine wiles and the dissolution of the self, served as a larger metaphor for an invincible and imperialist nation-state. It influenced Boccioni's resolutely virile images of muscular athletes, whose masses are reconfigured by velocity into mechanistic rhythms and sheathlike planes. Against this hypermasculine vision of armored bodies, however, one must juxtapose the art of Balla, whose dedication to the sentiments of domestic life, encouragement of women artists, and pursuit of decorative arts countered the provocative misogyny of the Futurist movement.[81] This is but one internal contradiction that prevents a reductive interpretation of Futurist attitudes toward women in theory and practice, in public posturing and in private life.

Despite his vituperative prose, Marinetti's scorn for the opposite sex had decidedly protofeminist features. He initially supported votes for women in the cynical belief that this would accelerate the downfall of the liberal parliamentary system, outworn social institutions, and stifling bourgeois mores. By the time of the official "Manifesto-Program of the Futurist Political Party" (1918)—advocating universal suffrage, anticlericalism, quick divorce, and the abolition of "marital authority"—he genuinely desired the liberation of both women and men from oppressive gender roles. Moreover, the provocative words of Futurism obscured its actual innovations. Through his journal *Poesia*, Marinetti was one of the most serious patrons of women writers in either mainstream or avant-garde publishing. During and immediately after World War I, women were attracted to Futurism for the opportunities it offered them to challenge social conventions and debate issues of sexual difference. The journal *L'Italia Futurista*, which was published from 1916 to 1918, had numerous women contributors and became an important forum for feminist concerns. Marinetti's supportive interaction with women authors (and later painters) prompted them to evolve what many scholars now define as a precocious "writing from the body," anticipating a postmodern *écriture feminine*.[82]

The Futurist movement put gender politics center stage, and it did so in Paris too, especially when the poet and performer Valentine de Saint Point launched her provocative "Manifesto of the Futurist Woman" (1912) and "Futurist Manifesto of Lust" (1913), further publicizing Marinetti's sexual politics and his infamous *serate*.[83] No such documents, debates, or equivalently radical stance existed within the Cubist movement. Nor did the Salon Cubists intentionally render problematic the social conventions of representing women. When the Futurist painters declared themselves "against the nude in painting, as nauseous and as tedious as adultery in literature," the Salon Cubists directly responded by openly embracing the nude as synonymous with the grand French tradition.[84] In the 1912 Salon des Indépendants, Delaunay exhibited his monumental *The City of Paris* (1912, fig. 7), with the Three Graces incongruously posed before the Eiffel Tower, their breasts and buttocks aflutter in the dynamism of urban life. In *The Bathers* (1912, fig. 8), shown at the same Salon, Gleizes similarly countered Futurist iconoclasm with a classical idyll that turned back the clock to a time before Gustave

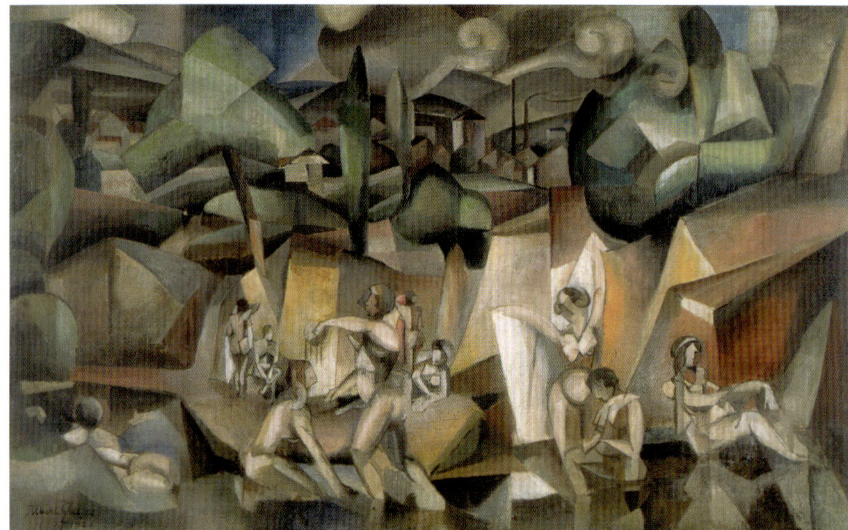

Fig. 8 Albert Gleizes
The Bathers (Les Baigneuses), 1912
Oil on canvas, 41⁵⁄₁₆ × 67⁵⁄₁₆ inches (105 × 171 cm)
Musée d'Art Moderne de la Ville de Paris

Courbet and Edouard Manet. The Futurist diatribe against tired flesh even prompted Léger to paint *Nude Model in the Studio*, claiming that the subject was irrelevant in any event; lady or locomotive, such subjects were mere pretexts for the superior art of "pure painting," versus the Futurist insistence on a modern, action-packed narrative.[85] The female nude appears in Picasso's Analytic Cubist paintings as an anonymous armature for pictorial invention (as opposed to his portraits of men, whose individual features and names are specifically inscribed in the images and titles). Beneath the surface, however, we know that the artist's misogynist attitudes permeate the disassembling of female anatomy and bawdy jokes of his papiers collés. Picasso's oeuvre is as much a personal, sentimental diary of his often disturbing erotic life as it is a history of art.[86]

Women painters of the Cubist movement such as Alice Halicka and Marie Laurencin were relegated to its margins, their achievements described within the discourse of the "decorative," not within the masculine realm of cultural innovation.[87] French avant-garde painting staunchly upheld the culture/nature dyad: man produced material and intellectual culture, while woman merely reproduced the race. Grounded in the theories of Friedrich Nietzsche and Otto Weininger, the Futurists similarly exalted the creative and activist forces of the male at the expense of a passive and domesticated female. But as we have seen with the Futurists, the strict division between masculine and feminine spheres was compromised by their positive valorization of mass culture, by the desire to play to the crowd. Futurist aesthetics, like Marinetti's call for free love, were predicated on the fast and easy, on the recourse to the common and emotive cheap thrill. Hence, any simple opposition between the sexes became mired in Futurism's undermining and inversions of this binary discourse. Marinetti referred to the crowd as a "stupid voyeur," implicating the impotence of the traditional male gaze. In paintings of the crowd such as Russolo's *Revolt* (1912), the "feminine" masses appear hard and resolute, with individuals reduced to standardized machine men. Indeed, anonymity was more telling than sexuality, for in Futurist activist politics, as in Georges Sorel's contemporaneous *Reflections on Violence* (1908), the crowd was a mere agent for revolt who presaged the actual revolution led by a "spiritual elite."[88] And despite the Futurists' cutting words against women, there is a notable absence of violent or debased sexualized imagery in their artwork. This lack in Futurism's visual repertoire contrasts sharply with German painting of the same period, where the female body is dismembered for the sake of gestural expressionism and *Lustmord* (sex murder) narratives.

Nowhere is the dialectic — rather than duality — between male and female more apparent than in Boccioni's oeuvre, in which the figure of the prostitute or scenes of mass transit and entertainment compete with the all-consuming image of his mother. Though the contrast between aberrant and chaste female sexuality falls securely within fin-de-siècle stereotypes, his truck with teeming street life, that is, with a feminized mass culture, elides this dominant dichotomy. Moreover, Boccioni's mother was a woman far past her sexual prime, whose finest reproductive achievement was giving birth to the artist himself. For all of his virile posturing, images of men and masculine power appeared only toward the end of his career, and the machine (by contrast to Balla's imagery) was virtually absent. In addition, psychosexual theories about the dissolution of the masculine self and the projected annihilation of the female "other" must be squared with Bergson's views on the indivisibility of all life, ideas with which Boccioni was intimately familiar. For Bergson, creative and organic evolution all formed part of the extended *élan vital*; though obviously perceived according to retrograde patriarchal values, the singular role of the female as procreator was nonetheless valued and instrumental to those who create. Of maternal love, Bergson wrote, "some have seen the great mystery of life. . . . It shows us each generation leaning over the generation that shall follow. It allows a glimpse of the fact that the living being is above all a thoroughfare, and that the essence of life is the movement by which life is transmitted."[89]

Boccioni's images of his mother, above all *Materia*, betray the creative tension within Futurist gender politics. In *Materia*, the artist's mobilizing perceptions gave life to inert matter, unifying the resistant and attracting forces of private and public, female and male, reproductive and innovative — in true reciprocal action, mother and son giving life to each other.[90] To be sure, culture is the prerogative of the male, but Boccioni's mother was anything but incidental material. The contrast to Le Fauconnier's *Abundance* (1910, fig. 9), shown at the 1911 Salon des Indépendants (and "perhaps the best-known Cubist picture in Europe before 1914"),[91] is instructive. Also influenced by Bergson's ideas, Le Fauconnier's allegory ties the fruitful female body to the earth in a worn and tired conceit. Though ungainly in its Cubist faceting and discretely swelling belly, the figure in *Abundance* follows the conventions of the academic nude and hence distances and depersonalizes the female form. Boccioni's figure, however, need not be undressed to assert her primitive matriarchal power, and she holds her own amid the action and blinding lights of the modern city. Like Picasso's *Gertrude Stein* (1906), which Boccioni saw at Stein's home on

Fig. 9 Henri Le Fauconnier
Abundance (*L'Abondance*), 1910
Oil on canvas, 75⅜ × 48⁷⁄₁₆ inches (191.5 × 123 cm)
Gemeentemuseum Den Haag

Fig. 10 *Victory of Samothrace*, Hellenistic, ca. 190 BCE
Marble, 129½ inches (328 cm) high
Musée du Louvre, Paris

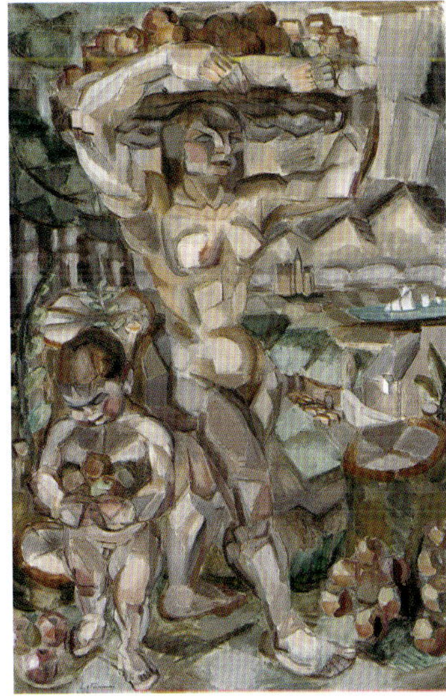

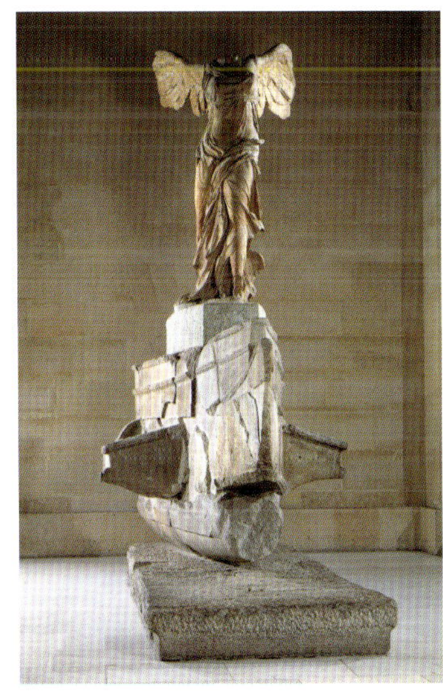

rue de Fleurus, the face in *Materia* is masklike and impenetrable, the body massive and secure onto itself. Whereas Picasso struggled with portraying a lesbian visage, Boccioni faced a post-procreative one.[92] In either case, the desexualized woman became a formidable force to be reckoned with. With her implacable presence and phallic thrust of the hands, Boccioni's figure is less "threatening lack" (representing fear of castration in Freudian terms) than an image of monumental womb envy, especially from an artist who famously expressed his recurrent frustration over creative impasse.

The female figure is not only Boccioni's central subject but is also integrally related to the evolution of his pictorial style; his progression toward abstraction emerges out of a dialogue with feminine form. In his earlier Divisionist images of modern life, including prostitution and feminized mass culture, the undulating surfaces yield under penetrating and dissolving brushwork, but then in *Materia* and related works of 1912 his mother's inviolable body is the site of a newly resistant mass. Only with the elimination of the female in the subsequent series of male athletes surging through space—the soccer player, the runner, the cyclist did Boccioni achieve abstract fields of pulsating color and unimpeded, self-propelling form. In sexual identity and pure movement, his depictions of athletes are directly related to his efforts in sculpture, culminating in *Unique Forms of Continuity in Space* (1913, cat. no. 40).

Even in *Unique Forms of Continuity in Space*, which Boccioni considered his finest sculptural achievement, woman is present in her absence. The figure of the striding warrior directly transposes *Victory of Samothrace* (ca. 190 BCE, fig. 10), the irrepressible force of Nike, alighting on the prow of a ship, her drapery blown and body defined by the counterforce of the wind. As installed in the Musée du Louvre, *Victory of Samothrace* stands on a block—a device repeated by Boccioni—surmounted on a prow. The connection to the original was made explicit by Marinetti in his "Multiplied Man and the Reign of the Machine," where he alludes to Boccioni's being of "omnipresent velocity," whose "outward swell" develops in the form of a prow.[93] For all the interpretations of Boccioni's sculpture as proto-Fascist vision of an inhumane ballistic warrior, the fact remains that the figure is well under life-size and significantly less imposing than the Hellenistic Nike. The planes of Boccioni's figure appear to flutter as much as cut through space, and the womanly body template is implicit in the concave breast cavity of the mechanistic man.

In "The Founding and Manifesto of Futurism," Marinetti had compared *Victory of Samothrace* unfavorably to the new beauty of a racing automobile, channeling the sexual charge of woman into the metallic eroticism of the machine: "You must caress them, treat them respectfully, never mishandle or overtire them. If you behave like this, your machine of fused iron and steel, this motor built to exact specifications, will give you not only what you put into it, but double or triple."[94] Fast women and fast cars have now become a cliché of modern advertising. No mere misogynist trope, Marinetti's image calculates the burgeoning economy of desire and the explicit "sex of things" that would drive modern society's collective libido.[95] Fear of biological destiny, of old age and death, is sublimated onto the consumer product, whose designed obsolescence fulfills the promise of the always available, newer model. That Nike would return as one of the most formidable, global products of late capitalism—for the runner no less—is an irony that would not have been lost on the Futurists.

Modernism/Modernity

Let us review the major points of contact between Cubism and Futurism. After their initial visit to Paris in October 1911, Futurist artists returned for the opening of their first international exhibition at Galerie Bernheim-Jeune in early February 1912 and stayed on through March. Boccioni traveled to the French capital again in early November, possibly in time to see the end of the Salon d'Automne,[96] and in summer 1913 to open an exhibition of his sculpture at Galerie La Boëtie. During these years, the Futurists' propaganda campaign of cultural imperialism and creative one-upmanship continued to be unleashed in France. Marinetti's "Technical Manifesto of Futurist Literature," dated May 1912, was excerpted in various French newspapers in early July.[97] After much advance publicity in the press, Boccioni's "Technical Manifesto of Futurist Sculpture," dated April, appeared in France at the beginning of October.[98] Therein, he advocated "utilizing any and every element of reality itself" to increase the plastic force of sculpture. Boccioni's move was not inspired by Braque's paper constructions, which were elaborated in the privacy of the studio, nor was it a response to specific, more publicly known, Cubist inventions.[99] Rather, his mixed-media sculpture was a logical internal development, progressing from the fictive representation of intersecting planes to their actual inclusion; brute matter now entered into the work of art. With his words-in-freedom, Marinetti similarly advocated the insertion of unmediated sounds and pure phenomenon unfettered by syntactical logic or subjective mood: "To substitute for human psychology, now exhausted, the lyric obsession with matter."[100]

Arguably, both of these 1912 manifestos codified the collage practice before its systematic application in Cubist or Futurist circles.[101] The Futurist precedence was acknowledged, albeit in a backhanded way, in a small but significant notice in *L'Intransigeant* on October 14. The occasion was the first exhibition of a Cubist collage, Juan Gris's *Le Lavabo* (1912), when awareness of the new medium and its challenge to originality and artistic genius entered into the public domain (as opposed to Braque and Picasso's intensely private experiments of that same autumn). As the anonymous reviewer gloated:

> *You will recall our discussion of the technical manifesto of Futurist sculpture. Therein, M. Boccioni boasted of using any and all materials to make a work of art. The small Salon of the Section d'Or has allowed the Parisian Cubists "to pull the rug from under the feet" of their Italian confreres. M. J. Gris has introduced a highly entertaining little oddity: to simplify the handiwork in his art he has simply pasted real objects onto his canvas.*[102]

In his manifesto, Boccioni heralded the end of the traditional unity of materials (the refined statuary of marble and bronze) and, with it, sublimity of subject matter. "Let's split open our figures and place the environment inside them," proclaims the text. Any number of diverse and mundane materials, even moving parts, could now vivify the "attraction and collision of planes." Along these lines, Boccioni's initial assemblages of late 1912–early 1913 (e.g., *Antigrazioso*) transposed the motifs and narrative drama of *Materia*. In *Fusion of a Head and a Window* (1912–13, destroyed; fig. 58.11), he drove actual pieces of window casement, hair, a glass eye, and wire into the gesso bulk of a head. Contrary to Boccioni's intentions, the lack of integration among unrelated materials stops all potential for action or a metaphoric unfolding of things. As a result, his subsequent sculptures each treat a single figure prolonging itself into space and—rather than construct with abstract elements, as does Picasso's *Guitar* (1912)—transpose an essentially pictorial synthesis of planes into an object seen in the round. Nonetheless, Boccioni's sculptures and manifesto opened up the possibility of a new form of unmediated artistic expression: the substitution of readymade materials and objects for creative labor.

The inclusion of mass-produced and heterogenous bits prompted an acrimonious debate between Boccioni and Papini in the open forum of *Lacerba* in early 1914. Papini posed the question, in so many words, "can a work of art be made out of something which is not a work of art?"[103] With specific reference to the collages of Picasso and Severini and Boccioni's mixed-media sculptures, Papini lamented that "instead of the lyrical or rational transformation of things, they have substituted the things themselves. . . . Art reverts to brute reality; invention becomes mere action." In other words, the circle of creation closes in on itself; authentic artistic means and labor are abandoned. Boccioni defended the inclusion of extraneous materials as a novel means of creative representation—of turning dross into gold—and not a recapitulation to primitive mimesis. Yet Papini had the last word: "If this tendency is pursued and elaborated in that given direction (that is, putting the things themselves in place of the things to be represented), then we will end up at the point of no return."[104] Unbeknownst to French and Italian avant-gardes, Duchamp had arrived there in 1913 with the interpenetration of a bicycle wheel and a kitchen stool. Duchamp's readymade was the logical consequence of merging art and life, though in a different manner from Futurist spectacle. Among the most notable failures in the history of art, Boccioni's widely seen and reviled assemblages nonetheless revealed the limits and potential of aesthetic transformation. In 1914, Picasso would return to sculpture in the round, placing a real absinthe spoon on the top of a modeled bronze for his *Absinthe Glass*.

Futurist collage was inevitably enriched by Cubist examples, especially in 1914 after Boccioni, Carrà, Papini, and Soffici again visited Paris. The primogeniture of Marinetti's words-in-freedom in relation to their collage aesthetic, however, was acknowledged in numerous collages in which Futurist artists cut and pasted words from his literary manifestos and *Zang Tumb Tuuum*. As Christine Poggi has shown, the mimetic function of word and image, the emphasis on verbal and visual patterns, unites Futurism's destruction of syntax in literary and pictorial domains, distinguishing it from Cubism's ironic play with language, fragment, and the commodity. By contrast with the unstable meaning and ambiguity of Braque and Picasso's papiers collés, the Futurists incorporated bits of newspaper for documentary fact—imparting specific political messages—or to agitate or mesmerize the viewer. Futurist words-in-freedom poems and paintings also reached a larger audience because many were reproduced in the mass press, as well as in the pages of *Lacerba*. Still rooted in an *arrière-garde* Symbolist aesthetic of lyrical expression, Poggi argued, the Futurists understood collage only pictorially, not metaphorically; collage was a means to create surface disunity, density, and texture, all to ends of visual simultaneity, rather than for multiplicity of meaning.[105] Even in mixed media then, Futurists failed to measure up to the intellectual rigor and linguistic transformations of Cubism. Yet it was precisely in their assault on precious aesthetic sensibilities that their finest influence on Cubism lay.

Predictably, the exhibitions at Bernheim-Jeune and La Boëtie provoked hostile or hilarious reactions from French critics, who were quick to defend national primacy in matters of fine art. Aside from a few ethnic slurs—Futurists were "risotto mouths" and their exhibitions "rooms of macaroni"—the popular press lampooned the pretensions of the catalogue texts and manifestos, barely addressing the art itself. "Drunk on sensations," the Futurists displayed "a complete lack of sensibility." The unfortunate spectator emerged "bruised," or with a "violent migraine," after barely escaping from the center of the picture.[106] The most damning criticism came from prestigious art critics such as the poet Roger Allard, a conservative nationalist and champion of the Salon Cubists. Allard dismissed the Futurists as mediocre talents, "as offshoots of a debased Wagnerism." They embraced spectacle—the blurring of boundaries between art and life—to detract from their lack of an authentic style. "Nothing is more odious to those who ignore technique in art," wrote Allard, "than the notion of the distinctions between genres. Hence the efforts of the barbarians to abolish them." Futurists reduced literature to a "kind of Esperanto" and art to "a Morse code of sensations." Quality, the privileges of taste, and the clarity of reason separated the connoisseur from the crowd. Preempting the later modernist criticism of Clement Greenberg and Michael Fried, Allard identified "aesthetic confusions" and theatricality as the greatest affronts to the purity and autonomy of the genuine artwork. And the Futurists were established as the most egregious bashers of the canon.[107]

The Parisian critics did protest too much, betraying their own "anxiety of influence."[108] Years later, Severini opined that the French were loath to admit their debt in the face of the Italians' "frenetic race for priority" and their "lack of tact and aggressive behavior."[109] In Giovanni Lista's more blunt assessment, French chauvinism, "as expressed by the arrogant and nationalist bourgeoisie of the Third Republic," would never have accepted the poor and backward Italians as cultural equals. But the fact remains that Cubism as a public avant-garde phenomenon existed only in relation to Futurism's activist model.[110] Futurist manifestos prompted Gleizes and Metzinger to formulate their own theoretical position and group identity with the publication of "Du Cubisme" (1912). From Ricciotto Canudo's "Manifeste de l'art cérébriste" (1914) to Le Corbusier and Amédée Ozenfant's postwar "Après le cubisme" (1918), the manifesto genre made avant-garde synonymous with movement, or group.

Even Apollinaire paid homage, if tinged with obligatory parody, in his "L'Antitradizione futurista" (1913)—having already lifted Marinetti's typographical and poetic innovations for his poem "Zone" (1912) and subsequent *calligrammes* such as "Lettre-Océan" (1914).[111] Indeed, Apollinaire emerged as the key aesthetic arbiter through whom members of the Parisian avant-garde such as Delaunay, Léger, and even Picasso could have surreptitiously borrowed from the Futurists. When he championed the progress made in Delaunay's pictures of early 1913 with their new subjects—airplanes, billboards, and rugby players—he praised them in no uncertain *Futurist* terms: "His painting, which appeared to be wholly intellectual (to the great joy of the German *Privatdozents*), now has a definitely popular character. I believe that this is one of the highest tributes one can bestow on a painter today."[112]

Rosalind Krauss has suggested that Picasso's specific, and expressed, hostility to the Futurists inspired his incorporation of newspaper within the papiers collés. Futurism represented the apex of anti-Mallarmé poetics, which had been on the rise from 1897 to 1914, advocating the deliberate contamination of artistic purity and devaluing genius of the ivory-tower variety. Increasingly threatened by Apollinaire's "conversion to the Futurist repertoire of images"—but sensitive to the the printed daily's formalist potential, which Mallarmé did not envision—Picasso usurped the banal and ephemeral, turning them into the exquisite stuff of enduring fine art.[113] Rather than addressing a public audience, Picasso's columns of newsprint served as austere formalist devices, while current events clipped and pasted on the artist's sheet became fodder for his Cubist inside jokes. In short, Cubism dirtied its hands with the cultural other, only to reinscribe its own aesthetic and social difference.

Krauss's supposition allows us to speculate further: Could Picasso and Braque's sudden inclusion of aviation puns and imagery in spring 1912 have been a direct response to Marinetti's literary manifesto, in which airplane flight as the metaphor of a revolutionary modern art enters public discourse for the first time?[114] At the very same moment, right after the garish Futurist exhibition at Bernheim-Jeune, Braque and Picasso reintroduced brilliant color into their monochrome canvases. Are not Picasso's *The Scallop Shell: "Notre Avenir est dans l'air"* (May 1912) and *Landscape with Posters* (July 1912) also direct responses to Futurism's onslaught? The use of color in these pictures is pointedly restricted to motifs of modern dynamism and the commodity. Of course, Picasso's wry use of ripolin enamel house paint instead of the venerable artist's medium of oil trumps the Futurists at their own commercial game. The notion that Futurist "states of mind"—the emotive depiction of fragmented memory images—did not figure into Braque and Picasso's strictly conceptual compositions is also erroneous. As Pepe Karmel has observed, it is probably not a coincidence that the two Cubist paintings richest in personal allusions—Picasso's *Violin, Wineglasses, Pipe, and Anchor* and its pendant,

Souvenir du Havre (both May 1912)—were painted after the Futurist exhibition.[115] "Havre" and "Honfleur," which appear as inscriptions in these paintings, refer to a trip Picasso made with Braque that April. The subject of "travel memory" was introduced in canvases exhibited at the Futurists' Bernheim-Jeune debut: Severini's *Souvenirs de Voyage* (1910–11) and Boccioni's triptych *States of Mind* (1911, figs. 20–22), consisting of *The Farewells*, *Those Who Go*, and *Those Who Stay*.

This is not to become embroiled in the question of "who did what first?" although the intense dialogue between Cubists and Futurists was motivated by just such a competition. Historically, as we have seen, Futurist claims have been attributed to mere bluster, pace Picasso's admission "when there is something to steal, I steal."[116] Yet even when acknowledged, the Cubist debt to Futurism is seen in parodic terms, as behooves the ironic wit, intellectual *jeu d'esprit*, and prodigious innovative capacity of Picasso. The Futurists have the dubious identity of vulgarians at the gate, whose threatening proximity served to entrench the already antagonistic positions between high art and popular culture, sincerity and bluff. To their folly and improvisation are juxtaposed French genius and deliberation. But this interpretation of Cubist exclusivity has its price. For all its internal play with linguistic signs, Cubism folds in on itself and becomes a unified signifier for aesthetic modernism. Instead, Futurism emerges as a complex of signifiers; it is as diverse, contradictory, and open-ended as modern life. To paraphrase Reyner Banham, Futurism changed the way the world was seen; Braque and Picasso's Cubist pictures were hardly seen at all.[117]

Though not elitist in questions of audience or taste, the Futurists were anything but populists. Unlike practitioners of the Russian avant-garde, Futurist painters never gave up traditional fine-art mediums for the anonymity and mass reproduction of photography; they never repudiated traditional values of individual style, nor what they vaunted as the Italian "racial" trait of superior creative genius. The utopian prototype for machine production, as well as the nihilistic readymade, did not enter the Futurists' lexicon. They did, however, extend their aim of merging art and life into direct political activism, beginning with their history as Socialists or Anarchic-Syndicalists, then Interventionists, and finally Fascists. The Futurists transformed the subjective aesthetic experience from object to event and, with it, created a new art of persuasion. Informed by the theories of Gustave Le Bon and Sorel, they perceived the public, not as being constituted of rational individuals capable of critical reasoning, but as an emotive collective whose desires could be directed and controlled. The political value of their movement ultimately lay in its innovative and aggressive means of shaping public opinion, in the totalizing fabric of the spectacle. While accepting the demise of the traditional ivory tower aesthete, Futurists retained the privileged position of fashioning an image and, through it, reality. Above all, Futurism concerned itself with fashioning the image of a new Italy, a goal that sealed the movement's fate with that of Fascism.

Notes

Two colleagues were extraordinarily generous in the preparation of this essay: Jeffrey Weiss, who allowed me to peruse his compendium of French criticism on Futurism in the years before World War I, and Pepe Karmel, who gave me access to an advance copy of his book *Picasso and the Invention of Cubism* (New Haven: Yale University Press, 2003). I am also indebted to them both for ideas and comments; any missteps are my own. Lucia Re and Marilyn McCully provided essential help with translation and documentation, and I am grateful to Peter Gay for his comments on the manuscript. Many of the ideas herein were developed in my lectures on Cubism and Futurism at the Graduate Center, CUNY, and have benefited from the dynamic input of my students, especially Vivien Greene. Last, I am grateful to Laura Mattioli Rossi for insisting that I write this essay and to an anonymous collector who has obliged me to look continually at Cubist pictures and not just read about them. All translations are by the author unless otherwise indicated.

1 Giovanni Papini, "Contro il futurismo," *Lacerba*, March 15, 1913, pp. 48, 46.

2 Guillaume Apollinaire, "Futurism," in Leroy C. Breunig, ed., *Apollinaire on Art: Essays and Reviews 1902–1918*, trans. Susan Suleiman (New York: Da Capo Press, 1972), p. 255; originally published in French in *L'Intermédiare des chercheurs et des curieux*, October 10, 1912.

3 The phrase "jackdaw [or "jay"] in peacock's feathers" comes from Apollinaire, "The Salon d'Automne," in Breunig, *Apollinaire on Art*, p. 114; originally published in French in *Poésie* (autumn 1910). Apollinaire first denounced the Salon Cubists and then went on to champion them as part of his attempt to be associated with all the advanced painters, including the Futurists. The rift between Braque and Picasso on one side and the Salon Cubists on the other, and the politics of the art world that conspired to keep them apart, are recounted in John Richardson, with the collaboration of Marilyn McCully, *1907–1917: The Painter of Modern Life*, vol. 2 of *A Life of Picasso* (New York: Random House, 1996), pp. 207–19.

4 William Rubin, *Picasso and Braque: Pioneering Cubism*, exh. cat. (New York: Museum of Modern Art, 1989), p. 11. In his definitive narrative of the artists' creative partnership (pp. 15–62), Rubin commented that he did not "regard the two artists as equals. Braque is one of the great modern painters, but we must go back to the most prodigious Renaissance masters for the like of Picasso" (p. 15). That Picasso was the more innovative artist was also the opinion of critics at that time, as per Rubin's account (pp. 41–47).

5 See essays and debates in Lynn Zelevansky, ed., *Picasso and Braque: A Symposium* (New York: Museum of Modern Art, 1992). See also the bibliography in Zelevansky for the groundbreaking, if orthodox, studies on Cubism and semiotics by Yve-Alain Bois and Rosalind Krauss. The finest application of poststructuralist and semiotic approaches, both for clarity of analysis and richness of interpretation, can be found in Christine Poggi, *In Defiance of Painting: Cubism, Futurism, and the Invention of Collage* (New Haven: Yale University Press, 1992). For a significant revision and elaboration of the linguistic model, see Pepe Karmel, *Picasso and the Invention of Cubism* (New Haven: Yale University Press, 2003).

6 Gertrude Stein, *The Autobiography of Alice B. Toklas* (1933; New York: Vintage Books, 1990), p. 102. Going against the grain of contemporary criticism, which found the Futurists irritating or sensationalist, Stein demurred, "In any case everybody found the futurists very dull" (p. 125). To which, Gino Severini countered, "They *were* boring really, with their impossible 'petit-nègre' French, but Miss Stein, although highly intelligent, was probably unaware of how much more amusing she was in her books than at her parties. In fact, it always amazed me that Picasso, a maniac about independence, could put up with her." Severini, *The Life of a Painter*, trans. Jennifer Franchina (Princeton: Princeton University Press, 1995), pp. 92–93.

7 The profound influence of Marey on art and its paradoxical interaction with Bergson's philosophy are documented in Marta Braun, *Picturing Time: The Works of Etienne-Jules Marey (1830–1904)* (Chicago: University of Chicago Press, 1992), especially chapter 7.

8 However, Balla joined Boccioni, Carrà, Russolo, and Severini in signing the exhibition's catalogue text, "Les Exposants au public" (published as "The Exhibitors to the Public" for the London Sackville Gallery show in March) as he had joined them in 1910 in signing the "Manifesto of the Futurist Painters" and "Futurist Painting: Technical Manifesto"; he was unquestionably aligned with Futurism.

9 Giacomo Balla and Fortunato Depero, "Futurist Reconstruction of the Universe" (March 11, 1915), in Umbro Apollonio, ed., *Futurist Manifestos*, trans. Robert Brain (New York: Viking Press, 1970), pp. 197–200.

10 See Estera Milman, "Futurism as a Submerged Paradigm for Artistic Activism and Practical Anarchism," *South Central Review* 13 (summer–fall 1996), pp. 157–79. For a significant early exception to the formalist pattern, see Reyner Banham, *Theory and Design in the First Machine Age*, 2d ed. (Cambridge: MIT Press, 1960). Banham positioned Futurism as the engine of twentieth-century theories of design and cultural modernity. Along with Lawrence Alloway, whose tastes were also congenial to Futurism, Banham was part of the British Independent Group (often characterized as British Pop), which valued consumerism and technology over aesthetic modernism. Curiously Banham's text, one of the most fundamental on the machine age, has not been cited in any of the recent Anglo-American revisionist texts on Futurism and Futurist historiography, including Milman's.

11 See Ester Coen, *Umberto Boccioni*, exh. cat. (New York: Metropolitan Museum of Art, 1988); and Anne Coffin Hanson, *Gino Severini*, exh. cat. (New Haven: Yale University Art Gallery, 1996). Futurist surveys were organized by the Museum of Modern Art, New York, in 1961, the Guggenheim Museum, New York, in 1973, the Philadelphia Museum of Art in 1980, and the Yale University Art Gallery in 1983; the latter three shows relied heavily on the Winston-Malbin Collection, the singular American collection of Italian Futurism, now dispersed.

12 The Italian literature on Second Futurism is extensive. Anglo-American studies on Second Futurism have focused on its relationship to Fascism and on women Futurists; a comprehensive art historical account of Futurism in the 1920s and 1930s, including Aeropittura, remains to be done. In English, see *Futurism Aeropittura*, exh. cat. (Philadelphia: Tyler School of Art, Temple University, 1987); *Futurism in Flight*, exh. cat. (London: Accademia Italiana delle Arti e delle Arti Applicate, 1990); *La Futurista: Benedetta Cappa Marinetti*, exh. cat. (Philadelphia: The Galleries at Moore, Moore College of Art and Design, 1998); and Gabriella Belli, ed., *Depero Futurista* (Milan: Skira Editore, 1999).

13 See, for example, *South Central Review* 13 (summer–fall 1996) and *Modernism/modernity* 1, no. 1 (September 1994), issues devoted to Futurism; Walter Adamson, *Avant-Garde Florence: From Modernism to Fascism* (Cambridge: Harvard University Press, 1993); Günther Berghaus, *Italian Futurist Theatre* (Oxford: Oxford University Press, 1998); Berghaus, *Futurism and Politics: Between Anarchist Rebellion and Fascist Reaction 1909–1944* (Providence: Berghahn Books, 1996); and Cinzia Blum, *The Other Modernism: F. T. Marinetti's Futurist Fiction of Power* (Berkeley: University of California Press, 1996).

14 Renato Poggioli, *The Theory of the Avant-Garde* (Cambridge: Harvard University Press, 1968); and Peter Bürger, *Theory of the Avant-Garde*, trans. Michael Shaw (Minneapolis: University of Minnesota Press, 1984)—standard texts on the historical avant-garde—both avoid discussion of the Italian Futurists for ideological reasons.

15 See F. T. Marinetti, "The Variety Theatre" (September 29, 1913), in Apollonio, *Futurist Manifestos*, pp. 126–31. Severini stated, "Marinetti . . . had become something of a 'manager' to a variety show and was organizing exhibitions in London, Berlin, Bruxelles, and Holland. . . . In this respect, that is, in subordinating everything to an extrinsic end, to a 'given effect,' Marinetti was master and innovator." Severini, *Life of a Painter*, pp. 93, 104. The relationship between Marinetti, the musical hall, and the identity of the avant-garde is thoroughly explored in Jeffrey Weiss, *The Popular Culture of Modern Art: Picasso, Duchamp, and Avant-Gardism* (New Haven: Yale University Press, 1994), pp. 39–43.

16 See Marjorie Perloff, *The Futurist Moment: Avant-Garde, Avant-Guerre, and the Language of Rupture* (Chicago: University of Chicago Press, 1986), pp. 81–115. This remains the definitive study of the manifesto as modernist literary form, demonstrating, in particular, how Marinetti blurred boundaries between traditional genres and mediums.

17 The key treatment in English of Marinetti's role as entrepreneur is Claudia Salaris, "Marketing Modernism: Marinetti as Publisher," *Modernism/modernity* 1 (September 1994), pp. 109–27. Salaris used the word "factory" (with obvious allusions to Andy Warhol) to describe Marinetti's production of books, magazines, and leaflets, a prodigious output that defined Futurist culture as a consumable "product."

18 F. T. Marinetti, "Technical Manifesto of Futurist Literature" (May 11, 1912), in Marinetti, *Let's Murder the Moonshine: Selected Writings*, ed. R. W. Flint, trans. Flint and Arthur A. Coppotelli (Los Angeles: Sun & Moon Press, 1991), pp. 93, 94, 96.

19 See Jeffrey Schnapp, "Politics and Poetics in F. T. Marinetti's *Zang Tumb Tuuum*," *Stanford Italian Review* 5, no. 1 (1985), pp. 75–92. Schnapp described Marinetti's performances as a new form of agit-prop wherein the power of the word, reinforced by the bodily presence of the declaimer "will flow unhindered between author and readerly mass" (pp. 82–83).

20 F. T. Marinetti, "Destruction of Syntax—Imagination without Strings—Words-in-Freedom" (May 11, 1913), in Apollonio, *Futurist Manifestos*, pp. 98, 105.

21 Quotations from Marinetti, "Variety Theatre," pp. 126–27.

22 See Berghaus, *Futurism and Politics*, pp. 48–52, 73–83.

23 M.L., "Une conférence futuriste," *Homme libre*, June 23, 1913, p. 2; and "La Loufoquerie sans fils," *Les Hommes du jour*, July 12, 1913, p. 6.

24 Marinetti, "Variety Theatre," p. 127. In defense of the Futurists, Papini wrote, "The buffoonery of the Futurist evenings is not so much the fault of the Futurists than of the listeners.... *The public amuses itself on its own*—that is, with its shouts, its guffaws and hurling of vegetables." Papini, "Contro il futurismo," *Lacerba*, March 15, 1913, p. 45.

25 Weiss, *The Popular Culture of Modern Art*, pp. 56–57. Weiss established the connection made in the critical press between avant-gardism and the insincerity of *bluff* and *réclame* (publicity).

26 Guillaume Apollinaire, "The Italian Futurist Painters," in Breunig, *Apollinaire on Art*, pp. 199, 200; originally published in French in *L'Intransigeant*, February 7, 1912. For similarly disparaging language, see Apollinaire, "Art News: The Futurists," in Breunig, pp. 200–205; originally published in French in *Le Petit Bleu*, February 9, 1912.

27 Daniel-Henry Kahnweiler, *My Galleries and Painters*, trans. Helen Weaver (New York: Viking Press, 1971), p. 42. Kahnweiler also stated, "Around 1914 there were some who were more quarrelsome than the surrealists who came after them, namely the Futurists, who actually had fist fights with their enemies at all their meetings; but this was exactly the opposite of what we wanted. My friends asked only to work; they had no wish to provoke, they knew what they were doing, and they only wanted to do their work.... They worked quietly, but, as I said, with absolute conviction" (p. 42).

28 See Richardson, *Painter of Modern Life*, p. 213; and Michael FitzGerald, *Making Modernism: Picasso and the Creation of the Art Market for Twentieth Century Art* (Berkeley: University of California Press, 1996).

29 See, for example, the opinion of Hélène d'Oettingen (Roche Grey), patron of *Les Soirées de Paris*, intimate of Picasso's circle, and contributor to *Lacerba*: "Individual aggression yearns for solidity of spirit, penetrated by unshakable faith—rare qualities that create mass movements and subordinate them. The first, that which bears the term inventor, the best led and the best organized, that which engendered all the others, was Futurism. For the first time in the sphere of Art they employed the means which were until then known only in commerce.... A team of fighters, the Futurists did not have the qualities to create masterpieces, but they left in the world of arts and letters the memory of their brilliant and tumultuous gatherings, of their celebrity and their influence." Roche Grey in Giovanni Lista, ed., *Futurisme: Manifestes, Proclamations, Documents* (Lausanne: L'Age d'homme, 1973), p. 435; originally published in French in *Paris* 1 (November 1924).

30 See Ardengo Soffici, "Picasso e Braque," *La Voce*, August 24, 1911, pp. 635–37; Soffici also translated a piece on Cubism by the French critic Henri Des Pruraux, which appeared a few months later as "Intorno al cubismo" in the December 7 issue of *La Voce*. For the exchange between Soffici and Prezzolini, see Alessando Del Puppo, *"Lacerba" 1913–1915: Arte e critica d'arte* (Bergamo: Lubrina Editore, 2000), p. 44. Lista noted that the first Cubist pictures likely seen by Boccioni were as illustrations reproduced in an article by Roger Allard in the June 1911 issue of *Les Marches du sud-ouest*: Léger's *Nus dans le forêt*, a nude by Gleizes, and a landscape by Le Fauconnier. See Lista, *Manifestes, Proclamations, Documents*, p. 50.

31 See Braun, *Picturing Time*, pp. 275–81, 291.

32 Umberto Boccioni, Carlo Carrà, Luigi Russolo, Giacomo Balla, and Gino Severini, "Futurist Painting: Technical Manifesto" (April 11, 1910), in Apollonio, *Futurist Manifestos*, p. 27.

33 "In the eyes of other countries, Italy is still a land of the dead, a vast Pompeii, white with sepulchres. But Italy is being reborn. Its political resurgence will be followed by a cultural resurgence." Umberto Boccioni, Carlo Carrà, Luigi Russolo, Giacomo Balla, and Gino Severini, "Manifesto of the Futurist Painters" (February 11, 1910), in Apollonio, *Futurist Manifestos*, p. 25.

34 In discussing the importance of Soffici's "Picasso e Braque," Rubin referred to it as "the earliest description of Cubism as something of joint venture of Picasso and Braque." See Rubin, *Picasso and Braque*, pp. 43–44.

35 Soffici referred to "tactile values" and Bernard Berenson's use of this term in writing about Florentine Renaissance painters. See Soffici, "Picasso e Braque," p. 636. The link between the Italian primitives and the primordial pictorial values of mass and volume anticipated Soffici's latent and reactionary Tuscan regionalism, which emerged full-blown during World War I. More immediately, it complicated one aspect of the dialogue between Cubism and Futurism: Futurists scorned the "static classicism," or compacted volumes, of their French peers, at the same that they claimed Italian primogeniture over autonomous "plastic values."

36 Daniel-Henry Kahnweiler, *Les Sculptures de Picasso* (Paris: Editions du Chêne, 1948), unpaginated. The historical and conceptual links between Symbolist theories of the sign and Picasso's radical exploitation of visual metaphor, metonymy, and synecdoche are detailed in Karmel, *Picasso and the Invention of Cubism*.

37 See David Cottington, *Cubism in the Shadow of War: The Avant-Garde and Politics in Paris 1905–1914* (New Haven: Yale University Press, 1998), pp. 123–43, especially p. 132.

38 Marinetti, "Destruction of Syntax," p. 105.

39 Boccioni, Carrà, Russolo, Balla, and Severini, "Manifesto of the Futurist Painters," p. 25.

40 Ardengo Soffici, "Chicchi del Grappolo," *Lacerba*, April 15, 1913, pp. 77–78. For a detailed account of the evolution of Soffici's aesthetics in relation to both Cubism and Futurism, see Del Puppo, *"Lacerba" 1913–1915*.

41 F. T. Marinetti, "The Founding and Manifesto of Futurism" (February 20, 1909), in Apollonio, *Futurist Manifestos*, p. 21.

42 See Leo Steinberg, "The Philosophical Brothel," *October* 44 (spring 1988), pp. 7–74; William Rubin, Hélène Seckel, and Judith Cousins, *Les Demoiselles d'Avignon* (New York: Museum of Modern Art, 1994); and David Lomas, "A Canon of Deformity: *Les Demoiselles d'Avignon* and Physical Anthropology," *Art History* 16 (September 1993), pp. 424–46.

43 Umberto Boccioni, "Fondamento plastico della scultura e pittura futuriste," *Lacerba*, March 15, 1913, p. 51.

44 Ibid., p. 51. Soon after Boccioni championed *antigrazioso*, and also in *Lacerbo*, Balilla Pratella offered a similar definition of *il grazioso* as being "of bourgeois origins and feminine indolence; it has many connotations: the refined, the pretty, the ladylike, the noble etc.... *joli* in France." Pratella, "Contro il *Grazioso* in musica ... e di altro ancora," *Lacerba*, May 15, 1913, p. 103.

45 Despite repeated efforts, the Italians did not have a colonial empire in Africa until the conquest of Libya in 1912 and then Ethiopia in 1936. Futurist imperialist discourse, which was rabid, was not explicit in their visual art until the Aeropittura movement of the 1930s.

46 The term "soft primitivism," in reference to Gauguin's work, is used in William Rubin, *Les Demoiselles d'Avignon*, p. 39. For the differences between Oceanic and African art as interpreted by western European artists, see Rubin, "Picasso," in Rubin, ed., *Primitivism in 20th Century Art: Affinity of the Tribal and the Modern* (New York: Museum of Modern Art, 1984), vol. 1, pp. 241–343. See also Tamar Garb, "'To Kill the Nineteenth Century': Sex and Spectatorship with Gertrude and Pablo," in Christopher Green, ed., *Picasso's Les Demoiselles d'Avignon* (New York: Cambridge University Press, 2001), pp. 55–75. Garb argued that Gertrude Stein was one of the few to appreciate Picasso's *Demoiselles* for its potent force of "ugliness" and that this ugliness evidenced not only the positive struggle of its creation but also death to the old way of viewing things: "What the painting represented to her [Stein] was an attack on a genre, not an attack on women" (p. 59). The violent metaphor of Garb's essay title (which is unwittingly Futurist) and the weight she assigned to Stein's aesthetic of the ugly underscore what Boccioni saw in *Demoiselles* as well; in *Materia* and other *Antigrazioso* works, he amalgamated this ugliness with high Analytic Cubist form.

47 Marinetti, "Technical Manifesto of Futurist Literature," p. 97.

48 Umberto Boccioni, Carlo Carrà, Luigi Russolo, Giacomo Balla, and Gino Severini, "Prefazione al catalogo della prima esposizione di pittura futurista," in Boccioni, *Pittura scultura futuriste (Dinamismo plastico)* (Milan: Edizioni Futuriste di "Poesia," 1914), p. 387; originally published as "Les Exposants au public," in *Les Peintres futuristes italiens* (Paris: Galerie Bernheim-Jeune, 1912). A similar phrase also appears in Boccioni, "What Divides Us from Cubism," in Coen, *Umberto Boccioni*, p. 247; originally published in Italian in *Pittura scultura futuriste*.

49 A photograph of Picasso in his studio, datable to autumn 1911, shows *Head (Fernande)* (in bronze). See Rubin, *Picasso and Braque*, p. 17. Boccioni could have also viewed it that fall in Ambroise Vollard's gallery.

50 Henri Bergson, *Matter and Memory*, trans. Nancy Margaret Paul and W. Scott Palmer (5th ed., 1908; New York: Zone Books, 1988), p. 9. From the extensive literature on Bergson and the avant-garde, see the fundamental study, Mark Antliff, *Inventing Bergson: Cultural Politics and the Parisian Avant-Garde* (Princeton: Princeton University Press, 1993); Linda Dalrymple Henderson, *The Fourth Dimension and Non-Euclidean Geometry in Modern Art* (Princeton: Princeton University Press, 1983); and Braun, *Picturing Time*.

51 Marinetti, "Technical Manifesto of Futurist Literature," p. 96; and Marinetti, "Destruction of Syntax," pp. 102–03.

52 Boccioni, "What Divides Us from Cubism," pp. 243, 244.

53 The phrase is from Roberto Longhi, "I pittori futuristi," *La Voce*, April 10, 1913. Longhi was reviewing favorably Boccioni's *Elasticity*, which was exhibited, along with *Materia*, at the Teatro Costanzi. See also Longhi, *Scultura futurista: Boccioni* (Florence, 1914).

54 Boccioni, "What Divides Us from Cubism," p. 243.

55 See collection of the period's French criticism in Giovanni Lista, *Il futurismo* (Milan: Jaca, 1986). Rubin defined Cubism as "the twentieth-century embodiment of Leonardo's definition of painting as a *cosa mentale*" in his *Picasso and Braque*, p. 15.

56 See Marinetti's writings "We Abjure Our Symbolist Masters, the Last Lovers of the Moon" (1911–15), "Multiplied Man and the Reign of the Machine" (1911–15), and "Geometric and Mechanical Splendor and the Numerical Sensibility" (March–April 1914), in Marinetti, *Let's Murder the Moonshine*, pp. 74–76, 98–101, 105–11.

57 Boccioni, Carrà, Russolo, Balla, and Severini, "Prefazione," p. 384.

58 The defacement of *The Laugh* is recorded in Coen, *Umberto Boccioni*, pp. 107–09. According to Nell Walden, who acquired *Forces of the Street* from Herwarth Walden, an irate viewer punctured a small hole in the canvas (likely with an umbrella) while it hung in the Futurist exhibition at Walden's Der Sturm gallery in Berlin in 1912. Boccioni apparently chose not to restore it fully; the hole in the upper right was left uncovered, though the canvas's torn edges were touched up with blue and violet paint. When she sold the painting, Nell Walden passed this information on to the new owners, and I thank Paolo Baldacci for bringing it to my attention.

59 Boccioni, "What Divides Us from Cubism," p. 243; and Boccioni, Carrà, Russolo, Balla, and Severini, "Prefazione," p. 389.

60 It is possible that Boccioni met Marcel Duchamp during the Futurist exhibition at Galerie Bernheim-Jeune in early February 1912; see Coen, *Umberto Boccioni*, p. xliv. Although the literature stresses the resemblance of Boccioni's cyborg figure to Duchamp's *Nude Descending a Staircase (No. 2)* (1912, cat. no. 15), it is much closer to the *King and Queen Traversed by Swift Nudes* of May 1912 (whose title would have appealed to Boccioni). At the request of Gleizes, *Nude Descending a Staircase (No. 2)* was pulled from the 1912 Salon des Indépendants around the time of the opening on March 20, so it is unclear whether Boccioni even saw it while he was in Paris in February–March. Boccioni may have seen both paintings in Duchamp's studio when he returned to Paris later in 1912. Severini, in *The Life of a Painter*, p. 110, dated this trip to late June–early summer, but there is no documentation to that effect. Instead, Boccioni likely visited the French capital in the fall. According to letters dated November 9 and 15, and analyzed in Maurizio Calvesi and Ester Coen, *Boccioni. L'opera completa* (Milan: Electa, 1983), p. 108. Boccioni was in Paris briefly that month to see the Salon d'Automne. The question remains whether he managed to see *Nude Descending a Staircase (No. 2)* and/or *The King and Queen Traversed by Swift Nudes*, which had both been on view October 10–30 in the Section D'Or at Galerie La Boëtie. The Futurists' influence on Duchamp (excluding their common knowledge of Marey's photographs) is discussed in Linda Dalrymple Henderson, *Duchamp in Context: Science and Technology in the Large Glass and Related Works* (Princeton: Princeton University Press, 1998), pp. 16, 243 n. 6.

61 The accusation that the Futurist depiction of movement was "cinematic" was ubiquitous in the contemporaneous criticism in Italy and France. On the conflict between Boccioni and Balla over the use of photographic images and Balla's friendship with photographer Anton Giulio Bragaglia, see Braun, *Picturing Time*, pp. 296–311. Bragaglia's interests were infused with spiritualism and the occult; for the link in Futurist practice between occult beliefs and science of that time, see *Okkultismus und Avantgarde: Von Munch bis Mondrian, 1900–1915* (Frankfurt: Schirn Kunsthalle, 1995); and Simona Cigliana, *Futurismo esoterico: Contributi per una storia dell'irrazionalismo italiana fra otto e novecento* (Naples: Liguori, 2002).

62 Boccioni, Carrà, Russolo, Balla, and Severini, "Prefazione," p. 383.

63 See Cottington, *Cubism in the Shadow of War*, pp. 87–122; Antliff, *Inventing Bergson*; and Antliff, "Organicism against Itself: Cubism, Duchamp-Villon, and the Contradictions of Modernism," *Word and Image* 12 (July–September 1996), pp. 366–88.

64 Marinetti had close ties with these writers in his Parisian days as a Symbolist poet. See Marianne Martin, "Futurism, Unanimism and Apollinaire," *Art Journal* 28 (spring 1969), pp. 258–68. Martin compared "the artistically feeble renditions of 'modern epics'" painted by the Salon Cubists in 1910–11 "and the much more vital, synthetic works executed after they had seen the Futurist works and evidently had thought and talked at length about the aims of the Italians" (p. 167).

65 Umberto Boccioni, "I futuristi plagiati in Francia," *Lacerba*, April 1, 1913, pp. 66–68. This piece was a reaction to Apollinaire, "Through the Salon des Indépendants," in Breunig, *Apollinaire on Art*, pp. 286–93; originally published in French in *Montjoie*, March 18, 1913. Virginia Spate wrote that the sheer force of the Futurists' words and images made Delaunay reconsider issues of representing dynamism, simultanism, and the subjects of modern life. See Spate, *Orphism: The Evolution of Non-Figurative Painting in Paris 1910–1914* (Oxford: Clarendon Press, 1979), pp. 29–30. See also Calvesi and Coen, "Precisazioni e inediti sulla polemica tra Apollinaire e Boccioni e sul Manifesto dell'Antitradizione," in *Boccioni*, pp. 124–28.

66 As Christopher Green noted, Delaunay's "literary simultanism" of late 1912–13 was a response to Blaise Cendrars, especially his Futurist-inspired collage poem "La Prose du transsibérien" (1913) and to Apollinaire's new appreciation of Futurism. See Green, *Léger and the Avant-Garde* (New Haven: Yale University Press, 1976) pp. 77–79. After championing "pure painting" in 1912, Apollinaire, in "Through the Salon des Indépendants," declared the return of the subject in painting in 1913.

67 Léger's *Study for Three Portraits* was on view at the 1911 Salon d'Automne. Boccioni, in "Il dinamismo futurista e la pittura francese," *Lacerba*, August 1, 1913, pp. 169–71, commented favorably on Léger, claiming that his recent article in *Montjoie* was "a true act of Futurist faith." See also note 30 above.

68 The account in Green, *Léger and the Avant-Garde*, of Léger's development in the prewar years has been one of the few to detail the specifics and degree of Futurist influence on the Parisan avant-garde. As Green noted (pp. 42–44), changes made in Léger's *Le Noce* of 1912, for example, show a direct response to Futurist canvases seen at Galerie Bernheim-Jeune in February of that year. Already in 1909–10, the Futurist manifestos prompted innovations in Léger's "dynamic Cubism."

69 Marinetti argued for the role of laughter in diverting humanity from "material and moral grief" in his "Variety Theatre," p. 127. Comic effects are the basis for distraction and amusements, for "conquering resistances" (p. 128). As the main effect of the revue, laughter "destroys the Solemn, the Sacred, the Serious, and the Sublime in Art with a capital A" (p. 129). Bergson, in his *Le Rire* (1900)—which may have influenced Boccioni's painting *The Laugh*—claimed laughter to be a critical tool for navigating social life. An earlier precedent can be found in Charles Baudelaire, "On the Essence of Laughter" (1855–57) in Baudelaire, *The Painter of Modern Life and Other Essays*, trans. Jonathan Mayne (London: Phaidon, 1964), pp. 147–65. On the comic force of the modern revue, see Weiss, *Popular Culture of Modern Art*, pp. 39–41.

70 Marshall Berman, *All that Is Solid Melts into Air: The Experience of Modernity* (New York: Simon and Schuster, 1981).

71 Boccioni, Carrà, Russolo, Balla, and Severini, "Futurist Painting: Technical Manifesto," p. 29. The three canvases exhibited in Paris were *The Laugh*, *The Modern Idol*, and *The Roundup*.

72 Ibid.; and Boccioni, Carrà, Russolo, Balla, and Severini, "Prefazione," p. 387.

73 Roderich Hellman, "Della Prostituzione," excepted and translated from *Über Geschlechtsfreiheit* (Berlin, 1878), in *Lacerba*, November 1, 1913, p. 245. Hellman's piece was part of a larger inquiry into sexuality—including sexual perversion, prostitution, motherhood, and sex education—that began in the Florentine *La Voce* and continued in its more belligerent-toned offspring, *Lacerba*. See, for example, Tavolato, "Elogio della prostituzione," *Lacerba*, May 1, 1913, pp. 89–92. Marinetti aimed to "systematically prostitute all of classic art on the stage," as he wrote in his "Variety Theatre," p. 130.

74 See Charles Baudelaire, "The Painter of Modern Life," in Baudelaire, *Painter of Modern Life*, pp. 1–40. The characterization of Marinetti is from Apollinaire, "Art News: The Futurists," p. 201.

75 See Baudelaire, "Painter of Modern Life," p. 13, and on women and prostitutes, pp. 34–38. Salaris connected Marinetti's embrace of commodity culture to Baudelaire's prescient understanding of the outmoded role of traditional art and artist in the age of mass society, as articulated in his prose poem "Perte d'auréole" (1869) from the collection *Le Spleen de Paris*. See Salaris, "Marketing Modernism," pp. 109–10.

76 Though Baudelaire's flaneur exists in the "heart of the multitude," he remains "hidden from the world," and "incognito." Baudelaire, "Painter of Modern Life," p. 9. On the leap from the flaneur to the activist, see Walter Benjamin: "His thirst for the new is quenched by the crowd, which appears self-impelled and endowed with a soul of its own. In fact, this collective is nothing but appearance. This 'crowd' in which the flâneur takes delight, is just the empty mould with which, seventy years later, the *Volksgemeinschaft* [People's Community] was cast." Benjamin, *The Arcades Project*, trans. Howard Eiland and Kevin McLaughlin (Cambridge: Harvard University Press, 1999), pp. 345–46.

77 For a summary of the nineteenth-century origins of associating mass culture with the feminine, see Andreas Huyssen, *After the Great Divide: Modernism, Mass Culture, Postmodernism* (Bloomington: Indiana University Press, 1986), especially pp. 44–62; and a more extensive analysis in Rita Felski, *The Gender of Modernity* (Cambridge: Harvard University Press, 1995).

78 Boccioni to his family, April 17, 1906, in Coen, *Umberto Boccioni*, p. xliii.

79 Cinzia Sartini Blum, *The Other Modernism: F. T. Marinetti's Futurist Fiction of Power* (Berkeley: University of California Press, 1996). In her excellent, largely psychoanalytic analysis of Marinetti's rhetoric, Blum identified an ideological construct of individual and national regeneration achieved through the annihilation of the sexual other. Futurist misogyny was the result of "a profound destabilization of the western ideal of the separate, bound, and autonomous subject" (p. ix). In this, she and other recent interpreters of the

proto-Fascist Futurist body have been influenced by the German model analyzed by Klaus Theweleit in his landmark *Male Fantasies*, trans. Stephan Conway, Erica Carter, and Chris Turner, 2 vols. (Minneapolis: University of Minnesota Press, 1987–89). As Blum also admitted, "Futurist rhetoric's abjection of the 'feminine other' does not conform to the actual standing of women within the movement" (p. xi).

80 Marinetti, quoted in Balla and Depero, "Futurist Reconstruction of the Universe," p. 198.

81 See Christine Poggi, "Dreams of Metallized Flesh: Futurism and the Masculine Body," *Modernism/modernity* 4, no. 3 (September 1997), pp. 19–43. The incompatibility of Balla's art with the misogyny of Marinetti's Futurism was the subject of my paper "Balla and Benedetta: Problems in Futurist Gender Theory," at the symposium *Futurism, Feminism, and the Work of Benedetta Marinetti Cappa*, Moore College of Art and Design, Philadelphia, September 1998.

82 See Lucia Re, "Futurism and Feminism," *Annali d'Italianistica* 7 (1989), pp. 253–71; Re, "Impure Abstraction: Benedetta as Visual Artist and Novelist," in *La futurista: Benedetta Cappa Marinetti*, pp. 31–47. Walter Adamson, "Futurism, Mass Culture and Women: The Reshaping of the Artistic Vocation, 1909–1920," *Modernism/modernity* 4 (January 1997), pp. 89–114; and Mirella Bentivoglio and Franca Zoccoli, *Women Artists of Futurism: Almost Lost to History* (New York: Midmarch Arts Press, 1997).

83 For more on Valentine de Saint-Point, see Lista, *Manifestes, Proclamations, Documents*, pp. 51–57; and Nancy Locke, "Valentine de Saint-Point and the Fascist Construction of Women," in Matthew Affron and Mark Antliff, eds., *Fascist Visions: Art and Ideology in France and Italy* (Princeton: Princeton University Press, 1997), pp. 73–100.

84 Umberto Boccioni, Carlo Carrà, Luigi Russolo, Giacomo Balla, and Gino Severini, "Futurist Painting: Technical Manifesto," in Apollonio, *Futurist Manifestos*, p. 30. See also Green, *Léger and the Avant-Garde*, pp. 45–48.

85 See Green, *Léger and the Avant-Garde*, p. 56.

86 John Richardson, *A Life of Picasso*, 2 vols. to date (New York: Random House, 1991 and 1996), has proven the indispensability of the biographical approach to Picasso's work. Biography, however, is anathema to scholars who emphasize the semiotics and formalist autonomy of Cubism, for example, Rosalind Krauss, "In the Name of Picasso," in Krauss, *The Originality of the Avant-Garde and Other Myths* (Cambridge: MIT Press, 1985), pp. 23–40.

87 See, for example, Apollinaire's reviews "Art News: The Decorative Arts and Female Painting" and "Art News: Women Painters," in Breunig, *Apollinaire on Art*, pp. 208–10, 227–30; originally published in French in *Le Petit Bleu*, March 13, 1912, and April 5, 1912, respectively.

88 For the links between the prewar Futurist movement and Fascism, see Emilio Gentile, "The Conquest of Modernity: From Modernist Nationalism to Fascism," *Modernism/modernity* 1 (September 1994), pp. 55–87; and Emily Braun, "Mario Sironi's Urban Landscapes: The Futurist/Fascist Nexus," in Affron and Antliff, *Fascist Visions*, pp. 101–33.

89 Henri Bergson, *Creative Evolution* (1911; New York: Modern Library, 1944), p. 142.

90 See Virginia Spate, "Mother and Son," in Terry Smith, ed., *In Visible Touch: Modernism and Masculinity* (Chicago: University of Chicago Press, 1997), pp. 107–38. For birthing metaphors and Futurist political ideology in Futurism, see Emily Braun, "Renaissance and Renascences: The Rebirth of Italy, 1911–1921," in *Masterpieces from the Gianni Mattioli Collection* (Venice: Peggy Guggenheim Collection, 1997), pp. 21–48.

91 Cottington, *Cubism in the Shadow of War*, pp. 87–92. Le Fauconnier's image was inspired by Alexandre Mercerau's poem, "Paroles devant la femme enceinte," in Mercerau, *Paroles devant la vie* (1912).

92 See Robert Lubar, "Unmasking Pablo's Gertrude: Queer Desire and the Subject of Portraiture," *Art Bulletin* 79 (March 1997), pp. 56–84.

93 "From now on we can foresee a bodily development in the form of a prow from the outward swell of the breastbone, which will be the more marked the better an aviator the man of the future becomes." Marinetti, "Multiplied Man and the Reign of the Machine," p. 99.

94 Ibid.

95 See Victoria de Grazia, ed., *The Sex of Things: Gender and Consumption in Historical Perspective* (Berkeley: University of California Press, 1996).

96 There is scarce documentation regarding what or whom Boccioni saw on his second 1912 visit to Paris. Severini (erroneously dating the trip to late spring, instead of early November) remembered that Boccioni "expressed a particular interest in sculpture ... I took him to visit Archipenko, Agero, Brancusi and Duchamp-Villon." Severini, *Life of a Painter*, p. 110. See also note 60 above.

97 Marinetti's "Technical Manifesto of Futurist Literature" was originally issued in Italian as a flyer, dated May 11, 1912. The first notices in the French press appeared in *Le Figaro* and *L'Intransigeant* on July 7; it was printed in its entirety in French in the latter paper the next day. See Lista, *Manifestes, Proclamations, Documents*, p. 137.

98 Umberto Boccioni, "Technical Manifesto of Futurist Sculpture," (April 11, 1912), in Apollonio, *Futurist Manifestos*, pp. 51–65. This manifesto was written by July 1912; see Flavio Fergonzi, *The Mattioli Collection: Masterpieces of the Italian Avant-Garde* (Milan: Skira, 2003), pp. 160. From mid-September on it was mentioned some twenty-nine times in French journals, and, according to Lista, *Manifestes, Proclamations, Documents*, p. 177, first published in full in French in *Je dis tout*, October 6, 1912. It may have appeared even earlier in *Les Tendences nouvelles* 57 (July–August 1912), pp. 1382–86, though I was unable to verify this dating against the original issue (versus the reprint edition). It was first published in the Italian press in *L'Italia*, September 30, 1912.

99 As Boccioni emphasized, his sculptural concept of objects intersecting with and modified by the environment owed much to the precedent of the sculptor Medardo Rosso. See Boccioni, "Technical Manifesto of Futurist Sculpture," p. 62.

100 Marinetti, "Technical Manifesto of Futurist Literature," p. 95.

101 Rubin documented that Braque was the first do to paper reliefs (possibly in 1911, though there is no secure evidence for this). See Rubin, *Picasso and Braque*, pp. 30–41. As to Picasso's *Still Life with Chair Caning* of May 1912, which is technically the first Cubist collage, Rubin characterized it as an anomalous work: "He does not immediately follow up on this idea however. During the later spring and summer, collage remains in abeyance as Picasso explores the introduction of color into Cubism" (p. 39). The dates of Boccioni's 1912 visits to Paris in February–March and early November do not allow for the possibility that he may have seen Braque's paper constructions (which were not made of heterogeneous materials in any event). There is no evidence that Boccioni visited Braque's studio, even though the French artist was Severini's neighbor. In 1912, moreover, Braque was often absent from Paris and in either Le Havre or Céret for much of the winter through early June and again in early November. It is generally conceded that around October 9, 1912, Picasso constructed the cardboard *Guitar* and shortly thereafter turned to papier collé (after the publication of the Futurist manifestos). A papier collé using newspaper dates from mid-November. See Rubin, pp. 407, 410. In addition to the difficulty in establishing a precise chronology for these inventions, Braque and Picasso did not exhibit them and were notoriously private about their experiments.

102 "Préfuturisme," *L'Intransigeant*, October, 14, 1912, p. 2.

103 This is the central question raised by Duchamp's "invention" of the readymade, as discussed in William Camfield, *Marcel Duchamp: Fountain* (Houston: Menil Collection, 1989), especially pp. 116–26.

104 Giovanni Papini, "Il cerchio si chiude," *Lacerba*, February 15, 1914, pp. 49–50; Umberto Boccoini, "Il cerchio non si chiude!" *Lacerba*, March 1, 1914, pp. 67–69; and Papini, "Cerchi aperti," *Lacerba*, March 15, 1914, pp. 83–85.

105 See Poggi, *In Defiance of Painting*. In this landmark study of Futurist collage and its dialogue with Cubist efforts, Poggi minimized the degree and kind of Futurist influence on Cubism. Because her thesis is framed expertly within the discourse of post-structuralism and semiotics, the Futurists' emphasis on sensation and the literal is viewed as aesthetically inferior. Picasso is credited with bringing high and low into a new level of exchange, while the repercussions of the same on the Futurists' larger social project remains unexplored. The bias of this interpretative model is one that has existed historically since Futurism burst on the Parisian scene.

106 For these and other characteristic examples, see "Cubism ultramontain," *Gil Blas*, February 4, 1912, p. 4; Henri Genet, "Les Peintres futuristes italiens," *L'Opinion*, February 10, 1912; Thiébault-Sisson, "La Peinture des états d'âme: L'exposition des futuristes italiens," *Le Temps*, February 8, 1912, p. 4; Louis Vauxcelles, "Les Futuristes," *Gil Blas*, February 6, 1912, p. 4; "Exposition des 'futuristes' italiens," *L'Art décoratif*, February 20, 1912, pp. 2–3; Jacques des Gachons, "La Peinture d'après-demain," *Je sais tout*, April 15, 1912, pp. 349–56; and André Warnod, "Les Sculptures futuristes de Boccioni, les tableaux de Thomas Couture," *Comoedia*, June 21, 1913, p. 4.

107 See Roger Allard, "Les Arts plastiques. Futurisme, simultanéisme et autres métachories," *Les Ecrits français*, February 5, 1914, pp. 254–58. Allard's diatribe against the Futurists was aggravated by the performances of Valentine de Saint-Point.

108 See Harold Bloom, *The Anxiety of Influence: A Theory of Poetry*, 2d ed. (New York: Oxford University Press, 1997).

109 Severini, *Life of a Painter*, p. 122.

110 Giovanni Lista, "The Activist Model; or The Avant-Garde as Italian Invention," *South Central Review* 13 (summer–fall 1996), pp. 21–22.

111 See Guillaume Apollinaire, "L'Anti-tradizione futurista," *Lacerba*, September 15, 1913, pp. 202 – 3. For influence of Marinetti on Apollinaire, see Poggi, *In Defiance of Painting*, pp. 95 – 201.

112 Apollinaire, "Through the Salons des Indépendants," p. 291. Regarding Apollinaire, Severini made this revealing statement: "I believe he was also aware of the 'life' element in Futurism, as opposed to the 'idea' factor which was then at the roots of Cubist and Picassian 'subjectivism,' and that these two elements could, essentially, stop being incompatible and become complementary." Severini, *The Life of a Painter*, p. 114.

113 Rosalind Krauss, "The Motivation of the Sign," in Zelevansky, *Picasso and Braque*, pp. 277 – 82.

114 "Wilbourg" (or "Wilburg") after Wilbur Wright was used by Braque and Picasso as a nickname for Braque, beginning in May 1912. See Judith Cousins, with the collaboration of Pierre Daix, "Documentary Chronology," in Rubin, *Picasso and Braque*, p. 393. Aside from general fascination with the Wright brothers' "conquest of the air," Rubin suggested that the appearance of aviation puns were associated with Braque's new invention of paper sculptures (p. 33). As per note 100, the dates for these sculptures are difficult to confirm. Robert Wohl wrote, "No one went further than Marinetti in seeking to spell out the implications of aviation for literature and art." Wohl, *A Passion for Wings: Aviation and the Western Imagination 1908–1918* (New Haven: Yale University Press, 1994), p. 264.

115 See Karmel, *Picasso and the Invention of Cubism*, p. 186. In his memoirs, Severini recalled that Picasso had shown special interest in his *Souvenirs de voyage* (1910–11) during a studio visit (and which he tentatively placed before the Futurists' Bernheim-Jeune show). Severini acknowledged the stylistic, if not the thematic, differences between his *Souvenirs* and that of Picasso, as well as Braque's reaction when Picasso subsequently unveiled his new work, *Souvenir du Havre* (1912): "Braque was present and seemed surprised at the painting. In a sweet-and-sour tone he said, 'The rifle has changed shoulders,' but Picasso held his tongue. He went on smoking his pipe behind us, wearing that typical smile of his which probably meant something like, 'How do you like my little joke?'" Severini, *Life of a Painter*, p. 96.

116 Françoise Gilot and Carlton Lake, *Life with Picasso* (New York: McGraw Hill, 1964), p. 317.

117 Banham wrote that Cubist aesthetics were "in no way as revolutionary as those of Futurism — chiefly because Cubism was a revolution within painting itself, and not a profound reorientation towards a changed world." Banham, *Theory and Design in the First Machine Age*, p. 109.

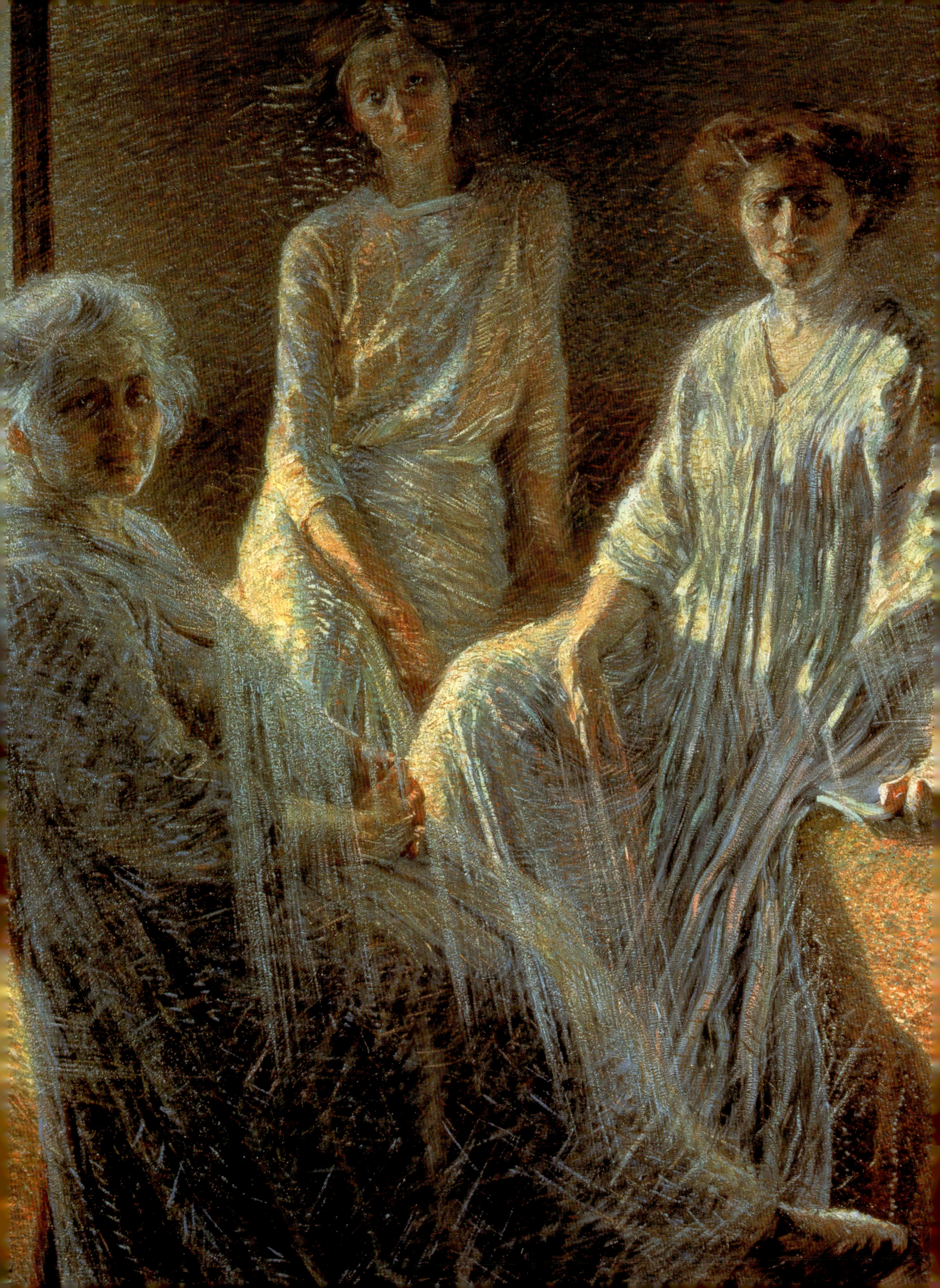

The Path to Universal Synthesis: Boccioni's Development from Divisionism to Futurism

VIVIEN GREENE

And so it is that Divisionism, like polyphony in music, like a stanza orchestrated in free verse in poetry, represents an effort of greater intensity and artistic complexity, a vehement aspiration toward what we call the symphonic and polychromatic unity of the picture that becomes ever more a universal synthesis.

—UMBERTO BOCCIONI[1]

Facing page
Detail of Umberto Boccioni, *Three Women*, 1909–10 (fig. 12)

In grandiloquent prose, Umberto Boccioni described the potential to represent universal synthesis in painting[2]—a concept intrinsic to Futurism, whereby simultaneous scenes and sensations are collapsed into a single unified image. He was emphatic in his assertion that Divisionism is the means to reach this end. The Divisionist method, which was grounded in scientific color theory and consisted of divided strokes of generally complementary colors, fit appropriately with several of the Futurists' goals. The swiftly applied filigree of pigment implied movement and coincided with the Futurist desire to depict motion, speed, and dynamism. The often luminous brushwork, especially when used to represent light effects, also came close to approximating the presence of energy or current, both symbols of modernity and topics of great interest to the Futurists. Perhaps most important for this discussion, the integrative quality of the brushstrokes lent itself to the Futurist ideal of visually fusing subject and action.

Divisionism, a movement that developed in Italy almost parallel to French Neo-Impressionism, was initially essayed by Giovanni Segantini with his *Ave Maria on the Lake* (1886).[3] The first generation of Divisionists subsequently emerged in the north of Italy during the 1890s. While not a self-proclaimed group, these painters all practiced a painting technique based in varying degrees on the chromatic treatises of Michel Eugène Chevreul and Ogden Rood to execute optically vibrant images. Some, such as Angelo Morbelli and Giuseppe Pellizza da Volpedo, embraced positivist thought and addressed the social issues of the day in their painting. Others followed a less materialist, more Symbolist vein. Notably, Segantini went on to create evocative rural and alpine landscapes, and Gaetano Previati, the main theorist on Divisionism, pursued metaphoric religious thematics.

Divisionism provided both a stylistic and a conceptual framework for Boccioni. This is particularly evident with regard to the notion of universal synthesis that he extolls in his writings. The idea that painting could bring together polyvalenced experiences extending beyond the simply visual and two-dimensional plane has its roots, at least in part, in the art and thought of Symbolism, a movement that overlapped with Divisionism in Italy. In fact, much Divisionist and Symbolist work sought to evoke synesthetic experience in holistically conceived images, with characteristically curvilinear brushstrokes and undulating forms weaving together figure and ground into an organic whole.

The Futurists' bond with Divisionism was a conflicted one, for in their content and objective, the emerging Futurists diverged from their immediate forerunners in a schism that signaled one of the many contradictions inherent in the premises defining Futurism.[4] So while the Futurists initially admired some of the proponents of Divisionism, their later iconoclastic rhetoric, which called for an eradication of everything associated with the past in favor of the modern, repudiated much of what the Divisionists produced because it was rooted in previous artistic traditions. Moreover, the Futurists railed against the idealized, mystical, or decadent subject matter of Symbolism and, by extension, Divisionism. Nevertheless, the older style was closely intertwined with Futurism during the first decade of the twentieth century. Among the Futurists, Boccioni's brushwork remained most closely bound to the Divisionist mode of pigment application until his untimely death in 1916. A look at the moments of contact Boccioni had with his Italian predecessors as well as an examination of the development of his own theories and paintings through the end of 1911 demonstrate the centrality of Divisionism to his art

Fig. 11 Umberto Boccioni
The City Rises (La città sale), 1910–11
Oil on canvas, 78 7/16 × 118 1/2 inches (199.3 × 301 cm)
The Museum of Modern Art, New York, Mrs. Simon Guggenheim Fund

Fig. 12 Umberto Boccioni
Three Women (Tre donne), 1909–10
Oil on canvas, 66 15/16 × 48 13/16 inches (170 × 124 cm)
Collezione Banca Intesa, Milan

Fig. 13 Gaetano Previati
L'Eroica, 1907
Oil on canvas, central panel 74 13/16 × 90 9/16 inches (190 × 230 cm); lateral panels 74 13/16 × 61 inches (190 × 155 cm) each
Associazione Nazionale Invalidi e Mutilati di Guerra, Rome

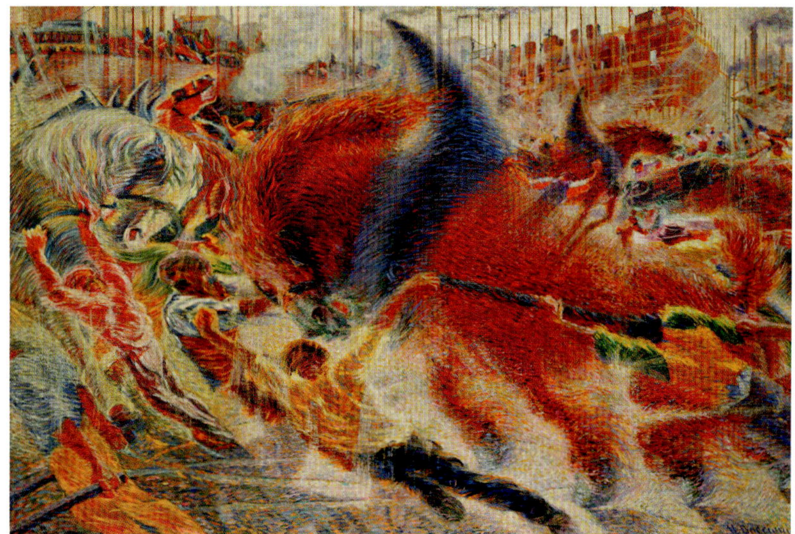

until he first encountered Cubist work in Paris that October.

At the beginning of the century, Boccioni lived in Rome, where, along with Gino Severini and Mario Sironi, he was schooled in the Divisionist mode of painting by Giacomo Balla, a slightly older artist who initially served as a bridge between the previous generation and the Futurist upstarts.[5] Enthusiastically embracing this relatively new, empirically-based style, these young men also looked directly to the work of the major Divisionist artists—among them, Previati, Morbelli, and Segantini—as models for their own nascent artistic production. Once the Futurists had coalesced into a self-proclaimed group, they demonstrated admiration for the art of Previati and Segantini in their "Manifesto of the Futurist Painters" of February 11, 1910. In the course of their diatribe against the current state of artistic taste in Italy, they criticized the establishment for ignoring the artists they deemed worthwhile: "Ask these priests of a veritable religious cult, these guardians of old aesthetic laws, where we can go and see the works of Giovanni Segantini today. Ask them why the officials of the Commission have never heard of the existence of Gaetano Previati. Ask them where they can see Medardo Rosso's sculpture."[6] Two months later, in their "Futurist Painting: Technical Manifesto" of April 11, they declared Divisionism to be a necessary component of Futurist painting: "We conclude that painting cannot exist today without Divisionism. This is no process that can be learned and applied at will. Divisionism, for the modern painter, must be an *innate complementariness* which we declare to be essential and necessary."[7]

Boccioni may have learned of Divisionism through his lessons with Balla, but he quickly pursued the progenitors of the movement on his own. His diary entries from 1907 indicate that he was closely reading Previati's *La tecnica della pittura* (1905).[8] In that same year, he had the opportunity to view Divisionist works firsthand on a trip to Paris, where he admired the work of Carlo Fornara, Previati, and Segantini at the exhibition *I pittori divisionisti a Parigi*.[9] His diary entries from 1908 reveal visits to Previati, whom Boccioni looked to as a mentor, and recount long conversations between the two.[10]

Previati's art and theories continued to loom large for Boccioni,[11] even in the work traditionally identified as Boccioni's first truly Futurist painting, *The City Rises* (1910–11, fig. 11),[12]—an image that serves as an antecedent to the less extreme urban activities visible in *Materia* (1912, cat. no. 27). In *The City Rises*, fine Divisionist brushwork and the coupling of intense complementary colors are employed to portray a frenzied scene of workers struggling to control their horses in an industrial setting. The most direct source for this canvas is Previati's triptych *L'Eroica* (1907, fig. 13),[13] which greatly impressed Boccioni when he saw it in the 1907 Divisionist exhibition in Paris. The surging horses are a quotation of the equine subjects in the central panel of *L'Eroica*.[14] The prostrate figures in Previati's left panel are analogous to the straining men on the left of *The City Rises*. Boccioni also appropriated compositional elements from Previati by translating the fiery curving form in the triptych's right panel into the sweeping blue harness of his central horse. In subject, the images are comparable as well: one extolling the heroism of war, the other that of labor and the modern city. Both thematics are ultimately connected to notions of nationalism that were central to the Italian zeitgeist of the era.

Previati was not the only artist whom Boccioni approached around this time, for by 1910 he had gone to Vittore Grubicy de Dragon for potential guidance, beginning a relationship that, to date, has been virtually undocumented. Grubicy, a painter, critic, and gallerist, was an instrumental figure in the dissemination of Divisionism in Italy and elsewhere in Europe. Correspondence between the two men documents that Grubicy provided at least one critique of Boccioni's work at an important moment in the artistic development of the younger man. Following a visit to Boccioni's studio, Grubicy wrote in July 1910:

> *Your picture of the three figures, since I last saw it in your studio, has come a long way and taken a pleasing turn of development. If I had assign a number to it, I'd say it has advanced from a 4 to a 10!*
>
> *As for the other one, which is fine as far as the figure of your mother is concerned, in those places where Futurism is allowed to parade its triumphs—in the sky—the result is entirely negative.*[15]

The first work to which he referred is *Three Women* (1909–10, fig. 12).[16] A portrait of Boccioni's mother Cecilia, his sister Amelia, and a woman friend, Ines, this transitional work for the artist demonstrates radical, if understated, Futurist strategies in the rendering of light effects upon the figures. However, it still belongs in the realm of Divisionism, and its traditional subject and relatively tame palette pleased Grubicy. But the older artist's deprecating assessment of Boccioni's other portrait, one that probably employed more expressionistic colors and an abstracted background, indicates his disapproval regarding Boccioni's forays into the experimental waters of Futurism.[17] The Divisionist's discouraging commentary should not have come as a surprise to Boccioni, for Grubicy made public his negative opinion on Futurism in April of that year, in a general article on the movement he authored for *Il Secolo*, in which

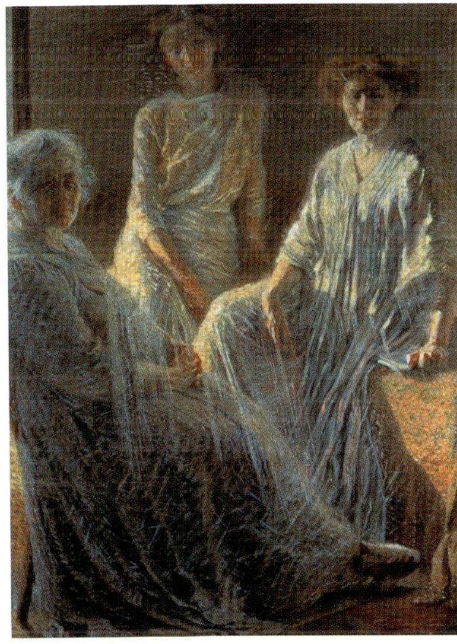

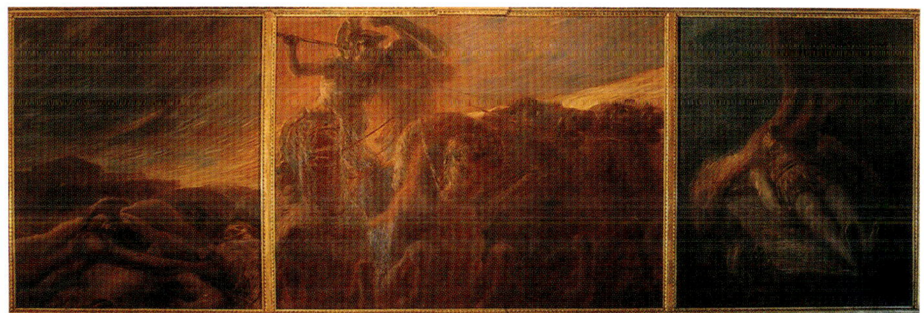

he acknowledged the young Futurists' enthusiasm in a somewhat patronizing tone that disparaged their bombastic philosophies: "Such resonant words as 'rebellion,' 'nausea,' and 'disdain,' follow hard upon one another, swelling the 'manifesto' with youthful boldness; [the text], however, demonstrates a substratum of deplorable ignorance on the part of young people who would arrogate to themselves the exacting role of standard-bearers for the Art of tomorrow."[18] Boccioni saw Grubicy as a powerful figure who had helped the careers of other artists, and later in 1910—despite the rebuke of July—he must have asked for Grubicy's support and been rejected. This is clear from a letter Boccioni sent Grubicy in January 1911:

> *Your letter did not surprise me. The entire conversation and the manner in which we said good-bye led me to intuit that you would not be able to do for me what you have so generously done for dead and living artists great and small.*
>
> *No matter! I've never been helped by anyone, and it is fated that this should continue to be so.*
>
> *I shall try to go it alone as I have always done. In the meantime, dear Mr. Grubicy, I sincerely thank you for your letter and for what positive things you have said in my regard.*[19]

Although his art developed in a fashion that Grubicy viewed as anathema to Divisionist painting, Boccioni still maintained an allegiance to this earlier style, identifying its key role in achieving certain essential pictorial aspects of Futurism. As the principal theorist of the Futurists, he articulated these ideas in "La pittura futurista," a lecture he gave in Rome in 1911.[20] Interestingly, a version of this text may have had as its working title "Sul divisionismo."[21] Here, Boccioni parsed out that which separated the Futurists from the Divisionists and the ways in which the latter were essential to the former. He pronounced, "Divisionism is not a technique. Divisionism is an attitude of the spirit."[22] With this oft-quoted statement, Boccioni suggested that Divisionism was a way of understanding the world, not simply a method of painting. He amplified this by explaining: "Indeed those theorists, instead of perceiving divisionistically like us, first looked at the world with conventional eyes (that is, such as culture had formed them), then applied, artificially, the technique of complementary colors to the canvas."[23] Boccioni maintained that the Futurists incorporated the premise of innate complementarism into their manner of perceiving reality, while the older Divisionists used the technique in a more formulaic manner, trapped by artistic conventions. His antimaterialist theory—that perception and creation were embedded in intuition—was also in contradistinction to the notion that art should imitate nature.[24] He elaborated that "we [the Futurists] recognize that our age finds its spiritual expression in Divisionism. Indeed, the dotting, the little brushstrokes, the striations that horrify the partisans of surface facility unquestionably give painting greater expressive and communicative force, in as much as every mark, however small, bears within itself the stamp of the individual. And in this respect we are, therefore, superior naturalists [*veristi*], since we intuitively imitate the action of light-rays when they strike bodies and give them color. And this, for us, is the only way to conceive the imitation nature."[25]

Related to Boccioni's aversion to art as a mimetic tool to replicate nature or reality was his denial of the empirically-based positivist dimension of Divisionism.[26] In fact, he argued

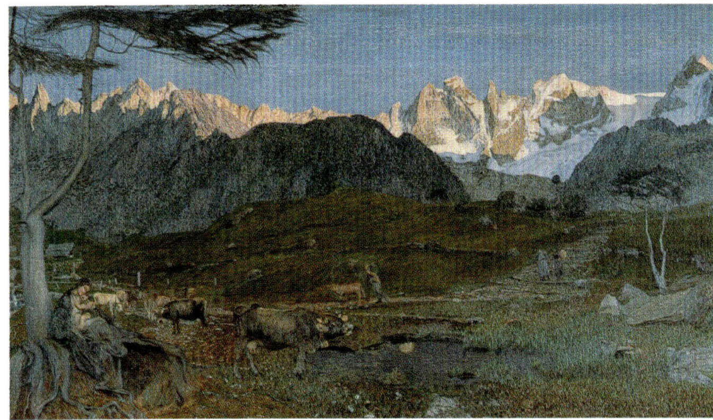

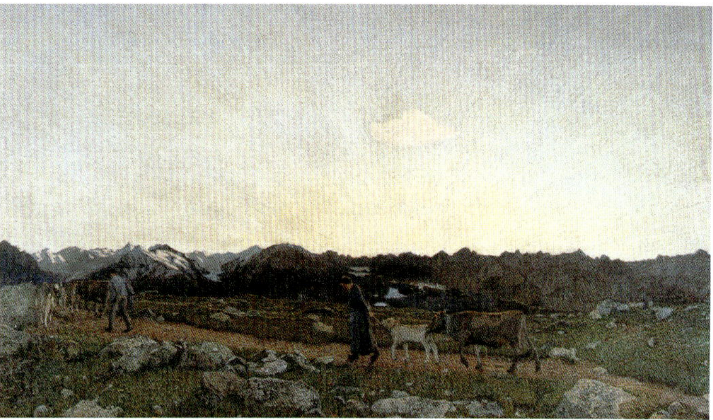

that art could not be anchored in science as this stripped it of its individuality and its expressive power, further claiming: "The unbending application of scientific processes of this sort in an absolutely intuitive field such as art, produced oppressive grays and monotony, embalming objects and discouraging the artists and the observer."[27] These distinctions were essential to Boccioni, yet, as with many Futurist philosophies, they highlight certain paradoxes. Significantly, the color theories in which Divisionism was based were scientific, and the Futurists themselves extolled science as being the liberating force bringing forth the modern world from the old, staid one: "scientific discoveries have *completely remade the fabric of the human mind*."[28]

Boccioni did endeavor to separate the style of painting he and his colleagues practiced from the Divisionism of the previous generation. With the perspective offered by hindsight, he would further clarify the distinctions between Futurism and Divisionism in later writings, obviously seeking to establish a certain distance between the two movements. In his book *Pittura scultura futuriste (Dinamismo plastico)*—published in 1914, although drafted in 1912—in chapter 14, entitled *Complementarismo dinamico*, he wrote:

> *In our 1st technical manifesto of painting ["Futurist Painting: Technical Manifesto" (April 11, 1910)] in diametrical opposition to the ideas then current in France, we said "a congenital complementarism" is necessary to the modern painter, just as it is an "absolute necessity for painting." Many, of course, thought we were simply latecomers to pointillism.... What we wanted, instead, was a dynamic contrast of forms corresponding to the dynamic contrast of complementary colors. We wanted a complementarism of form and color. Thus we fashioned a synthesis of the analysis of color (Divisionism of Seurat, Signac and Cross) and the analysis of form (Divisionism of Picasso and Braque).*[29]

But the importance of Divisionism is evident with this statement, for it concurrently differentiates Pointillism or Divisionism from Futurism and intimates that the Futurists' conception of dynamism was realized through the marriage of Divisionist and Cubist idioms.

Certainly, until 1911, Boccioni's work relied in myriad ways on Divisionist precepts (several of which came to bear upon *Materia*). Among these was his adoption of a common Divisionist pictorial format, that of the triptych. The triptych, customarily used for religious themes, experienced a resurgence throughout Europe in the 1890s and was adopted for less orthodox spiritual subjects or even secular imagery. Some triptychs, as in the case of Previati's *L'Eroica*, followed a traditional format and were conceived as a single three-part painting within a tabernacle frame. Segantini, instead, realized his monumental *Triptych of Nature* on the nature-bound cycle of life as three separate canvases, which were hung together: *Life* (1896–99), *Nature* (1897–99), and *Death* (1898–99) (figs. 14–16).[30] Grubicy took the multiple painting concept further when he assembled eight Alpine landscapes in the musically-themed polyptych *Winter in the Mountains* (1894–1911, figs. 17 and 18). Balla pursued the triptych format as early as 1904 with *The Day of the Worker* (1904–05, fig. 19). In this socially-minded meditation on the hopeless life cycle of the urban worker, he varied the tripartite composition in an asymetrical manner by juxtaposing a single image split into two smaller squares with a vertical rectangular one.

Boccioni seems to have taken his cue from Previati with the first of the triptychs he executed, *Triptych: We Venerate the Mother* (1907–08, cat. no. 2),[31] which is a clear precursor in subject to *Materia*. In this work, a woman, whom we recognize to be Boccioni's mother from her heavy body type and white, gathered hair, occupies the central panel, flanked by two allegorical figures. Her children appear in the smaller subsidiary panels. On the left, Umberto is portrayed reading by a window, while on the right, Amelia, his sister, is shown sewing by lamplight. This conception of a tripartite composition, depicting three separate but related scenes, could have easily contributed to Boccioni's eventual conflation of multiple narratives into a single scene; in fact, this seems to be the case with the earlier *The City Rises*, painted in 1910–11, which was originally conceived as a triptych in preparatory drawings but was then realized as one image. Boccioni persisted in his experimentation with three-part painting as late as 1911 with *States of Mind* (figs. 20–22).[32] However, the final version of this trilogy—portraying aspects of the psychologically fragmented experience of a farewell defined by the speed, anxiety, and chaos of urban experience—definitely breaks from Divisionism in style. We know that Boccioni reworked the *States of Mind* paintings after his trip to Paris in October of that year, the geometric forms and splintered space in each canvas belying his discovery of Cubism.[33]

During the 1910s, Boccioni also continued to use a very popular Divisionist subject that would have specific relevance to his development of the visual tropes that become full blown in *Materia*. This subject is that of a solitary figure, almost always female, seated in a darkened interior and set against a sunny window or balcony.[34] The placement of a sitter, especially a woman, in a window, had its modern roots in the work of artists such as Jean-François Millet, but it also can be linked to later nineteenth-century sources closer to Boccioni, as with Morbelli's *The Old People's Home (Knitting)* (1890, fig. 23), one of his many

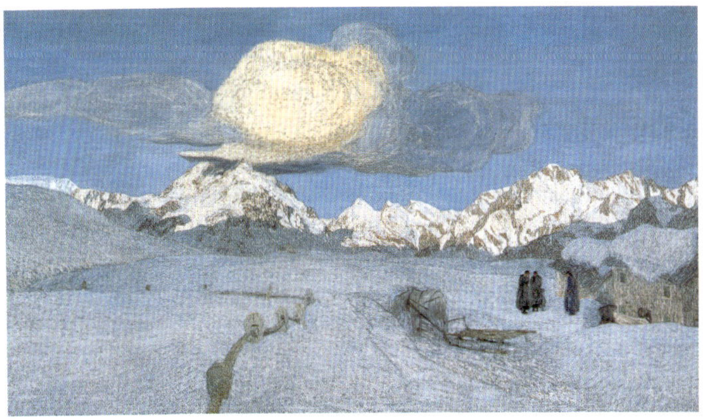

Fig. 14 Giovanni Segantini
Triptych of Nature: Life (*Trittico della natura: La vita*), 1896–99
Oil on canvas, 74 13/16 × 126 3/4 inches (190 × 322 cm)
Property of the Eidgenössische Kommission der Gottfried Keller-Stiftung, deposed at Segantini-Museum, Saint Moritz, Switzerland

Fig. 15 Giovanni Segantini
Triptych of Nature: Nature (*Trittico della natura: La natura*), 1897–99
Oil on canvas, 92 1/2 × 158 11/16 inches (235 × 403 cm)
Property of the Eidgenössische Kommission der Gottfried Keller-Stiftung, deposed at Segantini-Museum, Saint Moritz, Switzerland

Fig. 16 Giovanni Segantini
Triptych of Nature: Death (*Trittico della natura: La morte*), 1898–99
Oil on canvas, 74 13/16 × 126 3/4 inches (190 × 322 cm)
Property of the Eidgenössische Kommission der Gottfried Keller-Stiftung, deposed at Segantini-Museum, Saint Moritz, Switzerland

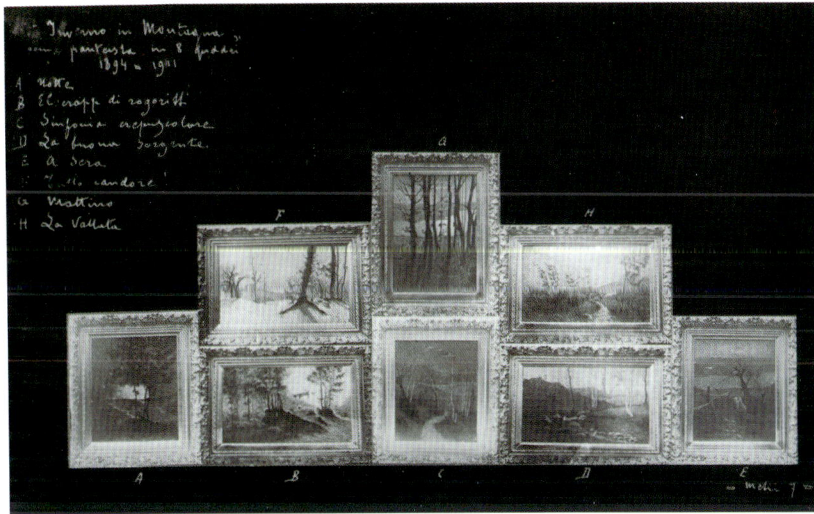

Fig. 17 Vittore Grubicy de Dragon
The polyptych *Winter in the Mountains*, 1911
Photograph, 13 3/8 x 16 15/16 inches (34 x 43 cm)
Museo di Arte Moderna e Contemporanea di Trento e Rovereto
The artist's notations list the titles of each painting in the polyptych.

Fig. 18 Vittore Grubicy de Dragon
Moonlight (*Poema invernale*), 1903
Oil on canvas, 25 3/8 × 21 7/8 inches (64.5 × 55.5 cm)
Civiche Raccolte d'Arte, Galleria d'Arte Moderna, Milan
This painting is at the far left in Grubicy's photograph of *Winter in the Mountains* (fig. 17).

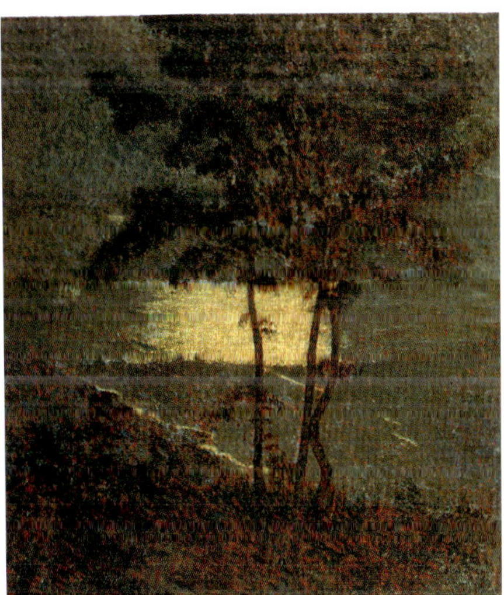

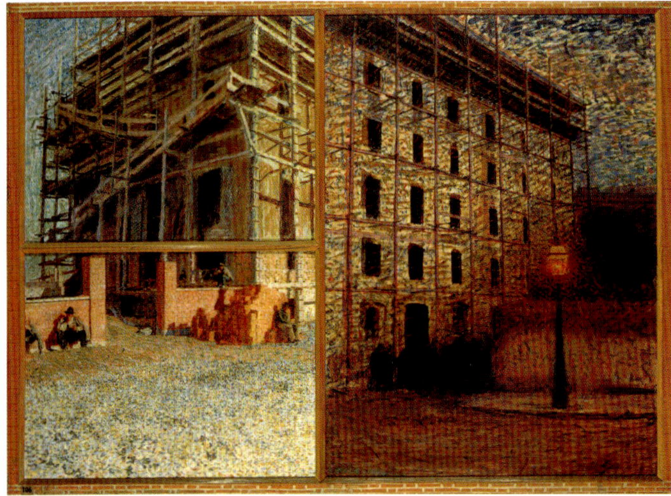

Fig. 19 Giacomo Balla
The Day of the Worker (*La giornata dell'operaio*), 1904–05
Oil on paper, 41¾ × 57³⁄₁₆ inches (106 × 145.2 cm), including artist's painted frame
Private collection, Courtesy of Massimo Martino Fine Arts & Projects, Mendrisio, Switzerland

portrayals of women in Milan's Pio Albergo Trivulzio, a state-funded hospice for the elderly. The strategic positioning of a sitter with sun entering and striking him or her allows for the full exploitation of the prismatic effects of light upon form and thus corresponded with Boccioni's visual objectives.[35]

Boccioni's quasi-obsessive focus on this subject emphasized its importance with regard to the specific pictorial concepts he was formulating. Granted, from a practical perspective, the typical household scene of a woman sewing or man reading provided a regular and ready model for painters, since people, of necessity, performed domestic tasks or passed time close to a window to benefit from the available natural illumination. Yet the very construction of the scene, whereby the figure is in one space but set against another, embodies those tenets Boccioni and the other Futurist signatories lay out in "Futurist Painting: Technical Manifesto."[36] This compositional arrangement enabled Boccioni to conceive of an image in which interior and exterior spaces and actions, which actually occur in separate spheres, exist simultaneously, as one would experience them optically but not literally in a spatial sense. This allowed him to arrive at the universal synthesis central to his notion of art. As he developed this idea, he finally merged the two environments physically and elided them temporally. By tracing the genealogy of this visual trope within Boccioni's own oeuvre, it is possible to follow his evolution during the first decade of the century.

Boccioni first explored this type of composition with an early drawing, *Young Woman Sewing* (1902–03, fig. 24).[37] In this naturalistic depiction, a young woman's back is turned to the viewer as she works by the light of a window in a spare setting reminiscent of Dutch seventeenth-century domestic interiors. Over the next decade, Boccioni's treatment of this arrangement would undergo extensive and radical transformations, culminating in his realization of *Materia*.[38] A woman posed in a window with her sewing is picked up again in 1908 in *The Story of a Seamstress* (cat. no. 3).[39] This painting of Boccioni's woman friend Ines (with whom he had an intimate relationship), shows the sitter reading next to a table with a sewing machine, and reprises, in part, *Triptych: We Venerate the Mother*. The artist's major concern with this work and the reason for choosing this arrangement yet again was light. What distinguishes *The Story of a Seamstress* is his obvious desire to show the play of light itself in its shifting permutations as it strikes the interior and, in particular, Ines's dress. In addition to the golden light that bathes the wall behind Ines, bright white seems to almost reflect off the front of her dress and down along the contour of her thigh and knee, while thin, white brushstrokes ripple across the folds of the dress's skirt. The resulting brilliance illustrates Boccioni's words regarding this painting: "I detest dark tones. Light, light, light!"[40]

Earlier that year, Boccioni worked on a similar theme with *Signora Massimino* (fig. 25),[41] in which one can see how he more fully realized its possibilities. This commissioned portrait maps many of the elements that would later provide the structure for *Materia*, including a single female figure who faces out from the composition and is seated in a window with a prominent wrought iron railing through which are visible a variety of urban sights: people walking hurriedly, a horse drawing a carriage, a tram.[42] The scene taking place on the street below, at a lower vantage point than that from which we see the sitter, could not realistically occupy the same frame as Signora Massimino given the angle from which she is painted. The physical impossibility of the sitter and exterior events

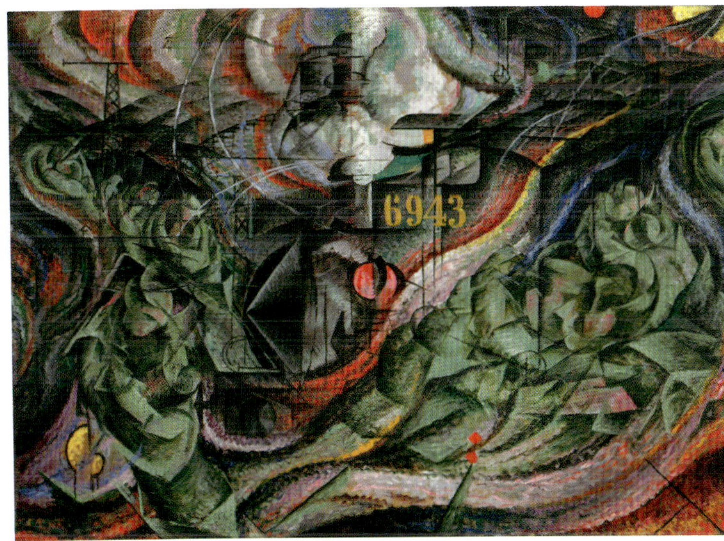

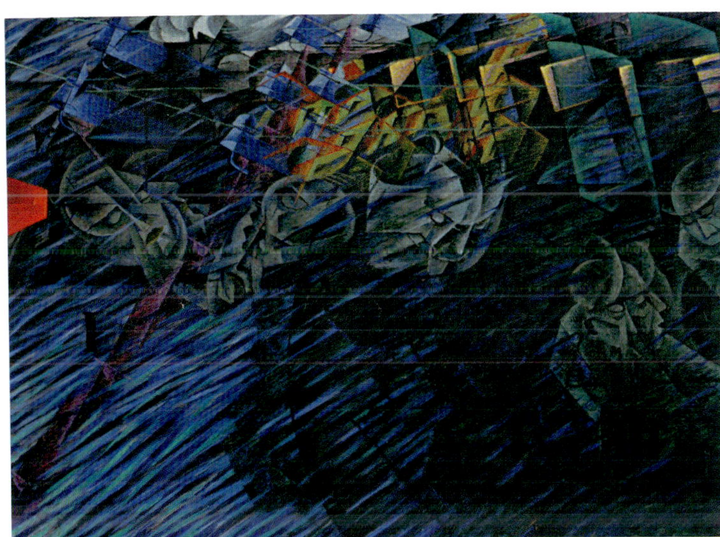

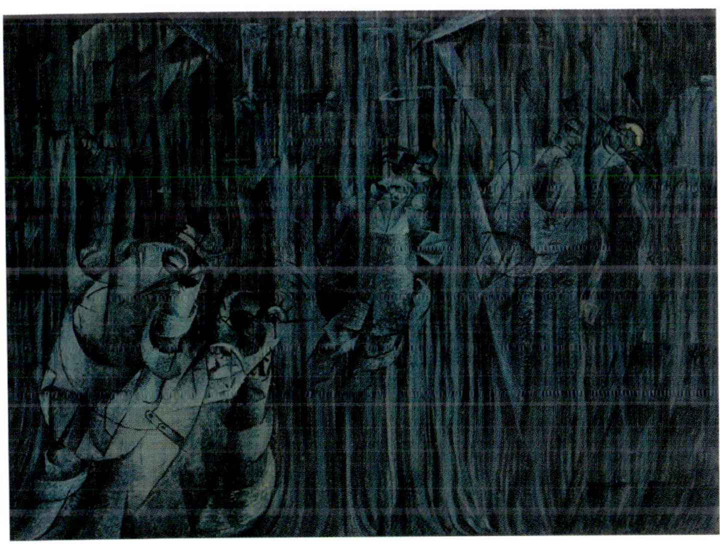

Fig. 20 Umberto Boccioni
States of Mind I: The Farewells
(*Gli addii: Stati d'animo II*), 1911
Oil on canvas, 27¾ × 37⅞ inches (70.5 × 96.2 cm)
The Museum of Modern Art, New York,
Gift of Nelson A. Rockefeller

Fig. 21 Umberto Boccioni
States of Mind II: Those Who Go
(*Quelli che vanno: Stati d'animo II*), 1911
Oil on canvas, 27⅞ × 37¾ inches (70.8 × 95.9 cm)
The Museum of Modern Art, New York,
Gift of Nelson A. Rockefeller

Fig. 22 Umberto Boccioni
States of Mind III: Those Who Stay
(*Quelli che restano: Stati d'animo II*), 1911
Oil on canvas, 27⅞ × 37¾ inches (70.8 × 95.9 cm)
The Museum of Modern Art, New York,
Gift of Nelson A. Rockefeller

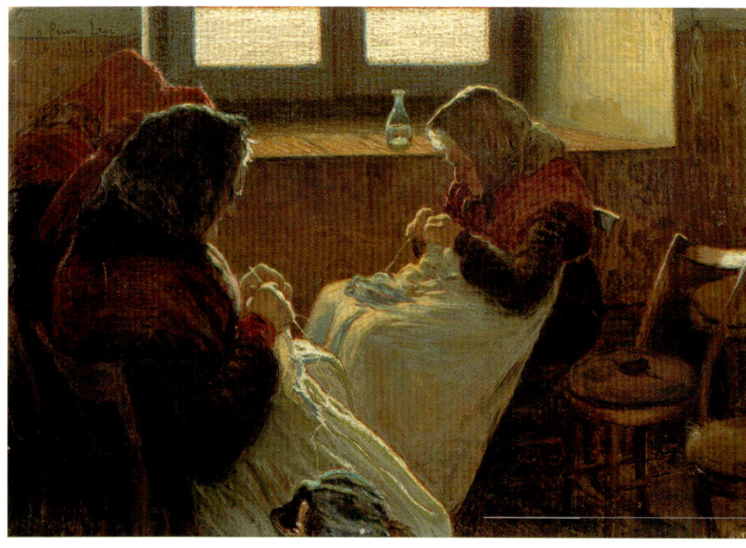

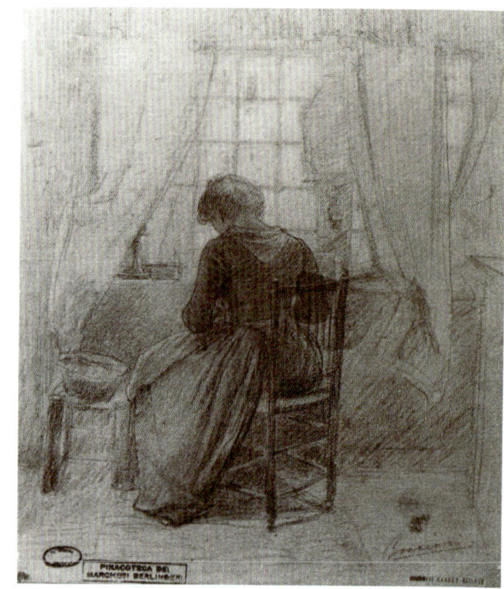

existing in the same visual space demonstrates that Boccioni was already taking multiple viewpoints and merging these into one image. In fact, this was a painting with which Boccioni struggled for quite some time, and he recounted his travails in his diary. In particular, he sounded pained in an entry dated March 18, 1908:

> *Who knows what that poor portrait will be worth? It's a step, I'm sure of that, but what an effort! What a paucity of resources, what distance between what I wanted to make and what I made. . . . The head, I've probably scraped down thirty times; the drawing, I've probably moved around another ten times. One day, after I'd finished all the iron bars of the balustrade, which give onto the shadow of the piazza (and with what efforts of proportion . . .), I found the entire perspective of the panes to be wrong. I wavered a day and a night then I scraped it all down and moved everything.*[43]

His difficulty with the resolution of the pictorial issues and the time it took him to complete this portrait presage its success as an image and its importance as a prototype for things to come.

The artist revisited a similar composition in *Sister on the Balcony* (1909, cat. no. 6),[44] in which he placed his sister Amelia at the very balcony where he would paint his mother for Materia. Here, with quick daubs of vibrant hues, Boccioni more consciously fused figure and background, eliminating perspectival clues so the city scene is almost on the same plane as Amelia's arm. This strategy was clearly intentional. A preparatory drawing includes notations on which colors would denote the depth and the desired perspectival construction of the composition.[45]

Boccioni's application of a distinctly Divisionist stroke is most articulated in a highly intimate portrait of his mother, *Controluce* (1909, cat. no. 5),[46] and the previously mentioned *Three Women*.[47] While none of the sitters are framed by a window, they are posed near one; both pictures depend upon natural sunlight to obtain the divided coloristic effects created by the light striking the women's forms.[48] In *Controluce*, the artist used the same fluid dashes of brilliant blue, orange, green, and yellow for his mother's bare back and face as he did for the unspecific background. The direction of the brushstrokes are the primary element that differentiates her plump body from her surroundings. In *Three Women*, Boccioni interprets the rays shining upon the women through the window or balcony as translucent veils of shimmering pigment with quasi-faceted layers of light. These are the precursors to the force lines of later Futurist work.

By thus expanding Divisionist strategies, Boccioni achieved the goals outlined in his writings. With his deployment of refracted light and divided filaments of color he seemed to imply the molecular constitution of his sitters and their surroundings. This allowed him to disintegrate his forms just enough to meld them better with their environment, so as to realize a fusion between subject and setting.

It is at this point that Boccioni's rupture with Divisionism truly begins. The works that immediately preceded *Materia* in the lineage of women at balconies are telling in this regard. The 1911 painting *The Street Enters the House* (cat. no. 7)[49] depicts the sitter's circular, all-encompassing experience of the activities on the street by structuring them so they literally interpenetrate the interior space she occupies. This intended impression was not lost on Boccioni's public and critics. When this work was shown in the exhibition *Intima* in Milan in 1911, Margherita Sarfatti wrote, "at La Famiglia Artistica, Boccioni is exhibiting a painting entitled *At the Balcony* [later retitled *The Street Enters the House*], in which he means to present a comprehensive synthesis of all the impressions the woman who is at the center of the painting can experience when looking out her window, including not only the buildings she sees in front of her, but also those she knows to be beside her and behind her."[50] *Simultaneous Visions* (cat. no. 8),[51] also from 1911, reproduces the same subject, the woman's face repeated twice (the result of her reflection in the glass of the window through which she looks), as she surveys a street scene from dual viewpoints. These paintings reveal a less divided brushstroke and a more complex treatment of spatial relationships with their broader planes of color, faceted forms, fractured space, and the more obvious collapse between subject and setting, interior and exterior.

Such elements reached their apex in *Materia*. Here, Boccioni's mother, the balcony of his studio, and the world outside are essentially joined in a confluence of energized, activated forms. Yet tiny divisionist strokes still play an important role, most evident in areas where light strikes solid forms, as in the geometric shapes of the buildings that extend onto the mother's figure and in her projecting hands and dress sleeves. They lend a sense of electrified movement to this composition in which Boccioni succeeds in the Futurist objective of placing the spectator at the center of the action and conveying the immediacy of sentient experience.

As the works produced from 1911–12 onward testify, Boccioni followed a course that led him away from a strict application of Divisionism. Nonetheless, the technique itself remained evident in his facture, he sustained his belief in the necessity of innate complementarism, and he held true to his overarching philosophy of universal synthesis. All of which allowed him to develop

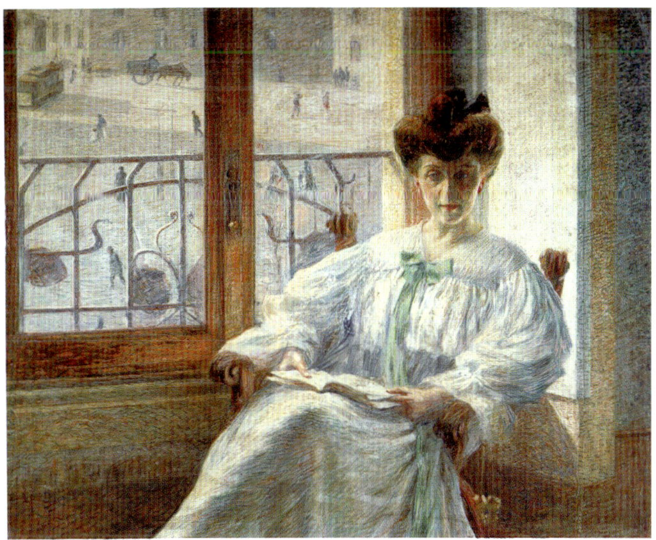

Fig. 23 Angelo Morbelli
The Old People's Home (Knitting)
(*All'ospizio [Il lavoro a maglia]*), 1890
Oil on canvas, 12 3/16 × 17 5/16 inches (31 × 44 cm)
Private collection, Italy

Fig. 24 Umberto Boccioni
Young Woman Sewing (*Giovane che cuce*), 1902–03
Pencil on paper, 14 3/16 × 11 13/16 inches (36 × 30 cm)
Private collection

Fig. 25 Umberto Boccioni
Signora Massimino (*La signora Massimino*), 1908
Oil on canvas, 48 7/16 × 59 7/16 inches (123 × 151 cm)
Private collection, Courtesy of Galleria dello Scudo, Verona

his aesthetic theories regarding the coalescence of subjects and objects with their environments. Traces of Divisionism's ongoing influence can be identified in several chapters of *Pittura scultura futuriste (Dinamismo plastico)*. For example, in chapter 6, "Perché non siamo impressionisti,"[52] Boccioni proclaimed that the Futurists' reelaboration of the "unity-object" (*unità–oggetto*) permitted them to better express the relationship between object and environment in their art and stated, "We thereby create a new conception of the object: the object-environment [*oggetto-ambiente*], conceived as a new, *indivisible unity*."[53] The artist continued with a similar premise in chapter 7, "Che cosa ci divide dal cubismo,"[54] observing, in a phrase that hearkens back to the notion of perceiving divisionistically, "Today our mental evolution no longer permits us to see an individual or object as isolated from their environment."[55] Even in the book's later chapters, in which complex, multilayered conceptions of objects, motion, and spatial relationships are addressed, Divisionism makes its latent impact felt. In fact, Boccioni's theoretical constructs of continuity and dynamism evidence Divisionism's artistic legacy; the threadlike, mobile brushwork persisting in his Futurist work implies states of temporal and spatial flux that were key to the evolution and depiction of his ideas.[56]

That an avant-garde painting style from the late nineteenth century had proven to be such a touchstone for Boccioni was a testament to its adaptability in a different era. His co-option of Divisionist strategies underscored his recognition of their inherent modernist possibilities. The older avant-garde movement supplied the foundational visual and theoretical principles that were indispensable to Boccioni's realization of universal synthesis in his art.

Notes

I could not have written this essay without the help of several individuals whom I must thank here: Laura Mattioli Rossi, for her ongoing guidance, perceptive suggestions, and generosity in sharing research; Emily Braun, for her encouragement and advice; Domenica Lo Monte, for transcribing a crucial Boccioni text; Lisa Panzera, for patiently listening to ideas and reading drafts; Giovanna Ginex, for her insights on Boccioni and the Divisionists, especially Gaetano Previati; Sergio Rebora, for providing his opinions on the relationship between Boccioni and Vittore Grubicy de Dragon; and Bea Zengotitabengoa, Francesca Grassi, and, especially, Anna Schultz, for their assistance with research matters. I also extend special thanks to Karole Vail and Ilaria Duprè for their tenacious efforts in locating the illustrations for this essay. Translations from Italian are by Stephen Sartarelli unless otherwise noted.

1 Umberto Boccioni, "Futurist Painting" (1911), in Ester Coen, *Umberto Boccioni*, exh. cat. (New York: Metropolitan Museum of Art, 1988), p. 236; for original text in Italian, see Boccioni, "La pittura futurista," in Zeno Birolli, ed., *Umberto Boccioni: Altri inediti e apparati scritti* (Milan: Feltrinelli, 1972), p. 22.

2 Boccioni's preoccupation with the linked concepts of universality and synthesis can be traced back at least as early as 1907, when he wrote about it in his diary: "I am becoming more and more aware that the fundamental flaw of Modern Art is its lack of universality, or at least that is how I call that sense of poetry dominant in ancient works, which makes the artist's song forever extend with amorous exaltation over all of creation. The tremendous analysis made in our century has renewed us by creating specialists. This explains the lack of universality in the modern artwork. I believe that what we need is a vast mind with the courage and strength to synthesize modern knowledge and create the true work of art." Boccioni diary, July 7, 1907, in Zeno Birolli, *Umberto Boccioni: Gli scritti editi e inediti* (Milan: Feltrinelli, 1971), p. 248. This point is noted in Luciano Caramel, "Dal divisionismo al futurismo a Milano: Boccioni, Carrà, Russolo," in Museo d'Arte Moderna e Contemporanea di Trento e Rovereto, *Divisionismo italiano*, exh. cat. (Milan: Electa, 1990), p. 395.

3 See entry for this work in Annie-Paule Quinsac, ed., *Giovanni Segantini: Light and Symbol, 1884–1899*, exh. cat. (Milan: Skira, 2000), p. 54. The literature on Divisionism, while vast, primarily exists in Italian, and the major publications in this language include Gabriella Belli and Franco Rella, eds., *L'Età del divisionismo* (Milan: Electa, 1990); Belli and Quinsac, *Carlo Fornara: Un maestro del divisionismo*, exh. cat. (Milan: Skira, 1998); Fortunato Bellonzi, *Il divisionismo nella pittura italiana* (Milan: Fratelli Fabbri, 1967); Gianfranco Bruno, *Plinio Nomellini*, exh. cat. (Milan: Stringa, 1985); Luciano Caramel, *Angelo Morbelli*, exh. cat. (Milan: Mazzotta, 1982); Teresa Fiori, *Archivi del Divisionismo*, with an introduction by Fortunato Bellonzi, 2 vols. (Rome: Officina Edizioni, 1968); Giovanna Ginex, *Emilio Longoni: Catalogo ragionato* (Milan: F. Motta, 1995); Ginex, *Giovanni Sottocornola: Dal realismo sociale al quotidiano familiare*, exh. cat. (Milan: Edi Artes, 1985); Fernando Mazzocca, ed., *Gaetano Previati, 1852–1920: Un protagonista del simbolismo europeo*, exh. cat. (Milan: Electa, 1999); Quinsac, *Segantini: Trent'anni di vita artistica europea nei carteggi inediti dell'artista e dei suoi mecenati* (Oggiono, Lecco: Cattaneo, 1985); Quinsac, *Segantini: Catalogo generale* (Milan: Electa, 1982); Quinsac, *La Peinture divisionniste italienne: Origines et premiers développements, 1880–1895* (Paris: Klincksieck, 1972); Sergio Rebora, *Vittore Grubicy De Dragon: 1851–1920* (Milan: Jandi Sapi, 1995); Aurora Scotti Tosini (née Aurora Scotti), *Angelo Morbelli: Tra realismo e divisionismo*, exh. cat. (Turin: GAM, 2001); Scotti Tosini, *Giuseppe Pellizza da Volpedo*, exh. cat. (Turin: Hopefulmonster, 1999); Aurora Scotti, *Angelo Morbelli* (Soncino: Edizioni dei Soncino, 1991); Scotti, *Pellizza da Volpedo: Catalogo generale* (Milan: Electa, 1986); and Scotti, *Catalogo dei manoscritti di Giuseppe Pellizza da Volpedo provenienti dalla donazione eredi Pellizza* (Tortona: Tipografia Ferrari Occella, 1974).

4 For the paradoxical rapport between the two movements, see Maurizio Calvesi and Ester Coen, *Boccioni: L'opera completa* (Milan: Electa, 1983), p. 44.

5 See Maurizio Fagiolo dell'Arco, *Giacomo Balla 1895–1911: Verso il Futurismo*, exh. cat. (Venice: Marsilio, 1998), pp. 20–21.

6 Umberto Boccioni, Carlo Carrà, Luigi Russolo, Giacomo Balla, and Gino Severini, "Manifesto of the Futurist Painters" (February 11, 1910), in Umbro Apollonio, ed. *Futurist Manifestos* (New York: Viking, 1973), p. 26. Also in 1910, Boccioni visited the Previati retrospective held at the Società per le Belle Arti ed Esposizione Permanente in Milan. See Giovanna Ginex, "Un sogno che svanisce nella luce della modernità: Gaetano Previati nella lettura critica, dalle suggestioni antipositive all'influsso su Umberto Boccioni," in Mazzocca, *Gaetano Previati, 1852–1920*, p. 69.

7 Umberto Boccioni, Carlo Carrà, Luigi Russolo, Giacomo Balla, and Gino Severini, "Futurist Painting: Technical Manifesto" (April 11, 1910), in Apollonio, *Futurist Manifestos*, p. 29.

8 On December 21, 1907, Boccioni wrote in his diary, "I'm reading Previati's the 'Tecnica della pittura' and feel humbled in the face of so much technical erudition." In Birolli, *Gli scritti editi e inediti*, p. 270. Again, on January 8, 1908, he wrote, "I'm reading Previati 'La tecnica della pittura,' and have enjoyed it very much." In Birolli, p. 273. While Previati wrote *I principi scientifici del divisionismo* (1906) specifically on Divisionism, Boccioni chose to focus on *La tecnica della pittura*, Previati's more didactic and general publication, perhaps because he had not had a formal academic education and felt the need for a more solid grounding in the basics of painting. Previati is mentioned in numerous entries in Boccioni's diary. See Birolli, pp. 101, 114, 281–82, 297. Previati's importance for Boccioni is well documented. In addition to Ginex's indispensable "Gaetano Previati nella lettura critica" (see note 6 above), among more recent publications, see Calvesi and Coen, *Boccioni*, especially the section "La poetica dello stato d'animo: Boccioni e Previati," pp. 53–57. Judith Ellen Meighan, *The "Stati d'Animo" Aesthetic: Gaetano Previati, Umberto Boccioni and the Development of Early Futurist Painting in Italy* (Ph.D. diss., Columbia University, 1998), traces the influence of Previati on Boccioni, particularly that of his writings. Ilaria Schiaffini recently addressed Boccioni and Previati as part of a larger discussion of Boccioni's early career, contextualizing his work within the Symbolist and spiritualist movements still prevalent in the first decades of the 1900s. See Schiaffini, *Umberto Boccioni: Stati d'animo. Teoria e pittura* (Milan: Silvana, 2002). Her investigation and my own share interesting affinities, although our goals ultimately differ. While she seeks to situate Boccioni alongside European contemporaries such as Vasily Kandinsky, the present essay focuses on the specific co-option of Divisionist tenets by Boccioni and the Futurists and negates the accepted teleological argument whereby Divisionism is validated only as a precursor to Futurism. As Schiaffini's book only became available when this essay was going to press, a greater consideration of our respective studies was precluded.

9 "The Divisionist exhibition in Paris, extremely interesting—the canvases by Segantini [are] marvelous, those by Previati very bold, those by Fornara and others respectable—They dealt me the decisive blow—Balla is finished." Boccioni diary, October 17, 1907, in Birolli, *Gli scritti editi e inediti*, p. 266. The exhibition, *I pittori divisionisti italiani a Parigi*, was held in September–October 1907 at the Società Dante Alighieri and organized by the gallerist Alberto Grubicy (estranged brother of Vittore Grubicy de Dragon).

10 For entries written at length about Previati, see Boccioni diary, March 2 and June 19, 1908, in Birolli, *Gli scritti editi e inediti*, pp. 287, 308–09. Previously, in 1906, Boccioni met another Divisionist, Giuseppe Pellizza da Volpedo, through Giovanni Cena, a mutual friend from Turin. Pellizza, however, was an artist he admired less among the Divisionists: "I'd met him in Rome and we discussed a lot. As an artist he wasn't very good." Boccioni diary, June 16, 1907, in Birolli, p. 246.

11 Boccioni expressed admiration for Previati as late as 1916 in a review he wrote of a Previati exhibition held in Milan. See Umberto Boccioni, "Le esposizioni collettive di Gaetano Previati e Carlo Fornara a Milano–L'arte di Gaetano Previati," *Gli Avvenimenti*, March 19–26, 1916, p. 3.

12 Among others, Calvesi and Coen identified this as Boccioni's first truly Futurist work. See Calvesi and Coen, *Boccioni*, p. 44. Hereafter, for all Boccioni works cited, the catalogue raisonné number (referred to as "Calvesi and Coen, no.") is provided; *The City Rises* is Calvesi and Coen, no. 675.

13 This fact has been noted previously by Calvesi and Coen, *Boccioni*, p. 46. While Boccioni ultimately painted a single-canvas work, he considered a triptych format in an earlier conception of *The City Rises*, as is evident from the 1910 drawings *La notte, il giorno, l'alba* (Calvesi and Coen, no. 673), in pencil, and *L'alba, il giorno, la notte* (no. 674), in ink.

14 Boccioni's fascination with the dynamic possibilities of the galloping horse are manifest throughout his work, and the Divisionist Segantini can also be cited as a source for this. As an early, undated drawing *Studi da Segantini e da Andrea del Sarto* (Calvesi and Coen, no. 17) demonstrates, Boccioni copied the horse from Segantini's painting *Cavallo a galoppo* (n.d., probably 1887–89). See Maurizio Calvesi, "Boccioni prima del futurismo," in Calvesi, Ester Coen, Antonella Greco, eds., *Boccioni prefuturista*, exh. cat. (Milan: Electa, 1983), pp. 18–19.

15 Unpublished letter, Vittore Grubicy to Boccioni, July 27, 1910, Box 1, Folder 29, Umberto Boccioni Papers, Research Library, The Getty Research Institute, Los Angeles (880380).

16 Calvesi and Coen, no. 455.

17 While I have been unable to determine definitively the work to which Grubicy referred, this might be the undated *La madre* (Calvesi and Coen, no. 456).

18 Vittore Grubicy, "Pittori futuristi," *Il Secolo*, April 19, 1910, n. 15803, p. 3. Sergio Rebora kindly provided a copy of this article.

19 Unpublished letter, Boccioni to Vittore Grubicy, January 17, 1911, Fondo Benvenuti-Grubicy, #78, Archivio del '900, Museo di Arte Moderna di Trento e Rovereto. I thank the museum's director, Gabriella Belli, for access to Grubicy's papers, and Paola Pettenella and Francesca Velardita for their kind assistance at the archives.

20 For the complete lecture in English, see Boccioni, "Futurist Painting," in Coen, *Umberto Boccioni*, pp. 231–39; in Italian, see Boccioni, "La pittura futurista," in Birolli, ed. *Altri inediti e apparati scritti*, pp. 11–29.

21 Boccioni, unpublished notes entitled "Sul divisionismo–frammenti," Box 3, Folder 4, Manuscript 5, Umberto Boccioni Papers, Research Library, The Getty Research Institute, Los Angeles (880380). Schiaffini has identified the document's handwriting as that of Decio Cinti, the Futurist movement's secretary, and further suggested that this is likely a partial transcription of the 1911 "La pittura futurista" lecture in Rome and was executed so Boccioni could have a clear copy from which to read. See Schiaffini, *Umberto Boccioni*, pp. 71–77, 158–59. The title "Sul divisionismo" and designation "frammenti" appear to be written on the manuscript title page in yet a different hand, and were probably added posthumously. It is unknown whether Boccioni intended using this title. While several drafts of this lecture in various states of completion are known to exist, given the possibility that "Sul divisionismo" may have been a working title and that it was the version Boccioni may have actually read in Rome, I examine this specific incarnation within my analysis.

22 Boccioni, "Sul divisionismo – frammenti," p. 73.

23 Ibid., pp. 81–82.

24 Ibid., p. 74.

25 Ibid., pp. 100–103.

26 However, not all Divisionists embraced positivism; for example, Previati maintained an anti-materialist view and was influential for Boccioni in this regard. See Ginex, "Gaetano Previati nella lettura critica"; and Meighan, *"Stati d'Animo" Aesthetic*, especially pp. 201–03.

27 Boccioni, "Sul divisionismo – frammenti," p. 90.

28 Ibid., p. 15.

29 Boccioni, *Pittura scultura futuriste (Dinamismo plastico)*, in Birolli, *Gli scritti editi e inediti*, p. 165; originally published as a separate volume by Edizioni Futuriste di "Poesia," Milan, in 1914

30 This triptych remained incomplete at the time of Segantini's death in 1899. However, highly finished drawings for it were included in the 1907 exhibition *I pittori divisionisti a Parigi*, which Boccioni visited in Paris. See Quinsac, *Segantini: Catalogo generale*, pp. 513–19.

31 Calvesi and Coen, no. 292. For a close analysis of this work, see Flavio Fergonzi, catalogue entry no. 8, in Laura Mattioli Rossi, ed., *Boccioni 1912 Materia*, exh. cat. (Milan: Mazzotta, 1991), p. 156.

32 Calvesi and Coen, nos. 723–25.

33 See Calvesi and Coen, *Boccioni*, p. 397.

34 For an examination of this trope, with Boccioni's *The Story of a Seamstress* (1908, cat. no. 3) as its focus, see Aurora Scotti, "Boccioni 1908: Del vero naturale alla materia in espansione," in Mattioli Rossi, *Boccioni 1912 Materia*, pp. 115–35. See also the section "La figura e la finestra," in Mattioli Rossi, p. 169; and entry for *La madre con l'uncinetto* (1907), no. 57, in Flavio Caroli and Ada Masoero, eds., *Dalla scapigliatura al futurismo*, exh. cat. (Milan: Skira, 2001), pp. 176–77. These images of women confined in domestic interiors also bring up the issue of the gendering of public and private spaces, the home being the obvious feminine domain. Already by the end of the nineteenth century, as women became more conspicuous in the public sphere and the suffrage movement gained momentum, traditional gender roles were destabilized and threatened. Many domestic interiors in painting became claustrophobic or repressive, reflecting male desire to contain women and keep binary identities well defined. However, Boccioni's interiors—those depicting his mother in particular—increasingly blurred boundaries between the home and the street in a less polarized conception of traditional feminine and masculine realms. For a specific discussion of gender in Boccioni's images of his mother, see Virginia Spate, "Mother and Son: Boccioni's Paintings and Sculpture 1906–1915," in Terry Smith, ed., *In Visible Touch: Modernism and Masculinity* (Chicago: University of Chicago Press, 1997), pp. 107 38. For the role of women in Futurism, see, for example, the section "The Futurist Wo(mb)man," in Emily Braun, "Vulgarians at the Gate," in the present publication, pp. 10–13.

35 A variation on this subject that bears mentioning is the nighttime version, such as Segantini's *Ritratto di Carlo Rotta* (1897), which employs interior light to illuminate the sitter but to the same end.

36 Specifically, in providing an example supporting their points, the Futurists wrote, "The sixteen people around you in a rolling motor bus are in turn and at the same time one, ten, four, three: they are motionless and they change places; they come and go, bound into the street, are suddenly swallowed up by the sunshine, then come back and sit before you, like persistent symbols of universal vibration. How often have we not seen upon the cheek of the person with whom we are talking the horse which passes at the end of the street." Boccioni, Carrà, Russolo, Balla, and Severini, "Futurist Painting: Technical Manifesto," p. 28.

37 Calvesi and Coen, no. 18.

38 Other works repeating this compositional arrangement are Boccioni's pastels of his grandmother, *The Old Woman* (1905–06; Calvesi and Coen, no. 51), and mother, *Mother* (1906; no. 244). In 1906, prior to *Mother*, he realized more ambitious variations in oil portraits of nonrelatives: *Portrait of Doctor Kopcick* (no. 235), in which the doctor is seated before the open doors of a balcony, and *Portrait of Sophie Popoff* (no. 241), with its sitter shown sewing by a window. Boccioni continued to repeat the arrangement in the 1907 pastels *Mother* (no. 247), *Sister Sewing* (no. 267), and *Mother Crocheting* (no. 276)—which return to his mother and sister, who were frequent models—and *Signora Sacchi* (no. 271). His *Two Seated Old Women* (no. 277), as Aurora Scotti has already pointed out, not only reiterates the subject but also appears to be a direct quotation of Morbelli, another Divisionist who looked to Millet for this composition type. See Scotti, "Boccioni 1908," p. 122. Interestingly Boccioni employed a similar arrangement in a self-portrait, *Portrait of a Sculptor* (1907; no. 250).

39 Calvesi and Coen, no. 309. For an extensive discussion of this work, see Scotti, "Boccioni 1908," pp. 115–35. As Scotti has noted, the title of this work is inspired by Thomas Hood's 1843 poem "The Song of the Shirt," a compassionate Victorian tale of the plight of women forced to do piece work at home to earn a meager living. This popular poem inspired several paintings, such as *The Song of the Shirt* (1902) by British artist Albert Rutherston. Unlike Rutherston, who depicts a sad, overworked seamstress, Boccioni portrays a genteel woman. However, the reference is of interest when one considers that Boccioni's mother and sister earned a necessary income sewing and doing other handiwork at home.

40 Translation by author. Boccioni diary, April 1, 1908, in Birolli, *Gli scritti editi e inediti*, p. 299. Boccioni acknowledges Previati's influence in this work as well, mentioning in his diary entry for May 28, 1908 that the figure recalled the Divisionist artist. Birolli, p. 306.

41 Calvesi and Coen, no. 299.

42 See entry for *Signora Massimino* in Caroli and Masoero, *Dalla scapigliatura al futurismo*, pp. 178–80.

43 Boccioni diary, March 18, 1908, in Birolli, *Gli scritti editi e inediti*, pp. 292–93. For other diary entries addressing the execution of this portrait in depth, see December 21, 1907 (in Birolli, p. 270), December 24, 1907 (p. 271), and January 8, 1908 (pp. 273–75).

44 Calvesi and Coen, no. 442.

43 Calvesi and Coen, no. 443.

46 Calvesi and Coen, no. 434.

47 Another related work from 1909 is *Female Portrait* (Calvesi and Coen, no. 435).

48 Boccioni would continue on the same tack with the portrait *Portrait of Signora Meta Quarck* in 1910 (Calvesi and Coen, no. 467).

49 Calvesi and Coen, no. 745.

50 Margherita Grassini Sarfatti, "Cronache d'Arte. L'Esposizione 'Intima' alla Famiglia Artistica," *Avanti*, December 13, 1911. I thank Laura Mattioli Rossi for supplying me with this article.

51 Calvesi and Coen, no. 744.

52 Boccioni, *Pittura scultura futuriste (Dinamismo plastico)*, in Birolli, *Gli Scritti editi e inediti*, pp. 109–21.

53 Ibid., p. 120.

54 Ibid., pp. 121–37.

55 Ibid., p. 124.

56 It could even be argued that Divisionism provided Boccioni with a concrete base upon which to develop his theories regarding the absolute motion of an object and its state of becoming within a fourth dimension, theories culled from Henri Bergson's writings regarding the duration of an object within the fourth dimension. For more on Boccioni's theories, see the chapters "Moto assoluto e moto relativo" and "Dinamismo" in *Pittura scultura futuriste*, pp. 181–91 and 195–208 in the original 1914 edition. For more on Boccioni and Bergson, see Flavio Fergonzi, "On the Title of the Painting *Materia*," in the present volume, pp. 48–53. For a specific discussion of Boccioni and the fourth dimension, see Mark Antliff, "The Fourth Dimension and Futurism: A Politicized Space," *The Art Bulletin* 82 (December 2000), pp. 720–33; and for the Futurists and Bergson, see Antliff, *Inventing Bergson: Cultural Politics and the Parisian Avant-Garde* (Princeton: Princeton University Press, 1993), pp. 155–66. See also Linda Dalrymple Henderson, *The Fourth Dimension and Non-Euclidean Geometry in Modern Art* (Princeton: Princeton University Press, 1983), pp. 110–16; and Brian Pertrie, "Boccioni and Bergson," *The Burlington Magazine* 116 (March 1974), pp. 140–47.

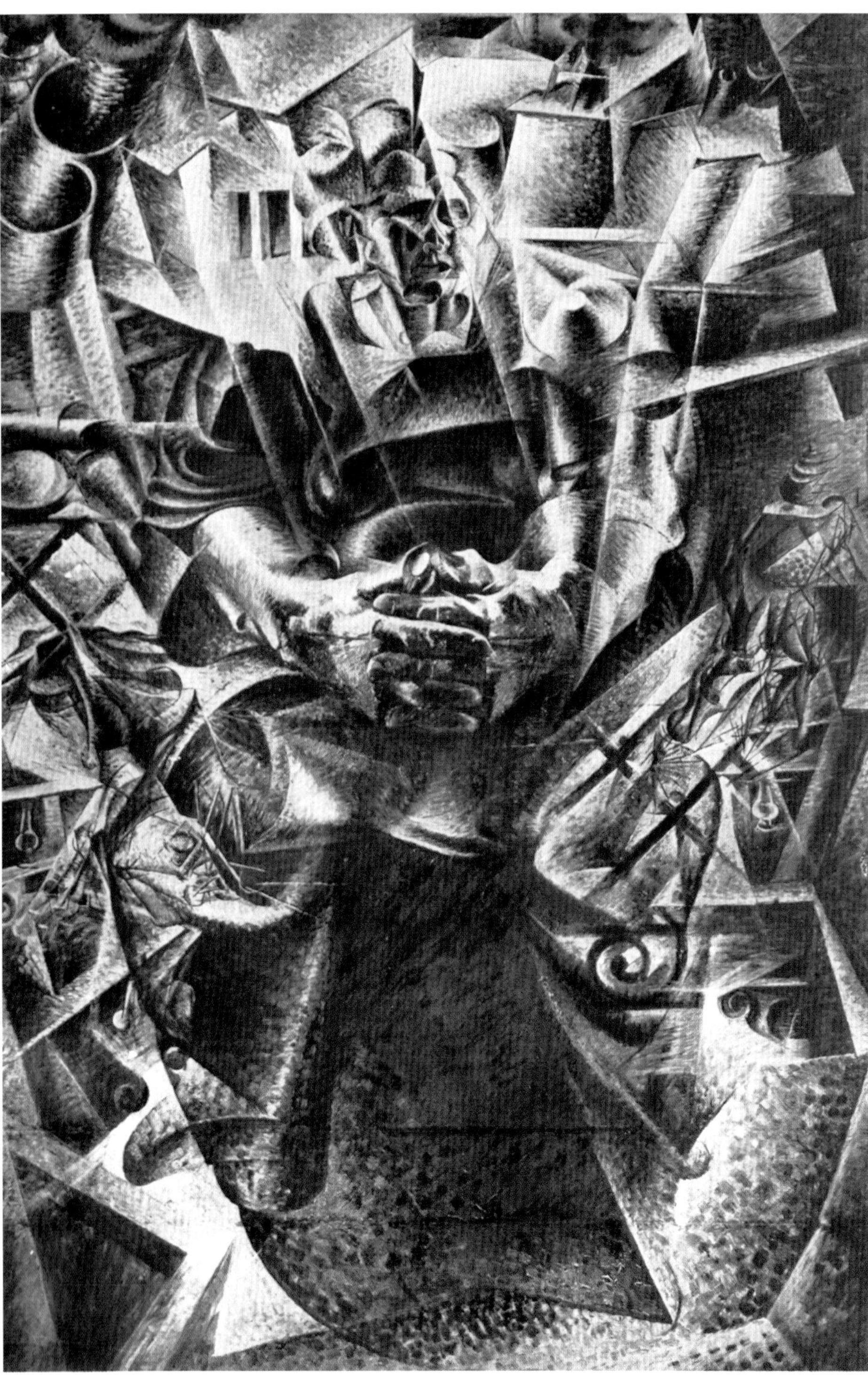

Fig. 26
Umberto Boccioni's *Materia* before the 1913 changes. Photograph reproduced in *Cahiers d'Art* 25, no.1 (1950), p. 35.

Boccioni Between Painting and Sculpture

LAURA MATTIOLI ROSSI

On March 15, 1912, Boccioni wrote from Paris to a friend and patron, Vico Baer, "These days I'm obsessed with sculpture! I believe I've seen a total renewal of this mummified art."[1] With the preface to the catalogue of his first exhibition of Futurist sculpture, he signed himself—for the first time—as "Umberto Boccioni, *painter and sculptor.*" The text, dated May 9, 1913, appeared in French when this exhibition was held at Galerie La Boëtie in Paris from June 20 to July 16;[2] it was published in Italian when his second sculpture show opened in December at Giuseppe Sprovieri's Galleria Futurista in Rome.[3] Included in Rome was the last major plaster Boccioni made, *Human Forms in Movement* (1913; destroyed).[4] During the period between spring 1912 and the end of summer, he also painted the large canvas entitled *Materia* (1912, cat. no. 27), universally recognized as one of the pinnacles of the artist's production and an uncontested masterpiece of Futurism.[5]

In *Materia,* Boccioni realized in pictorial form many of the artistic theories expressed in writings by Boccioni, Carlo Carrà, Luigi Russolo, Giacomo Balla, and Gino Severini—"Manifesto of the Futurist Painters" (published February 11, 1910), "Futurist Painting: Technical Manifesto" (April 11, 1910), and "Les Exposants au public" (February 5, 1912), the catalogue preface for their group exhibition at Galerie Bernheim-Jeune in Paris[6]—and by Boccioni himself. *Materia* also responded to new ideas that arose from Boccioni's contacts with artists working in Paris and from his own experiments in sculpture. A particularly compelling work also for its imposing size, *Materia* stands at the center of Boccioni's artistic development: it was painted right after the triptych *States of Mind* (1911–12, figs. 20–22) and falls between the equally monumental *The City Rises* (1910–11, fig. 11) and *Dynamism of a Soccer Player* (1913).[7]

Materia portrays the painter's mother, Cecilia Forlani Boccioni, seated on an armchair, hands crossed in her lap, in front of a French door. Behind her, the balcony railing marks the separation between the interior space of the room and the outside, while to the sides, the open windows reflect the activity in the street below: a horse passing to the left; a man walking to the right. The urban landscape occupying the upper portion of the canvas corresponds precisely with what could be seen in 1912 from the top-floor apartment at via Adige 23, on the southern outskirts of Milan, where Boccioni had been living since September 1908:[8] rooftops of multistoried residential buildings of recent construction, the double entrance of the Besozzi Marzoli mill, and the smokestacks of the power plant located in the piazza Trento.[9] The realistic details of this distant vista also include the profile of the Duomo and mill wheels sinking in the waters of the Naviglio canal.

Both a female figure in front of a window and a scene drawn from everyday life were not unusual in the artist's repertoire of images. In line with the goals of the "Manifesto of the Futurist Painters," Boccioni often depicted what he saw from his window: "Living art draws its life from the surrounding environment.... How can we remain insensible to the frenetic life of our great cities?"[10] After *Sister on the Balcony* (1909, cat. no. 6), Boccioni started *The City Rises,* which took its cue from the excavations being done in piazza Trento, where work began in June 1910 on two large tanks necessary for the running of the adjacent power plant.[11] The construction of the Besozzi Marzoli mill, begun in July 1911 right in front of Boccioni's home, appears in *On the Balcony*, the painting shown in the *Esposizione intima annuale* at the Famiglia Artistica in Milan that December. The title was later changed to *The Street Enters the House* (1911, cat. no. 7), a Futurist description that better evokes the aural and visual qualities of the scene. The canvas caught the attention

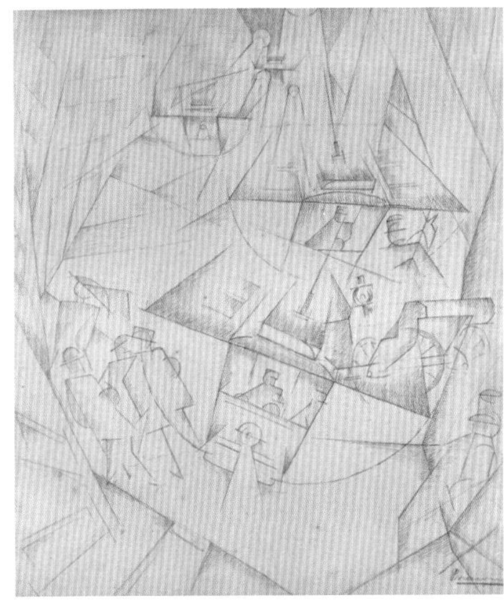

Fig. 27 Umberto Boccioni
Study for *The Forces of a Street* (*Le forze di una strada*), 1911
Pencil on paper, 17¼ × 14⁹⁄₁₆ inches (43.8 × 37 cm)
Civiche Raccolte d'Arte, Gabinetto dei Disegni, Milan

of the critic Margherita Sarfatti, an important Italian cultural figure during the first decades of the twentieth century, who judged it harshly for approximating the qualities of cinema rather than painting.[12] Nonetheless, it has certain elements that relate to *Materia*, such as the square format, which Boccioni often used, and the point of view, corresponding to the balcony itself. In *The Street Enters the House*, the heads of two horses slip within the volutes of the balcony railing, while rays of summer light and the profile of a fan pass through the mother's figure—all clear examples of the theorized interpenetration of bodies.

In 1911, shortly after *The Street Enters the House*, Boccioni painted two other urban views: *The Forces of a Street*,[13] which represents a tram pushing forward amid carriages and passersby under the glow of the streetlamps strung between buildings; and *Simultaneous Visions* (cat. no. 8), in which the face of a woman looking from above onto the street below is reflected in the window pane. Both are very similar in format and dimensions, and many of the details present in *The Forces of a Street*—the design of the tram, the carriage alongside it, the stylized, anonymous figures in the street—are repeated (but in diurnal form) in *Simultaneous Visions*, so much so that one concludes the artist used the same preparatory drawing (fig. 27) for both paintings. Nevertheless, in *Simultaneous Visions*, the tighter, less analytical composition, the solidity of the volumes rendered through Divisionist technique, and the still life in the foreground with pitcher and plate (prefiguring the helicoidal structure of *Development of a Bottle in Space* [1912, cat. no. 37]), lead one to date the work shortly after *The Street Enters the House* and immediately following *The Forces of a Street*—that is, before Boccioni's trip to Paris in mid-October 1911. Indeed, the Galerie Bernheim-Jeune catalogue preface was presented to his Futurist colleagues for approval on October 11, 1911,[14] and, in turn, had been inspired by the lecture Boccioni gave in Rome on May 29, 1910.[15] Statements in the preface correspond precisely with paintings:

> *Painting someone on the balcony, seen from inside, we do not limit ourselves to what the window frame allows us to see; rather, we endeavor to convey the whole aggregate of plastic sensations felt by the painter on the balcony: the sunlit bustle of the street, the double row of houses extending to the left and right, the balconies with flowers, etc. Which means a simultaneity of environment, and thus a dislocation and dismemberment of objects and a scattering and fusion of details freed from common logic and independent of one another.*
>
> *To make the spectator live at the center of the painting, as we expressed it in our manifesto, the painting must be a synthesis* of what one remembers and what one sees.[16]

The paintings do not presuppose a direct knowledge of the Cubist breakdown of forms and derive stylistically from what Boccioni might have seen in reproductions available among the Futurists.

For Boccioni, 1912 was a particularly intense year. As he described it in a letter from Rome to Baer, dated February 19, 1913, "The year of the Paris exhibition [which opened on February 5, 1912] has just come to a close. What I did seems like nothing to me, and yet to others it seems huge! Aside from the plunge into life: shows in Paris, London, Berlin, Brussels, Hamburg, Amsterdam, the Hague, Munich, Vienna, Budapest, and now Rome, which I'm preparing! Trips abroad. Manifesto and sculpture. Six paintings. Lecture. The reconciliation in Florence. Finished the book on painting."[17] He was recounting the Futurist exhibition that was held at Galerie Bernheim-Jeune in February–March 1912, which included ten of his canvases; he had accompanied the exhibition to London and Berlin during its extensive itinerary traveling to the cities mentioned in his letter. He subsequently visited Severini in Paris during early November to see the Salon d'Automne. In the letter to Baer, "Manifesto and sculpture" refers to "Technical Manifesto of Futurist Sculpture," dated April 11 but drafted by July;[18] "the reconciliation in Florence," the agreement reached with Ardengo Soffici and Giovanni Papini that had led to the publication of the first issue of the review *Lacerba* on January 1, 1913; and "finished the book on painting," to the first draft of book *Pittura scultura futuriste (Dinamismo plastico)*, which would be published in 1914.

The "six paintings" include those presented at the Futurist painting exhibition, which opened on February 21, 1913,[19] in the foyer of the Teatro Costanzi in Rome, and which replaced the works he had sold the previous year. The canvases were *Materia*, chosen to open the sequence owing to its recognized prominence within the group, the triptych *States of Mind*, which had already been shown in the 1912 traveling exhibition and which the artist had not wanted to sell, *Elasticity* (1912, fig. 28), *Decomposition of Figures at a Table* (1912; location unknown),[20] *Horizontal Construction* (1912, cat. no. 28), *Antigrazioso* (1912, fig. 29), and *Abstract Dimensions* (1912, cat. no. 21).[21] In the catalogue, the paintings are listed in the preceding order, which may be chronological[22]—although *Materia*'s position as incipit is unchanged—or it may correspond only to their sequence in the show, where they were installed in thematic groups. I lean toward the latter hypothesis, which places *Materia* in juxtaposition with *States of*

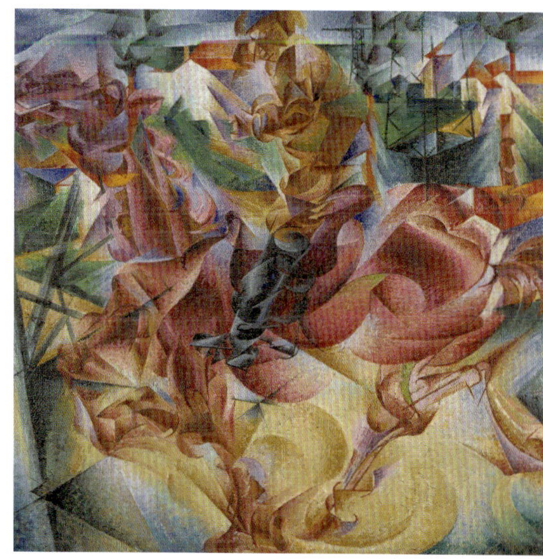

Fig. 28 Umberto Boccioni
Elasticity (*Elasticità*), 1912
Oil on canvas, 39³⁄₈ × 39³⁄₈ inches (100 × 100 cm)
Civiche Raccolte d'Arte, Museo d' Arte Contemporanea, Jucker Collection, Milan

Mind because Boccioni considered the triptych to be his prior masterpiece. That would have left, on the two remaining walls, first, the two typically Futurist subjects *Elasticity* and *Decomposition of Figures at Table*, and then the three portraits, of which the two placed at the ends were once again of his mother, *Horizontal Construction* and *Abstract Dimensions*, with *Antigrazioso* in between. *Horizontal Construction* would therefore have been separated from *Materia*, underlining the conceptual break that lies between them, despite their visual similarity.

Existing documentation does not allow us to establish with any absolute certainty the chronological order of the six paintings that Boccioni made between his first Paris show and the Teatro Costanzi exhibition. Nor is it possible to assign a specific time period to any of them. Even Boccioni's references to when he began working on his sculptures remains extremely vague, and the lack of certitude is compounded by the contradictions in the artist's own writings. In fact, he predated his first mixed-media sculptures to 1911[23] — at least a year before their actual execution — in order to assert Italian predominance over French experimentation at a moment when Guillaume Apollinaire's support for Orphism had increased hostilities between the two avant-gardes.

Given these circumstances and the numerous theories advanced by other art historians,[24] and well aware of retracing a purely hypothetical itinerary myself, I shall proceed by way of inference and comparison to reconstruct as coherent an order as possible. In anticipation of my conclusion, I believe that in 1912 and 1913, Boccioni created works in dialogue with one another — paintings, drawings, and three-dimensional sculptural groups — and often concurrently, continually testing different possibilities and solutions.[25] To begin, *Elasticity* certainly preceded the realization of *Materia*. A considerably important image in both subject and size (the same square dimensions as *The Street Enters the House*), it expresses a typical Futurist conception of dynamism, but for stylistic reasons likely dates from before mid-summer 1912. Subsequently, Boccioni became more interested in the interpenetration of planes than in the movement of bodies; when he revived his experimentation in dynamism with the virile sculptures of 1913, he elaborated the syntheses and deformations created by motion, as also evidenced by the drawings of the period. In *Elasticity*, the movements of a trotting horse and bouncing horseman are still rendered by mixing multiple images and anatomical analyses of musculature in three-dimensional syntheses. To reproduce more than merely the motion of man and animal, Boccioni sought to invent a visual equivalent of the rhythmical sensation created by the particular pace of the horse. The fusion of the figures with their surroundings is limited by comparison to other pictures, such as *Simultaneous Visions* and *Materia*, while the naturalistic details are instead quite numerous: the cloth placed between the saddle and the animal's skin, the urban landscape once again depicting the smokestacks of the via Adige area, and the iron pylons of the piazza Trento power plant.

Preceded by a large study in the same square format,[26] *Elasticity* could not have been executed during his short stay (less than a month) in Milan that spring. In all likelihood, it was painted at the beginning of the summer, right after the artist returned to Milan. A horse's head, neck, and hind leg appear in very similar form on the left side of *Materia* and in a study for *Materia* (1912, cat. no. 26), which is also known as a study for *Horizontal Construction*. In all, the animal's muzzle is cut off by the edge of the canvas.

Abstract Dimensions is characterized by a square, though smaller, format, by a clearly constructed design, and by large brushstrokes of color covering only part of the canvas, giving the whole an unfinished look. Here again, the painting is difficult to date precisely and is generally placed among the last works of 1912. It was probably realized during Boccioni's interval in Milan during the spring, roughly between April 20 and May 20. At that time, for reasons both practical and technical, Boccioni was unable to work in sculpture, the medium that had so "obsessed" him since mid-March. Instead, he went back to painting his favorite model — his mother — who also sat for his initial works in three dimensions. *Abstract Dimensions* shows a direct knowledge of Cubism, especially in the facial features, as well as a vigorous three-dimensionality of volumes, both in the body and the modeling of hair. The latter element is important in clarifying the painting's chronology because it is the prototype for the treatment found in the sculpture *Antigrazioso* (1912–13, cat. no. 31), with its individually rounded, massive locks, and *Materia*, with its rays of light impinging on the emphatically modeled hair.[27] The "unfinished" status of *Abstract Dimensions* can perhaps be explained by the brevity of Boccioni's stay in Milan that spring; he was unexpectedly called back to Berlin to settle the sale of all the works in the traveling Futurist show to the banker Albert Borchardt.[28]

On June 1, 1912, Boccioni was with F. T. Marinetti in Brussels, giving a lecture on Futurism. Upon his return to Milan, he could finally turn to sculpture. Our most reliable accounting of the evolution of his sculpture comes from Roberto Longhi, who wrote a long review of Boccioni's show at Sprovieri's Galleria Futurista, entitled *Scultura futurista: Boccioni,* and published by Libreria de "La Voce" in 1914. The first sculpture to be completed was certainly *Antigrazioso*, which

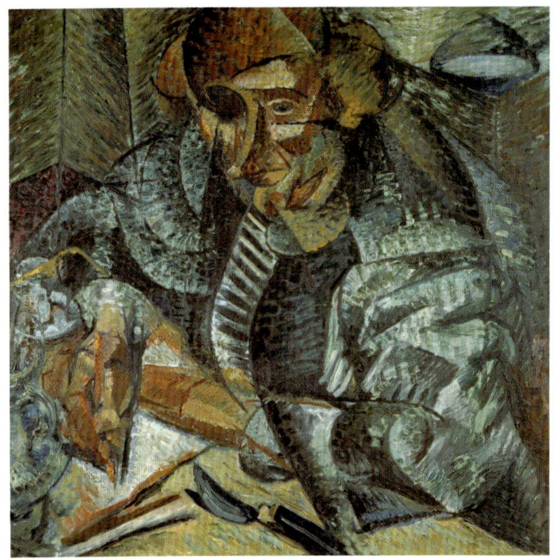

Fig. 29 Umberto Boccioni
Antigrazioso, 1912
Oil on canvas, 31½ × 31½ inches (80 × 80 cm)
Private collection

Longhi identified as a trial piece, still under the influence of Post-Impressionism, and a somewhat confused attempt to develop a new sculptural form.[29] He wrote, "The dense lumpiness of the flesh weighs heavily in certain cavities, whose delineation clearly derives from a skeletal structure that emerges here and there, suggesting the hidden, if definite construction underneath."[30] Such structure had been the object of study in Boccioni's recent *Abstract Dimensions*, and the correspondence between painting and sculpture is evident in the rendering of the mother's mouth, cheeks, and eyes found in both works. As Longhi noted, the awkward, massive nose, seen up close, recalls Medardo Rosso's *The Concierge* (1883, fig. 30). Longhi also called attention to "hints of unresolved elements in the background, out of which radiates, rather uselessly, two paperlike segments,"[31] a reference to the interpenetration of the mother's head and the facades of the houses in front of the via Adige apartment's windows. As Boccioni had theorized in "Technical Manifesto of Futurist Sculpture," "Sculpture must, therefore, make objects live by showing their extensions in space as sensitive, systematic and plastic.... Let's ... proclaim the ABSOLUTE AND COMPLETE ABOLITION OF FINITE LINES AND THE CONTAINED STATUE. LET'S SPLIT OPEN OUR FIGURES AND PLACE THE ENVIRONMENT INSIDE THEM."[32]

This is where specific preparatory drawings come into play, although it is probable that many have been lost. While the fine study for *Abstract Dimensions* (1912, fig. 31) defines the overall subject of the painting in exacting strokes, some sketches, which can be dated to the summer of 1912 (or earlier), specifically address the theme of the interpenetration of head and window that is found in the sculpture *Antigrazioso* and in *Materia*. These include *Mother's Head* [33] drawn on the back of a letter from Marinetti to Boccioni, *Seated Mother with Hands Folded (Half-Length Portrait of Mother)* (1911–12, cat. no. 22), and *Study of Head*,[34] in which architectural elements fuse increasingly with the figure's mass.

Among the various studies, the one associated with both *Materia* and *Horizontal Construction* constitutes a point of arrival after the first experiments in sculpture and a point of departure for the two paintings. Boccioni used the same preparatory work to generate both, as he had done previously with a study used for *Forces of a Street* and *Simultaneous Visions*. The edges of the study for *Materia* and *Horizontal Construction* are rounded out to create a circular composition that roughly corresponds to the central subject of *Materia*. The head of the central, seated figure of the mother grazes the top of the drawing sheet, while her skirt touches the base. To the left, iron railing merges with her elbow, resting just above a horse, while to the right, the railing reappears just below her knees, near the protruding structure of a balcony—beneath which the flattened figure of a passerby, with a hat on his head, brings to mind the silhouettes featured in *Simultaneous Visions*. The urban landscape displays no distinguishing features except for the long wall of a street and some summary indications of houses in the background. A few strokes of the pen, likely added after an initial version in pencil only, underscore and echo parts of the composition, transforming it in a manner similar to that of *Horizontal Construction*: the two vertical jambs that reduce the breadth of the visual field to the central part of the scene, the underscoring for the curve of the mother's shoulders and fullness of her bosom, and the suggested position of her elbow on the left. Boccioni also used pen to heighten the appearance of the wall, which is grafted onto the left shoulder like a wing, and the dark hollow of the dress above the thumbs. Last, a few clear strokes trace the profile of the left hand, cut the composition off at knee level, and shade the lower area of the dress.

The lack of documents makes it difficult to determine when Boccioni completed *Materia*. The only *terminus ante quem* is the book cover he designed for Balilla Pratella's *Musica futurista* (1912, fig. 32), which Marinetti sent to Pratella on November 26, 1912, and which reprises the upper part of the painting.[35] It is likely that *Materia* was begun during July or August and completed in September or October. When Boccioni returned home after a visit to Paris in early November, the already cold Milan weather would have precluded long sittings in front of the open window, a risk to the health of his elderly mother.

Boccioni planned from the start to make a particularly large and demanding painting—162 by 150 centimeters—almost square in format but slightly higher than wide. It only assumed its definitive, vertical format over the course of execution, which must have begun from the center, in the area around the hands, and continued outward. Boccioni's incessant creative drive propelled him to gradually increase the size of the painted surface: first, he added a strip of canvas to the top; then, two strips to the bottom, without changing the width, until it reached its current height of 226 centimeters. *Dynamism of a Soccer Player* (1913) similarly acquired its final dimensions through the addition of canvas. It was not unusual for Boccioni to work instinctively, elaborating as he went along, unconstrained by the preparatory studies, which provided only a general or initial idea. In the case of *Materia*, the female figure grew to monumental dimensions as he repeatedly confronted the subject, so that at a certain point, the imposing head could not fit within the original parameters of the canvas.

Fig. 30 Medardo Rosso
The Concierge (*La portinaia*), 1883
Plaster, 15³⁄₁₆ × 13⁹⁄₁₆ × 7¹⁄₁₆ inches (38.5 × 34.5 × 18 cm)
Museo Medardo Rosso, Barzio, Italy

Fig. 31 Umberto Boccioni
Study for *Abstract Dimensions* (*Dimensioni astratte*), 1912
Pencil on paper, 8³⁄₈ × 6⁵⁄₈ inches (21.3 × 16.9 cm)
Private collection

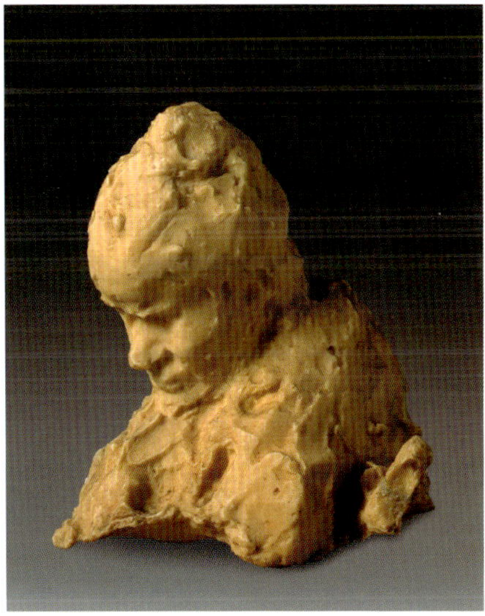

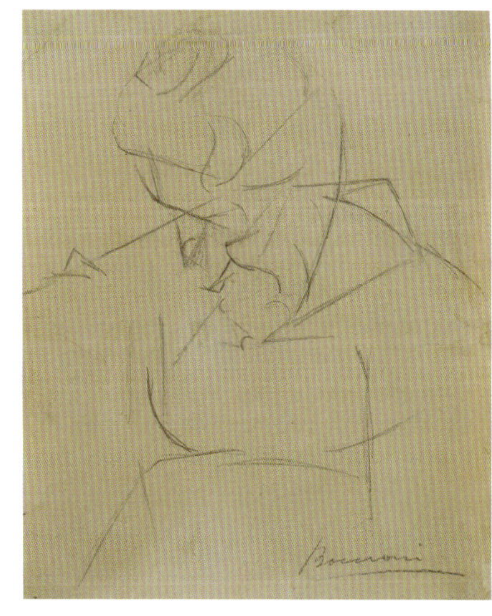

The mother's majesty is underscored by the rapt, detached expression of the face. She projects a sense of austere calm, quite unlike the smiling but caricature-like expression of the sculpture *Antigrazioso* and the greatly distorted physiognomies of the portraits that immediately followed. The surface of *Materia* is articulated by alternating concave and convex spaces, drawing in and repelling the viewer's gaze; for example, the hands in the foreground project outward, while simultaneously enclosing the mysterious depth of the mother's lap. The surroundings unfold in a circular motion radiating from the area of the skirt, which dominates the center of the composition with its dark presence. The entire painting is saturated with color, thanks to the exceptional intensity of Boccioni's Divisionist technique. Reflections from the windowpanes cut into the upper part of the figure with distinct bands of light, which also seem to radiate directly from the distant buildings. The planes of the armchair and floor fuse with those of the balcony projecting out onto the street. To the right, a male figure, totally liberated from the silhouette he had assumed in previous works, is foreshortened from behind. The synthesis of limbs and motion corresponds to Boccioni's drawings of human dynamism, some of which he had apparently already executed in 1912. As with the fleeting figure in *Materia*, they anticipate the muscular, striding figures developed in plaster in 1913.

As Marisa Dalai Emiliani has shown, Boccioni began painting his mother from the perspective of standing at his easel in front of her.[36] He then moved the easel and himself to where she had been sitting in order to render what he saw reflected in the panes of the open window. This exchange of position between painter and sitter is fundamental to the spatial construction of the work; it actually cancels out the distance between the view of the observer (and the artist) and the object of representation, a distance on which traditional, so-called Albertian perspective had been based for centuries. In this ingenious way, Boccioni fulfilled the aim of the Futurists' "Futurist Painting: Technical Manifesto" to "put the spectator in the center of the picture."[37] It was a fundamental accomplishment, since the Futurists had been working long and hard on various interpretations of this idea. Boccioni himself had moved increasingly closer to the body of the sitter, placing himself right behind his mother in the 1911 views. Cubist perspective was totally different, being influenced by theories of non-Euclidean geometries; it broke down the object, different points of view recombining on one plane.[38] The Cubist painters transposed onto the canvas what they knew and remembered about the object after circling around it, but Boccioni painted what he perceived while standing at the center of the composition, in the position of the object itself.

For the viewer, the method applied in *Materia* can elicit a sensation of being pulled into the work's vortex. As discussed by Fausto Petrella, this method also conveys the psychological implications, the symbolic power, of the artist fully identifying with his mother, becoming one with her.[39] At the same time, Boccioni himself became Nature-Matter and, above all, the Creator, generating a new reality: a painting that no longer renders the merely visible but instead creates the world according to its own laws and revolutionary freedom.

Horizontal Construction portrays the same subject as *Materia* in a square format that is smaller in size and compositional focus. The mother, seated in her usual armchair, is visible down to the knees. The railing behind her separates inside from outside, the latter dominated by buildings whose square profiles interpenetrate with the contours of her figure. *Horizontal Construction* has been interpreted by some scholars as a preparatory work for *Materia*; others consider it an earlier version of what was realized in the larger painting through the addition of thematic layers. I maintain, however, that *Horizontal Construction* comes after *Materia* and was painted upon the artist's return from Paris in November 1912. Boccioni presented it at the Teatro Costanzi exhibition in Rome in 1913, together with two other portraits of his mother (*Materia* and *Abstract Dimensions*), though its pictorial interests differ from the preceding works. Indeed, it is directly related to the conception and execution of the mixed-media sculpture *Head + House + Light* (1912, destroyed; fig. 58.12).

Horizontal Construction was conceived through a process of subtraction, as indicated by the pen-and-ink overdrawing of the study (used by Boccioni for both this painting and *Materia*), which emphasizes central aspects of the composition while ignoring individual details such as the horse and male figure that were part of the original whole. As evidenced in the final painting, Boccioni was most interested in precisely the parts he redrew in pen and in the angle of the building in front of the window, which overlays with the top of the woman's head to create a dark triangle. These elements, as well as the concentration of light in a single band and the nose delineated in two distinct parts, all appear in *Horizontal Construction* and *Head + House + Light* and are elaborated in a series of graphic studies made in 1912: *Mother*, a preparatory drawing for *Horizontal Construction* (fig. 33), *Study*,[40] *Mother*,[41] and a study for *Head + House + Light*.[42]

It is precisely the mother's head in *Horizontal Construction* that makes it difficult to imagine Boccioni simply got the measurements wrong in starting with a canvas of 162 by 150

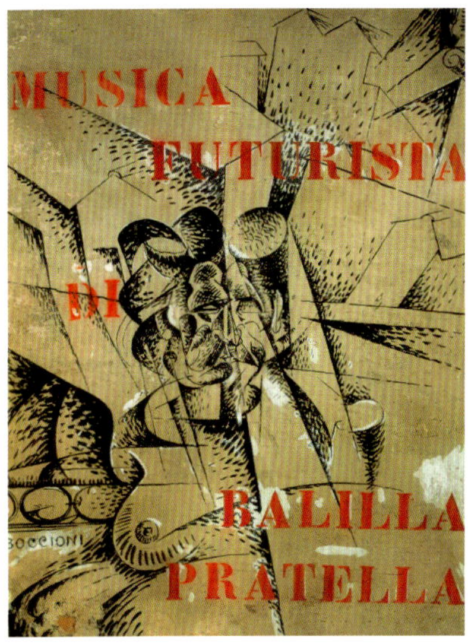

Fig. 32 Umberto Boccioni
Cover for Balllla Pratella's *Musica futurista*, 1912
Tempera and ink on paper, 20⅞ × 15⅜ inches (53 × 39 cm)
Private collection, Courtesy of Galleria dello Scudo, Verona

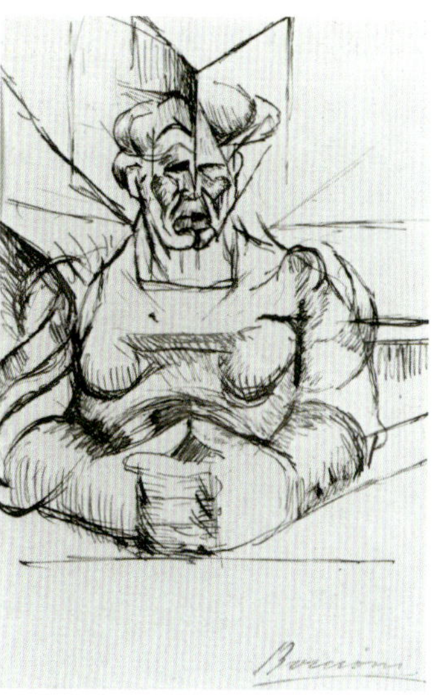

centimeters for *Materia* (assuming *Materia* comes afterward in the chronology). More logically, in returning to an already proven subject, he wanted to update it and did so by experimenting with the recent developments he saw in French painting. In addition, *Horizontal Construction* is characterized by a colder, more restrained color scheme, solidly defined volumes, and, as Fergonzi has pointed out, by a long brushstroke similar to the one Boccioni used in *States of Mind*;[43] only in the face and hands of the mother does it approach the carefully wrought brushwork of *Materia*.

Among the details of greatest interest in *Horizontal Construction* —and ones that are directly related to the three-dimensional volumes of Boccioni's sculptures—are the letters and numbers indicating different planes and measurements internal to the composition: "1p" painted on the mother's abdomen refers to *primo piano* (foreground); and "2p" on the breast, *secondo piano* (background). Distances between things are also indicated: on the right, "m. 122" and "70 cent." (122 meters and 70 centimeters), with "60 passi" (60 paces) below them; and on the left, "m. 200" (200 meters). Similar inscriptions were painted on the sculpture *Head + House + Light*: "45°" at the top of the woman's head, measuring an angle where the building with windows abutted with the triangle formed by light rays; "PARAPETTO" (parapet), marking the horizontal plane branching off from the left shoulder like a wing (the same delineation in *Horizontal Construction* is marked "m. 200"); and "MURO" (wall), appearing twice to mark triangular planes in the left foreground—all in block letters or numerals, in keeping with Cubist practice. "6 cent" appears twice in cursive in the drawing *Table + Bottle + Block of Houses* (1912, cat. no. 36), which was rendered at the same time as the studies of interpenetration of bodies and the sculpture *Development of a Bottle in Space*.

The inscriptions shared by paintings, sculptures, and drawings correspond directly with a passage in "Technical Manifesto of Futurist Sculpture": "A piece of Futurist sculpture will contain all those wonderful mathematical and geometrical elements of which objects are composed in our own times. And these objects will not be juxtaposed with a statue, like explanatory attributes or detached decorative elements, but, following the laws of a new concept of harmony they will be encapsulated inside the muscular lines of a body."[44] The same argument appears in Boccioni's preface written in 1913 for the sculpture exhibitions at Galerie La Boëtie and Galleria Futurista: "By broadening the concept of the sculptural object to the plastic resultant of object and environment, we will achieve the necessary abolition of the distance that exists, for example, between a figure and a house 200 meters away. We will achieve, moreover, the extension of a body into the ray of light striking and the entrance of *emptiness* into the *fullness* passing before it."[45]

According to Longhi, *Head + House + Light* was Boccioni's second sculpture.[46] Very similar in iconography to *Horizontal Construction*, it represented—in three-dimensional terms—the interpenetration of bodies and the solid rays of light, in accordance with the artist's own theories: "from this day forward clay, too, will be able to shape the atmosphere surrounding things."[47] The insertion of the housing block on top of the head recalled the sculpture *Antigrazioso*, but with the lines of force branching out from the sides. Following his own proscriptions in "Technical Manifesto of Futurist Sculpture," Boccioni added actual iron and wooden elements, including a piece of railing, to the plaster figure: "This new plastic art will then be a translation, in plaster, bronze, glass, wood or any other material, of those atmospheric planes which bind and intersect things."[48] In the extant photographs from the Galerie La Boëtie exhibition, the work appears varnished, again echoing his writings: "I can have the outside of a sculptural group shaded, have the outer contours colored black or gray with lighter gradations toward the center. In this way I create an auxiliary chiaroscuro that gives me a nucleus in the surrounding atmosphere."[49] Even more detailed information can be drawn from "Petites Curiosités," a review of the exhibition published in *Le Figaro* on June 21, 1913:

> *Boccioni shows the public half a woman's head surmounted by a wall made up of pieces of wood which indicate that beyond this wall there is a roof, sky, clouds, planets, stars, etc. The ray of light is represented by an egg-yolk yellow pigment which covers the other half of the figure. On the bust a real, authentic stairway, with wrought iron and a railing, specifies the "ambiance." Then the walls reappear, becoming streets on which little dolls are placed to represent the passersby. In consideration of the laypeople, the sculptor has glued labels along his sculpture and one can read useful information on these labels:* walls, street, *etc.*[50]

Head + House + Light is already modeled in plaster, yet unfinished in its details, in photographs (figs. 56.3–.7) taken of Boccioni's studio at Bastioni di Porta Romana 35; he took possession of this space in January 1913, actually moving in that March.[51] The fine drawing *Head + House + Light* (1913, cat. no. 33) was apparently done after the sculpture's initial modeling and as a detailed study of radiating bands of light. Further connections are manifest in the cover for Pratella's *Musica futurista* from late November 1912, which combines the head of *Materia* and the bare breast

Fig. 33 Umberto Boccioni
Mother (La madre), 1912
Ink on paper, 8¹¹⁄₁₆ × 5½ inches (22 × 14 cm)
Location unknown

Fig. 34 Umberto Boccioni
Controluce, 1910
Pencil and pen on paper,
14¾ × 18⅞ inches (37.5 × 48 cm)
Private collection

Fig. 35 Umberto Boccioni
Study for *Fusion of a Head and a Window (Fusione di una testa e di una finestra)*, 1912
Ink on paper, 12³⁄₁₆ × 8¼ inches (30.9 × 21 cm)
Location unknown

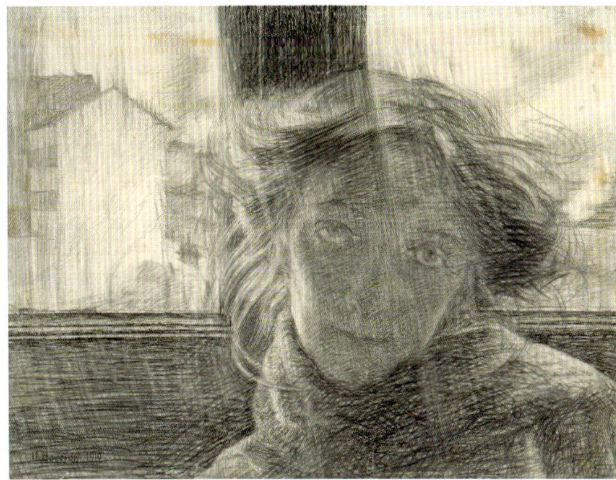

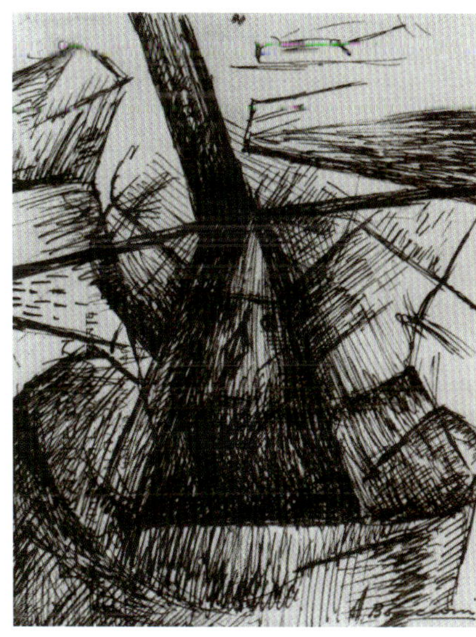

rendered in the drawing for *Head + House + Light*. In developing the cover design, Boccioni made several sketches in 1912—a study for the *Musica futurista* cover (cat. no. 24), *Study*,[52] and *Study for Head + Light*[53]—which tentatively moved away from *Materia* and toward the sculptures *Head + House + Light* and *Fusion of a Head and a Window* (1912–13, destroyed; fig. 58.11).

The emphatically graceless aspect of the mother, underlined by the title of the first sculpture, *Antigrazioso*, similarly characterizes the second plaster. Boccioni used the title *Antigrazioso* again, this time in a painting dating from the period between mid-November 1912 and late January 1913. Here, the facial features were influenced by the more aggressive aspects of Pablo Picasso's work, such as *Les Demoiselles d'Avignon* (1907) and related studies. Boccioni also looked to Carrà's *Portrait of Marinetti* (1911), which circulated in the traveling Futurist exhibition in 1912. In Carrà's portrait, the pose of the figure at the desk is reversed and—in its early version—less solidly constructed in form.[54] The painting *Antigrazioso* portrays Sarfatti, writing at her desk under the light of a lamp, her red hair cut at the ears and framing the face.[55] Relations between Boccioni and Sarfatti were not always friendly. In spring 1910, they met in Milan at the *Mostra annuale degli artisti lombardi*, held at the Palazzo della Permanente, and in 1911 worked together organizing *Mostra d'arte libera: La manifestazione collettiva dei futuristi* at the Ricordi Pavilion.[56] Boccioni was offended, however, after she panned his painting *On the Balcony* in the pages of *Avanti!* in December. He subsequently derided her in a March 15, 1912, letter to Vico Baer, written from Paris;[57] Carrà dismissed her with a similar tone in an April 14, 1912, letter to Boccioni.[58] Nonetheless, Boccioni and Sarfatti had a mutual interest in promoting "synthetic values" in painting and reconciled some time during the winter, after the success of the European tour of the Futurists' 1912 exhibition. Their rapprochement may well have occurred over a meal at the famed Milanese restaurant Savini, since *Study of a Head* (1912–13),[59] a sketch for *Antigrazioso*, is on Savini letterhead.

A word of masculine gender, "*Antigrazioso*" was used by Boccioni for his painted and sculpted depictions of women, the gender being in agreement with the art object itself, be it painting, portrait, or canvas—all masculine nouns in Italian—and not with the person portrayed. The artwork rather than the person is graceless; however, the female subject was inevitably deprived of those pretty traits deemed cloying by the Futurists and most appreciated by people ignorant of contemporary art. In the polemical opening of "Technical Manifesto of Futurist Sculpture," Boccioni wrote of traditional sculptural form, "These concepts, along with such famous catchwords as 'ideals of beauty,' which everyone speaks of in hushed tones, are never separated from the glorious periods of ancient Greece and its later decadence."[60]

Sarfatti regarded *Materia* as Boccioni's masterpiece, so much so that she tried to convince Benito Mussolini to buy the painting.[61] Already by 1912, Sarfatti owned an important drawing by Boccioni, *Controluce* (1910, fig. 34), which the artist used as the starting point for his third sculpture, *Fusion of a Head and a Window*. There exists a series of preparatory sketches (including fig. 35)[62] for the sculpture as well as an a posteriori watercolor (cat. no. 34), which again portrays the artist's mother sitting in front of the window, through which she is assaulted by rays of light. *Fusion of a Head and a Window* was composed of an actual wooden window-frame with an iron latch and part of the glass, a rolled up braid of hair, and a glass eye that emitted sinister reflections. An extant photograph of the Galerie La Boëtie installation shows an airy profile drawn in iron wire (fig. 58.6), which resembles the mother's features in the sculpture *Antigrazioso*. Other elements of *Fusion of a Head and a Window* relate directly to *Materia*: the house block hinted at the left, the spiral cone corresponding to the right shoulder, and the multiple bands of light falling from above. The radical move of incorporating real materials finds precise explanation in "Technical Manifesto of Futurist Sculpture":

> *Thus transparent planes, glass, strips of metal sheeting, wire, streetlamps or houselights may all indicate planes—the shapes, tones and semitones of a new reality....*
>
> *[One must] deny sculpture any attempt at realistic, episodic structures; affirm the absolute necessity of using all elements of reality in order to rediscover the basic elements of plastic sensitivity. By thus considering bodies and their parts as PLASTIC ZONES, any Futurist sculptural composition will contain planes of wood or metal, either motionless or in mechanical motion, in creating an object; spherical fibrous forms for hair, semicircles of glass for a vase, wire and netting for atmospheric planes, etc....*
>
> *[One must] maintain that, in the intersecting planes of a book and the corner of a table, in the straight lines of a match, in a blind drawn across a window, there is more truth than in all the tangled muscles... which are still the main inspiration of our demented modern sculptures.*[63]

Boccioni, however, soon rejected the inclusion of nonartistic materials and jarring fragments of reality because they worked against a sculptural synthesis of form.

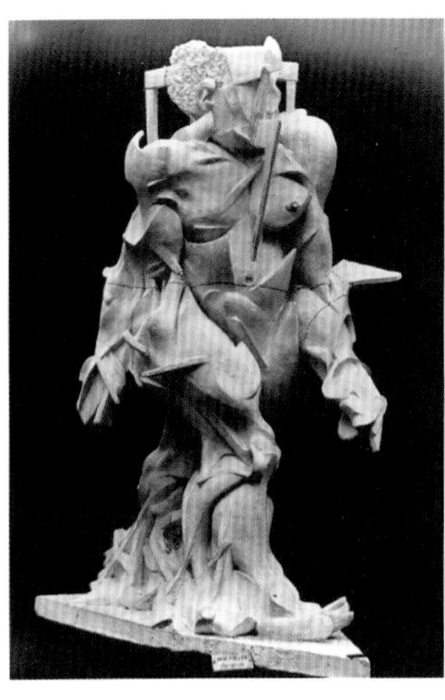
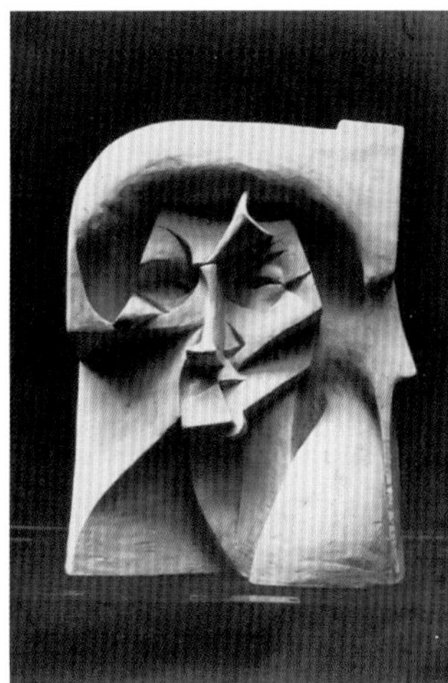
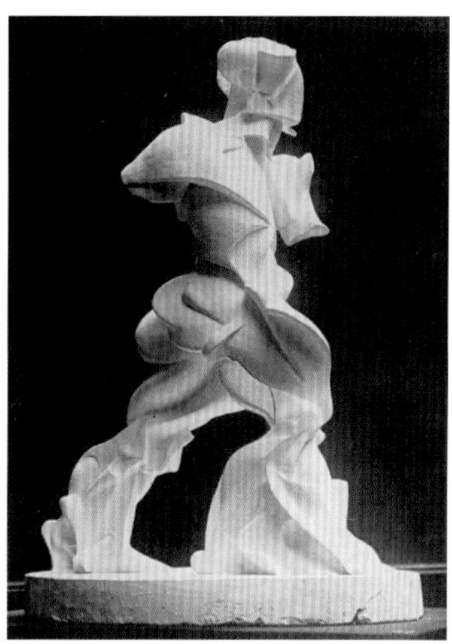
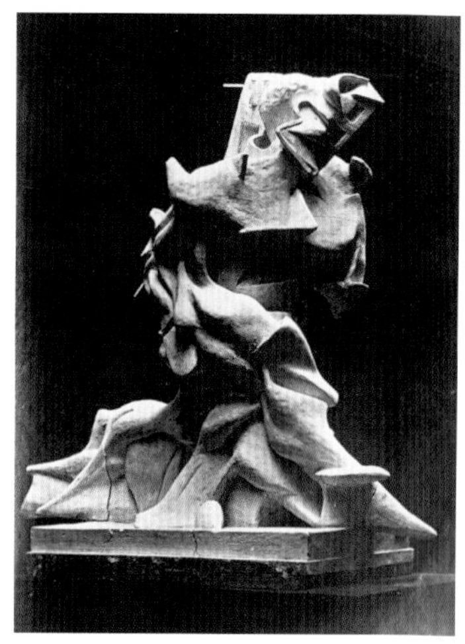

Based on the information found in Longhi's 1914 essay, a hypothetical sequence for the artist's subsequent sculptures can be suggested: *Development of a Bottle in Space* (in two versions, one subtitled *by Means of Form*, and the other, varnished in red, subtitled *by Means of Color*); *Synthesis of Human Dynamism* (1913, destroyed; fig. 36); *Empty and Full Abstracts of a Head* (1912, destroyed; fig. 37); *Spiral Expansion of Muscles in Motion* (1913, destroyed; fig. 38;); *Muscles in Speed* (1913, destroyed; fig. 39); *Force-Forms of a Bottle* (1913, destroyed);[64] and *Human Forms in Movement*. Two series of photographs taken in Boccioni's studio at Bastioni di Porta Romana 35 during March–May 1913 confirm this chronology: the first group (figs. 56.1–.8) shows the space half-empty, while the second (figs. 57.1–.14) documents the artist, his mother, Giacomo Balla, and a plasterer and his young assistant in a studio thronging with works.

Boccioni rented the new studio because his via Adige apartment was too small to house his sculptures of muscular figures in motion (or, for that matter, his large-scale canvases), and the photographs show the sculptures *Synthesis of Human Dynamism*, already finished and certainly the first of the striding figures, given the residual realistic details; *Spiral Expansion of Muscles in Motion*; *Antigrazioso*; *Muscles in Speed*, in the process of being realized; and *Development of a Bottle by Means of Color*, which does not yet have its patina. Sitting on an easel, the a posteriori gouache of *Empty and Full Abstracts of a Head* (1913, cat. no. 35) stands in for the already completed plaster sculpture. *Force-Forms of a Bottle* and *Unique Forms of Continuity in Space* (1913, figs. 40–42 and 58.10, cat. no. 40) had not yet been made, and *Fusion of a Head* and *Development of a Bottle in Space* had been sent to the Futurist exhibition in Rotterdam, from May 18 to June 15, 1913, where *Materia* was also included.[65]

In the summer, when all the sculptures and paintings were returned to Milan, Boccioni significantly revised *Materia*, his 1912 masterpiece, especially in the area of the lower left, where he eliminated the original, luminous mandorla-shaped form that Longhi had negatively described as too similar to "the radiant rhythm of any ordinary country-church monstrance."[66] During this time, using the automatic shutter release, he took photographs in which he is seen improvising a playful, suggestive pantomime with the painting itself (figs. 59.4–.7):[67] Boccioni being given birth by the Great Mother; the painter placing his palette over Mother Nature's hands; and the man who has engendered Mother Painting.

Translated from the Italian by Stephen Sartarelli.

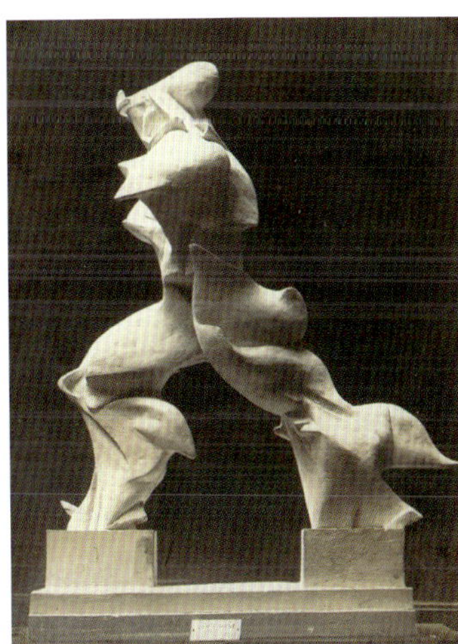

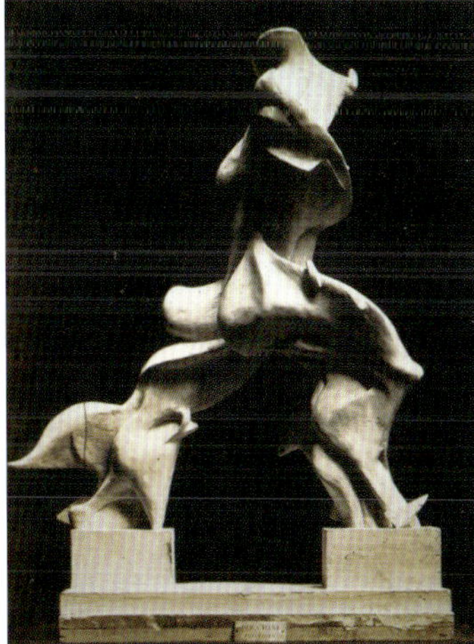

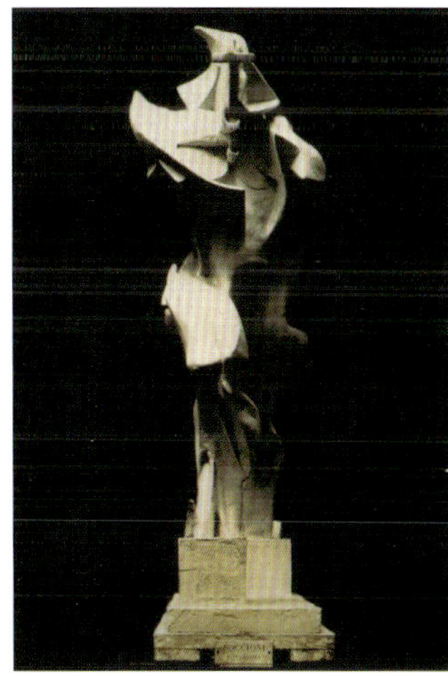

Fig. 36 Anonymous
Umberto Boccioni's *Synthesis of Human Dynamism,* 1913
Gelatin-silver print, 9¼ × 6⅜ inches (23.5 × 16.2 cm)
Private collection

Fig. 37 Anonymous
Umberto Boccioni's *Empty and Full Abstracts of a Head,* 1913
Gelatin-silver print, 6½ × 4¾ inches (16.5 × 12 cm)
Calmarini Collection, Milan

Fig. 38 Anonymous
Umberto Boccioni's *Spiral Expansion of Muscles in Motion,* 1913
Gelatin-silver print, $9\frac{5}{16}$ × 6⅜ inches (23.7 × 16.2 cm)
Private collection

Fig. 39 Anonymous
Umberto Boccioni's *Muscles in Speed,* 1913
Gelatin-silver print, 9¼ × 6⅜ inches (23.5 × 16.2 cm)
Private collection

Fig. 40 Anonymous
Umberto Boccioni's *Unique Forms of Continuity in Space,*
lateral view from left, 1913
Gelatin-silver print, 6½ × 4¾ inches (16.5 × 12 cm)
Calmarini Collection, Milan

Fig. 41 Anonymous
Umberto Boccioni's *Unique Forms of Continuity in Space,*
lateral view from right, 1913
Gelatin-silver print, 6½ × 4¾ inches (16.5 × 12 cm)
Calmarini Collection, Milan

Fig. 42 Anonymous
Umberto Boccioni's *Unique Forms of Continuity in Space,*
frontal view, 1913
Gelatin-silver print, 6½ × 4¾ inches (16.5 × 12 cm)
Calmarini Collection, Milan

Notes

1 Boccioni to Baer, March 15, 1912, in Zeno Birolli, ed., *Umberto Boccioni: Gli scritti editi e inediti* (Milan: Feltrinelli, 1971), p. 349.

2 See Boccioni, preface to *1re Exposition de sculpture futuriste du peintre et sculpteur futuriste Boccioni*, exh. cat. (Paris: Galerie La Boëtie, 1913), pp. 3–9.

3 See Boccioni, preface to *Esposizione di scultura futurista del pittore e scultore futurista Boccioni*, exh. cat. (Rome: Galleria Futurista, 1913), pp. 3–9.

4 *Human Forms in Movement*, executed apparently in the period falling between the Galerie La Boëtie and Galleria Futurista shows (that is, between June and November 1913), was later exhibited at Galleria Gonnelli, Florence, March–April 1914, as attested by the catalogue (*Esposizione di scultura futurista del pittore e scultore futurista U. Boccioni* [Florence: Galleria Gonnelli, 1914], p. 28, no. 12) and on the occasion of the large posthumous exhibition at Palazzo Cova, Milan, December 28, 1916–January 14, 1917 but under a different title, *Essential Forms of a Footballer*, as documented by the catalogue (*Grande esposizione Boccioni pittore e scultore futurista*, with writings by Boccioni and preface by Marinetti [Milan: Galleria Centrale d'Arte (Palazzo Cova), 1916], p. 58, no. 7). There are no known photographs of this sculpture, which must certainly have been lost in 1917, not long after the Palazzo Cova show, along with most of Boccioni's other sculptural works, which were made in plaster and fell victim to the rain.

5 For complete *Materia* bibliography and the critical debate over the work, see Flavio Fergonzi, "Umberto Boccioni: *Materia*, 1912," in Fergonzi's catalogue raisonné *The Mattioli Collection: Masterpieces of the Italian Avant-garde* (Milan: Skira, 2002), pp. 155–77. I am particularly indebted not only to Fergonzi's research but also to Marco Rosci, "La materia e lo stato d'animo plastico," in Laura Mattioli Rossi, ed., *Boccioni 1912 Materia*, exh. cat., Galleria dello Scudo, Verona (Milan: Mazzotta, 1991), pp. 43–64; and Marisa Dalai Emiliani, "Dalla trasparenza della mimesis alla opacità della poiesis," in Mattioli Rossi, pp. 65–82.

6 See Umberto Boccioni, Carlo Carrà, Luigi Russolo, Giacomo Balla, and Gino Severini, "Les Exposants au public," in *Les Peintres futuristes italiens*, exh. cat. (Paris: Galerie Bernheim-Jeune, 1912), pp. 1–14. This exhibition was held February 5–24, 1912, and subsequently traveled to London and other cities in Europe.

7 Maurizio Calvesi and Ester Coen, *Boccioni: L'opera completa* (Milan: Electa, 1983), no. 895. Hereafter, when the catalogue raisonné number for a Boccioni work is provided it is referred to as "Calvesi and Coen, no."; *Dynamism of a Soccer Player* is Calvesi and Coen, no. 895.

8 Umberto's father, Raffaele Boccioni, left his wife, Cecilia Forlani Boccioni, in 1899 to live with Virginia Piacenti, with whom he had two daughters. Umberto lived at his aunt Colomba Boccioni Procida's house in Rome until the end of March 1906, when he went first to Paris and then to Russia. He reached Padua in early December that same year, where his mother and sister, Raffaella Amelia, were living. After a brief period in Venice (April to mid-August 1907) and a brief sojourn in Munich, Boccioni moved to Milan, where he lived at via Castel Morrone 7 from November 1907. In September1908, he moved with his mother and sister to the apartment at via Adige 23, where he stayed until March 1913. Amelia married Guido Callegari on March 28, 1910, and moved back to Padua, where her mother often stayed with her as a guest. Regarding via Castel Morrone 7 and via Adige 23, see my "Boccioni in Milan," in the present volume, pp. 142–45.

9 For more about the power plant and its smokestacks, see Leonardo Capano and Antonello Negri, "Via Adige 23," in Mattioli Rossi, *Boccioni 1912 Materia* (1991), pp. 253–55.

10 Umberto Boccioni, Carlo Carrà, Luigi Russolo, Giacomo Balla, and Gino Severini, "Manifesto of the Futurist Painters," in Umbro Apollonio, ed., *Futurist Manifestos*, trans. Robert Brain et al. (London: Thames and Hudson, 1973), p. 25.

11 See Leonardo Capano and Antonello Negri, "Ancora su via Adige," in Laura Mattioli Rossi, ed., *Boccioni 1912 Materia*, exh. cat., Fondazione Antonio Mazzotta, Milan (Milan: Mazzotta, 1995), pp. 258–59.

12 See Margherita Grassini Sarfatti, "Cronache d'Arte. L'Esposizione 'Intima' alla Famiglia Artistica," *Avanti!*, December 13, 1911.

13 Calvesi and Coen, no. 747.

14 See Birolli, *Gli scritti editi e inediti*, p. 157.

15 Ibid.

16 Boccioni, Carrà, Russolo, Balla, and Severini, "Les Exposants au public," pp. 4, 6.

17 Boccioni to Baer, February 19, 1913, ibid., p. 366.

18 See Fergonzi, "Umberto Boccioni: *Materia*, 1912," p. 176 n. 37.

19 See *Prima esposizione pittura futurista*, exh. cat. (Rome: Galleria Giosi, 1913), p. 21.

20 Calvesi and Coen, no. 796; the location of this work is now unknown.

21 The identification of this work is considered uncertain in Fergonzi, "Umberto Boccioni: *Materia*, 1912," pp. 158–59, paragraph 1, and p. 176 n. 26.

22 See ibid., p. 159, paragraph 2, where Fergonzi seems to favor this hypothesis.

23 In the 1914 edition of his *Pittura scultura futuriste (Dinamismo plastico)* (Milan: Edizioni Futuriste di "Poesia," 1914), Boccioni published three series of illustrations to accompany his text titled, respectively, "First series of Futurist paintings," "Second series of Futurist paintings," and "Boccioni's plastic ensembles exhibited in Paris." In the captions for the last series, he dated *Head + House + Light* and *Fusion of a Head and a Window* as 1911, *Synthesis of Human Dynamism*, *Development of a Bottle in Space*, and *Empty and Full Abstracts of a Head* as 1912, and *Force-Forms of a Bottle*, *Spiral Expansion of Muscles in Motion*, *Muscles in Speed*, and *Unique Forms of Continuity in Space* as 1913. Boccioni probably moved back the dates of his first five sculptures to affirm the precedence of his own experimentation over that of the French during a moment in which the polemic with Orphism was particularly heated.

24 Fergonzi, "Umberto Boccioni: *Materia*, 1912," pp. 156–66, summarizes the chronological question precisely. Boccioni's movements in 1913 are documented by correspondence published in Birolli, *Gli scritti editi e inediti*, pp. 363–73.

25 Boccioni's movements in these two crucial years are known with some accuracy; for 1912, they are reconstructed in Fergonzi, "Umberto Boccioni: *Materia*, 1912," pp. 159–60, paragraph 3. The artist traveled to Paris in February 1912 for the Futurist group show at Galerie Bernheim-Jeune, then to London and Berlin. He was in Milan for roughly a month between the last ten days of April and May 20, after which he returned to the German capital. From June to November—when he traveled to Paris to see the Salon d'Automne—he was living and working steadily at his via Adige residence. He remained in Milan until mid-February 1913, except for two days in Rome before Christmas. In mid-February, he went back to Rome to organize the show at the Teatro Costanzi, and stayed there until March 9, when he took part in a Futurist soirée that ended in a brawl. Back in Milan, he left the via Adige residence and moved definitively to Bastioni di Porta Romana 35 before the end of March. In the second half of June, he traveled to Paris for a show of his own sculpture; and finally, he was in Rome from early December until the end of the year for his show at Sprovieri's Galleria Futurista.

26 Calvesi and Coen, no. 798.

27 These observations on his mother's hair in various different works cast into doubt the authenticity of the painting *Mother* (1912; Calvesi and Coen, no. 753).

28 See Boccioni to Carrà and Russolo, [May 29, 1912], in Birolli, *Gli scritti editi e inediti*, p. 355.

29 Roberto Longhi, *Scultura futurista: Boccioni* (Florence: Libreria de "La Voce," 1914), pp. 10–11.

30 Ibid., p. 10.

31 Ibid., p. 11.

32 Boccioni, "Technical Manifesto of Futurist Sculpture," in Apollonio, *Futurist Manifestos*, pp. 52, 63.

33 Calvesi and Coen, no. 956, where it is undated.

34 Calvesi and Coen, no. 835, where it is undated.

35 Fergonzi, "Umberto Boccioni: *Materia*, 1912," p. 160, paragraph 5.

36 See Dalai Emiliani, "Dalla trasparenza della mimesis alla opacità della poiesis," pp. 65–82.

37 Umberto Boccioni, Carlo Carrà, Luigi Russolo, Giacomo Balla, and Gino Severini, "Futurist Painting: Technical Manifesto," in Apollonio, *Futurist Manifestos*, p. 28.

38 See Linda Dalrymple Henderson, *The Fourth Dimension and Non-Euclidean Geometry in Modern Art* (Princeton: Princeton University Press, 1983).

39 See Fausto Petrella, "La 'materia' inquieta e le sue trasformazioni. Appunti per una ricerca," in Mattioli Rossi, *Boccioni 1912 Materia* (1991), pp. 83–114. See also Petrella, "Mater Materia Prima: Clinical and Critical Remarks," in the present volume, pp. 54–61.

40 Calvesi and Coen, no. 758.

41 Calvesi and Coen, no. 759.

42 Calvesi and Coen, no. 760.

43 See Fergonzi, "Umberto Boccioni: *Materia*, 1912," p. 162, paragraph 8.

44 Boccioni, "Technical Manifesto of Futurist Sculpture," p. 62.

45 Boccioni, preface to *Esposizione di scultura futurista del pittore e scultore futurista Boccioni*, in Birolli, *Gli scritti editi e inediti*, p. 35.

46 Longhi, *Scultura futurista Boccioni*, p. 44.

47 Boccioni, "Manifesto tecnico della scultura futurista," in Birolli, *Gli scritti editi e inediti*, p. 30. The mention of clay makes explicit the fact that Boccioni, following a traditional practice, would make a clay sketch (*bozzetto*) first, before proceeding to execute the model in plaster, which the artist would later revise, either with refinishings in the modeling or with colored varnishes. For the plaster execution, he would avail himself of a specialized craftsman, the *gessatore* who appears in photographs together with Balla (figs. 57.8 and 57.12). Boccioni never executed any bronze castings of his models; those in existence were made posthumously.

48 Boccioni, "Technical Manifesto of Futurist Sculpture," p. 52.

49 Boccioni, preface to *Esposizione di scultura futurista*, p. 35.

50 Le Masque de fer, "Petites Curiosités," *Le Figaro*, June 21, 1913, p. 1.

51 For more about Boccioni's studio/residence at Bastioni di Porta Romana 35, including photographic documentation, see Giovanna Ginex, "Snapshots from Umberto Boccioni's Studio," in the present volume, pp. 62–81.

52 Calvesi and Coen, no. 767.

53 Calvesi and Coen, no. 772.

54 The first version of Carrà's *Portrait of Marinetti* is reproduced in Maria Druidi Gambillo and Teresa Fiori, eds., *Archivi del futurismo* (Rome: De Luca Editore, 1962), vol. 2, p. 281.

55 The subject of the painting *Antigrazioso*, which became the property of the Sarfatti estate, was correctly recognized to be Margherita Sarfatti by Emily Braun (oral communication). My father, Gianni Mattioli, who was a friend of Sarfatti from 1921 onward, told me the painting was a portrait of her. This also becomes clear from the Mattioli-Sarfatti correspondence of the early 1950s, when Mattioli tried in vain to purchase this work

56 See Margherita Grassini Sarfatti, *Acqua passata* (Bologna: Licinio Cappelli Editore, 1955), p. 93.

57 See Boccioni to Baer, March 15, 1912, in Birolli, *Gli scritti editi e inediti*, p. 351: "Signora Sarfatti has started writing to me again, and is nice to the point of irritation. . . . It's strange that Signora Sarfatti is compelled to slip and hobble in life, as when she speaks of art. . . . Fortunately the tumbles she takes on the stairs are less serious than those she takes when loftily protesting against abstraction. . . . It's enough to break one's neck!

58 See Carrà to Boccioni, April 14, 1912, in Mattioli Rossi, *Boccioni 1912 Materia* (1995), p. 270: "Another disgusting little thing: yesterday I saw the foul Sarfattis at Savini's. I didn't even deign them so much as a glance. Christ, when I think I used to like them, I begin to despise myself and my primordial naiveté."

59 Calvesi and Coen, no. 791.

60 Boccioni, "Technical Manifesto of Futurist Sculpture," p. 51.

61 Information regarding negotiations with Mussolini for the purchase of *Materia* on the part of *il Duce*—certainly pursuant to prompting by Marghertia Sarfatti during the period when the two were romantically tied—is drawn from a manuscript letter dated July 12, 1929, written from Verona by Guido Callegari to Giovanni Scheiwiller. The letter is in a private collection. I thank Giovanna Ginex for bringing this document to my attention.

62 Calvesi and Coen, nos. 764 and 768; fig. 34 is no. 766.

63 Boccioni, "Technical Manifesto of Futurist Sculpture," pp. 63–65.

64 Calvesi and Coen, no. 853.

65 See *Les Peintres et les sculpteurs futuristes italiens*, exh. cat. (Rotterdam: Rotterdamsche Kunstkring, 1913), p. 34. That *Materia* was absent from Boccioni's studio from February to summer in 1913—having been sent directly to Rotterdam from the Teatro Costanzi exhibition in Rome—is verified by Fergonzi, "Umberto Boccioni: *Materia*, 1912," pp. 161–62, paragraph 7, p. 176 n. 48. Indeed, the painting never appears in any of the photographs of Boccioni's studio from this period.

66 Longhi, *Scultura futurista Boccioni*, p. 17. For the difference between the two versions of *Materia*, see Marco Rosci, "La materia e lo stato d'animo plastico," in Mattioli Rossi, *Boccioni 1912 Materia* (1991), p. 47; and Leonardo Capano, *Materia* entry, in Mattioli Rossi, pp. 200–205.

67 The photographs have been studied in Rosci, "La materia e lo stato d'animo plastico," pp. 45–47.

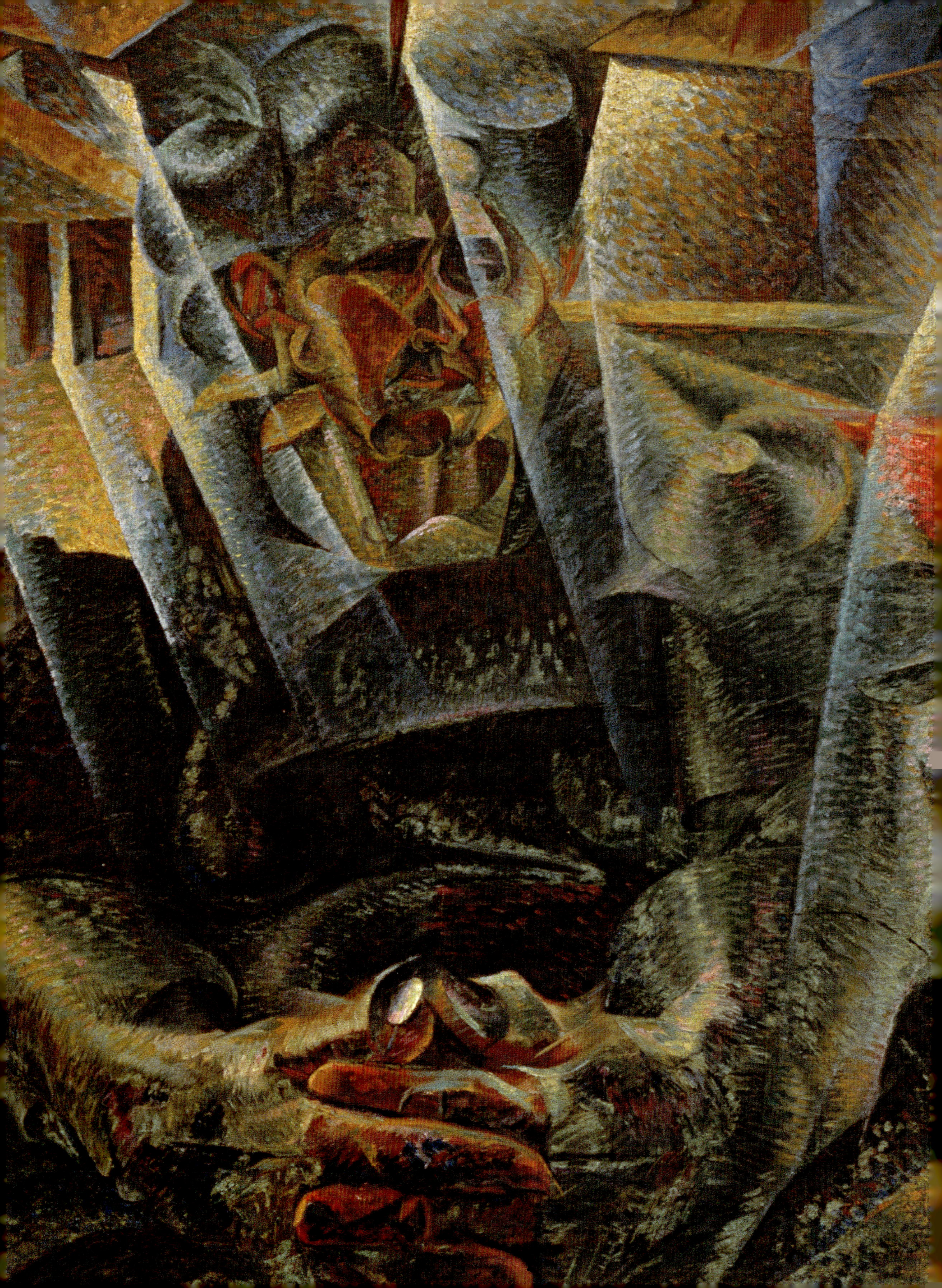

On the Title of the Painting *Materia*

FLAVIO FERGONZI

Futurist artists attached particular importance to the titles of their works. Among the various strategies they used to provoke the viewer—unsettling subject matter, brash colors, rejection of the academic canon—the title was one of the finest exploited, amplifying rather than mediating the conflict between the average, passéist, prejudicially hostile audience and ostensibly indecipherable, modernist content. The choice of wording for a title was intended as a further affront to any viewer who, while gazing at the image, happened to come across it on an exhibition label or accompanying a catalogue reproduction.

The shock was even greater in the backward and recalcitrant cultural climate that was Italy in February 1913, when Boccioni's *Materia* (1912; cat. no. 27) was first shown as part of the Futurists' group exhibition in the foyer of Teatro Costanzi in Rome. In the years before World War I, few were accustomed to reading an artwork's formal qualities—known as the aesthetics of pure visibility in Italy—save for an educated elite. But almost everyone knew how to read a title to find a logical explanation of the content or a means of penetrating it. Visitors to the Teatro Costanzi exhibition expected a title that described or suggested a mood (as did, for example, Mario Calderini's *Autumn Evening* [1911], shown at the first Secessione romana in 1913), emphasized a visual detail (Cipriano Efisio Oppo's *The Beam of the Train* [1912], at the Circolo artistico Internazionale di Roma in 1913), or provided a plain description of the composition (the case even in Henri Matisse's radically modernist *Goldfish* [spring–summer 1912], also at the Rome Secession, where it generated much controversy).[1]

The Futurist paintings shown at Teatro Costanzi constituted a new, unsettling experience for the public. Viewers found themselves confounded by titles that defied logic and common sense: Boccioni's *Abstract Dimensions* (1912, cat. no. 21; but dimensions of objects are geometrically determined, therefore concrete and measurable); Carrà's *The Street Walks* (1912; people walk, streets do not), Luigi Russolo's *Solidity of Fog* (1912; fog is gaseous, not solid); and Giacomo Balla's *Little Girl Multiplied by the Balcony* (1912; a nonsensical mathematical operation). The next step for viewers—to overcome the challenge of the images—was already impeded. The public grew indignant because it was provoked; Roberto Longhi wrote with amusement of the "flowers of idiocy" coming from the lips of the most pompous spectators.[2] Others played along with the Futurists, trying to match the titles with passages they managed to recognize in a canvas, as did one Milanese journalist writing a feature on the Teatro Costanzi opening for *Corriere della Sera*.[3]

Futurist titles fulfilled another function as well, that of formulating the terms of a pictorial problem in order to stress its successful resolution. Before giving the titles of the most current works, the catalogue of the Futurist exhibition in Rotterdam in May–June 1913 (immediately following the one in Rome) listed the paintings shown at prior venues, beginning with Galerie Bernheim-Jeune in Paris in February 1912.[4] It was a savvy publicity stunt to show that the paintings had already been seen and sold on a prestigious international tour, but the Futurists also wanted to emphasize forcefully that the rules of the artistic game had changed. They made the public aware of how the previous cycle of works had resolved complex issues of representation, such as the skyward yearning of a new urban quarter under construction (Boccioni's *The City Rises* [1910–11, fig. 11]), the interpenetration of interior and exterior spaces (Boccioni's *The Street Enters the House*, [1911, cat. no. 7]), the evocation of voices, perceptions, and states of mind (Carrà's *What*

Facing page
Detail of Umberto Boccioni, *Materia*, 1912 (cat. no. 27)

the Streetcar Told Me [1911]), the persistence of an image over time and space (Russolo's *One Head Three Times* [1911]), and the combination of disjointed and distant travel memories in a single picture (Severini's *Souvenirs de Voyage* [1910–11]). The title had value all by itself as a veritable declaration of poetics, and there were even a few visitors who seem to have taken this process too literally. For example, an attentive Roman cultural journalist, Federico Mastrigli, writing on Carrà's *Speed Breaks Up the Horse* (1912), took pains to demonstrate that speed in itself does not break up forms, and that, in any event, the painter's task is to put them back together again in a coherent arrangement.[5]

The titles used by the Futurists did not start out so rebellious or novel. "Futurist Painting: Technical Manifesto," with its reckless assertions, had already been written by April 1910, but at his one-man show at Ca' Pesaro in Venice that year, Boccioni's *Landscape* (1909) and *A Drama Teacher* (1910, fig. 53) hardly broke with conventional titles found at established events such as the Biennale or the Brera.[6] In their group exhibition at the Padiglione Ricordi, Milan, in May 1911—no catalogue was printed, but the titles appeared in newspaper reviews[7]—the Milanese Futurists wavered between longstanding humanitarian socialist beliefs (Boccioni's *Work* [1910–11]), anarchist sympathies (Carrà's *Funeral of the Anarchist Galli* [1911]), a new take on history painting motivated by rising anti-Austrian sentiment (Carrà's *The Martyrs of Belfiore* [1910–11]), traditional salon painting (in title and subject, Boccioni's *The Laugh* [1911, fig. 6] echoed the well-known and critically hailed canvas by Philip Maljavine, *The Laugh* [1899], which was exhibited at the 1901 Venice Biennale and thereafter in the permanent collection of the Ca' Pesaro museum), and the omnipresent tinge of Symbolism (Boccioni's *Mourning* [1910] and Russolo's *The Dying Man* [n.d.] and *Music* [1910–11]), which still hovered over everything. Reviewing the show, the Florentine Ardengo Soffici, who was uniquely current with the latest Cubist developments in France, allowed himself some heavy-handed irony regarding the "innovative title" of Boccioni's *Beloved Whores* (1910; known today as *The Roundup*),[8] the sort of title well in keeping with the outworn tropes of the Scapigliatura (the Disheveled Ones), the Milanese-based, French-Symbolist-inspired writers of the 1870s. As Soffici proved, the Futurists' claim to have renewed the arts was an empty boast because they drew on the worst sort of literary clichés from Symbolism to unanimism.

Only when Marinetti took the situation in hand did the artists realize how effective titles could be in their strategy of provocation. He made the arrangements for the Galerie Bernheim-Jeune exhibition in February 1912 and financed a reconnaissance trip to Paris for Boccioni, Carrà, and Russolo a few months before, in October 1911, during which they realized that the Futurists could trump the innovations of the Cubists by countering the staid nineteenth-century titles used at the Salon d'Automne (Fernand Léger's *Study for Three Portraits* [1910–11], Jean Metzinger's *Landscape* [1911] and *Femme à la cuiller* [1911], and Albert Gleizes's *Portrait of Jacques Nayral* [1911, cat. no. 13]). Provocative titles would also grab the attention of journalists and generate advantageous publicity.

Of course, Boccioni's key work at Galerie Bernheim-Jeune, the triptych *States of Mind* (1911, figs. 20–22) was still imbued with late-Symbolist traditions, and the individual titles of its three canvases—*The Farewells, Those Who Go,* and *Those Who Stay*—were borrowed almost verbatim from those of Charles Cottet's triptych *Aux pays de la mer* (1898): *Les Adieux, Ceux qui partent,* and *Ceux qui restent*. A version of Cottet's celebrated work was exhibited at the 1899 Venice Biennale, from which it was acquired by the Museo Bottacin in Padua.[9]

Nonetheless, there were signs of important change in the titles Boccioni gave to works included in the Galerie Bernheim-Jeune exhibition. For example, he rebaptized *Work* as *The City Rises* eight months after it had been exhibited under the first title. In doing so, human labor—no longer represented in the ideological terms of fin-de-siècle humanitarian socialism—was reduced to something "purely physical, to the parameters of energy and movement," according to Marinetti's new dictums.[10] More important, the renaming of *On the Balcony,* exhibited at a small show in December 1911, as *The Street Enters the House* shifted people's attention to the mechanisms of perception; the wording of the title coincided with a passage in the catalogue essay, explaining to the French audience that the Futurists wanted to represent, not the visible, but a combination of sensations experienced by the subject—in this case, a woman looking out from an apartment onto a street.[11] Other titles served the same didactic function, such as *Simultaneous Visions* (1911, cat. no. 8) and *The Forces of a Street* (1911), in which emphasis was placed on the almost-invisible passersby and the tram, and the physical forces they set into motion. In 1912, at least some of these titles led to accusations of *"peinture littéraire"* (literary painting) being hurled at the Futurists.[12] Significantly, the Paris-based Gino Severini, who was the most sensitive to this sort of criticism, realized that the strategy behind the titles detracted from the genuine innovations of the images themselves. In a letter concerning the 1913 Teatro Costanzi exhibition he asked Marinetti if he might list his series of six paintings in the catalogue simply as "Painting No. 1, Painting No. 2, etc.," but his request was denied.[13]

Materia, painted in 1912 and exhibited in February 1913 at Teatro Costanzi, opened a new chapter for the Futurists in the titling of their works. Here an abstract term, ennobled by a centuries-old tradition of philosophical and scientific debate, was used for an everyday, immediately recognizable image—a figure on a balcony—yet one that was monumental in scale and stylistically current with the international avant-garde. Within the development of Boccioni's works, this broke with the long sequence of plain thematic titles (*The Laugh* and *The Roundup*) and Symbolist ones (*The City Rises, The Modern Idol* [1911, fig. 2], and *Those Who Go*). Boccioni also moved beyond deliberate provocation (*The Street Enters the House*) and the flaunting of brand new technical jargon (*Simultaneous Visions* and *Abstract Dimensions*) to enter into a more intellectually ambitious realm. It should be emphasized that, in the Italian context, giving an abstract concept to a painting was utterly novel. The Teatro Costanzi exhibition featured at least three such instances—Boccioni's *Materia* and *Elasticity* (1912, fig. 28) and Russolo's *Solidity of Fog*—with titles insisting on properties of the physical world. In this way, the Futurists drew attention to the fact that their works, no longer concerned with depicting external reality, delved instead into the essence of the things represented.

In the case of *Materia,* no documentation exists—no letters, no diary—to ascertain whether the title came before the painting or vice versa: did Boccioni begin with the aim of illustrating the concept, or did he create the image of his mother against the balcony and then call it *Materia*? The latter hypothesis is more likely, given the painting's enlargement through the addition of canvas, and its pivotal role in the constellation of works that includes *Horizontal Construction* (1912, cat. no. 28), *Head + House + Light* (1912, destroyed; fig. 58.12), and several related studies. It appears that Boccioni began to focus on a subject dear to him—his mother on the balcony—and that the choice of such an imposing title emerged as the painting developed into an important ideological manifesto.

When Boccioni was making and naming his picture, the Italian *materia* was a word of disparate and disputed meanings. *Grand Dictionnaire universel Larousse,* the popular encyclopedic compendium of late nineteenth-century knowledge, linked the French *matière* with "the Sanscrit *matram*—'measure' and 'matter'—from the root *ma,* to make with the hands, to construct, to measure."[14] The word also derived from the Latin *mater* (mother), and was still understood by Italians in this way, as witnessed by its inclusion in 1937 in Ottorino Pianigiani's etymological dictionary: "others connect this word directly back to the Latin *mater,* mother, which derives from the same root [*matram*], to wit, the prime matter from which others are formed."[15] A family of three words—*materia* (matter), *madre* (mother), and *mano* (hand)—and their etyma are inextricably linked in Boccioni's painting. In his psychoanalytic reading of *Materia,* Fausto Petrella demonstrated how the words' etyma activate metaphorical thought and images on a subconscious level, triggering the latent meanings that are submerged in day-to-day linguistic usage.[16] Boccioni's mother herself, with whom he shared an unusually intense relationship—"he loved his mother more than anything in the world," stated Carrà[17]—and who had become his preferred model years before, likely triggered the chain of connections. He deformed the physique of the *mother,* drawing attention to her enormous *hands* in the foreground through grotesque exaggeration, while emptying her of all symbolic primacy by emphasizing her relation to the surrounding *matter*. Recent studies analyzed Boccioni's ambivalent depiction of the mother's body, one fraught with latent violence and fear of castration[18] and acknowledged his explicit debt to Marinetti's poetics, whereby passive matter, gendered feminine, awaits penetration by an active masculine force.[19]

The relationship between the object represented (mother) and the painting's title (matter or material), however, exhausts only one possible interpretation. The viewers of *Materia*—first, in Rome (in 1912), then, in Rotterdam (1913), London (1914), and San Francisco (1915)—were aware, even if only in some general or uninformed manner, that *materia* was a fashionable word at the center of a fervent cultural debate, a word whose meaning had radically changed over a decade. The scientific literature directly or indirectly accessible to Boccioni had remarkably widespread diffusion, and one should not exclude the possibility that a few of the ideas developed in these books had a direct bearing on the execution of the painting. It is no coincidence that around the same time Boccioni gave the title *Materia* to a painting in which his mother is dramatically linked to the background by rays of light, he used the title *Horizontal Construction* for a smaller, analogous image, in which similar light effects do not appear.

In the book *L'Evolution de la matière* (1905) by Gustave Le Bon—whose *Psychologie des foules* (1895; *The Crowd: A Study of the Popular Mind,* 1897) was a key ideological influence on the Futurist depiction of crowds—faith in the indestructibility of matter was overturned by a new theory of electronics. According to Le Bon, objects gave off "effluvia of particles similar to cathode rays," thereby connecting "ponderable bodies with the imponderable ether."[20] Charles Gibson's popular *Scientific Ideas of Today* (1909; translated into Italian in

1912) described matter as emitting rays of energy into the cosmos.[21] In Alberto Righi's *Radiant Matter and Magnetic Rays* (1909), one finds "elastic forces" arising from "special deformations" that emit electrical forces into the ether—a concept very similar to Boccioni's "lines of force."[22] The lecture by Henri Poincaré that ended the popular series *Les Idées modernes sur la constitution de la matière,* held in Paris in 1912 at the Société Française de Physique, explored, with great clarity and simplicity, Max Planck's theory of energy exchanges between matter and the ether.[23] All of these sources popularized the nineteenth-century electromagnetic theories of Michael Faraday and James Clerk Maxwell, as well as the electromagnetic bases of matter theorized by Friedrich Wilhelm Ostwald, the 1909 Nobel laureate whose principal work was translated into French in 1912.[24] Nevertheless, the "matter" that preoccupied Boccioni when he named his opus was more philosophical than physical and derived directly from the writings of French philosopher Henri Bergson, who defined *matter* as "the aggregate of images" perceived by someone, while the syntagma "perception of matter" represented the same aggregate but "referred to the eventual action of one particular image, my body."[25]

It is very likely that Boccioni became directly acquainted with Bergson's texts in 1912, precisely at the moment he conceived *Materia* and began the studies for it. Before this date, the word *materia* had never appeared in his writings or letters with any learned implication; for example, the "terror of matter [*materia*] that suffocates me," mentioned in a 1908 diary entry, refers merely to his fear of being unable to translate his ideas with the proper technique.[26] It is not until a letter to Carrà from Berlin, datable to mid-April 1912, that Boccioni used the word for the first time in a specifically Bergsonian sense, that is, as the combination of the images perceived and coordinated by the self: "There is no longer any truth except outside the pictorial (as I understood it until yesterday); *for the moment I'm not interested in anything but matter expressed according to myself... et tout le reste est littérature.*"[27]

Toward the end of the twentieth-century's first decade, Bergson's ideas dominated philosophical debates all over Europe, even in Italy. His fame reached its peak after his lecture tour through Italy and England in 1911 and 1912.[28] The formulations of the man who could with good reason be called "the fashionable philosopher"[29] had already passed into the language of art: in 1910, Soffici used Bergson's theory on the perception of things "in relation to our needs" to explain the perspectival distortions of Cubist painting.[30] During this same period, especially among the writers of *La Voce,* a pocket of resistance formed against a philosophy deemed too diffuse; there was, according to Giuseppe Prezzolini, a new "hunger for order and discipline," based on an opposite need, well expressed by Paul Cézanne in painting, to "give solidity, firmness, and cubicity to the shapes of things."[31]

In the course of his international travels in 1912, particularly visits to Paris, London, and Berlin during February–May, Boccioni found a receptive climate for the discussion of Bergson's concepts of duration, memory, and intuition, which were flourishing among artists. These ideas, drawn mostly from synopses in contemporary journals, and not from the original books, were widely adapted in interpretations of the new Cubist painting in articles by Roger Allard, Albert Gleizes, Jean Metzinger, and Tancrède de Visan.[32] Boccioni was certainly aware of these critical approaches, if only indirectly. In the space of a year, encouraged by their exploration of simultaneity in painting, references to Bergson became commonplace among the Futurists. In 1913, even Severini, a painter little given to theoretical speculation, could claim in the introduction to the catalogue for his solo exhibition at the Marlborough Gallery in London: "to perceive, says Bergson, is after all, nothing more than an opportunity to remember."[33]

Back in Milan in summer 1912, Boccioni apparently verified the ideas he had picked up second-hand against Bergson's original texts. Brian Petrie demonstrated the consistency of many concepts in Boccioni's *Pittura scultura futuriste (Dinamismo plastico)* (drafted that year and published in 1914) with Bergson's tenets; for example, Boccioni identifies the perceiving subject with the thing perceived; he speaks of the distinction between absolute and relative motion and of the theory of muscular sensation.[34] Bergson's notions of space and time also influenced the ideology behind Futurist mass politics, as Mark Antliff elaborated in a recent study.[35]

While the Bergson-Boccioni connection in 1912–13 may be indisputable, no one has investigated the artist's specific mode of access to the philosopher's texts. The issue is not unimportant; indeed, it is essential to try to understand how a painter who read a great deal—but in a somewhat disorderly fashion and without a firm cultural base—would have approached the complexity of Bergson's writings. How did Boccioni relate directly and continuously to the lofty level of the contemporary scientific debate? There is some evidence in an undated note published in 1971 by Zeno Birolli, the *terminus ante quem* being March 1913, when parts of this text were used in Boccioni's first article published in *Lacerba.*[36] Here, Boccioni transcribed a passage from Bergson's *Matter and Memory* (originally published in French as *Matière et mémoire* in 1896) on the condition of matter, largely to counter accusations that the

Futurists were engaged in cinematography rather than painting. Bergson claimed matter to be indivisible, "all division of matter into independent bodies with absolutely determinate contours is an artificial division,"[37] contradicting the common-sense meaning given it in most popular dictionaries of the time.[38]

The undated note, which contains other quotations and a list of readings, makes it possible to reconstruct Boccioni's path as a reader of Bergson through the libraries of Milan. Taking into account a slight error of transcription (7.4.D.41 instead of F.4.D.41), Boccioni wrote down the call number for *La filosofia dell'intuizione,* the Bergson anthology translated by Giovanni Papini in 1909 and available in the Biblioteca Nazionale Braidense of Milan. (The first edition of *Matter and Memory,* from 1896, could also be found in the Braidense library; see fig. 43) Boccioni's notations attest to the superficiality and rapidity with which he approached *La filosofia dell'intuizione;* they include, almost exclusively, only the brief sentences printed in italics, which served to sum up Bergson's important conceptual points. For example, he took notes from pages III, 4, 6, 74, 163, 213, 215, 218 (containing the passage on the indivisibility of matter quoted above), 225, and 252 (the first lines of the author's conclusion). Boccioni's quick schooling in Bergson's dense constructs nonetheless exposed him to key concepts and images that bore surprising fruit in the painting subsequently entitled *Materia.* In agreement with the concepts Boccioni read in Bergson's *Matter and Memory,* the image represented arises from the body's "center of action" (p. 4 in the 1896 edition); there is a continual relationship between centripetal and centrifugal forces binding the perceiver to the object perceived (p. 6); the image of the body occupies the center of the perceptual field, changing the images perceived as it moves (p. 10); the

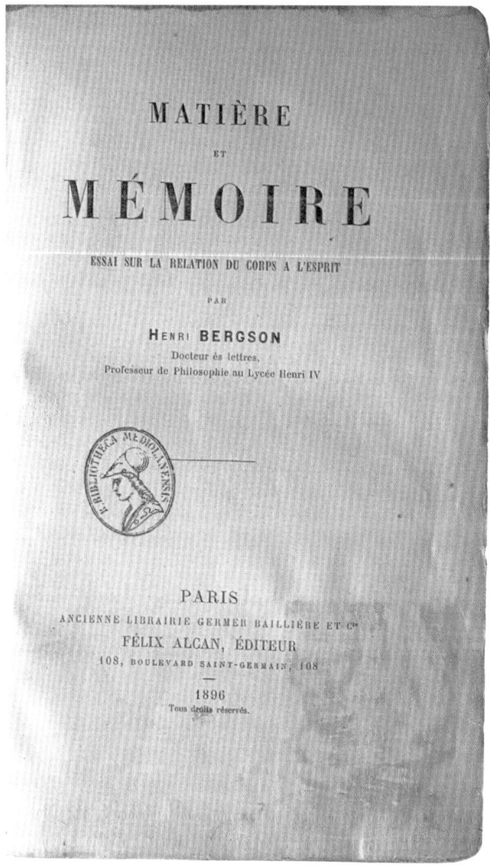
MATIÈRE

ET

MÉMOIRE

ESSAI SUR LA RELATION DU CORPS A L'ESPRIT

PAR

HENRI BERGSON

Docteur ès lettres,
Professeur de Philosophie au Lycée Henri IV

PARIS
ANCIENNE LIBRAIRIE GERMER BAILLIÈRE ET Cie
FÉLIX ALCAN, ÉDITEUR
108, BOULEVARD SAINT-GERMAIN, 108

1896
Tous droits réservés.

Fig. 43 Title page from first edition of Henri Bergson's *Matière et mémoire: Essai sur la relation du corps à l'esprit* (Paris: Alcan, 1896) in the Biblioteca Nazionale Braidense, Milan.

body's perceptual centers are linked to objects through actual extensions (p. 27); the body is experienced as a center from which is reflected, onto the surrounding objects, the forces that these objects exert upon it (p. 47); and there are no intervals delineated between the body and the objects it perceives (pp. 48–49).[39]

Even before Boccioni examined Bergson's original texts first hand, Marinetti had played an essential role in pushing Futurist artists to reflect on the philosopher's concept of matter. In Marinetti's "Technical Manifesto of Futurist Literature," dated May 11, 1912, and published as the introduction to his *I poeti futuristi* (1912), the word *materia* (as "matter") is obsessively repeated no less than nine times[40] and used in the precise Bergsonian sense of a network of perceptible images. Indeed, in a response dated August 11, 1912, Marinetti had to defend himself against those who accused him of being overly indebted to Bergson's philosophy.[41] In the literature manifesto, Marinetti evoked *materia* in terms very familiar to Boccioni. He wrote of a new "lyric obsession with *matter*" that would replace stale pandering to human psychology.[42] Matter would be freed from the subjectivity of the first-person narrative that is "contemplated by a cold, distracted *I*, too preoccupied with itself, full of preconceived wisdom and human obsessions."[43] He further described matter as possessing "an admirable continuity of impulse toward greater warmth, greater movement," and the need to penetrate its essence in order to "destroy the dumb hostility that separates it from us."[44]

Boccioni frequented Marinetti in Milan quite assiduously in summer 1912. During this period, the artist realized that the challenge to Cubism needed to rise above the mere oppositions of style—movement versus immobility, brilliant color versus monochrome, modern versus academic subjects—listed in the catalogue preface he signed with his fellow Futurists for their Galerie Bernheim-Jeune exhibition several months earlier, in February. By bestowing the title *Materia* to a grand image of his mother seated on a balcony, Boccioni laid claim, against Cubist theory, to the privileged relationship between Futurist art and Bergson's philosophy of time and space.

Translated from the Italian by Stephen Sartarelli.

Notes

1 For a precise reconstruction of artistic events in Rome in the first months of 1913, see Mario Quesada, "Roma dal 1912 al 1918: mostre e vicende artistiche" and "Archivio 'privato' della Secessione Romana," in Rossana Bossaglia, Mario Quesada, and Pasqualina Spadini, eds., *Secessione Romana 1913–1916,* exh. cat. (Rome: Palombi, 1987), pp. 31–33, 45–48, respectively. For the Italian reception of Matisse's *Goldfish* (that is, the painting now in the Statens Museum for Kunst in Copenhagen), see Flavio Fergonzi, "Firenze 1910–Venezia 1920: Emilio Cecchi, i quadri francesi e le difficoltà dell'impressionismo," in *Bollettino d'Arte del Ministero per i Beni Culturali e Ambientali*, 78, ser. 6, no. 79 (May–June 1993), pp. 1 26.

2 Roberto Longhi, "I pittori futuristi," *La Voce,* April 10, 1913.

3 See Civ. [Guelfo Civinini?], "L'esibizione del futurismo al Costanzi: Uno spettacolo burrascoso," *Corriere della Sera,* February 22, 1913: "curtain, curtain, curtain—waiter, a cognac!—greetings, hello, how are you?—turn and strut—I am the sun—gasps of dying stars—I am a dog walking along—walking along, with twenty-five legs—galleria vittorio emanuele—bedside-rug—23–34–52, bet on Naples, sure winners those three. And so on and so forth. It's perfectly clear."

4 See "Première série des tableaux futuristes exposés à Paris, Londres, Berlin, Hambourg, Amsterdam, La Haye, Munich, Vienne et Budapest et vendus," in *Les Peintres et les sculpteurs futuristes italiens*, exh. cat., Rotterdamsche Kunstkring (Rotterdam: De Jong, 1913), pp. 13–16.

5 See Federico Mastrigli, "La mostra futurista al 'Costanzi': Dinamismo, stati d'animo e linee-forza," *La Vita,* February 23–24, 1913, p. 3: "They all wanted to give the viewer the same impression of movement that Carrà, for example, attempted to capture in his painting *Speed Breaks Up the Horse*. Apart from the fact that speed doesn't break up anything, Carrà's painting raises a new and insurmountable problem . . . that of putting back together the horse that's been broken up."

6 These are the titles mentioned in Boccioni to Barbantini, June 21, 1910, in Zeno Birolli, ed., *Umberto Boccioni: Gli scritti editi e inediti* (Milan: Feltrinelli, 1971), pp. 339–40.

7 See D.b.[?], "Esposizione libera," *La Perseveranza,* May 1–2, 1911; C.c., "La prima esposizione di arte libera," *Il Secolo,* May 2, 1911; N. Barbantini, "L'esposizione libera di Milano," *L'Avvenire d'Italia,* May 19, 1911; "Esposizione d'arte libera," *L'Uomo di pietra*, May 6, 1911; and Ardengo Soffici, "Arte libera e pittura futurista," *La Voce,* June 22, 1911.

8 Soffici, "Arte libera e pittura futurista."

9 See Ester Coen, *Umberto Boccioni,* exh. cat. (New York: Metropolitan Museum of Art, 1988), p. 122. On the fame of Cottet's triptych, see Rodolphe Rapetti's entry for this work in Michel Laclotte, ed., *Polyptyques: Le tableau multiple du moyen-âge au vingtième siècle*, exh. cat. (Paris: Réunion des Musées Nationaux, 1990), p. 194.

10 As asserted in Maurizio Calvesi, "Un Boccioni ritrovato e il tema dialettico della spirale," *Paragone*, nos. 317–319 (July–September 1976), pp. 259–60.

11 The presence of *The Street Enters the House* at a show at La Famiglia Artistica, Milan in December 1911, under the title *Al balcone* (*On the Balcony*), is attested to in Margherita Grassini Sarfatti, "Cronache d'Arte. L'Esposizione 'Intima' alla Famiglia Artistica," *Avanti!*, December 13, 1911, a review in which the painting is described very precisely. Sarfatti's review was rediscovered thanks to Antonello Negri, "Uno sguardo circolare," in Laura Mattioli Rossi, ed., *Boccioni 1912 Materia*, exh. cat. (Milan: Mazzotta, 1995), pp. 31–32.

12 Gustav Kahn, "L'Art. Les Futuristes italiens," *Mercure de France*, March 1, 1912, p. 184. This review is not included in the rich anthology of French reviews of the Futurists' Galerie Berheim-Jeune exhibition in Giovanni Lista, *Les Futuristes* (Paris: Veyrer, 1988).

13 Severini to Marinetti, February 9, 1913, in A. Hanson, "Marinetti Papers: Letters and Postcards from Gino Severini to F. T. Marinetti, 1910–1915," in Anne Coffin Hanson, *Severini futurista: 1912–1917*, exh. cat. (New Haven: Yale University Art Gallery, 1995), pp. 144–45.

14 Pierre Larousse, *Grand Dictionnaire universel du XIXe siècle français*, vol. 10 (Paris: Administration du Grand Dictionnaire Universel, 1873), p. 1337.

15 Ottorino Pianigiani, *Vocabolario etimologico della lingua italiana*, (Milan: Sonzogno, 1937–38), s.v. "materia."

16 See Fausto Petrella, "La 'materia' inquieta e le sue trasformazioni: Appunti per una ricerca," in Mattioli Rossi, *Boccioni 1912 Materia*, p. 95.

17 Carlo Carrà, *Boccioni* (Milan: [no publisher], 1916), p. 23.

18 See Virginia Spate, "Mother and Son: Boccioni's Painting and Sculpture 1906–1915," in Terry Smith, ed., *In Visible Touch: Modernism and Masculinity* (Chicago: University of Chicago Press, 1997).

19 See Christine Poggi, "Dreams of Metallized Flesh: Futurism and the Masculine Body," in *Modernism/modernity* 4, no. 3 (September 1997), pp. 31–35.

20 See Gustave Le Bon, *L'Évolution de la matière* (Paris: Flammarion, 1905), pp. 6, 9.

21 See Charles Gibson, *Idee scientifiche d'oggi: Sulla natura della materia, elettricità, luce, calore, ecc. messe alla portata di tutti*, trans. Leopoldo Jung (Milan: Cogliati, 1912), p. 59.

22 Augusto Righi, *La materia radiante e i raggi magnetici* (Bologna: Zanichelli, 1909), pp. 9, 110.

23 See Henri Poincaré, "Les Rapports de la matière e de l'éther," in *Société Française de Phisique: Les Idées modernes sur la constitution de la matière. Conferences faites en 1912* (Paris: Gauthiers-Villars, 1913), p. 364.

24 The work of Wilhelm Ostwald, especially his *L'Évolution de l'électrochimie* (Paris: Alcan, 1912), is discussed in relation to Boccioni in F. Petrella, "La 'materia' inquieta," p. 101. On the theories of Faraday and Maxwell, see Linda Dalrymple Henderson, "Die Moderne Kunst und das Unsichtbare: Die verborgenen Wellen und Dimensionen des Okkultismus und der Wissenschaften," and Giovanni Lista, "Futurismus und Okkultismus," both in Veit Loers and Pia Witzmann, eds., *Okkultismus und Avantgarde. Von Munch bis Mondrian 1900–1915,* exh. cat. (Ostfildern: Edition Tertium, 1995), pp. 28, 443, respectively.

25 Henri Bergson, *Matter and Memory*, trans. N. M. Paul and W. S. Palmer (New York: Zone Books, 1988), p. 22.

26 Boccioni diary, in Birolli, *Gli scritti editi e inediti*, p. 304.

27 Boccioni to Carrà, [after April 12, 1912], in Birolli, *Gli scritti editi e inediti*, p. 353.

28 For an early framing of the question of Bergson's international fame, see Mark Antliff, *Inventing Bergson: Cultural Politics and the Parisian Avant-Garde* (Princeton: Princeton University Press, 1993), pp. 3–15.

29 Alessandro Chiappelli, "Il filosofo di moda," *Il Marzocco*, May 7, 1911.

30 Ardengo Soffici, "Divagazioni sull'arte," *La Voce*, September 22, 1910.

31 Giuseppe Prezzolini, "Io devo . . . ," *La Voce*, February 15, 1912.

32 This important question has been reconstructed from two different points of view: Maria Grazia Messina, "La formazione di cubisti tra filosofia e letteratura," in Maria Grazia Messina and Jolanda Nigro Covre, *Il cubismo dei cubisti: Ortodossi/eretici a Parigi intorno al 1912* (Rome: Officina, 1986), pp. 37–90; and Antliff, *Inventing Bergson*, pp. 16–105.

33 Gino Severini, introduction to *The Futurist Painter Gino Severini Exhibits His Latest Works*, exh. cat. (London: Marlborough, 1913), p. 3.

34 See Brian Petrie, "Boccioni and Bergson," in *The Burlington Magazine* 116, no. 852 (March 1974), pp. 140–47.

35 See Mark Antliff, "The Fourth Dimension and Futurism: A Politicized Space," *The Art Bulletin* 82, no. 4 (December 2000), pp. 720–33.

36 See Boccioni, "Libri da consultare-Bergson" (undated note), in Birolli, *Gli scritti editi e inediti*, p. 442; and Boccioni, "Fondamento plastico della scultura e pittura futuriste," *Lacerba*, March 15, 1913.

37 Boccioni, "Libri da consultare-Bergson," p. 442.

38 See Giuseppe Rigutini and Pietro Fanfani, eds., *Vocabolario italiano della lingua parlata* (Florence: Tipografia Cenniniana, 1875), p. 945; and Nicolò Tommaseo and Bernardo Bellini, *Dizionario della lingua italiana*, 6 vols. (Turin: Pomba, 1861–79), vol. 4, p. 147.

39 Pages cited are in Henri Bergson, *Matière et mémoire: Essai sur la relation du corps à l'esprit* (Paris: Alcan, 1896).

40 See F. T. Marinetti, "Manifesto tecnico della letteratura futurista," in Marinetti, *Teoria e invenzione futurista*, ed. Luciano De Maria (Milan: Mondadori, 1983), pp. 46–54. The manifesto must have appeared in print at least one month after its May 11 date since the first reviews of *I poeti futuristi* were from July, such as Alberto Calza, "Poeti futuristi . . . ma non tanto," *Il Giornale d'Italia*, July 21, 1912.

41 See F. T. Marinetti, "Risposta alle obiezioni," in Marinetti, *Teoria e invenzione futurista*, p. 55. The question is discussed in Luciano de Maria, "Marinetti poeta e ideologo," in *Teoria e invenzione futurista*, pp. 69–80.

42 F. T. Marinetti, *Let's Murder the Moonshine: Selected Writings*, ed. R. W. Flint (Los Angeles: Sun & Moon Press, 1991), p. 95.

43 Ibid., p. 96.

44 Ibid.

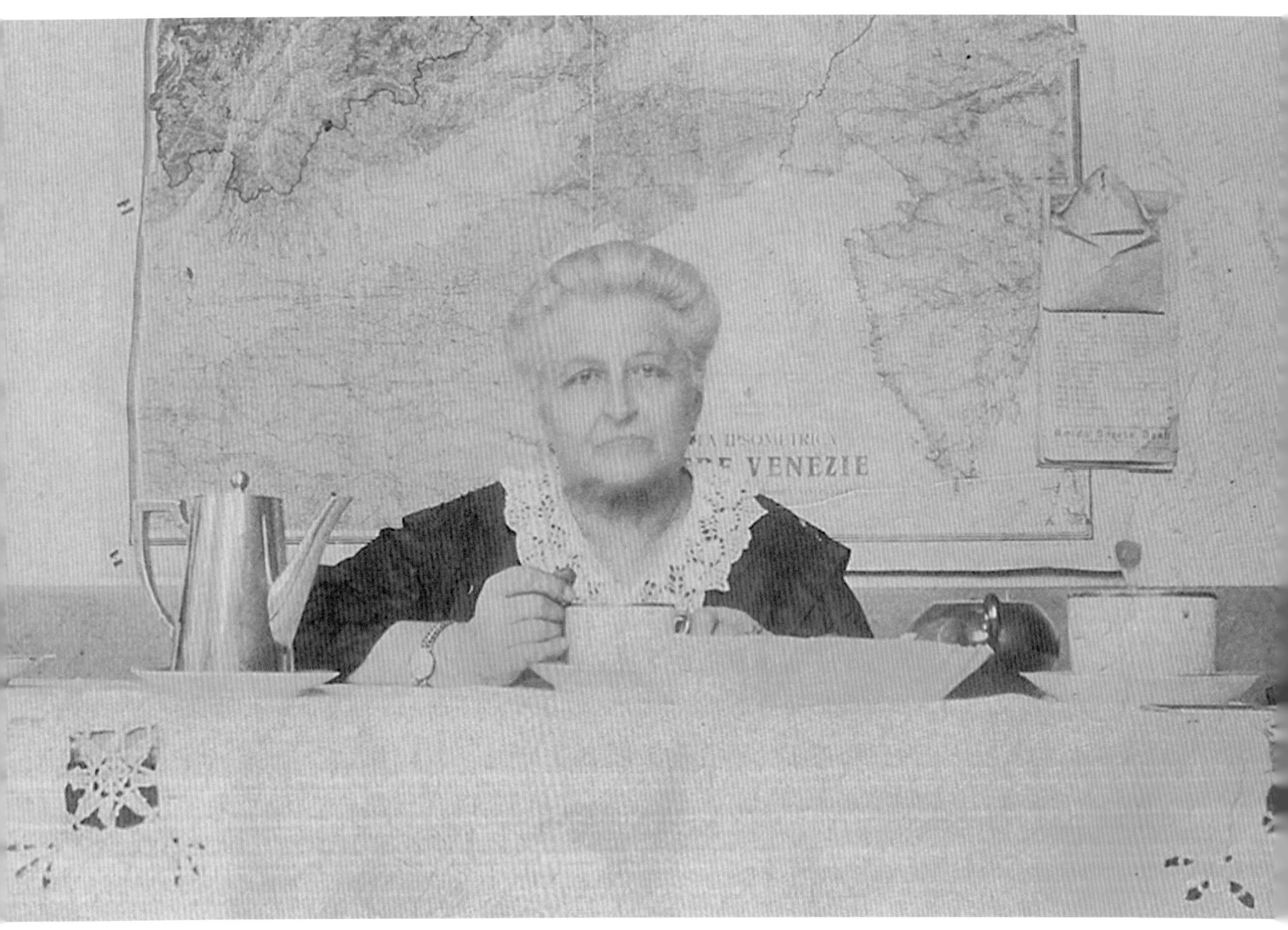
VENEZIE

Mater Materia Prima: Clinical and Critical Remarks

FAUSTO PETRELLA

It's the terror of matter that suffocates me.

—UMBERTO BOCCIONI[1]

Fig. 44 Umberto Boccioni
Boccioni's mother Cecilia photographed in front of Triveneto map, 1908
Collection of Fiorenzo Mancini

Concentrating on a great painting, Umberto Boccioni's *Materia* (1912; cat. no. 27)—reflecting on a single work's salient features and complex motivating factors—conveniently delimits the field. But once this delimitation has been made, our need for understanding soon compels us to look in many other directions. The result is a tangle of many threads: places near and far, the artist and the work, the heterogeneous documents accompanying them, the artist's writings, the responses of those who have enjoyed the work, and many other things.[2]

The clinician, like the critic and the art historian, is forced to follow different threads and make connections, evaluate, valorize, and even create them, establishing justifiable imaginative interactions and constructing plausible, coherent contexts.[3] One starts with the experience—the object and one's relationship to it—and constructs comparisons, differences, and links between the work and other considerations and works. If we want to focus attention on a single thread, for example, the artist's mother Cecilia Forlani Boccioni—an approach authorized by *Materia*'s explicit reference to her, whom it portrays—we realize that even here we are dealing not with one thread but with skeins made up of many (but not innumerable) threads.

How do we interrogate the work, the artist? This is the problem. In itself, the work is mute. Boccioni, of course, is no longer alive, and if he were, perhaps, rather than speak with them, he would prefer to portray a psychoanalyst or psychiatrist in a corner of some painting, maybe hidden among the others in some chromatic fold of *The Laugh* (1911, fig. 6).

I saw *Materia* for the first time in Venice many years ago. I well remember my initial, confused reaction to this imposing, enigmatic sphinx, who stops and questions the wayfarer. Lingering with it too long is dangerous. Something attracts yet repels, defying comprehension. This discussion cannot fail to bear in mind the sense of surprise, bother, and shock (related to the content, as Hermann Rorschach would describe it) of my first encounter. I have observed these prereflexive reactions in other viewers and noted the tremendous impression made by the painting's seriousness and complexity, by one's intuitive perception of a sacred profanation and challenge, one's confrontation with an absolute, troubling emotion. One also feels respect and admiration for the person capable of producing these emotions in us.

At this point begins identification with the artist, as Ernst Kris would say,[4] in addition to the simultaneous questioning as to the *how* and questioning of oneself/ourselves and the artist.

The Mother

With Boccioni, one thing immediately becomes clear: the mother became her son's preferred "model" and was directly and thematically involved in his work in an unusual way, over and over again throughout his artistic production. It is something well beyond the simple, occasional tribute that a great many famous painters paid to their mothers, especially in their early years. I cannot think of any other who elevated the mother to the status of privileged object of representation in such a direct and systematic way. For Boccioni, the mother is an almost ever-present reference, the starting point and end point of representation. Determining the meaning and function of this repetition is, of course, also a psychological problem, one that accompanies, step by step, the artist's stylistic and poetic evolution.

Biographies of artists, like our own memories, are usually scant in remembrances of childhood and references to the early stages. Biographical information tells us little

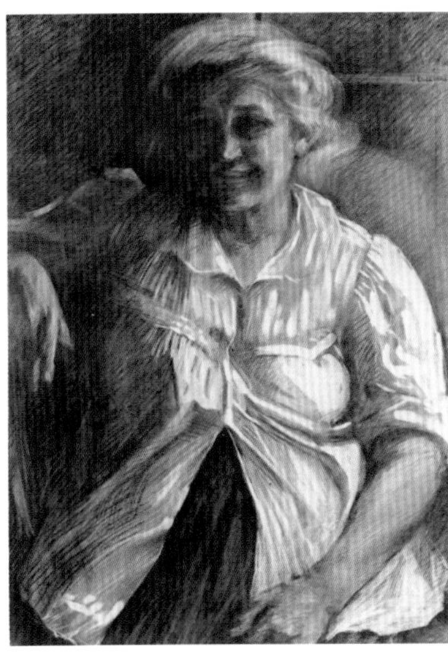

Fig. 45 Umberto Boccioni
Mother (La madre), 1908
Pastel and tempera on paper
Dimensions and location unknown

about childhood passions, the family system of care and support, and the strategies of emancipation and defenses against related anxieties. Artistic and creative activity is tied up with these aspects; artistic products become easily entangled in unfavorable psychological processes, often originating in childhood, and are aborted, or they liberate themselves from these problems and take off, transcending them in the successful work of art. In art history, references to the artistic and cultural environment abound, but there are almost none to the "enabling environment," as Donald Winnicott calls it,[5] of an artist's familial and parental relations, especially with the mother.

We know very little about Boccioni's father and not much about his mother either. What meaning are we to give to the insistent image of the mother in Boccioni's work and to the many documents attesting to the intensity of this bond? The psychoanalyst may think immediately of the persistence of the child's investment of love and of an especially intense fixation on the mother, obscure in origin. However, it is psychoanalytically important to assert ignorance and uncertainty, to accept not having any sure answers, rather than develop the one-sided hypothesis of an erotic and/or hostile fixation on the mother, about whom we actually know almost nothing.

Boccioni's intense bond with his mother is extremely explicit and in many ways also self-aware. Artworks, letters, and diaries show the artist solidly and passionately anchored to her. Photographs in which she appears, often with her son or with his works, show a serious woman with a face typically expressing sadness. The severe expression, an attitude characteristic of depression, is a constant in Boccioni's numerous drawings and paintings of her. But there is also a portrait, *Mother* (1908, fig. 45), that seems important inasmuch as it represents a significant exception. It effectively captures a woman laughing, relaxed in manner. Her overall posture and the position of her upper extremities signal an availability for embrace, allusively repeated in the upside-down V-shaped opening of her dress.

In a beautiful photographic self-portrait from 1913 (fig. 56.3), the artist is sitting in his studio, head resting on hand, eyes looking out at the viewer. Beside him stands his "mother"—that is, a bust of his mother, *Head + House + Light* (1912, destroyed; fig. 58.12), on a pedestal. We may ask ourselves, what interpretative discourse could fill the void separating this image of the artist, sitting triumphantly beside his creation, from the typical photograph of mother and child documenting, as if by requirement, almost everyone's childhood? Or even, for example, from Boccioni's own *Mother and Daughter (Portrait of Balla's Wife and Daughter)* (ca. 1906, fig. 46)?

In his 1907 diary, the artist wrote, "Yesterday morning Mama left, and I am alone and *bouleversé*,"[6] bearing witness to an attachment—here pronounced, elsewhere more secret, hinted at, or dissembled—that would last his entire life. Even in his last letters from the front in World War I, Boccioni's thoughts constantly turn to her: "My mother is my greatest anguish at this moment . . . , my only anguish, if anything bad should happen, is leaving Mama behind."[7] It is ironic that love for the motherland, "my Futurist ideal," as he called it, irresistibly drove him far away from his mother. Futurist ideal and patriotic ideal became one and the same, a play of idealizing, reparative tensions in which the bond with the mother is strongly implied. The motherland, debased, offended, and prostituted by fathers and their foolishness, will finally be made great. A great future awaits; we are inside a heroic and oedipal myth.

There are Boccioni's painful separation from his mother; the countless kisses he sends her in a passionate, playful letter during a Roman sojourn in 1901; the long period in 1907 and 1908 during which he lived with her and his sister Amelia in Padua; the indifference to other women, as declared in his 1907 diary: "no bond, no affection whatsoever, except for the great affection I feel (the most possible for me) for my Mother and my Sister."[8] Nonetheless, his relationship with his mother was stormy. He was intolerant of her "incurable worrying about with everything, her troubled face, her constant sighing, the continuous wretchedness of her life," and felt "terrible anguish" over her health, fearing she might die at any moment, without his having been able to make her happy.[9] Consistent with Boccioni's manifest Don Juanism[10] was a state of perpetual dissatisfaction, a feeling of not being loved or able to love, a sense of the painful, unavoidable transience of the amorous experience, which could not hold up to criticism when compared to his ideal, and, finally, a sense of the futility of life, which is not equal to devotion to Art. Boccioni's devotion to the Great Mother—which lost all connection to the person of his mother who, however, was constantly before his eyes—in the end appeared to him as an exalting religion of the Unknown.[11]

The Maternal Repertoire

Boccioni's many portraits of his mother are very different from one another. They range from Dürer-style drawing, with balance of solid volumes, to Cézannesque constructivism, taken to the point of Cubist faceting and disintegration of the viewpoints from which the mother's face is seen. There are also Impressionist-Divisionist representations such as *Controluce* (1909, cat. no. 5).

In 1908, Boccioni produced a vast inventory of his personal universe in *Beata solitudo* (fig. 47). The psychological interest of this

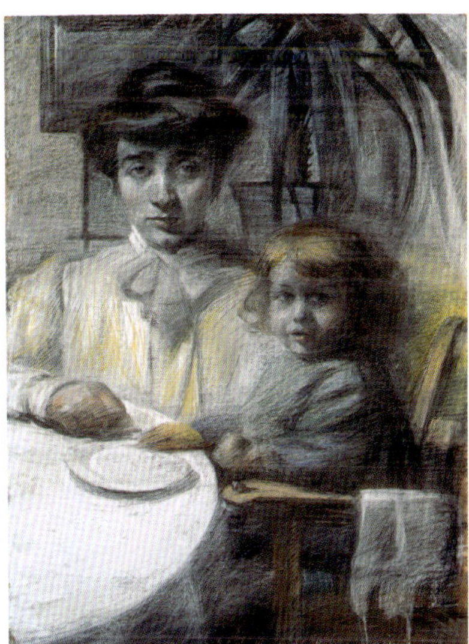

Fig. 46 Umberto Boccioni
Mother and Daughter (Portrait of Balla's Wife and Their Daughter)
(Madre e figlia [Ritratto della moglie di Balla con la figlia]), ca. 1906
Pastel on cardboard, 38 × 27 15/16 inches (96.5 × 71 cm)
Museo di Arte Moderna e Contemporanea di Trento e Rovereto

drawing lies in the stratigraphy it provides of the conflicting affective and ideological elements in the artist's inner world. What particularly stands out is the specific maternal dramaturgy, which is so typical of Boccioni and would shortly thereafter profoundly influence his Futurist vision, culminating in *Materia*. The vision presented in *Beata solitudo* brings together contrasting emotions and thoughts that are organized in an overly dense and rigid weltanschauung. The method adopted, a detailed analysis of the forces at work in human existence, is entirely different from the search for the intuitive synthesis of subject, object, and environment in *Materia*. Taking place in the light of day, *Beata solitudo* knows no shadow or darkness; everything appears formally resolved but devitalized. The allegory spatializes the opposition between beatific solitude and the chaotic world as one of above and below. Above is the thoughtful white figure of Solitude, severed from care and close to the ideal: the beaming sun, the regenerative mother-father symbol that combines all positive qualities. The horizontal split is underscored by the line of the sea. Below is the negative counterpart of the ideal: an erotic woman, a courtesan in the Beardsleyian style. In perfect alignment along the composition's central, vertical axis—beginning at the center of the sun and ending at the courtesan's pubis—are images of Milan's Duomo, Motherhood (a child at a mother's breast, flanked by figures of Brawl and Despair), and Death (on horseback). Pairings of erotic and destructive aspects—for example, the Lovers on the right and a bomb about to explode on the left—are strident but controlled by the rigidly right-angled composition. The many antinomies of modernity represented here— individual/couple/collectivity, culture/nature, Eros/destruction—are vertically coordinated by various articulations of the maternal feminine.

Two photographs (figs. 44 and 48), brought to my attention by Laura Mattioli Rossi, separately show *Beata solitudo* and the artist's mother in the same position, with a map of the so-called Triveneto (the Three Venetias) as background. These photographs underscore a certain identification of *Beata solitudo* with Boccioni's mother, an interchangeability between the two. The background map is itself especially relevant because the Triveneto region contained Trieste, Trent, and other Austrian territories populated by an Italian majority, and the demands that Italy annex it were growing more and more insistent at this time. Italian irredentism, to which Boccioni passionately subscribed, expressed an aspiration to rejoin to the motherland those "unredeemed" Italian populations that remained under foreign rule. The maternal constellation that lies at the origin of the artist's interventionist nationalism is particularly evident here.

The subsequent *Controluce* of 1909—comparable, for its emotional content, to the smiling portrait, *Mother*, of 1908—is striking for its soft treatment of the mother's nudity (itself so utterly audacious) and the sensuality with which the light caresses the shoulders and back. The isolation in which the mother is placed with respect to the rest of the space helps to highlight the skin and hair, in relation to the hands, for example. If, however, we consider such works as the paintings *Materia* and *Horizontal Construction* (1912, cat. no. 28) and the sculptures *Head + House + Light* and *Antigrazioso* (1912–13, cat. no. 31), we are faced with entirely different, though still explicit, inflections of the Boccionian maternal. In these Futurist works, the accent has often been shifted—by means of the title—onto the constructional aspects of the vision presented, but the mother remains the manifest reference of the experimentation, its solid ground.

Consider the contrast between the idealizing devotion to the mother and the process of turbulent profanation of the same object that leads from *Triptych: We Venerate the Mother* (1907–08, cat. no. 2) to subsequent Futurist statements. For the purpose of psychological evaluation, it is essential to examine *We Venerate the Mother*. The plans for this painting included a background for the central maternal part that would have consisted of "sunset, church, and ruins,"[12] a rather conventional allegory: sunset and church called upon to echo the mother in the landscape, in keeping with the devotional intention of the whole, and ruins (the object of Futurist scorn for the old), no less. It is revealing that the artist is the very same person who, only a few years later, would sing the ecstatic praises of modernity and the innovative delirium of the age. For Boccioni the Futurist, only by potently charging "new material" with new energies was it possible to conceive new experiences, to "perceive what until now had never been perceived."[13] It became necessary to detach oneself from the maternal, from parents, from the old—no more nostalgia, an end to "miserable powder-blue childhood memories, dark influences of atavism, white languors of puberty—all the idiocies: family upbringing, the imbecilic, classical-forty-eightish rhetoric [the liberalism of the revolutionary year 1848] that our parents and teachers imposed on us for so many years."[14] It was a question of removing oneself—and removing all lingerers, with kicks, whips, or whatever it took—from the forced worship of parents, from childhood, in short, and its regressive seduction. It was a question of turning to the modern, the machine, to the creative destruction of the old, and turning against restoration, conservation, charm, tenderness, etcetera.

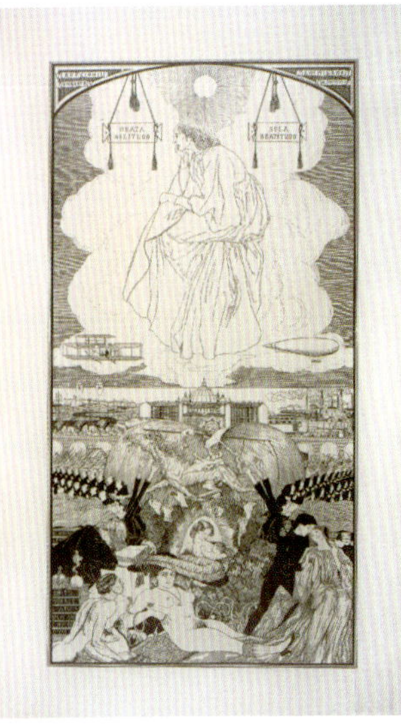

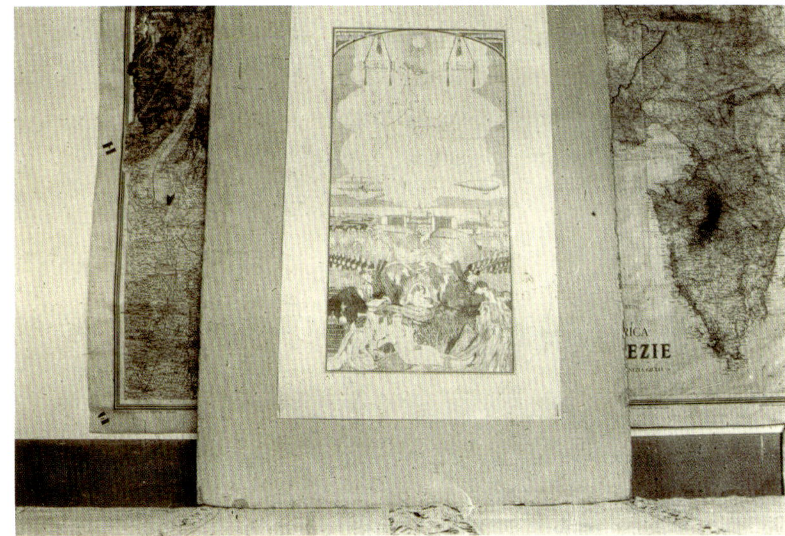

Boccioni the Theorist

Boccioni was a great, lucid theoretician of his own painting. It is fundamental to an understanding of his conception of the tasks of Futurist painting to consider that, even in the physiognomy and substance of reality, we again find the mother, her face, her body, her hands, her moods. One's relationship with the object, with the quality and stuff of the perceived world, with the need to enter, grasp, immobilize, animate it, and so on, all this stems from the maternal raw material with which reality is originally woven. On the subject of this material, hidden in language and in matter, Sigmund Freud observes that even wood, when it appears in dreams, can be interpreted as a symbol of the feminine, the motherly.[15]

In the tension-filled conception of matter that characterizes Boccioni's vision, forces and energies are simultaneously in motion, and conceived in extreme, grandiose terms. The conflicts thus called forth have their corresponding risks, and the tool of resolution, the stabilizing force, the remedy, is fragile and aleatory. Boccioni's object—a deformed one on which he inscribes the subject's projection, a postcatastrophic and persecutive "bizarre object" (in the sense described by Wilfred Bion)[16]—is the fruit of an aggregation and combination of interdependent, complementary plastic elements that nevertheless do not lose their characteristics, or the fruit of a deformation that may include chopping up or amalgamation. On the other hand, by conceiving the object from the inside, that is, by "living it," affirms Boccioni, we allow for its expansion, its power, its manifestation, simultaneously creating its relationship to the surrounding environment. The object's borders recede toward a periphery, toward surroundings of which the spectator (whether the artist or us) is the hospitable center.[17] Thus the object, its representation, and we (the spectators) are saved, moved, and stimulated; the pleasure of catastrophic penetration has been achieved, form conquered, time defeated but not mortified.

Boccioni keenly felt that that the entire operation involving the loss of customary reality and the conquest of the new, unheard-of dynamic reality was a risk; it occurred in a state of fear or terror of a catastrophe that at moments seemed inevitable. He thus put himself on the side of catastrophe in order to dominate and catalyze it:

> *Birth, growth, death, such is the fatalism that guides us. Not to march toward finality is to refuse evolution and death. Everything is heading toward catastrophe! We must therefore have the courage to surpass ourselves until death; enthusiasm, fervor, intensity, ecstasy are all aspirations to perfection, that is, to consummation. We must do away with negations through the terror of realizations.*[18]

To synthesize, in somewhat approximative fashion, the three risks of this dynamic energism are: depression from the loss of the object through the failure of its creative vitalization and one's relationship to it; catastrophic fragmentation of the self and the exploded object; and confusion of the field of experience, for various reasons. These are eventualities to be feared, signs that the equilibrium of the centrifugal-centripetal play of vision has been lost, that flight—designed to dominate matter's complexity, to dismember unity and unify multiplicity, to overcome time, to incorporate the object and incorporate oneself in it—implies the risks of falling, of psychosis, of death in the end.

The necessary stabilizing gesture asserted by Boccioni is of an intuitive-synthetic sort, and despite his considerable efforts at analysis and explanation, he preserves its secret. Intuition must grasp the unique form of the continuity of transformations in space. Boccioni is indeed the genius of painterly transformations of experience; the "dislocation and break-up of objects, the scattering and fusion of details liberated from common logic and independent of one another"[19] is the catastrophe to be produced and dominated. It is emotion that "gives the measure, restrains analysis, legitimates the will and creates dynamism. Emotion and subject are the same thing. The motion of the object was our concern! In its lyric interpretation (emotion) lies the happy medium, the fulcrum on which to stop the representation of reality without stopping life itself or falling into didacticism or into the chaos of a higher analysis."[20]

Materia Taken as a Whole

Materia seems like a strict application of the experience of the dynamic complexity of sight that Boccioni described and theorized. At the same time, the painting presents itself as an imposing and simultaneously dynamic whole that resists any overly analytical attitude on the part of the observer. Is it correct to assert that the artist was applying his conception of vision intellectualistically or, rather, that he derived his conception from the realized painting, managing (at least at certain moments) to "see" the world in this fashion? His vision actually appears to take its cue from a prereflexive/emotional nucleus, from a gaze that projected itself in a flash and instantaneously grasped what its own projection had transformed. The illusion of speed in stasis, of centrifugal motion within a general implosive collapse, produces a destabilization of the picture of the world, which nevertheless preserves the full recognizability of its referentiality.

In a general sense, one is struck by the contrast between the brightness at the top

Fig. 47 Umberto Boccioni
Beata solitudo, 1908
Ink on paper, 25³⁄₁₆ × 13 inches (64 × 33 cm)
Fondazione Antonio Mazzotta, Milan

Fig. 48 Umberto Boccioni
Beata solitudo (fig. 47) photographed propped against Triveneto map, 1908
Private collection, Courtesy of Galleria dello Scudo, Verona

of *Materia*, where the houses outside enter or radiate through the window into the room, and the darkness of the lower part. The mother's skirt hides depths worthy of a chthonic deity, leaving no hope for protective mercy. The gnarled, deformed hands, emphasized and thrust forward with a wide-angle effect, combine with the arms to delimit the vast space of a not very reassuring womb. These material, decidedly unpretty hands are the central, culminating point of an ironic overall deformation. The irony applies to the iconographic tradition of the great altarpieces, in which the Madonna, with or without the Christ child, sits enthroned against a paradisiacal landscape. Boccioni's anti-idealizing approach attacks every maternal attribute; materialization, from the height of idealization, has become profanation, abasement, even magnified negation.

Belonging to the painting's order of operation are urban background, home interior, and especially the potential eclipse of the distinction between inside and outside, a fusional movement achieved simultaneously with irradiation. From this, nothing chaotic, in my opinion, is generated, in that a higher degree of containment—the painting itself, its concept and realization—is proposed in place of the inside-outside differentiation, whose conceivable mingling is orgasmic in nature. In this visual orgasm and symbolic construction, there are the risks of dispersion and the attraction of nothingness in the excitement of the ego-object fusion. And there is the need to succeed despite the implicit violence.

Window, Railing, Balcony

The theme of window, with railing and balcony, is so recurrent, it becomes an essential element in the construction of many of Boccioni's works. The reasons for this predilection, which finds its most extreme, culminating moment in *Materia*, are manifold and would require a separate study to be properly discussed. I limit myself to synthesizing and observing that in general the window, for what it frames, is a double for the painting, a sort of painting within the painting; it is also the place where a painting's natural boundary, the frame, finds a way to be represented. In the window, a "functional phenomenon" is manifested, where the frame's containing function, as well as that of the seeing eye, is more or less consciously represented.[21] To paraphrase Freud and Herbert Silberer, one could say that the window is the painterly equivalent of the endopsychic representation of a function: vision, the seeing eye, which delimits, separates, and contains the experience. It is also the limen between inside and outside, the sign and place where this distinction can be revoked or taken in the most diverse directions.

Railings, balconies, and windows appear in dreams also as representative duplicates of the dreamer's body or of the object of desire, as Freud showed in *The Interpretation of Dreams* (1899/1900): as symbolic duplicates of the breast, the anaclitic support, the orificial openings that allow the projection and introjection of objects. These equivalencies on the fantasy level form the basis of the symbolic and expressive polyvalencies of the window in *Materia*. In the pre-Futurist Boccioni, a closed window, with its fine, calligraphic railing, can become the safe locus of a sometimes overly limiting visual summit from which to extend one's gaze on the outside, as in *Signora Massimino* (1908, fig. 25). The elevated viewpoint renders the presence of a horse in the street innocuous; the outside is kept at a distance. But later things change, and the street literally penetrates the domestic space with increasing force. The horse, which in *The Street Enters the House* (1911, cat. no. 7), for example, insinuates itself through the railing, ends up, in *Materia*, inside the house, in contact with the mother. The noise of the street synesthetically becomes vision, and the outside bursts into a defenseless room, creating a new, unusual symbolism.

On the subject of windows, Boccioni wrote, "the square of an open window becomes an irregular, variable body in which bodies, which live outside, on the horizon insert themselves through a conducting body (the atmosphere), which penetrates into the room in a form that the potentialities of the forms of bodies living outside have impressed on it."[22] Vision from above becomes something like a symbol for the possibility of grasping the whole simultaneously. The window frame may disappear (being identified with the painting's perimeter); the railing may also disappear or be only partially indicated,[23] as in *Materia*, where it merges with the armrests of the "throne." And then there is the thinning, to the point of breaking, of the barrier between inside and outside, the realization of the interpenetration of bodies, the vertigo of spiral ascents. The need to contain is exasperated at the moment of the boundaries' catastrophe, when the point of view becomes Luciferian, with objects rising up into the room, going inside and at the same time going outside, projecting into a space that the maternal womb cannot contain but seems to be generating.

Horse, Man in Motion

Within *Materia* are included two figures in motion. In the left-hand area close by the mother's joined hands there is a horse and on the right, a man. How did they get there? One might answer: from the road, from the actual presence of a staircase, from a memory, and so on. In any instance, if a horse passes noisily in the street outside, through the presence of its sound, it is "as if" it is inside the room. And so in *Materia* the horse itself is shown inside, present and moving, having got past the filter of the railing, the barrier of "as if," of analogy. The visual transformation of sound — the assumption of the racket from a visual "vertex," as Bion would say [24]—replaces the need for the horse (or the man) to be actually seen in the street.

With Boccioni, there are many transformations of this kind, too many to analyze here. In the act of painting, he sought the unique transformation, the instantaneous synthesis of possible connections and transformations, the omniscient/panoramic vertex of possible summits. The dividing membrane between inside and outside — which was solid in Boccioni, unlike for the psychotic — had to be broken to achieve unity, union with the complementary thing. Yet at the same time, the horse and man in motion are symbols, at least for the psychoanalyst, of the mother's and son's drives, of a secret sensuality, fearsome and untamable, and of the runaway fantasies that can form around all this. Just as the two small incandescent lamps (or baluster shapes?), symmetrical and reassuring, placed at either side of the mother, are most likely symbols of the maternal body that seem to have survived the violence of transformations. The plastic drama attempts to direct, on the synthetic, concentrated plane of vision, a complex dramaturgy — one with very remote origins.

In August 1912, Boccioni wrote to Gino Severini:

> *The commitment I've made is terrible, and the plastic mediums appear and disappear at the moment of realization... Is it the chaos of judgment? What is the law?... Is it inside? Is it outside? Is it sensation? Is it delirium? Is it the brain? Analysis? Synthesis?... I don't know what! — Forms upon forms — confusion— ... If were to continue in this vein I could only end up killing myself. Life certainly is becoming an unbearable torment.*[25]

Even Boccioni's subsequent war experience, at first exalting, would give way to growing disappointment and tension — in the form of a sense of the nothingness of existence — in the face of the unbearable crumbling of the euphoric plan to save the homeland, Italy, as the "good mother,"[26] an ideal purified of all contamination.[27] Only Art, in the end, will become worth the effort in his eyes — so soon before the unfortunate fall from an excited horse, which "forced his destiny" and cost him his life.

Translated from the Italian by Stephen Sartarelli.

Notes

1 Boccioni diary, April 25, 1908, in Zeno Birolli, ed., *Umberto Boccioni: Gli scritti editi e inediti* (Milan: Feltrinelli, 1971), p. 304; writings published in this source are cited as "in Birolli (1971)" in subsequent notes.

2 Two excellent volumes of Boccioni's writings, collected, arranged, and commented on by Zeno Birolli, are the sources for all my references to and quotations from Boccioni's diaries, letters, manifestos, and theoretical writings: Birolli, *Gli scritti editi e inediti*, and Birolli, ed., *Umberto Boccioni: Altri inediti e apparati critici* (Milan: Feltrinelli, 1972). An indispensable tool for getting to know Boccioni and his work is Maurizio Calvesi and Ester Coen, *Boccioni: L'opera completa* (Milan: Electa, 1983). For a more extensive treatment of *Materia*, see, among others, Fausto Petrella, "La 'materia' inquieta e le sue trasformazioni: Appunti per una ricerca," in Laura Mattioli Rossi, ed., *Boccioni 1912 Materia*, exh. cat. (Milan: Mazzotta, 1991). For a study on Boccioni's relationship with his mother and with women in general, see Virginia Spate, "Mother and Son: Boccioni's Painting and Sculpture 1906–1915," in Terry Smith, ed., *In Visible Touch: Modernism and Masculinity* (Chicago: University of Chicago Press, 1997). Spate shows notable similarities with my essay in Mattioli Rossi but perhaps too emphatically highlights the pre-Fascist and antifeminine aspects of the Futurist group.

3 For example, the author of the present essay is professor of psychiatry at the Università degli Studi at Pavia and a full member of the Italian Psychoanalytic Society and the International Psychoanalytical Association.

4 See Ernst Kris, *Psychoanalytical Explorations in Art* (New York: International Universities Press, 1952).

5 See D. W. Winnicott, *The Maturational Processes and the Facilitating Environment. Studies in the Theory of Emotional Development* (London: Hogarth Press and Institute of Psycho-Analysis, 1965).

6 Boccioni diary, March 28, 1907, in Birolli (1971), p. 238.

7 Boccioni to Vico Baer, mid-October 1915, and to Guido Callegari, October 22, 1915, in Birolli (1971), p. 381ff.

8 Boccioni diary, July 26, 1907, in Birolli (1971), p. 251.

9 Boccioni diary, Feburary 14, 1908, in Birolli (1971), p. 283.

10 Particularly important passages for understanding Boccioni's position toward women and love can be found in his diaries. Betraying art for women, he felt, clearly meant betraying the mother and losing the whole system of idealizations and support that depended on the idealized mother figure.

11 See Boccioni diary, January 2, 1908, in Birolli (1971), p. 273.

12 Boccioni diary, October 17, 1907, in Birolli (1971), p. 265.

13 Boccioni, *Pittura e scultura futuriste (Dinamismo plastico)*, in Birolli (1971), pp. 90, 89.

14 Ibid., p. 77.

15 In "Symbolism in Dreams," one of his introductory lectures delivered in 1916 and 1917, Freud, referring certainly to an etymological source in his possession, stated, "And, speaking of wood, it is hard to understand how that material came to represent what is maternal and female. But here comparative philology may come to our help. Our German word '*Holz*' seems to come from the same root as the Greek '[hulē]', meaning 'stuff' 'raw material.' This seems to be an instance of the not uncommon event of the general name of a material eventually coming to be reserved for some particular material. Now there is an island in the Atlantic named 'Madeira.' This name was given to it by the Portuguese when they discovered it, because at the time it was covered all over with woods. For in the Portuguese language '*madeira*' means 'wood.' You will notice, however, that *madeira* is only a slightly modified form of the Latin word '*materia*,' which once more means 'material' in general. But '*materia*' is derived from *mater*, 'mother': the material out of which anything is made is, as it were, a mother to it. This ancient view of the thing survives, therefore, in the symbolic use of wood for 'woman' or 'mother.'" Sigmund Freud, "Symbolism in Dreams," in Freud, *Introductory Lectures on Psycho-Analysis (Parts I and II)*, vol. 15 of *Standard Edition of the Psychological Works of Sigmund Freud* (London: Hogarth Press and Institute of Psycho-Analysis, 1968 [1963 ed.]), pp. 159–60. For a striking condensation of *madeira* and the feminine figure, which at this point should be considered a mother, see René Magritte's *Découverte* (1927), at the Musée d'Art Moderne, Brussels; in a disturbing metamorphosis, the heavy veining of wood appears on the white skin of the woman portrayed.

16 See W. R. Bion, "Differentiation of the Psychotic from Non-psychotic Personalities," *International Journal of Psycho-Analysis* 38, no. 266 (1957); also published in Bion, *Second Thoughts: Selected Papers on Psycho-Analysis* (London: Heinemann, 1967).

17 See Boccioni, *Pittura e scultura futuriste*, in Birolli (1971), pp. 173–74.

18 Ibid., p. 126.

19 Ibid., p. 179.

20 Ibid., p. 134.

21 On Herbert Silberer's "functional phenomenon," see Sigmund Freud, *The Interpretation of Dreams*, vols. 4 and 5 of *Standard Edition of the Psychological Works of Sigmund Freud* (London: Hogarth Press, 1953); and Fausto Petrella, "Percezione endopsichica/fenomeno funzionale," *Rivista di psicoanalisi* 39, no. 1 (1993). A particularly pointed example of the conscious game being played with "frame/window/world-in-the-frame" and with the imaginal status of pictorial realism can be found in many famous paintings by Magritte, with different variations on the theme.

22 Boccioni, *Pittura e scultura futuriste*, in Birolli (1971), p. 158.

23 See *The Street Enters the House* and *Simultaneous Visions* (1911, cat. no. 8).

24 See W. R. Bion, *Transformations: Changes from Learning to Growth* (London: Heinemann, 1965).

25 Boccioni to Severini, August 1912, in Birolli (1971), p. 359.

26 Boccioni to Vico Baer, mid-June 1913, in Birolli (1971), p. 369.

27 See Boccioni diary, March 22, 1908, in Birolli (1971), p. 296: "Oh! Ideal, you, you alone exist!"

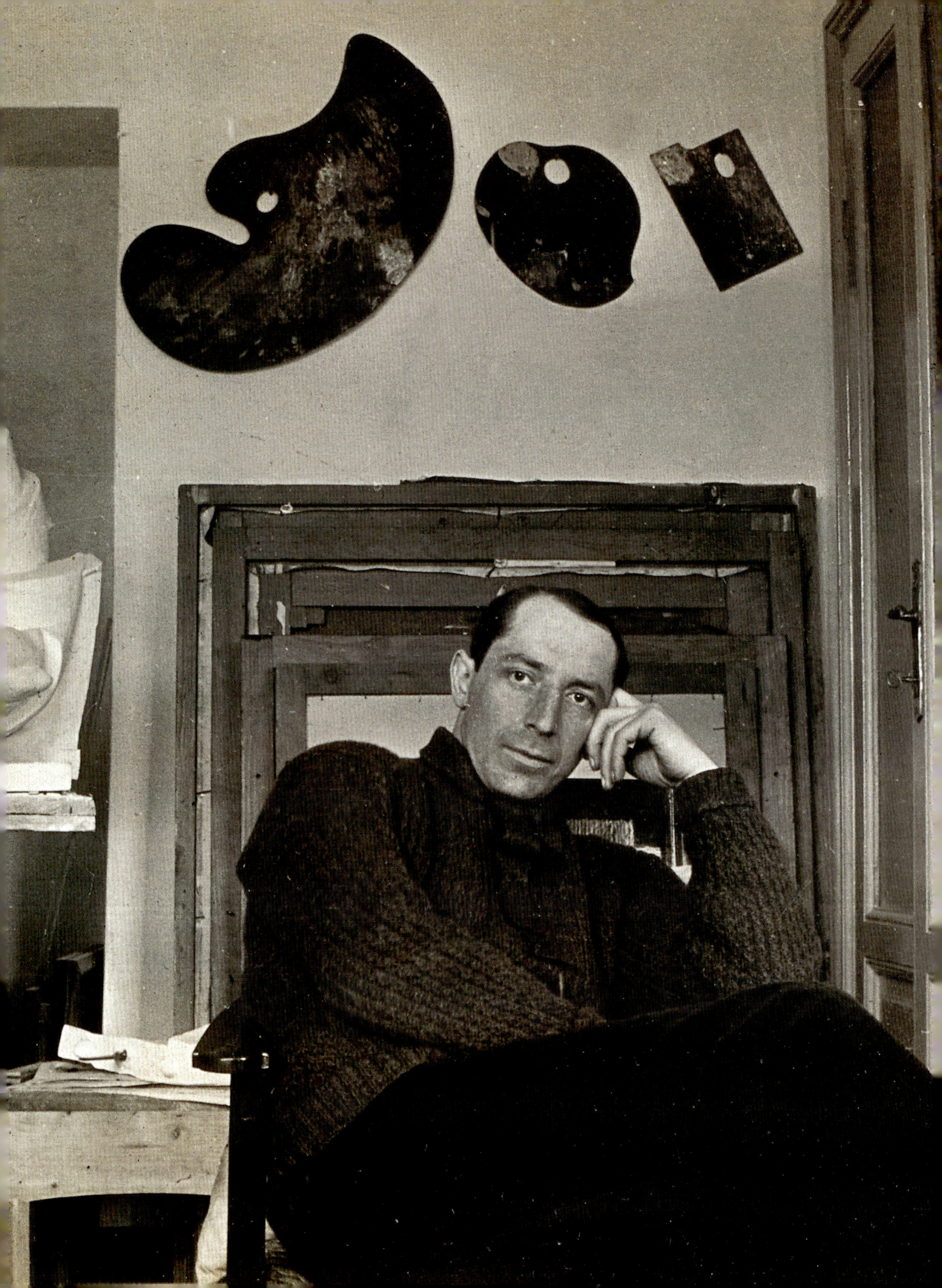

Snapshots from the Studio of Umberto Boccioni

GIOVANNA GINEX

The use of photography by artists after the announcement of the daguerreotype in 1839 has been analyzed by historians in two principal ways: as historical document (including art-historical document) and as a tool of artistic creation.[1] The same approaches hold true for the study of Futurist photography, especially in the most up-to-date scholarship.[2] Recent research into Umberto Boccioni's *Materia* (1912, cat. no. 27) has yielded new opportunities for reconstructing the artist's instrumental use of photography during the critical period when he worked on this painting and the related sculpture *Head + House + Light* (1912, destroyed; fig. 58.12). Until now, there has been no sequence established for Boccioni's studio photographs, most of which have been reproduced only in piecemeal fashion. Gathering the prints scattered about in various collections has been the cornerstone of the first phase of research; with almost all of the originals now located, it has been possible to begin grouping and dating them. The results are significant, for they allow insight not only into Boccioni's working method but also into the deliberate staging of his self image.[3]

Boccioni's Photography as Source and Document

Studies of artists' photographs, a rapidly growing field in the last two decades, have finally called attention to the recovery and conservation of the studio patrimony, that is, of surviving plates, original prints, and anything else related to photographic practice. The analysis of the relationship between photography, painting, and sculpture was often impeded, either by the scarcity of extant photographic materials or by the minimal importance granted them. Until very recently, art historians—the very people who were most likely, in the course of studies, to come across photographs made or used by artists in their work—disregarded the photographs' material importance. Moreover, old cameras, negatives, and original prints were often destroyed by heirs, who usually saved only family photos and sometimes an antique curio such as a plate holder or wooden camera.

Things were no different for Boccioni. The roughly 150 extant prints, which include both vintage and later prints, were found in diverse collections and a generally precarious state of conservation, indicating the carelessness or indifference with which these valuable resources were treated.[4] Of the photographs presented in sequence for the first time in this publication, most were already known but barely acknowledged. No attention had been paid to their technique, the circumstances of their execution, the number of copies from the same negative, their provenance, or even to their correct dating. They were made by the artist or by other technicians, either at his Milan studio/apartment from 1913 until possibly just after his death in 1916 or in the rooms of his exhibition at Galerie La Boëtie in Paris in summer 1913. Not under consideration here are earlier photographs such as portraits and views.

Finally, a technical point, unless otherwise noted, we are dealing with positive photographic prints on paper. Boccioni's originals can be generally subdivided into two rather homogeneous groups: small-format prints—for the most part aristotypes/printing out papers, including some with silver gelatins—characterize the amateur photographs; while the professional, medium-size, made-for-publication images are silver-bromide gelatin prints, many of them sepia-toned.[5] The original negatives have not been found and are probably lost; nevertheless, a comparative analysis of prints (some originating from the same negative) suggests celluloid and not glass negatives.[6]

Facing page
Self-portrait of Umberto Boccioni, March 1913 (detail of fig. 56.3)

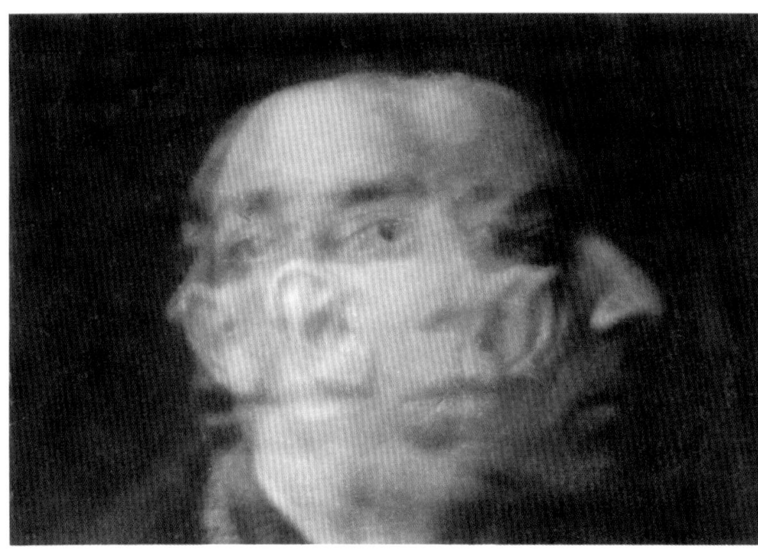

Fig. 49 Anton Giulio Bragaglia
Umberto Boccioni, 1911–12
Photograph, 4 13/16 × 6 11/16 inches (12.3 × 17 cm)
Calmarini Collection, Milan

The relationships between photography and an artist's work are varied and complex. They range from the purely instrumental use of the photographic image as an "objective" means of reproduction or visual documentation more faithful than any sketch from life, to the elaboration of the photograph—including painting over it—as a medium for original experimentation. Different artists turned to mechanical means of reproduction for different ends, and some were inspired to explore the innate qualities of the photographic medium itself. Boccioni was well aware of the possibilities that the camera offered to painting, specifically in the example of Etienne Jules Marey's chronophotography,[7] which was exploited in the work of Giacomo Balla and in the contemporaneous photodynamic experiments of the Bragaglia brothers, for whom Boccioni served as a willing model at least once (fig. 49).[8] Yet in the years just before World War I, Boccioni had a decidedly negative view of photography with regard to its role in fine art. As an amateur photographer, however, he made excellent use of the medium as a playful tool for the performance of the self and the recording of his artistic process. He also understood the critical role of professional photographic images as a means of publicizing himself and his most representative works.[9]

Research conducted in the invaluable archive of the artist's heirs has yielded a photographic document that makes Boccioni's relationship to the medium even more complex, and possibly explains his later, adamant rejection of it as the result of prior artistic experience. A photograph of his sister Amelia, datable between 1904 and 1908, was cropped and painted over in oils by Boccioni with the vibrant colors and long, fibrous strokes typical of his early Divisionist style (fig. 51). The figure's pose and clothing are strikingly close to the depiction of Amelia in the painting *Three Women* (1909–10, fig. 12) as well as in the pastel *Portrait of Sister Reading* (1909, fig. 50). Clearly, Boccioni, like the majority of Italian Divisionists, used photographs early on as sources for painting, especially portraits—a method that he was later loath to accept.

As for the photographs used in the careful diffusion of his own image and reproductions of his works, it must be emphasized that he always used established professionals such as the Milanese photographer Emilio Sommariva.[10] One of the most important figures in Italian photography, Sommariva took portraits of all of the Futurist artists in 1910 and 1911, and was also responsible for the portrait chosen by Boccioni for the frontispiece of his book *Pittura scultura futuriste (Dinamismo plastico)* in 1914 (fig. 52). In 1911, as demonstrated in the original inventories of his photographic studio, Sommariva also took shots of various works by Boccioni, of which only the original plate of *A Drama Teacher (Signora Maffi)* (fig. 53)—a painting that was neither signed nor dated by the artist—has been recovered thus far.[11] Boccioni also posed for another prominent Milanese photographer, Attilio Badodi, who made a portrait datable around 1914 (fig. 54).

In Boccioni's Studio: Spring 1913–Summer 1916

"From the ample windows of Boccioni's new studio, his pure white sculptural groups can clearly be seen from the Bastioni."[12] So wrote F. T. Marinetti of the studio and apartment that the artist first rented around January 1913. Boccioni moved into it definitively as of March that year, after his return from Rome: "I'm a wreck from changing house and studio," the artist wrote to Roberto Papini on April 2.[13] Boccioni left his cramped via Adige quarters, where he had been living since

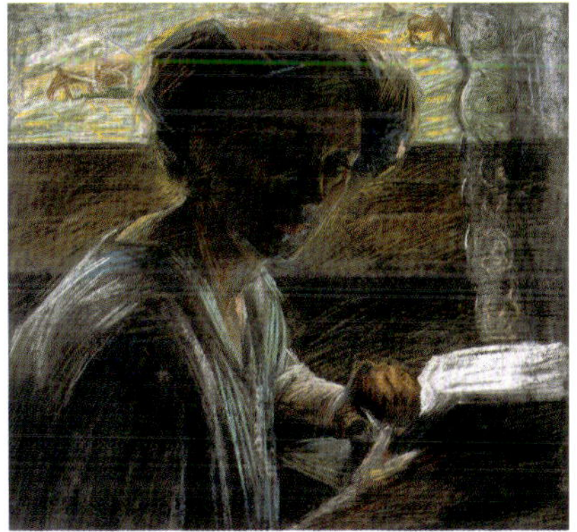

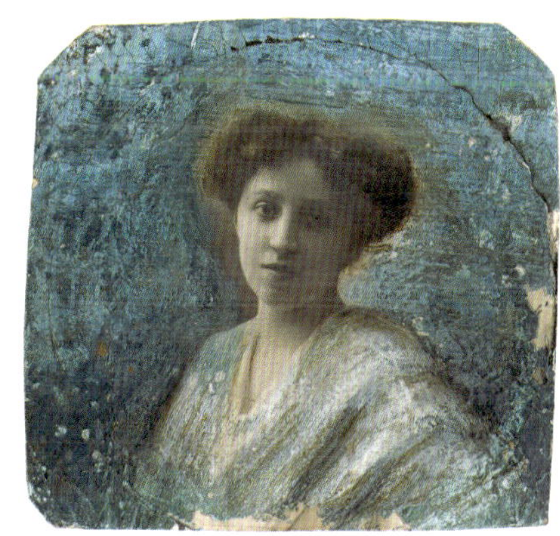

Fig. 50 Umberto Boccioni
Portrait of Sister Reading (Ritratto della sorella che legge), 1909
Pastel on paper, 21¹⁄₁₆ × 22³⁄₄ inches (53.5 × 57.8 cm)
Musei Civici Veneziani, Ca' Pesaro–Galleria Internazionale d'Arte Moderna

Fig. 51 Umberto Boccioni
Amelia Boccioni, 1904–08
Gelatin-silver print, glued on cardboard and painted in oil, 25⁵⁄₈ × 27⁹⁄₁₆ inches (65 × 70 cm)
Private collection

1909, but remained within Milan's southern quarter.[14] The architecture of the new building, Bastioni di Porta Romana 35 (whose street was later divided into the present-day viale Emilio Caldara and viale Regina Margherita, altering the original plan), was similar to the old. It was, in fact, another example of recent housing developments in the city's periphery, where apartments, businesses, and factories were on the rise. The *bastioni* (bastions, or walls, dating back hundreds of years), which divided the center of Milan from the periphery, were increasingly encroached upon by late nineteenth-century projects and the construction of broad boulevards. As part of the new urban plan, the *Regolamento d'igiene* (health regulation) issued in 1902 set guidelines for the facade and height of buildings, the inclusion of green spaces, and the hygienic standards of new apartments, including the one chosen by Boccioni.[15]

The demolition of the ancient city walls, beginning in the early twentieth century and continuing between World Wars I and II, as well as the massive bombardment suffered by Milan in the second war, spared very few of the buildings constructed at the turn of the century. In the short stretch of the former ring wall now called viale Regina Margherita, near the Rotonda di via Besana, only one fragment of the old rampart survives in isolation, and, fortunately, in front of it still stands the building in which Boccioni resided and worked. Never previously identified—undoubtedly because of the confusion created by the change in street names—the building at viale Regina Margherita 9 today corresponds almost exactly to images captured by Boccioni in the summer of 1913.

One bright, sunny day in late July or early August, Boccioni took at least two snapshots of a portion of his building's facade within which can be seen the windows of his new, spacious studio and living quarters (figs. 59.1 and 59.2). If we venture a hypothetical sequence, the artist crossed the street to the bastion and took the closer shot first, from a position almost directly across from the main door. The intention was to capture the image of two of his sculptures seen from the outside and framed by the two windows of his first-floor studio (the two lower levels being considered the ground and basement floors): *Development of a Bottle in Space* (1912) and *Unique Forms of Continuity in Space* (1913).[16] An enthusiastic amateur photographer, Boccioni attempted a shot beyond the technical capabilities of his camera, and especially beyond the possibilities offered by the optics, however versatile, of the portable cameras of the time. Although, in the photographer's mind, the sculptures were indisputably the main subject of the first, closer snapshot, they are barely legible in the print, appearing as light, minuscule shapes framed by the large windows. In the second shot, Boccioni broadened the field by standing farther back from the building but on the same axis with respect to the main entrance. The same view exists today, except that the building in Boccioni's images seems to sink lower (one sees the head and shoulders of a passerby at the height of the basement windows). The street was in fact elevated and later demolished in the lowering of the roadbed; hence, in Boccioni's photographs, the large windows of the basement appear lower than they actually are. The first-floor windows remain identical to what Boccioni saw through the lens: French windows, with railings adorned by a simple cast-iron decorative motif and wooden panels framing the upper sections.

Of the seven spacious windows corresponding to the rooms rented by the artist, six are captured in the second photograph. There is also a window on the right-hand side of the building, which may or may not have been

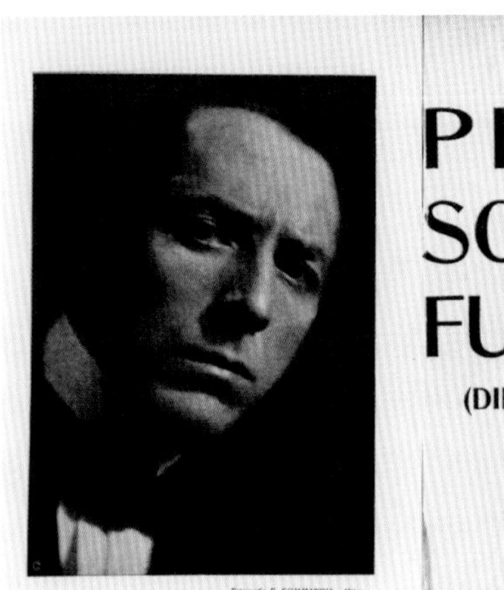

BOCCIONI
FUTURISTA

PITTURA
SCULTURA
FUTURISTE

(DINAMISMO PLASTICO)

CON 51 RIPRODUZIONI
QUADRI SCULTURE
DI BOCCIONI - CARRÀ
RUSSOLO - BALLA
SEVERINI - SOFFICI

EDIZIONI FUTURISTE
DI "POESIA"
MILANO - CORSO VENEZIA, 61

Fig. 52 Emilio Sommariva
Umberto Boccioni, ca. 1914; frontispiece in Boccioni, *Pittura scultura futuriste (Dinamismo plastico)* (Milan: Edizioni Futuriste di "Poesia," 1914)
Shown with facing title page.
Private collection

part of the original configuration of Boccioni's apartment, though it is certainly original to the complex. This side opens onto an old park, now partially occupied by the pavilions of the Policlinico, and the nearby Rotonda di via Besana. Whether or not Boccioni's space included this side window, the seven on the front assured exceptional morning and early afternoon light. Nor was there at any time any other structure blocking the sun; even the *bastioni* were too distant to cast a shadow on the facade. No wonder Boccioni was thrilled about his new space. Light was central to his experiments in spatial and volumetric interpenetration, and now he was able to try his hand at large-scale works, which would have been impossible in the cramped quarters on via Adige.

"The splendid apartment I rented before leaving fills me with hope for a year of *materially* greater work," Boccioni wrote from Rome to Vico Baer in February 1913.[17] He was undoubtedly taken by the large main room articulated by three of the sunlit windows, which he equipped as his studio. The workspace was separated from the other rooms by a corridor, accessible through two adjacent doors. As soon as he moved in, he immediately measured up the space with the camera's mechanical eye, exploring and registering his new surroundings with himself at the center, in time shaping it into an ideal configuration for creation, recreation, and family gatherings.

Boccioni set up the camera on a medium-height base near the middle of the studio room, beginning an identifiable sequence of seven original photographs that includes self-portraits taken by setting the automatic shutter release.[18] First is the image of the nearly empty studio, with the lens pointed toward the wall bordering the other rooms (fig. 56.1). This is followed by a self-portrait of Boccioni leaning against the wall, between the far door and stacks of various paintings and stretchers (fig. 56.2); two drawings of human dynamism are affixed to a stretcher, embodying some preliminary ideas for large sculptures.[19] He moved the camera closer and took three more self-portraits in mirrored poses—one of these unknown until now, in which the artist smiles in amusement—where he framed himself between the other door and *Head + House + Light*, which has a rectangular niche behind it (figs. 56.3–.5).[20] Next is the same plaster sculpture surrounded by the niche, an arrangement of anthurium and roses, canvases, and easels (fig. 56.6). Another self-portrait shows the artist in the act of sculpting and ends the session (fig. 56.7).

The narcissistic, if playful, self-staging can be interpreted in several ways. For our purposes, it is useful to consider the series as a deliberate set of clues left behind by the artist as to his life and work. Together the photographs allow us to reconstruct for the first time the floor plan and elevation of the studio where Boccioni produced all his works from 1913 until his death, and in particular where he completed *Materia* and either refinished or created the greater part of his sculptures. For the sake of identifying every angle of the studio, we must also consider shots that show the other end wall of the studio, which has a sofa flanked by two sets of shelves. The functional furnishings of the apartment, red in color, were designed by Boccioni himself.[21] Centered along the wall, the large sofa is covered by an oriental rug and pillows. In one photograph, a fur stole and the leather case of the artist's portable camera can be seen on the sofa (fig. 56.8).

A tentative chronology for Boccioni's paintings and sculptures can be gleaned already from the first image in the series (fig. 56.1). Against the end wall and close to the window, one can discern the modeling clay and supports that will soon give birth to large masculine figures in motion. On the shelves lie spatulas and other sculpting tools as well as two clay models that would be lost along with most of Boccioni's sculptural production. On a lower shelf in the left foreground, we can recognize the clay maquette for *Head + House + Light* and, next to it, a clay model bearing the approximate height and dimensions of *Empty and Full Abstracts of a Head* (for finished sculpture, subsequently destroyed, see fig. 37). The plaster version of *Head + House + Light*, still unvarnished, can be glimpsed at the upper left.

The sofa at the opposite end wall is the starting point for a large series of photographs from later in spring 1913 (figs. 57.1–.14), which includes several shots of Boccioni's mother Cecilia sitting there amid numerous drawings, such as *Muscles in Speed* (1913) on the right, and behind her, on the left, *Dynamic Decomposition* (1913).[22] A man's hat and raincoat and an umbrella are also strewn on the sofa. A piece of embroidery is draped on the arm of a chair on the right; an illegible detail, possibly one of the large sculptures, appears in the far upper right, near the wooden shelving unit that matches the one on the left (fig. 57.1). The sequence continues with Boccioni's mother seated in one of the nearby chairs and embroidering in an atmosphere of silence (figs. 57.2–.4). The new angle, with the camera pointed at the wall opposite the windows, reveals palettes arranged on the wall, portfolios, paints, and equipment, as well as an easel bearing a drawing made after *Empty and Full Abstracts of a Head* (1913, cat. no. 35).[23]

The mother then stands up (fig. 57.5), and Boccioni moves the camera in a straight line toward the other end of the room, to the area just before the two doors, leaving it aimed at the same wall in almost the same position as several months earlier (figs. 56.3–.7). He stages a scene—no longer silent but very animated—around the plaster model of *Spiral Expansion of Muscles in Motion* (1913, destroyed; fig. 38) and sets the automatic shutter release to take shots of the artist in work-smock with his mother and Balla and then joined by a plasterer and his young apprentice, who assisted in the execution of the large models (figs. 57.6–.8). Next we see Boccioni alone (fig. 57.9), at the feet of *Spiral Expansion of Muscles in Motion*, very smartly dressed in coat and tie, the inevitable cigarette between his fingers, and, at the far left, a detail of *Muscles in Speed* (1913, destroyed; fig. 39), a work in progress. The chronology of the sculptures, evidenced in the photographs, is further confirmed by Marinetti's eyewitness accounts: "In Boccioni's studio loom great muscles in speed, and especially polymaterial speeds, with the appearance of the first sculptures that solidify space, shadow, and light."[24]

The camera is then moved past the two doors to the farthest end of the room, and the sequence continues with quick, consecutive snapshots with a large sculpture as their fulcrum. Balla, Boccioni, his mother, and the two assistants move around the plaster model of *Synthesis of Human Dynamism* (1912, destroyed; fig. 36) while a large portion of *Spiral Expansion of Muscles in Motion* appears at the left (figs. 57.10–.12). A slight shift of the camera to the right gives us Boccioni posing alone with *Synthesis of Human Dynamism* (fig. 57.13), with an already finished *Antigrazioso* (1912–13, cat. no. 31) partially visible at the far right, and a shot of the sculpture by itself (fig. 57.14). In the wooden shelving in the background, on the left of the top shelf, is clearly visible the small plaster model, not yet painted red, of *Development of a Bottle by Means of Color* (1912), yet another of Boccioni's lost sculptures (figs. 57.11–.14).

Pictures at an Exhibition

From June 20 to July 16, 1913, Galerie La Boëtie in Paris mounted an exhibition of Boccioni's sculptures and drawings. It was the artist's second show in the French capital, after the Futurist group exhibition held the year before at Galerie Bernheim-Jeune.[25] The deadline propelled him to work furiously, producing several large plaster sculptures of the human figure in motion. From October 10 to October 30, 1912, Galerie La Boëtie had hosted the exhibition of the Salon de la Section d'Or, which brought together for the first time works by such artists as Robert Delaunay, Marcel Duchamp, Juan Gris, Marie Laurencin, Fernand Léger, Francis Picabia, and Jacques Villon, among others. The show triggered a critical firestorm but enjoyed such success that it was replicated in other cities in the years that followed. Boccioni possibly visited the Section d'Or—his visit to the contemporaneous Salon d'Automne is well documented—with his own forthcoming exhibition in mind and fully aware of the favorable opportunity created by the association of his show with the preceding one.

"To Umberto Boccioni / Souvenir of his / photographer / Lucette Korsoff." This handwritten dedication (fig. 55) most likely appeared at the front of a small album of thirteen photographs documenting Boccioni's Galerie La Boëtie exhibition (figs. 58.1–.13).[26] These images and his own snapshots were kept by Boccioni among his personal papers. Lucette Korsoff, who took the photographs, including some automatic shutter-release shots, was a Russian opera singer of international renown, who was in Paris to perform in Gaetano Donizetti's *Lucia di Lammermoor*.[27] The photographs provide precious documentation of the installation, including images of lost sculptures from various angles. A left-hand view (figs. 58.1–.3) of the already varnished *Head + House + Light* is documented

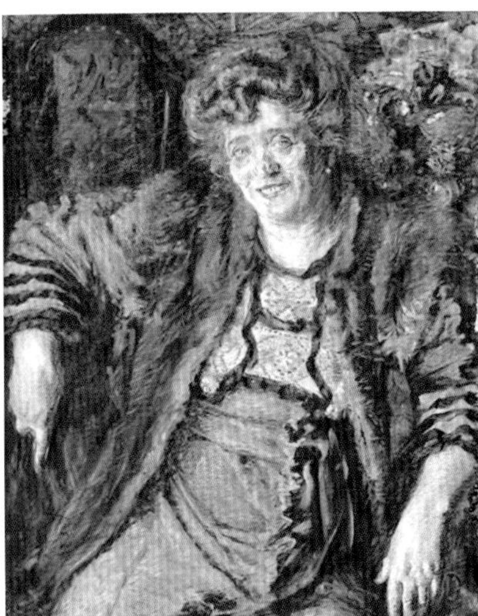

Fig. 53 Emilio Sommariva
Umberto Boccioni's *A Drama Teacher (Signora Maffi)*, 1911
Modern print from glass-plate negative, 9⁷⁄₁₆ x 7¹⁄₁₆ inches (24 x 18 cm)
Biblioteca Nazionale Braidense, Milan

as is a right-hand view (figs. 58.6 and 58.7) of *Fusion of a Head and a Window* (1912–13, destroyed; fig. 58.11) that reveals a previously undocumented profile created out of colored iron wire.

In addition to photographs of two unidentified people and other images of the gallery,[28] Korsoff must also have taken the extant close-up shots of the individual sculptures: an analysis of the background of the original prints reveals the unmistakable damasked wallpaper that lined the walls of the Parisian gallery. Some of these images also capture the small metal labels, inscribed in red, with the words "BOCCIONI / FUTURISTA," leaning against the sculptures (figs. 58.8, 58.11, and 58.13).[29] The photographs of *Force-Forms of a Bottle* show the mark where the sculpture broke in transit, an unfortunate story familiar to Boccioni scholars (figs. 58.8 and 58.9). Korsoff's original print documenting *Head + House + Light* clearly displays the stenciled words Boccioni had placed on different areas of the plaster (fig. 58.12). Over the years, all of these images have been manipulated and retouched from reproduction to reproduction, to the point of canceling out essential details, the date and context of their making, and the photographer. Only for *Force-Forms of a Bottle* did Boccioni himself have the photograph retouched in order to preserve the image of the destroyed work for posterity. He subsequently had medium-format professional photographs taken of the other plasters—executed by an unidentified photographer. These were done after the exhibition closed, while the works were held in Paris for a few months at the Sagot art storehouse, waiting to be shipped to the next venue (figs. 36–42).[30]

Materia and After

Between mid-July and September 1913, Boccioni was back in Milan, in his large, bright studio now stripped of sculptures (which were still in Paris) but packed with paintings, stacked by the dozens. Among these was *Materia*, which had just returned from the Futurist exhibition in Rotterdam. In preparation for definitive changes to the lower section,[31] Boccioni set up the large canvas in bright sunlight, leaning it against the long wall across from the windows; the painting almost blocks out the niche that appears behind *Head + House + Light* in the earlier series of studio photographs. Once again he staged a performance for the camera: with the lens pointed toward the sofa, he photographed himself sitting between the pillows (fig. 59.3), then moved down the length of the room and turned the lens toward the wall against which *Materia* stood majestically, ending with self-portraits in front of the almost finished work. There are four extant versions of theatrical poses that show the artist sitting and standing,[32] with and without his palette, and looking into the camera either smiling or pensive (figs. 59.4–.7). Here again the photographic images also read as significant chronological documents. Of the sketches, studies, and paintings that find their way into the frames of Boccioni's poses with *Materia* some appear unfinished, while others have since been lost.

There was scant photographic activity for many months. Boccioni fell ill, was arrested and taken to San Vittore prison for his involvement in an Interventionist demonstration, and suffered from depression, which he attempted to alleviate by enlisting in the army as a volunteer.[33] Three photographs, whose sequence is reconstructed for the first time here, were taken by the artist between spring 1914 and July 1915, before he went off to the front, and begin with his sister Amelia sitting alone in the studio near a stove (figs. 60.1–.3). Although some photographs are certainly missing, one can recognize the

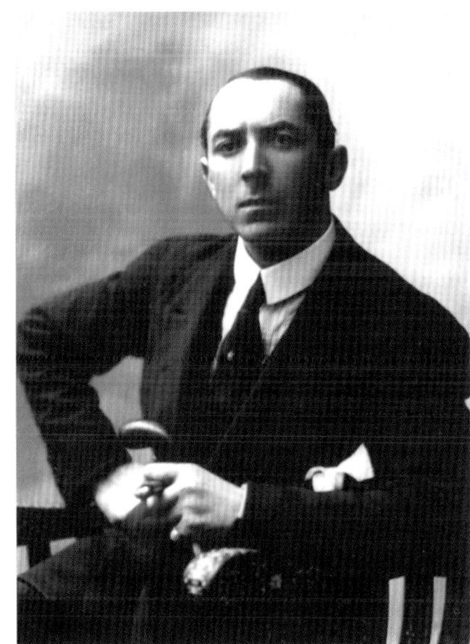

Fig. 54 Attilio Badodi
Umberto Boccioni, ca. 1914
Gelatin-silver print, 9¼ × 6¹⁵⁄₁₆ inches (23.5 × 17.7 cm)
Calmarini Collection, Milan

artist's typical arrangement and framing of the scene in two of them, in which the sculpture *Dynamism of a Speeding Horse + Houses* (1914–15),[34] at the center of the frame, is propped up alone on a small set of shelves in the corner of the studio habitually used for making sculpture (figs. 60.2 and 60.3).[35] The "actors" in the three extant photographs are Boccioni's mother and Amelia.

Between November 1915 and January 1916, Boccioni returned several times from the front, including some lengthy furloughs. During one of these visits, he staged another photo session (figs. 60.4–.9), this time featuring the sculpture *Synthesis of Human Dynamism*, which had been the protagonist once before in the second part of the sequence that included Balla (figs. 57.10–.14). Here Boccioni is in uniform, his facial expression melancholic. Even the studio furnishings have changed: the right-hand area with the niche, previously the preferred location for photographing, has a table in front of it and the stove to the right. The camera's position for shooting the automatic shutter-release frames has therefore shifted. The extant shots are less careful in their execution than Boccioni's previous standards. The image is partly blurred, and the framing off center. For some reason—probably the rearrangement of the furniture—his usual photographic session and self-portraits were rendered more difficult.

The artist's paternal aunt Colomba Boccioni Procida appears on the far right, seemingly by accident, in two of the uniformed self-portraits (figs. 60.5 and 60.6). Boccioni then deliberately included her in the automatic shutter-release shots that close the session. In these we see the artist posing with his mother, sister, and aunt in front of one of the doors to the studio (figs. 60.7–.9). The atmosphere is one of farewells; the hatbox, umbrella, and other articles of clothing near the door appear ready for the imminent departure.[36]

The last series of photographs, partially reconstructed here, is somber, even elegiac in mood (figs. 60.10–.13). Because the landscapes Boccioni painted at Pallanza between June and August 1916 are present, the photographs were taken some time after the summer but no later than December when these works were included in the posthumous Boccioni retrospective organized by Marinetti at Milan's Galleria Centrale d'Arte in Palazzo Cova—after which the plasters and certain paintings never made it back to the artist's studio.[37]

The subjects and framing are different in these images, especially in the photo of Boccioni's studio, now taken from an unusual, fuller angle, facing toward the end of the room with the sofa (fig. 60.10).[38] In the background one can see the poster for the July 1913 show at Galerie La Boëtie; in the foreground, right of center, is the plaster model of *Synthesis of Human Dynamism*, secured with cords to the ceiling, in the same position it has in the self-portraits (figs. 60.4–.6). To the left stands *Spiral Expansion of Muscles*. The sculptures are surrounded by various paintings turned to face the camera, including *Spiral Construction* (1913–14),[39] on the easel to the right, with one of the landscapes executed at Pallanza just below it and another on the easel to the left. The large plaster sculptures, the easels, and the paintings are adorned with wilted flowers generously strewn about, as if in remembrance.

The other photographs take us around the apartment, passing through the two doors, a threshold not previously crossed. Boccioni's bedroom, in perfect order, is shot from two different angles, to take in both sides of the room (figs. 60.12–.13).[40] One sees the furniture designed by the artist, as well as drawings, paintings, and sculptures. The large

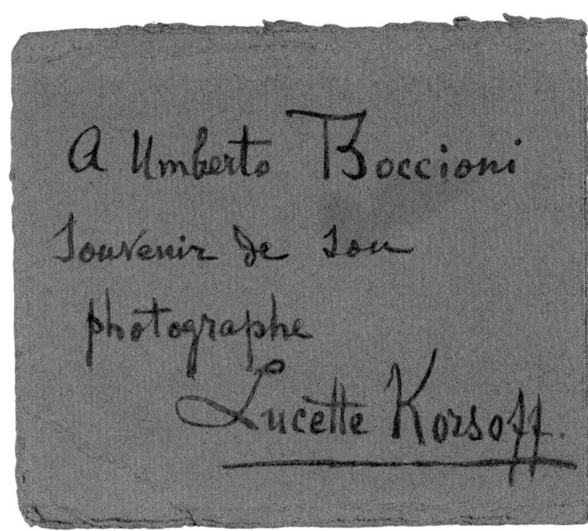

Fig. 55 Page from photo album, inscribed by Lucette Korsoff to Umberto Boccioni, 1913
Ink on cardboard
Private collection

mirror to the left of the bed at first may be mistaken for an open doorway (fig. 60.13).[41] Both rooms are empty of people. These last, poignant images—by a photographer unknown—are clearly in tribute to the artist, who died at the front on August 17, 1916.

In 1911, Marcel Duchamp painted *Dulcinée* (which depicts five silhouettes of the same woman), which Boccioni saw in Paris. That same year, the Bragaglia brothers started their first photodynamic experiments. These images were included in the 1913 theoretical manifesto by Bragaglia entitled "Futurist Photodynamism." This explicit reference to the Futurist movement, however, infuriated Boccioni, who angrily vetoed Bragaglia's admission to the group after the text was published.[42]

Yet already for many years, certain techniques—including those of Marey's chronophotographs—had made it possible to capture instantaneous images of motion in a single image, producing photographs that visually achieved what Boccioni and the Futurists had sought in their "Futurist Painting: Technical Manifesto" of 1910: "moving objects constantly multiply themselves: their form changes like rapid vibrations. . . . Thus a running horse has not four legs, but twenty."[43] Boccioni, however, refused to make room for photography in his mature artistic work, since he considered it an inadequate analytic tool. In this respect, his attitude was paradoxically passéist, being based on an unstated primacy of the "fine" arts over the new medium, at a time when photography was beginning to demonstrate, through avant-garde experiments, its ability to constitute a legitimate art with its own, specific language. The arguments made by Boccioni against photography as art may also seem contrary to his own artistic practice, especially when considered in the light of his bold mixed-media experiments in sculpture. Yet, in point of fact, Boccioni remained profoundly classical even in the most daring of his sculptural and painterly endeavors—*Materia* being the finest example of this. He did not accept mechanical reproduction as part of his own creative vision of reformulating the real. Instead, he thought the photographic medium (wrongly, we can say today) to be a crude mirror of reality.

Boccioni was a decent amateur photographer who recorded himself and his workspace, as well as the people dear to him, as a satisfying pastime. He carefully saved the unsteady snapshots made by friends at his major shows, but he hired established professionals who conformed to the tastes of the elite public when it came to the official circulation of his own image and works. It was left to Marinetti to reconsider the role and function of Futurist photography among the arts of the twentieth century. Yet, in "Manifesto of Futurist Photography," which he signed with Tato in 1930, his professed goals sounded inevitably like an epitaph: "All of these activities aim to make the science of photography cross the boundary into pure art, and, likewise, to favor its development in the fields of physics, chemistry, and war."[44]

Translated from the Italian by Stephen Sartarelli.

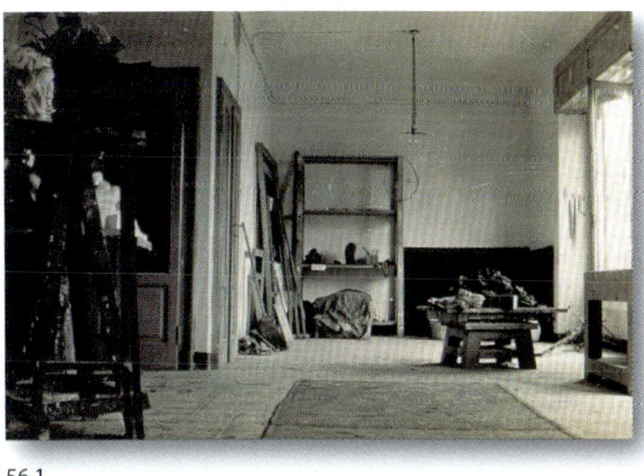

56.1

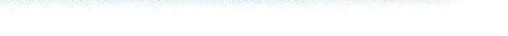

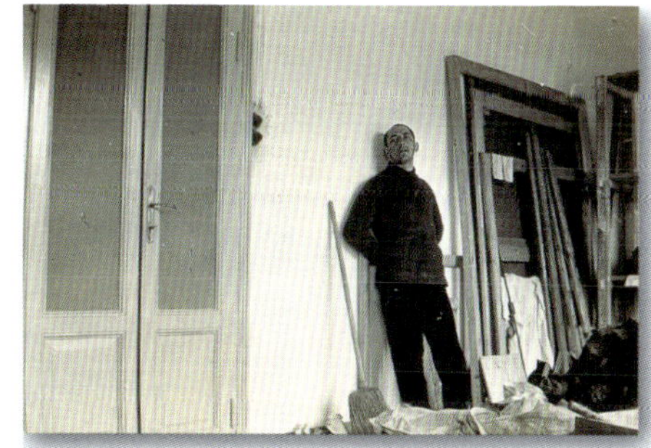

56.2

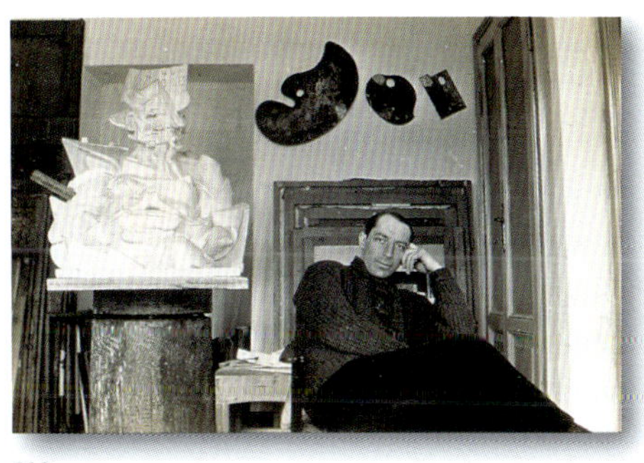

56.3

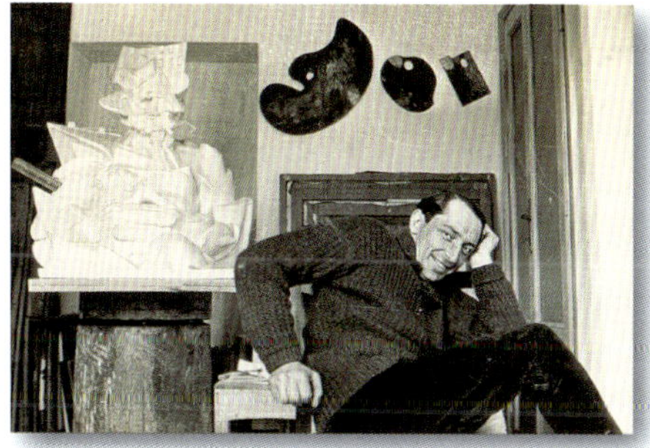

56.4

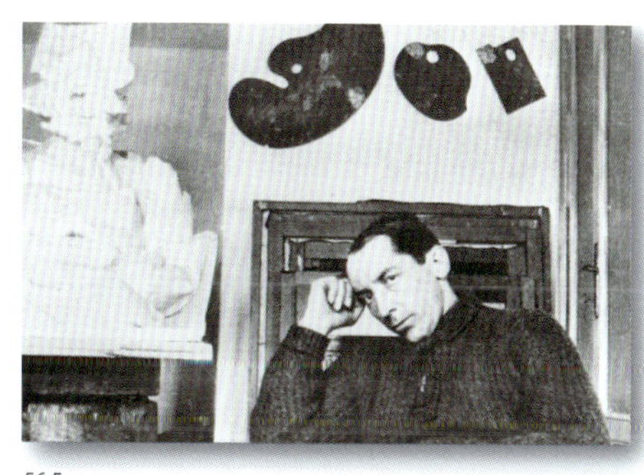

56.5

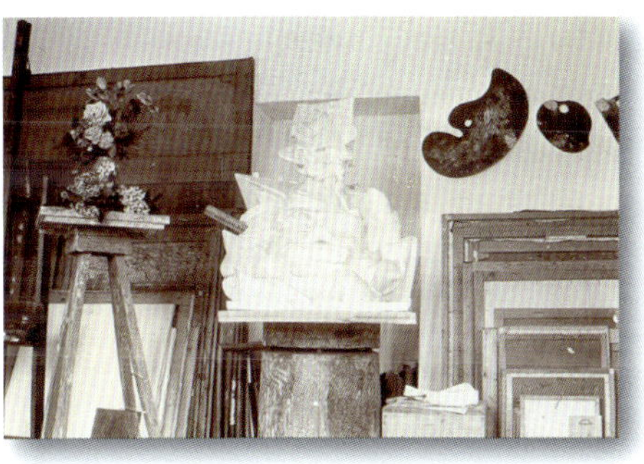

56.6

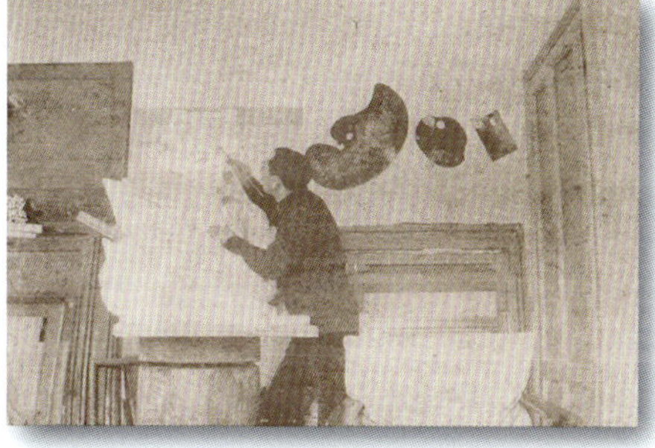

56.7

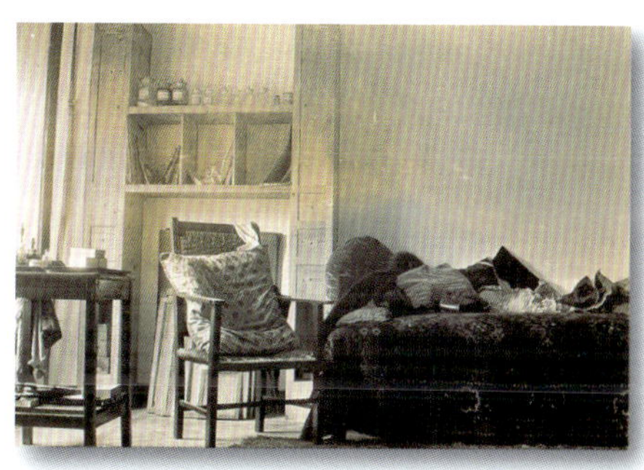

56.8

Figs. 56.1–.8. Photographs by Umberto Boccioni of his studio at Bastioni di Porta Romana 35 (now viale Regina Margherita 9), Milan, 1913

Fig. 56.1 Umberto Boccioni
On far left, plaster model of *Head + House + Light* with floral arrangement alongside; on shelves in background, to left of second shelf, two sculptural studies, March 1913
Gelatin-silver print, $2\frac{3}{8} \times 3\frac{3}{8}$ inches (6 × 8.5 cm)
On back: in pencil, "88"
Private collection
Another original print is in Calmarini Collection, Milan.

Fig. 56.2 Umberto Boccioni
Self-portrait; on right, affixed to stretcher with tacks, two drawings of figures in motion, March 1913
Gelatin-silver print, $2\frac{3}{8} \times 3\frac{3}{8}$ inches (6 × 8.5 cm)
On back: in pencil, "88"; in ballpoint pen, "27"
Private collection

Fig. 56.3 Umberto Boccioni
Self-portrait, seated (turned toward door) next to plaster model of *Head + House + Light*, March 1913
Gelatin-silver print, $2\frac{3}{8} \times 3\frac{3}{8}$ inches (6 × 8.5 cm)
Calmarini Collection, Milan

Fig. 56.4 Umberto Boccioni
Self-portrait, seated and smiling (turned toward door) next to plaster model of *Head + House + Light*, March/April 1913
Gelatin-silver print, $5\frac{11}{16} \times 7\frac{11}{16}$ inches (14.5 × 19.5 cm)
Private collection
Print is enlargement realized a few decades after the shot.

Fig. 56.5 Umberto Boccioni
Self-portrait, seated (back to door) next to plaster model of *Head + House + Light*, March 1913
Modern print
Archivio Pollini, Milan
Print is probably an enlargement of central part of a lost original. This would explain difference of proportions despite fact that framing is same as in related self-portraits (figs. 56.3 and 56.4).

Fig. 56.6 Umberto Boccioni
Plaster model of *Head + House + Light* with floral arrangement alongside, March 1913
Aristotypo, $2\frac{9}{16} \times 3\frac{9}{16}$ inches (6.5 × 9 cm)
Private collection

Fig. 56.7 Umberto Boccioni
Self-portrait, while working on plaster model of *Head + House + Light*, March 1913
Modern print
Private collection
The original has not been found.

Fig. 56.8 Umberto Boccioni
Furnishings at one end of studio, 1913
Gelatin-silver print, $2\frac{3}{8} \times 3\frac{3}{8}$ inches (6 × 8.5 cm)
On back: in pencil, "29"
Private collection

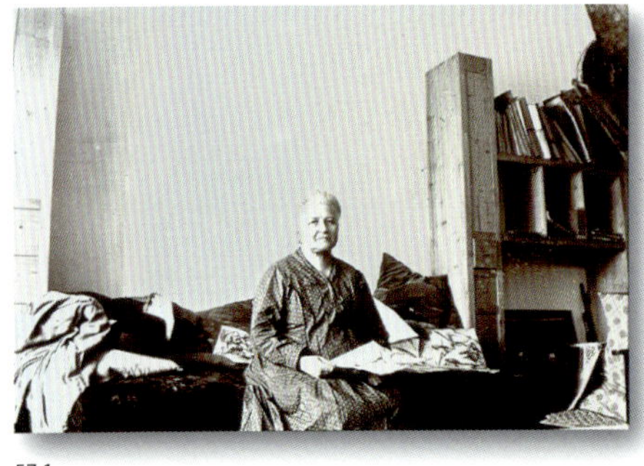

57.1

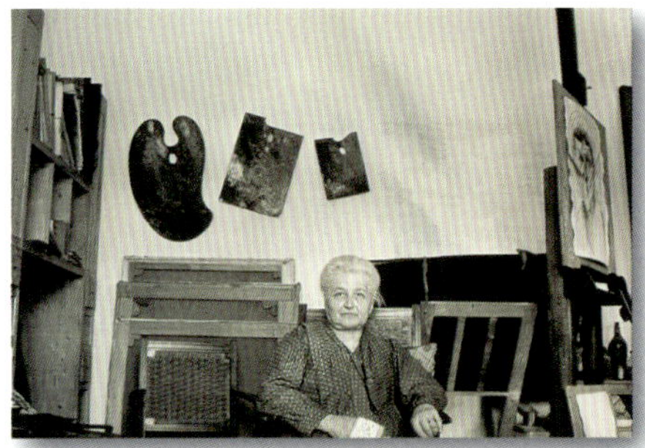

57.2

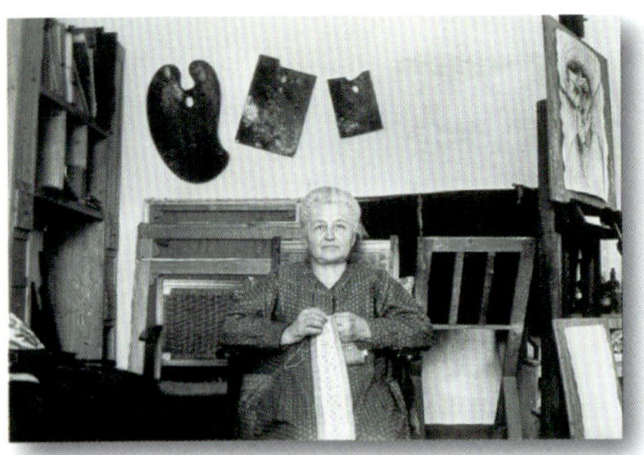

57.3

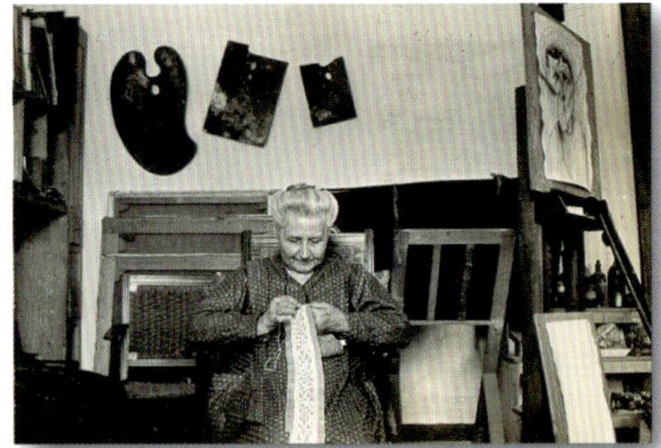

57.4

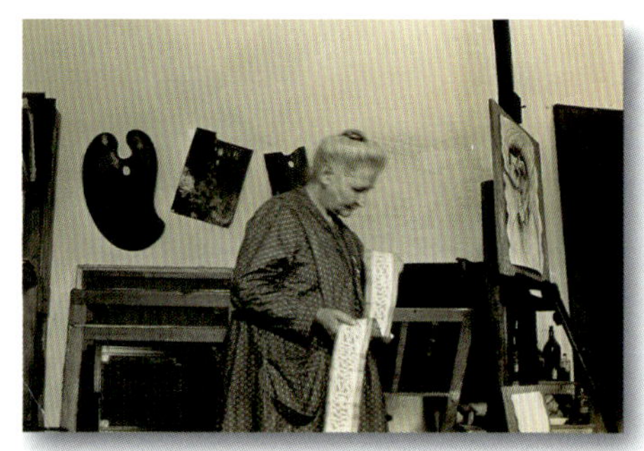

57.5

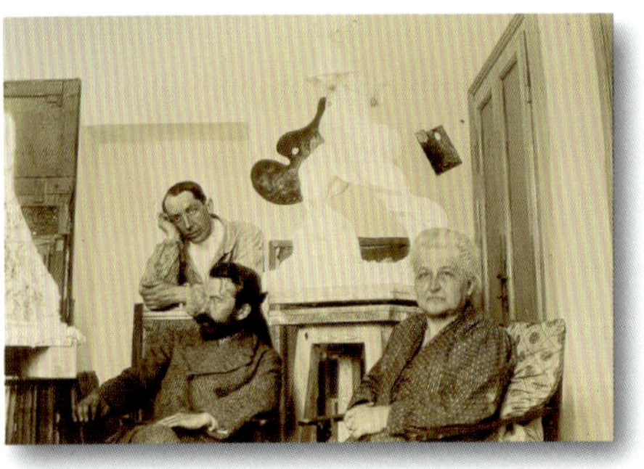

57.6

57.7

57.8

Figs. 57.1–.14. Photographs by Umberto Boccioni of his studio at Bastioni di Porta Romana 35 (now viale Regina Margherita 9), Milan, 1913

Fig. 57.1 Umberto Boccioni
Artist's mother Cecilia seated on sofa covered by rug; next to her, on right, the drawing *Muscles in Speed*; and behind her, on left, the drawing *Dynamic Decomposition*, April 12–May, 1913
Aristotype, $2\frac{5}{8} \times 3\frac{9}{16}$ inches (6.6 × 9.1 cm)
On back: in pencil, "mother"
Private collection

Fig. 57.2 Umberto Boccioni
Artist's mother Cecilia, having moved from sofa to chair, takes up embroidery and looks at camera; on right, on easel, is the drawing *Empty and Full Abstracts of a Head*, April 12–May, 1913
Gelatin-silver print, $2\frac{3}{8} \times 3\frac{7}{16}$ inches (6 × 8.7 cm)
On back: in pencil, "28"; in ballpoint pen, "13"
Private collection

Fig. 57.3 Umberto Boccioni
Artist's mother Cecilia, with embroidery in hand, looks at camera; on right, on easel, is the drawing *Empty and Full Abstracts of a Head*, April 12–May, 1913
Gelatin-silver print, $2\frac{1}{2} \times 3\frac{1}{4}$ inches (6.4 × 8.3 cm)
Research Library, The Getty Research Institute, Los Angeles (880380)

Fig. 57.4 Umberto Boccioni
Artist's mother Cecilia, while embroidering; on right, on easel, is the drawing *Empty and Full Abstracts of a Head*, April 12–May, 1913
Gelatin-silver print, $2\frac{7}{16} \times 3\frac{7}{16}$ inches (6.2 × 8.7 cm)
On back: in pencil, "28"
Private collection

Fig. 57.5 Umberto Boccioni
Artist's mother Cecilia stands up with embroidery in her hands; on right, on easel, is the drawing *Empty and Full Abstracts of a Head*, April 12–May, 1913
Gelatin-silver print, $2\frac{3}{8} \times 3\frac{7}{16}$ inches (6.1 × 8.7 cm)
On back: in pencil, "28"
Private collection

Fig. 57.6 Umberto Boccioni
Giacomo Balla and Boccioni's mother Cecilia seated, with Boccioni standing and resting his arms on back of Balla's chair; at center, plaster model of *Spiral Expansion of Muscles in Motion*, April 12–May, 1913
Aristotype, $2\frac{3}{8} \times 3\frac{9}{16}$ inches (6 × 9 cm)
On back: in ballpoint pen, "15"
Private collection

Fig. 57.7 Umberto Boccioni
Giacomo Balla and Boccioni's mother Cecilia seated; at center, Boccioni posing with plaster model of *Spiral Expansion of Muscles in Motion*, April 12–May, 1913
Aristotype, $2\frac{5}{8} \times 3\frac{9}{16}$ inches (6.6 × 9.1 cm)
Private collection

Fig. 57.8 Umberto Boccioni
Giacomo Balla and Boccioni's mother Cecilia seated; in background, Boccioni and two assistants posing with plaster model of *Spiral Expansion of Muscles in Motion*, April 12-May, 1913
Gelatin-silver print, $2\frac{1}{2} \times 3\frac{7}{16}$ inches (6.3 × 8.8 cm)
Private collection
Another original print is in Calmarini Collection, Milan.

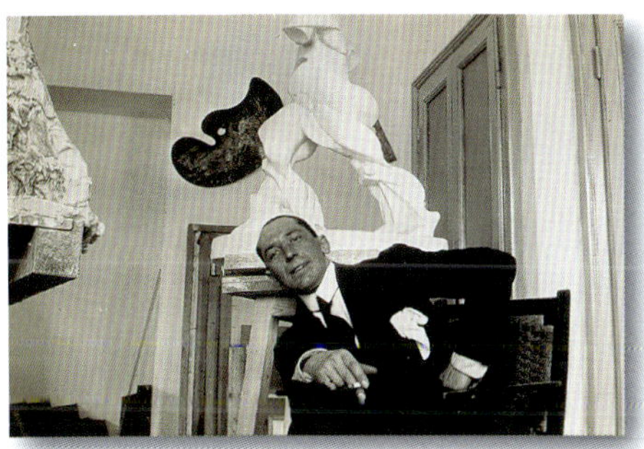

57.9

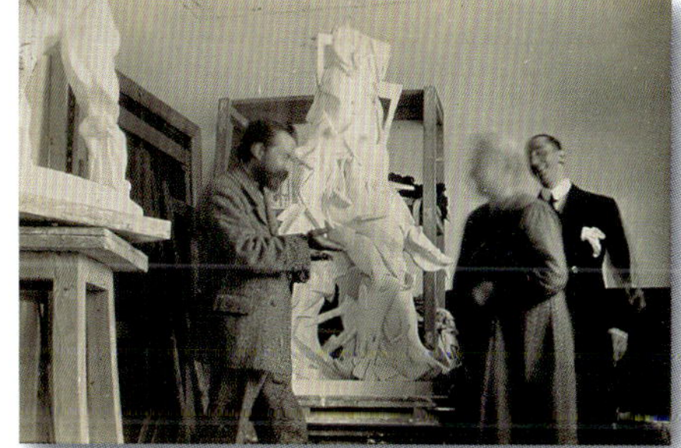

57.10

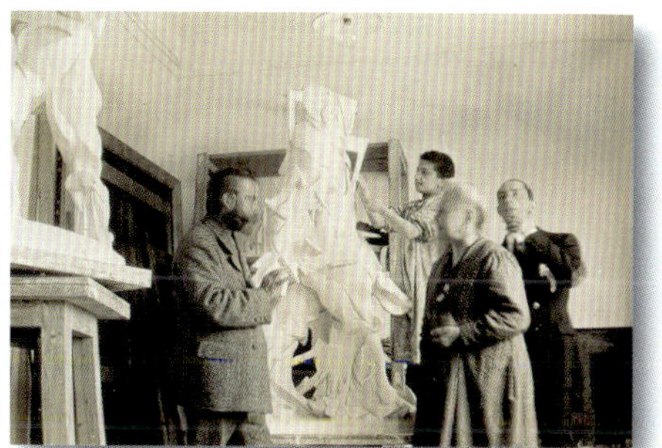

57.11

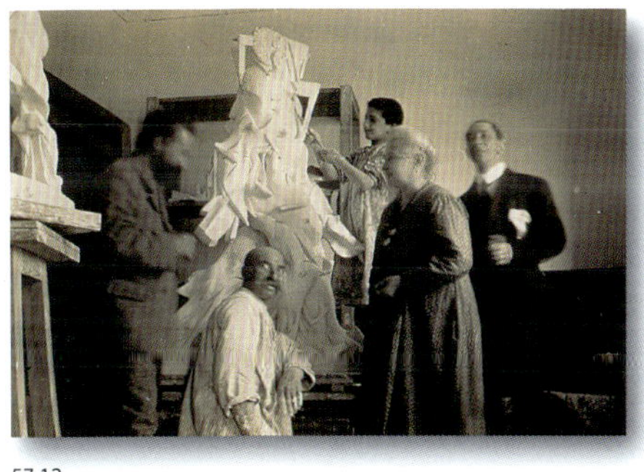

57.12

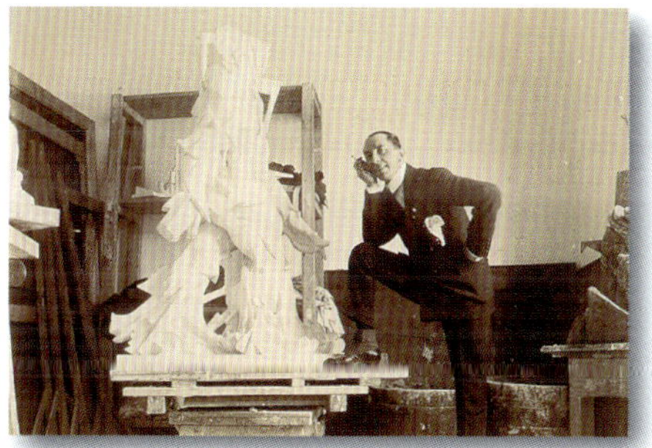

57.13

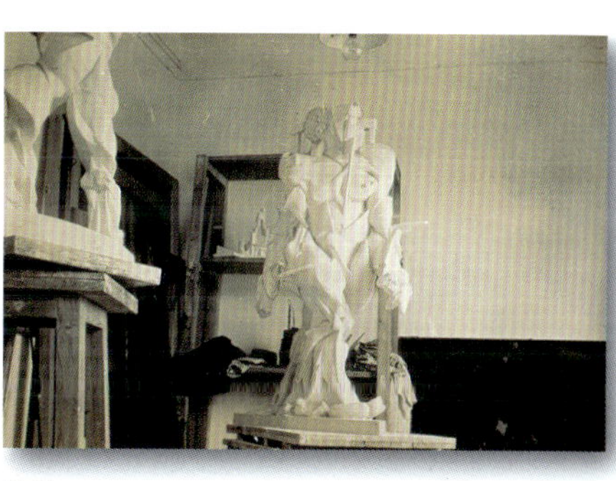

57.14

Fig. 57.9 Umberto Boccioni
Self-portrait, seated in front of plaster model of *Spiral Expansion of Muscles in Motion*, April 12 – May, 1913
Gelatin-silver print, $2\frac{7}{16} \times 3\frac{3}{8}$ inches (6.2 × 8.5 cm)
On back: in pencil, "28"
Private collection

Fig. 57.10 Umberto Boccioni
Giacomo Balla, Boccioni's mother Cecilia, and Boccioni standing around plaster model of *Synthesis of Human Dynamism*; on left, plaster model of *Spiral Expansion of Muscles in Motion*, April 12 – May, 1913
Gelatin-silver print, $2\frac{1}{2} \times 3\frac{7}{16}$ inches (6.3 × 8.8 cm)
Private collection

Fig. 57.11 Umberto Boccioni
Giacomo Balla, Boccioni's mother Cecilia, and Boccioni standing around plaster model of *Synthesis of Human Dynamism*, while assistant works on sculpture; on left, plaster model of *Spiral Expansion of Muscles in Motion*; and in background, on shelf, plaster model of *Development of a Bottle by Means of Color*, April 12 – May, 1913
Aristotype, $2\frac{3}{8} \times 3\frac{3}{8}$ inches (6 × 8.6 cm)
Private collection
Another original print is in Calmarini Collection, Milan, and came from the Boccioni heirs (silver-gelatin print; on back: in pencil, "31").

Fig. 57.12 Umberto Boccioni
Giacomo Balla, Boccioni's mother Cecilia, and Boccioni standing around plaster model of *Synthesis of Human Dynamism*, while one assistant works on sculpture and another crouches in front; on left, plaster model of *Spiral Expansion of Muscles in Motion*; and in background, on shelf, plaster model of *Development of a Bottle by Means of Color*, April 12 – May, 1913
Gelatin-silver print, $2\frac{3}{8} \times 3\frac{3}{8}$ inches (6 × 8.5 cm)
On back: in pencil, "28"
Private collection

Fig. 57.13 Umberto Boccioni
Self-portrait, posing with plaster model of *Synthesis of Human Dynamism*; on left, plaster model of *Spiral Expansion of Muscles in Motion*; on right, *Antigrazioso*; and in background, on shelf, plaster model of *Development of a Bottle by Means of Color*, April 12 – May, 1913
Aristotype, $2\frac{3}{8} \times 3\frac{9}{16}$ inches (6 × 9 cm)
On back: in ballpoint pen, "5"
Private collection

Fig. 57.14 Umberto Boccioni
Plaster model of *Synthesis of Human Dynamism*; on left, plaster model of *Spiral Expansion of Muscles in Motion*; and in background, on shelf, plaster model of *Development of a Bottle by Means of Color*, April 12 – May, 1913
Gelatin-silver print, $2\frac{7}{16} \times 3\frac{7}{16}$ inches (6.2 × 8.7 cm)
On back: in pencil, "28"
Private collection

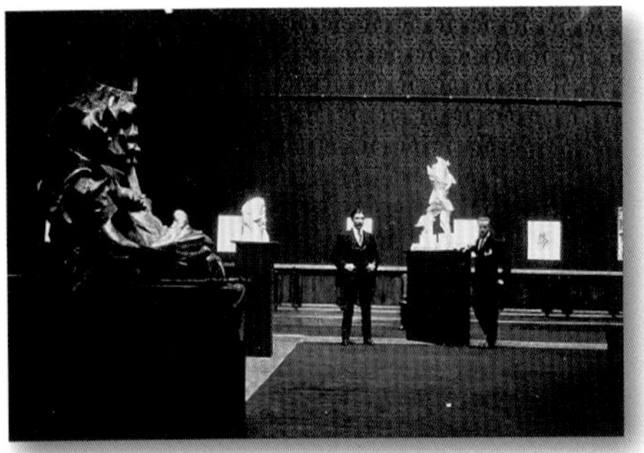

58.1

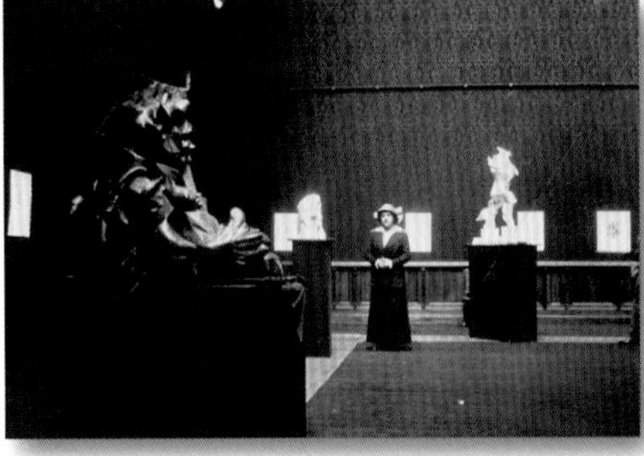

58.2

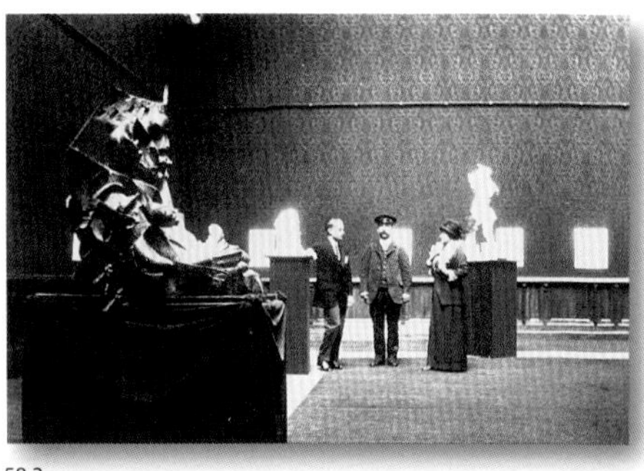

58.3

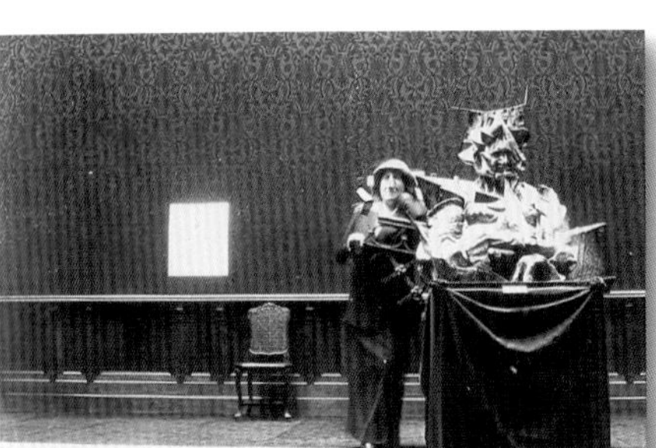

58.4

Figs. 58.1–.13. Photographs by Lucette Korsoff of installation and individual sculptures at Umberto Boccioni's exhibition of sculpture and drawings, Galerie La Boëtie, Paris, 1913

Fig. 58.1. Lucette Korsoff
Two unidentified men standing near plaster model of *Unique Forms of Continuity in Space*; on left, in background, *Empty and Full Abstracts of a Head*; and on left, in foreground, *Head + House + Light*, June 20–July 16, 1913
Gelatin-silver print, 2³⁄₈ × 3³⁄₈ inches (6.1 × 8.6 cm)
Private collection

Fig. 58.2. Lucette Korsoff
Korsoff standing in between *Empty and Full Abstracts of a Head* and plaster model of *Unique Forms of Continuity in Space*; on left, in foreground, *Head + House + Light*, June 20–July 16, 1913
Gelatin-silver print, 2³⁄₈ × 3³⁄₈ inches (6.1 × 8.6 cm)
On back: in ballpoint pen, "12"
Private collection

Fig. 58.3 Lucette Korsoff
Two unidentified men (one in braided uniform) and Korsoff standing in between *Empty and Full Abstracts of a Head* and plaster model of *Unique Forms of Continuity in Space*; on left, in foreground, *Head + House + Light*, June 20–July 16, 1913
Reproduced in Zeno Birolli, *Umberto Boccioni: Racconto critico* (Turin: Einaudi, 1983), fig. 23. The original has not been found.

Fig. 58.4 Lucette Korsoff
Korsoff standing near plaster model of *Head + House + Light*, June 20–July 16, 1913
Aristotype, 2⁹⁄₁₆ × 3⁹⁄₁₆ inches (6.5 × 9 cm)
Calmarini Collection, Milan
Provenance: Boccioni heirs

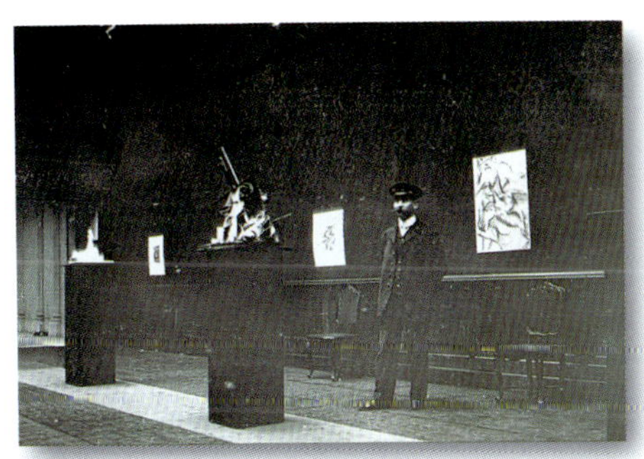

58.5

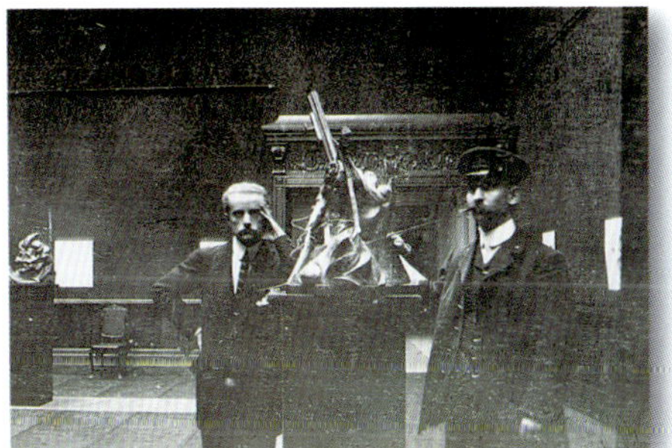

58.6

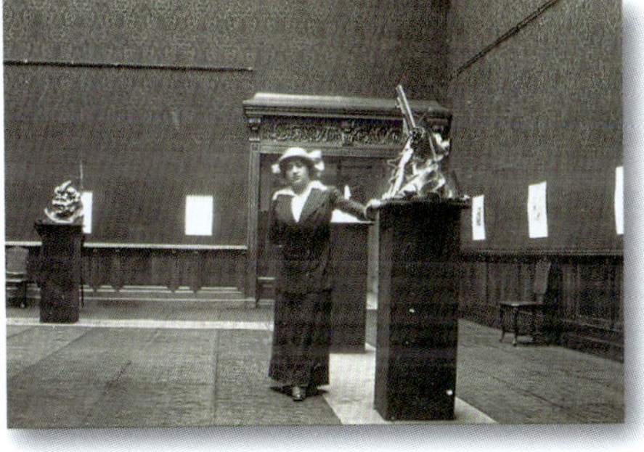

58.7

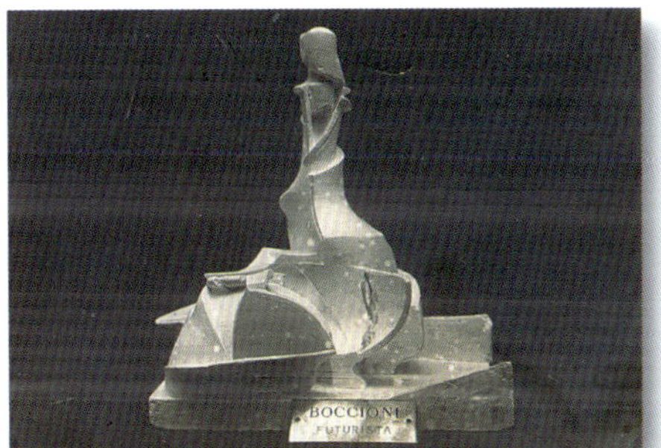

58.8

58.9

Fig. 58.5 Lucette Korsoff
Unidentified man (in braided uniform) standing near *Fusion of a Head and a Window*; on left, plaster model of *Force-Forms of a Bottle*; and on far right, on wall, *Muscular Dynamism*, June 20 – July 16, 1913
Gelatin-silver print, $2\frac{9}{16} \times 3\frac{9}{16}$ inches (6.5 × 9 cm)
On back: in ballpoint pen, "10"
Private collection

Fig. 58.6 Lucette Korsoff
Two unidentified men (one in braided uniform) standing next to *Fusion of a Head and a Window*; on left, in background, *Antigrazioso*, June 20 – July 12, 1913
Gelatin-silver print, $2\frac{11}{16} \times 3\frac{11}{16}$ inches (6.9 × 9.3 cm)
On back: in ballpoint pen, "8"
Private collection

Fig. 58.7 Lucette Korsoff
Korsoff standing next to *Fusion of a Head and a Window*; on left, in background, *Antigrazioso*; June 20 – July 12, 1913
Gelatin-silver print, $2\frac{3}{8} \times 3\frac{9}{16}$ inches (6.1 × 9 cm)
On back: in ballpoint pen, "9"
Private collection

Fig. 58.8 Lucette Korsoff
Force-Forms of a Bottle, June 20 – July 16, 1913
Gelatin-silver print, $4\frac{3}{4} \times 6\frac{1}{2}$ inches (12 x 16.5 cm)
On back: in pencil, "Boccioni – futurista / Forme forze di una bottiglia / N7 del catalogo"
Calmarini Collection, Milan

Fig. 58.9 Lucette Korsoff
Force-Forms of a Bottle, June 20 – July 16, 1913
Gelatin-silver print, retouched in india ink at sculpture's base and in ceruse on convex surfaces, $4\frac{3}{4} \times 6\frac{7}{16}$ inches (12 x 16.4 cm)
On back: in pencil, "6894 / 64 linee rame / con filo / – 9 –"
Private collection

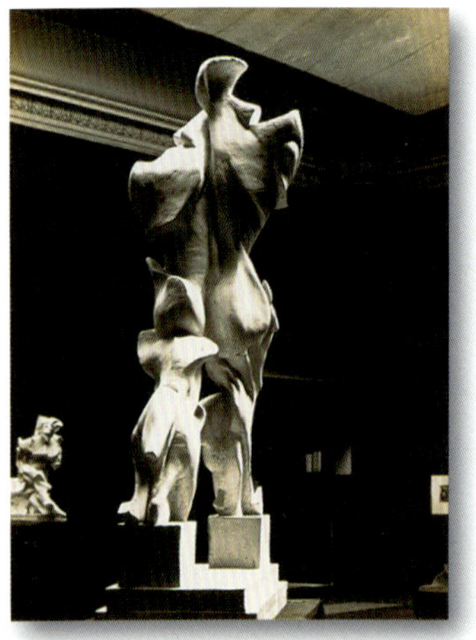

58.10

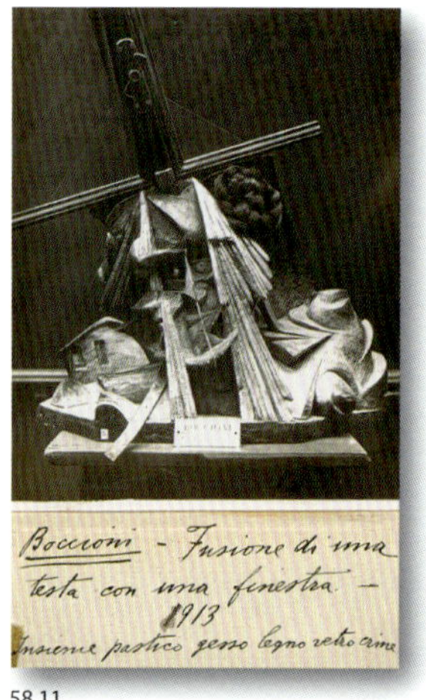

58.11

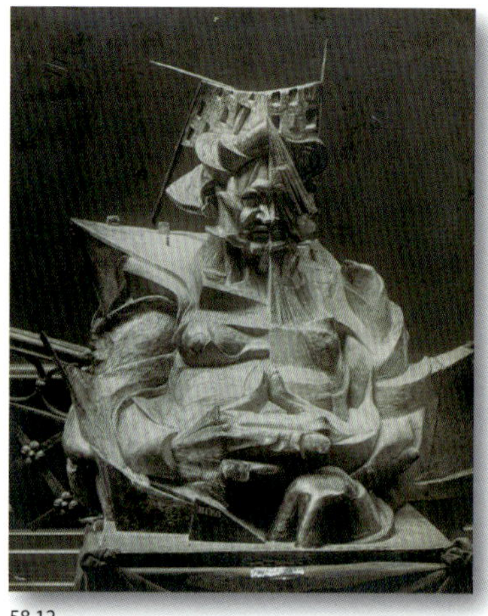

58.12

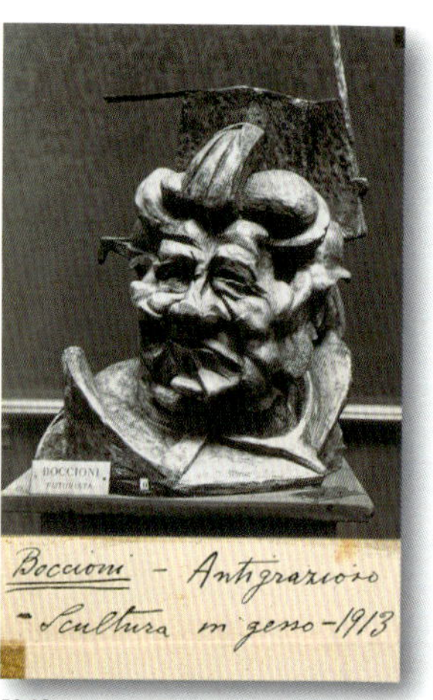

58.13

Fig. 58.10 Lucette Korsoff
Plaster model of *Unique Forms of Continuity in Space*;
on left, in background, *Muscles in Speed*, June 20-July 16, 1913
Gelatin-silver print, $6\frac{11}{16} \times 4\frac{15}{16}$ inches (17 × 12.6 cm)
On back: in pen, "foto proprietà sorella" (photo belonging to sister)
Private collection

Fig. 58.11 Lucette Korsoff
Fusion of a Head and a Window, June 20-July 16, 1913
Gelatin-silver print, $6\frac{3}{4} \times 4\frac{9}{16}$ inches (17.1 × 11.6 cm)
On original label, glued at bottom facing front: in pen, in Boccioni's hand, "Boccioni – Fusione di una / testa con una finestra – / 1913 / Insieme pastico [plastico] gesso legno vetro crine"
Private collection

Fig. 58.12 Lucette Korsoff
Head + House + Light, June 20 – July 16, 1913
Gelatin-silver print, retouched in lower center, $6\frac{1}{2} \times 4\frac{3}{4}$ inches (16.5 × 12 cm)
On back: in pencil, "Boccioni – futurista / Testa + casa + luce / N4 del catalogo"
Calmarini Collection, Milan

Fig. 58.13 Lucette Korsoff
Antigrazioso, June 20 – July 16, 1913
Gelatin-silver print, $6\frac{3}{4} \times 4\frac{9}{16}$ inches (17.1 × 11.6 cm)
On original label, glued at bottom facing front: in pen, in Boccioni's hand, "Boccioni – Antigrazioso / – Scultura in gesso – 1913"
Private collection

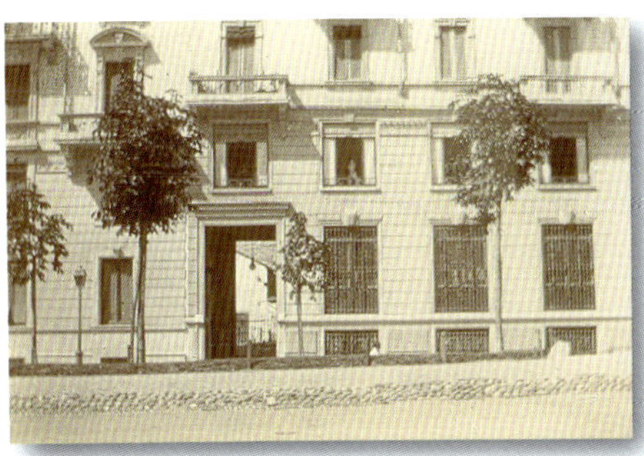

59.1

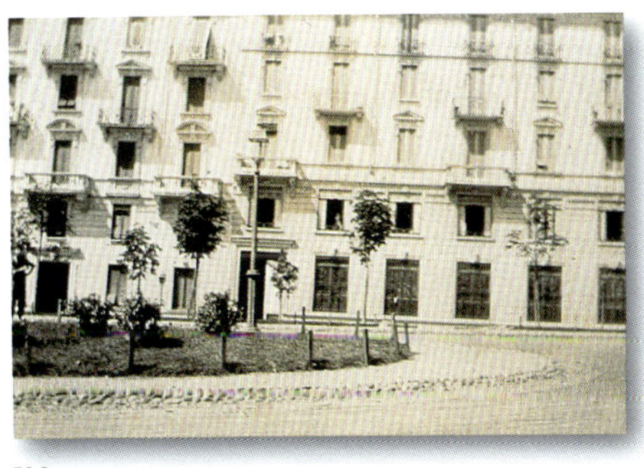

59.2

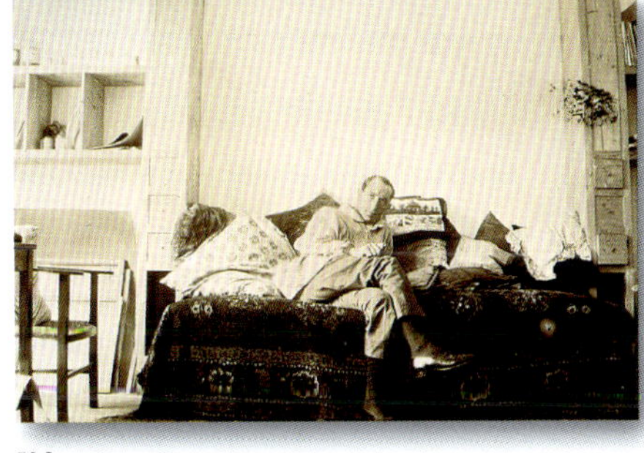

59.3

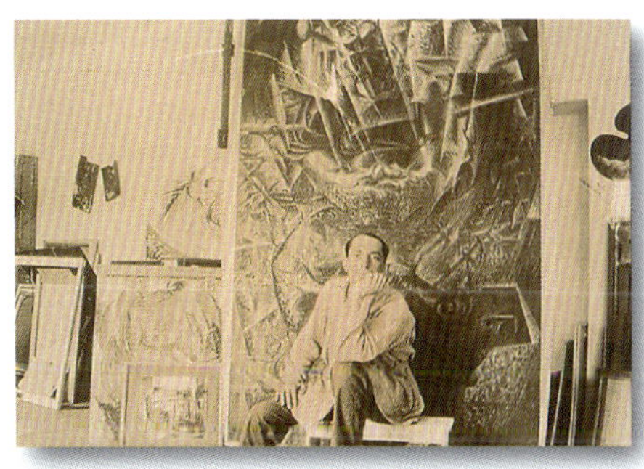

59.4

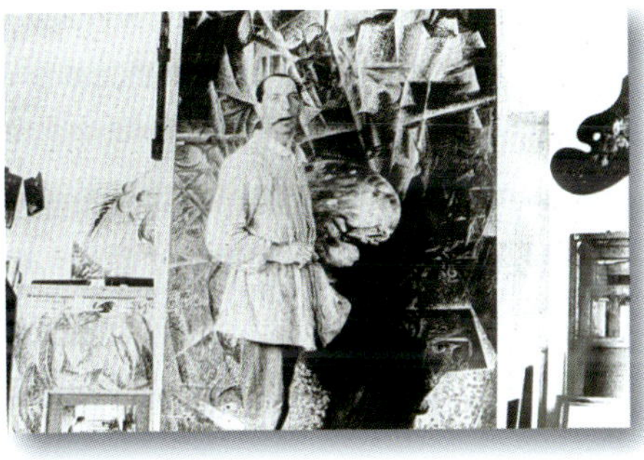

59.5

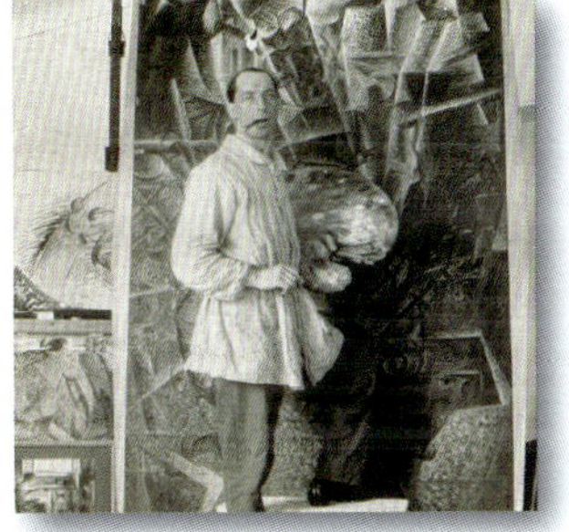

59.6

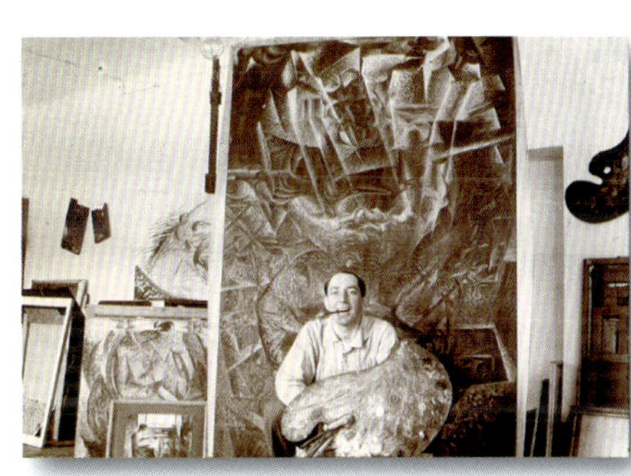

59.7

Figs. 59.1–.7. Photographs by Umberto Boccioni of exterior and his studio at Bastioni di Porta Romana 35 (now viale Regina Margherita 9), Milan, 1913

Fig. 59.1 Umberto Boccioni
Exterior view, July/August 1913
Aristotype, $1\frac{15}{16} \times 2\frac{15}{16}$ inches (4.9 × 7.5 cm)
On back: in pencil, "Dalla finestra centrale appare una statua futurista di Umberto Boccioni / casa di via Porta Romana"
Private collection

Fig. 59.2 Umberto Boccioni
Exterior view, July/August 1913
Aristotype, $2\frac{3}{8} \times 3\frac{3}{8}$ inches (6 × 8.6 cm)
Private collection

Fig. 59.3 Umberto Boccioni
Self-portrait, seated on the sofa, July 17 – September 29, 1913
Aristotype, $2\frac{3}{8} \times 3\frac{9}{16}$ inches (6 × 9 cm)
Private collection

Fig. 59.4 Umberto Boccioni
Self-portrait, seated in front of *Materia*, July 17 – September 29, 1913
Sepia print, $2\frac{1}{2}$ x 3 inches (6.4 x 7.6 cm)
Research Library, The Getty Research Institute, Los Angeles (880380)
Another print is reproduced in Gianfranco Bruno, *L'opera completa di Boccioni* (Milan: Rizzoli, 1969), p. 83, inscribed, on front, in Boccioni's hand, "Al caro e grande / [Balilla] Pratella / affettuosamente / fraternamente / Boccioni"

Fig. 59.5 Umberto Boccioni
Self-portrait, standing in front of *Materia*, July 17 – September 29, 1913
Modern print
Archivio Pollini, Milan
With the exception of a cropped print (fig. 59.6), the original has not been found.

Fig. 59.6 Umberto Boccioni
Self-portrait, standing in front of *Materia*, July 17 – September 29, 1913
Gelatin-silver print, $2\frac{3}{16} \times 2\frac{3}{16}$ inches (5.5 × 5.5 cm); left and right sides are cropped
On back: in pencil, "15"
Calmarini Collection, Milan
Provenance: Giannetto Bisi

Fig. 59.7 Umberto Boccioni
Self-portrait, seated in front of *Materia*, July 17 – September 29, 1913
Aristotype, $2\frac{9}{16} \times 3\frac{9}{16}$ inches (6.5 × 9 cm)
Private collection

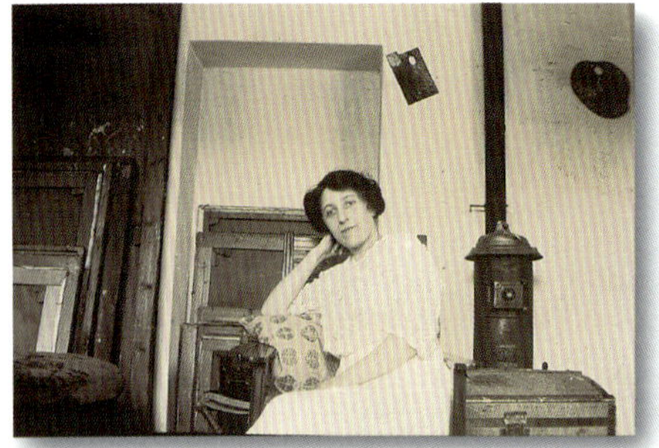

60.1

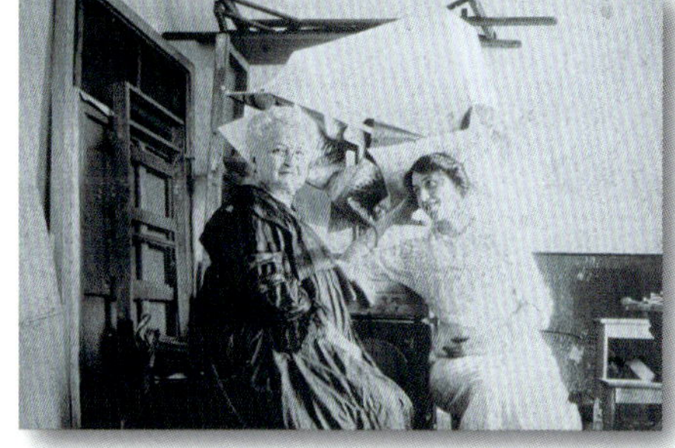

60.2

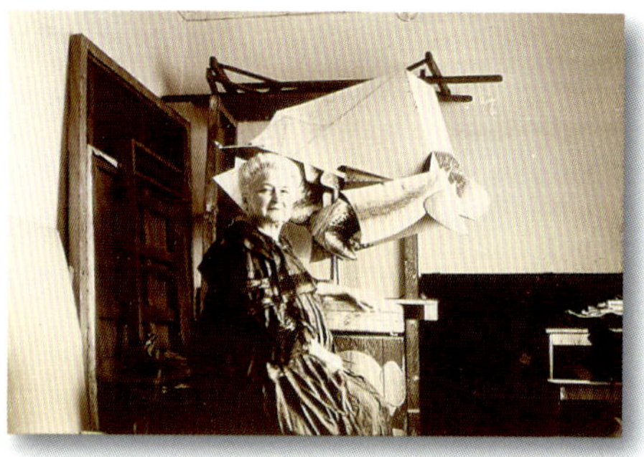

60.3

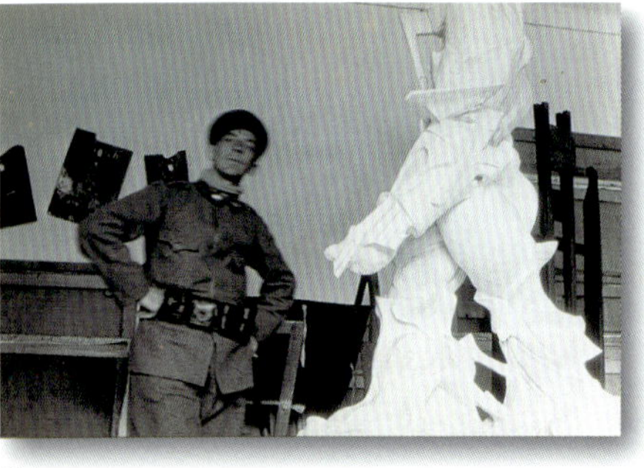

60.4

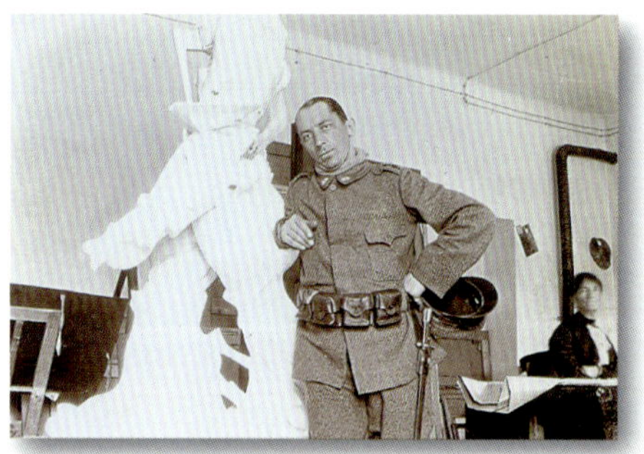

60.5

60.6

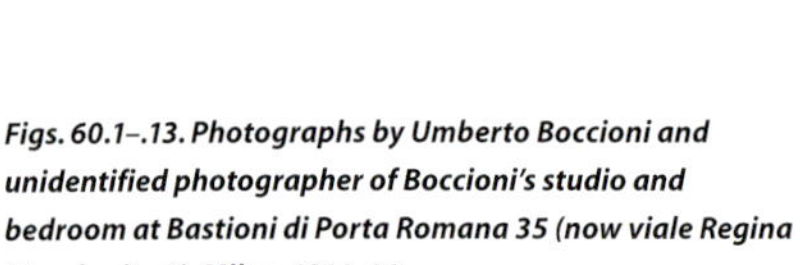

Figs. 60.1–.13. Photographs by Umberto Boccioni and unidentified photographer of Boccioni's studio and bedroom at Bastioni di Porta Romana 35 (now viale Regina Margherita 9), Milan, 1914–16

Fig. 60.1 Umberto Boccioni
Artist's sister Amelia, spring 1914 – July 1915
Aristotype on postcard-shaped light cardboard,
$2\frac{13}{16} \times 3\frac{7}{16}$ inches (7.1 × 8.7 cm)
On back: in pencil, "Amelia"
Private collection

Fig. 60.2 Umberto Boccioni
Artist's mother Cecilia and sister Amelia seated in front of *Dynamism of a Speeding Horse + Houses*, spring 1914 – July 1915
Gelatin-silver print, modern reproduction, $5 \times 6\frac{15}{16}$ inches (12.7 × 17.6 cm)
On front, at bottom [On back?]: in pencil, "Mamma Cecilia ed Amelia nello studio di V. Porta Romana – Milano"
Private collection

Fig. 60.3 Umberto Boccioni
Artist's mother Cecilia seated in front of *Dynamism of a Speeding Horse + Houses*, spring 1914 – July 1915
Aristotype, $2\frac{3}{8} \times 3\frac{7}{16}$ inches (6 × 8.8 cm)
Calmarini Collection, Milan

Fig. 60.4 Umberto Boccioni
Self-portrait, in military uniform, with plaster model of *Synthesis of Human Dynamism*, November 1915 – January 1916
Silver-gelatin print, $2\frac{3}{8} \times 3\frac{7}{16}$ inches (6 × 8.7 cm)
Private collection

Fig. 60.5 Umberto Boccioni
Self-portrait, in military uniform, with plaster model of *Synthesis of Human Dynamism*; on right, artist's paternal aunt Colomba Boccioni Procida, November 1915 – January 1916
Aristotype, $2\frac{9}{16} \times 3\frac{7}{16}$ inches (6.5 × 8.7 cm)
Calmarini Collection, Milan

Fig. 60.6 Umberto Boccioni
Self-portrait, in military uniform, with plaster model of *Synthesis of Human Dynamism*; on right, artist's paternal aunt Colomba Boccioni Procida, November 1915 – January 1916
Aristotype, $2\frac{1}{2} \times 3\frac{7}{16}$ inches (6.3 × 8.8 cm)
Calmarini Collection, Milan
Provenance: Giannetto Bisi

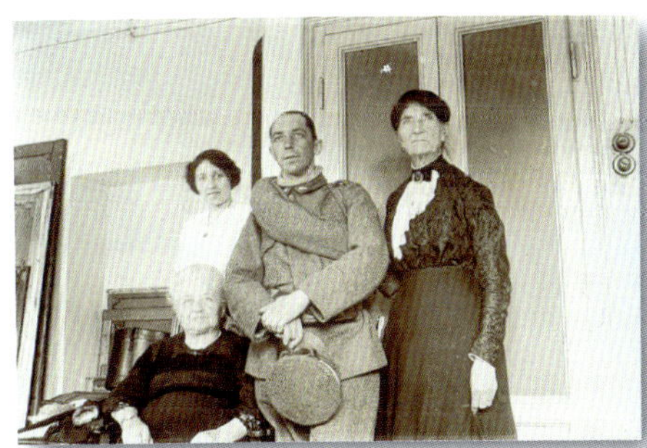

60.7

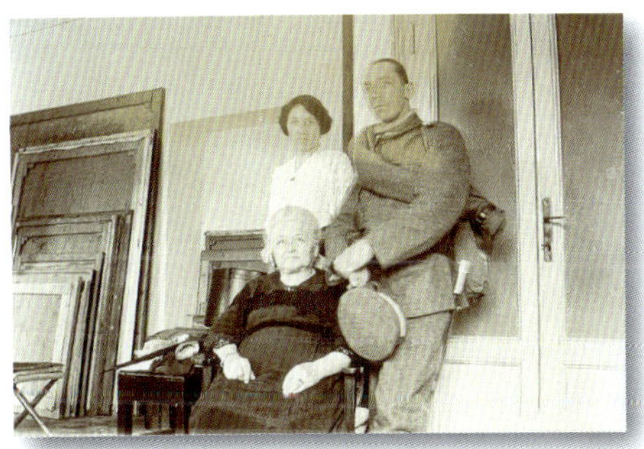

60.8

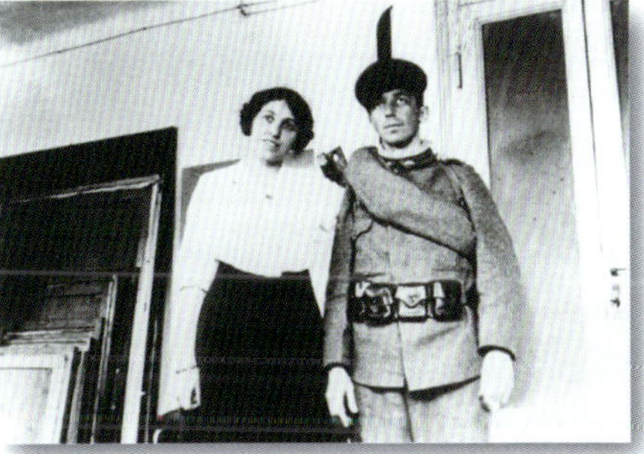

60.9

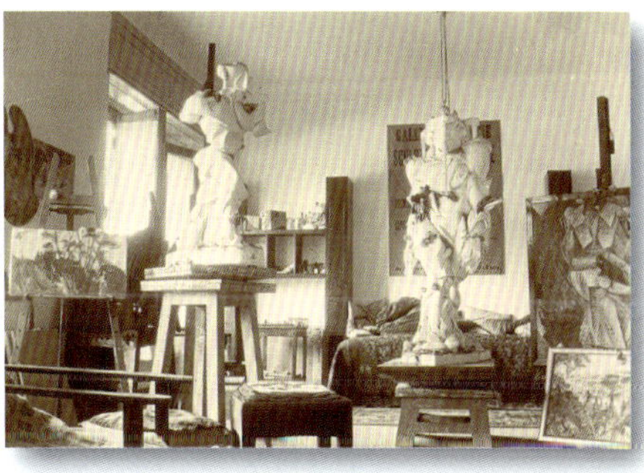

60.10

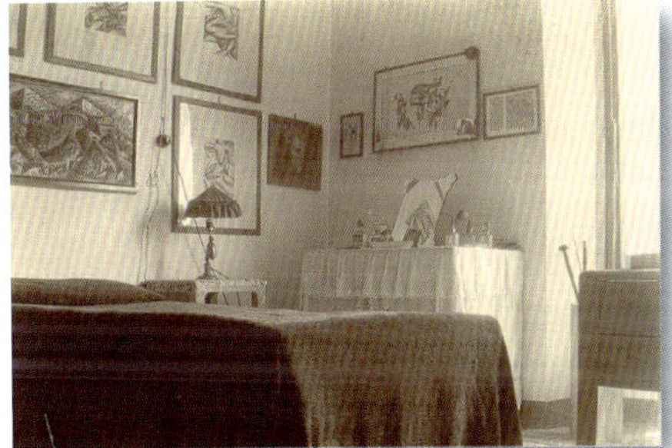

60.11

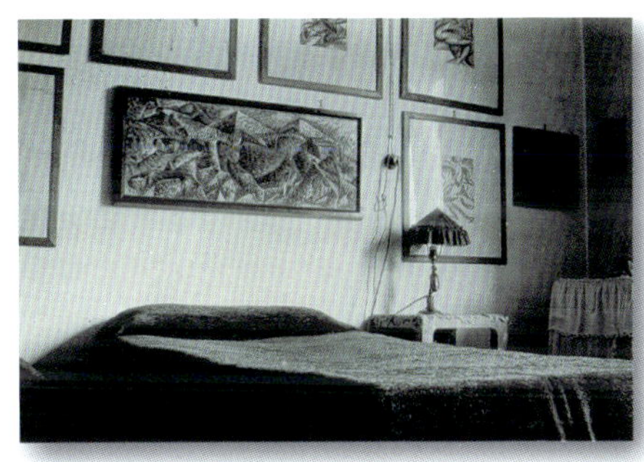

60.12

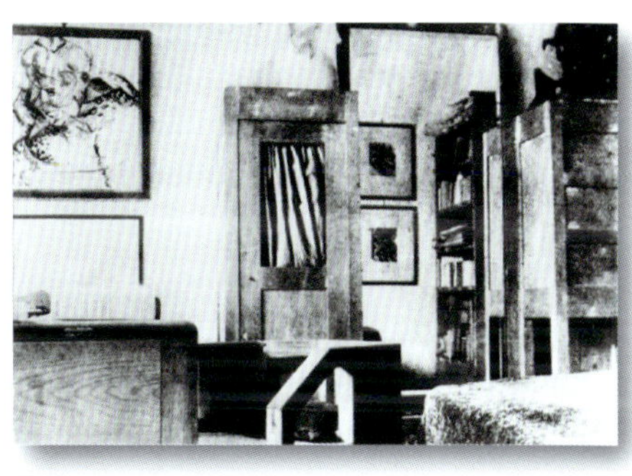

60.13

Fig. 60.7 Umberto Boccioni
Boccioni, in military uniform, with his mother Cecilia (seated), sister Amelia, and aunt Colomba Boccioni Procida, November 1915 – January 1916
Aristotype, $2\frac{5}{8} \times 3\frac{9}{16}$ inches (6.6 × 9 cm)
On back: in ballpoint pen, "1"
Private collection

Fig. 60.8 Umberto Boccioni
Boccioni, in military uniform, with his mother Cecilia (seated) and sister Amelia, November 1915 – January 1916
Aristotype, $2\frac{9}{16} \times 3\frac{9}{16}$ inches (6.5 × 9.1 cm)
On back: in ballpoint pen, "3"
Private collection

Fig. 60.9 Umberto Boccioni
Boccioni, in military uniform, with his sister Amelia, November 1915 – January 1916
Modern print
Archivio Pollini, Milan

Fig. 60.10 Anonymous
In background, poster for Umberto Boccioni's exhibition at Galerie La Boetie, Paris, June – July 1913, foreground, right, plaster model of *Synthesis of Human Dynamism*, adorned with wilted flowers; left, plaster model of *Spiral Expansion of Muscles in Motion*, also adorned with flowers; and various paintings, including, on easel at right, *Spiral Construction*, with one of the landscapes executed at Pallanza just below it and another on the easel to the left, June – December 1916
Aristotype, $2\frac{3}{8} \times 3\frac{9}{16}$ inches (6 × 9 cm)
Private collection

Fig. 60.11 Anonymous
Umberto Boccioni's bedroom; at head of bed, *Plastic Dynamism + Horse + Block of Houses*; above, *Muscular Dynamism* and *Dynamic Breakdown of Figure*; and behind the lamp, *Muscles in Speed*, followed by pastel *Mother* at right, 1916
Aristotype, $2\frac{3}{8} \times 3\frac{9}{16}$ inches (6 × 9 cm)
Private collection

Fig. 60.12 Anonymous
Umberto Boccioni's bedroom; at head of bed, *Plastic Dynamism + Horse + Block of Houses*; above, *Muscular Dynamism* and *Dynamic Breakdown of Figure*; and behind the lamp, *Muscles in Speed*, followed by pastel *Mother* at right, 1916
Gelatin-silver print, $2\frac{3}{8} \times 3\frac{9}{16}$ inches (6 × 8.5 cm)
On back: in ballpoint pen, "17"; in pencil, "783"
Private collection

Fig. 60.13 Anonymous
Umberto Boccioni's bedroom; on wall, far left, *Abstract Dimensions*; on armoire to left of mirror, plaster model of *Empty and Full Abstracts of a Head*; on chest of drawers to right, plaster model of *Antigrazioso*; and reflected in mirror, two drawings, 1916
Modern print
Archivio Pollini, Milan
Reproduced in G. Ballo, *Boccioni: La vita e l'opera* (Milan: Saggiatore, 1982), fig. 20, which is clearer than later reproductions. Print is in all likelihood enlargement of central part of a lost original.

Notes

1 On this vast subject, see the fundamental texts Aaron Scharf, *Art and Photography* (London: A. Lane, 1968); and Peter Galassi, *Before Photography: Painting and the Invention of Photography* (New York: Museum of Modern Art, 1981). See also the more recent Claudio Marra, *Fotografia e pittura nel novecento: Una storia "senza combattimento"* (Milan: Mondadori,1999); and Dorothy M. Kosinski, ed., *The Artist and the Camera: Degas to Picasso*, exh. cat. (Dallas: Dallas Museum of Art; New Haven: Yale University Press, 2000). Among the Italian sources of the period, see Gianni Beltrame, "La fotografia instantanea e l'arte," *Rivista scientifico-Artistica di fotografia* 1, no. 5, (Milan, 1892), pp. 139–40. On the Italian situation between the nineteenth and twentieth centuries, see, for the Divisionists, Giovanna Ginex, "Fotografia e pittura nel laboratorio divisionista," in Gabriella Belli and Franco Rella, eds., *L'età del divisionismo* (Milan: Electa, 1990), pp. 232–95 (with bibliography). Concerning sculptors, the case of Medardo Rosso is of great interest, especially in relation to Boccioni; on this subject, see *Medardo Rosso*, exh. cat., texts by Giovanni Anselmo, Gloria Moure, et al. (Santiago de Compostela: Centro Gallego de Arte Contemporánea, 1996).

2 See, for example, recent texts by Giovanni Lista: *Futurism and Photography*, exh. cat. (London: Estorick Collection, 2001); *Cinema e fotografia futurista*, exh. cat. (Milan: Skira, 2001); and "Futuristischer Film und futuristische Fotografie," in *Der Lärm der Strasse: Der italienische Futurismus 1909–1918*, exh. cat. (Hannover: Sprengel Museum Hannover, 2001), pp. 294–317.

3 I thank Laura Mattioli Rossi for the passionate and indispensable support she gave me over the course of this work. I also thank Vivien Greene, Flavio Fergonzi, and Silvia Bersolli.

4 In February 2002, the prints could be found in four different private Italian collections; a few originals are also in the Research Library, the Getty Research Institute, Los Angeles. Countless museums, publishers, and collectors, moreover, have and use modern reproductions of the images—often only of details, without determining their actual provenance, perpetuating often partial and imprecise information as to the dating, techniques, and subjects of the images.

5 For the technical characteristics of the prints reproduced here, I refer the reader to the captions.

6 The celluloid negatives produced from ca. 1895 onward, which were light and easier to use, proved particularly suitable for portable cameras and thus for amateur use. They were produced in rolls or in flat film. Some of the direct-contact aristotypes clearly show the celluloid boundary along the edges. One of them, in printing, also included the outer edge of the roll, recognizable by the convexity of the film toward the outside.

7 On Marey and the impact his research had on twentieth-century painting, see, Marta Braun, *Picturing Time: The Work of Etienne-Jules Marey (1830–1904)* (Chicago: University of Chicago Press, 1992).

8 In my opinion, the famous multiple photoportrait *I–We–Boccioni* (in the Calmarini Collection, Milan), dated ca. 1907–10 and always attributed to Boccioni—and which was made with the help of mirrors by using an illusionistic technique well familiar to street photographers and amateur photographers from the 1890s onward—does not portray the young Boccioni, as has always been stated. Instead it represents the journalist, writer, and amateur photographer Giannetto Bisi (1881–1919), husband of the painter Adriana Bisi Fabbri and a close friend of Boccioni, from whose collection the photo comes. This is borne out by comparison with other portraits of Bisi. What *is* in Boccioni's hand, however, is the writing in pen and the signature, a fact that may have caused the confusion between the source of the writing (and also perhaps of the shot) and the person portrayed.

9 Numerous sources document the fact that Boccioni kept and constantly updated a photo album of his works, which were photographed by professionals. See Zeno Birolli, *Umberto Boccioni: Racconto critico* (Turin: Einaudi, 1983), p. 111; and Maurizio Calvesi and Ester Coen, *Boccioni: L'opera completa* (Milan: Electa, 1983), p. 303: "The Marchesa Casanova wants to come to Milan to visit your home and to see my paintings. I brought my *album*" (Boccioni to Vico Baer, July 20, 1916; Boccioni was a guest of the Busoni family at the the Marchesi Casanova's villa in Pallanza).

10 After attending the school of painting at the Accademia di Brera of Milan, Sommariva (1883–1956) became a photographer and portraitist of the Lombard aristocracy and bourgeoisie, and was the favorite of artists as well. His most famous portraits, aside from those of Boccioni, include F. T. Marinetti and the entire group of Futurist artists, as well as Ada Negri, Massimo Bontempelli, Ugo Ojetti, Filippo Turati, Margherita Sarfatti, Giacomo Puccini, Luca Beltrami, Emilio Gola, Gaetano Previati, and Lyda Borelli. The Sommariva photographic archive, in the Biblioteca Nazionale Braidense in Milan, is currently in the process of being reorganized by the present author. On Sommariva, see Nicolas Monti and Mario Quadraroli, *Emilio Sommariva*, exh. cat. (Lodi: Banca Popolare, 1984); Giovanna Ginex, "Il fondo fotografico Emilio Sommariva, fotografo a Milan" and "Il fondo Sommariva," in Tiziana Serena, ed., *Per Paolo Costantini*, vol. 2, *Indagine sulle raccolte fotografiche* (Quaderni 9, Centro Ricerche Informatiche per i Beni Culturali) (Pisa: Scuola Normale di Pisa, 1999), pp. 55–56.

11 The subjects of the shots taken that day for Boccioni are indicated in Sommariva's accounts book: "Umberto Boccioni reproduced paintings. 'Three Women' and 'Signora Maffi.'" Calvesi was correct in 1953 when he suggested that the signature and date of 1909 now on *Portrait of Signora Maffi*, but not seen in Sommariva's photograph, were probably apocryphal and placed there after the artist's death. See Calvesi and Coen, *Boccioni: L'opera completa*, no. 464, p. 314. It is likely that in 1913, Boccioni had Sommariva take other photographs as well, probably of sculptures, which the artist had in possession by April of that year, that is, before the works were sent to Paris for his exhibition at Galerie La Boëtie. Boccioni wrote to Roberto Longhi on April 25, 1913, "Any chance you may be coming to Milan? I'd like to show you the sculptures before they leave. Would you like some photographs?" Longhi replied on April 30, requesting that he send "a few photographs, with a few explanations, if possible." In Luigi Tallarico, *Boccioni: Cento anni* (Rome: G. Volpe, 1982), pp. 238, 240. Three photographs—of *Synthesis of Human Dynamism, Spiral Expansion of Muscles*, and *Muscles in Speed*—were recently found at Fondazione Longhi. In 1914, Boccioni sent another series of photographs of the sculptures (now in the Calmarini Collection, Milan) to Giannetto Bisi, who at the time was chief editor of *Il Mondo*, the illustrated magazine of Sonzogno, and contributed to the reviews *Pagine d'Arte* and *Emporium*. They were accompanied by a note in the artist's hand, dated September 9, 1914: "Illustrious Friend, the photographs are ready. I'd like to speak with you: could you come by my studio? Phone me to make an appointment. / 11919 / Warm regards / and thanks / Boccioni." In January 1914, Bisi had published an article in *Emporium* on Boccioni's exhibition of Futurist painting and sculpture at Giuseppe Sprovieri's Galleria Futurista in Rome.

12 F. T. Marinetti, *La grande Milano tradizionale e futurista: Una sensibilità italiana nata in Egitto*, ed. Luciano De Maria (Milan: Mondadori, 1969), pp. 101–02.

13 Calvesi and Coen, *Boccioni: L'opera completa*, p. 124. On the Bastioni studio, see Gino Agnese, *Vita di Boccioni* (Florence: Camunia, 1996), which also quotes an oral testimony by Marco Bisi (1908–2002), Giannetto's son, on the arrangement of the rooms.

14 On the via Adige studio, see Leonardo Capano and Antonello Negri, "Via Adige 23," in Laura Mattioli Rossi, ed., *Boccioni 1912 Materia*, exh. cat. (Milan: Mazzotta, 1991), pp. 253–56, where the years Boccioni lived at via Adige are incorrectly given as 1909–12 instead of 1908–13.

15 See "Moderni edifici pubblici e privati: I Bastioni," in *Milano nel 1906* (Milan: Allegretti, n.d. [1906]), p. 93, 120–121.

16 Calvesi and Coen, *Boccioni: L'opera completa*, nos. 782a and no. 856. Hereafter, when the catalogue raisonné number for a Boccioni work is provided, it is referred to as "Calvesi and Coen, no."; *Development of a Bottle in Space* is Calvesi and Coen, no. 782a. Numbers are given for works not otherwise illustrated in the present volume.

17 Boccioni to Baer, February 19, 1913, in Zeno Birolli, ed., *Umberto Boccioni: Gli scritti editi e inediti* (Milan: Feltrinelli, 1971), pp. 365–66.

18 Artists often used the automatic shutter release to photograph themselves, family members, and friends in their studios. In this regard, among the Futurists, see the example of Fortunato Depero in Lista, *Cinema e fotografia futurista*, pp. 145–51, 177–82. It is especially interesting to compare Boccioni's snapshots with what we know of the photographs taken of Pablo Picasso from ca. 1901 to ca. 1920. See Anne Baldassari, *Picasso and Photography: The Dark Mirror*, exh. cat. (Paris: Flammarion; Houston: Museum of Fine Arts, 1997), fig. 6, p. 12; text on p. 14; fig. 10, p. 16; fig. 14, p. 21; figs. 73 and 74, pp. 64–65; fig. 87, p. 75; fig. 105, p. 90; fig. 127, p. 107; and figs. on pp. 134–41. The similarities between Picasso and Boccioni regarding the use of photography end here—Boccioni, unlike Picasso, never used photography in the development of his works.

19 These sketches clearly relate to the ideation of certain sculptures, yet we cannot identify them conclusively with any extant works. They do, however, look very similar to Calvesi and Coen, nos. 877 and 880.

20 The reconstruction of the entire photographic sequence, as well as the evident photographic style of Boccioni make it possible to rule out absolutely the previous attribution of fig. 56.3 to Studio Badodi, as maintained in Lista, *Cinema e fotografia futurista*, p. 141, caption.

21 Among the various testimonies in agreement on this point, I mention specifically that of Marco Bisi, the recently deceased son of the actress Adriana Bisi Fabbri (maternal cousin of Boccioni) and Giannetto Bisi. The recording of a recent interview with Marco Bisi is in a private collection.

22 Calvesi and Coen, nos. 875 and 882.

23 The exact dating—now verified—of the photo sequence allows us to recognize the drawing as subsequent to the sculpture, in keeping with Boccioni's characteristic studio practice.

24 Marinetti, *La grande Milano tradizionale e futurista*, p. 297. For possible chronology of Boccioni's sculpture, see, above all, Roberto Longhi, *Scultura futurista: Boccioni* (Florence: Libreria de "La Voce," 1914); and Laura Mattioli Rossi, "Boccioni: Between Painting and Sculpture," in the present volume, pp. 34–45.

25 See *Les Peintres futuristes italiens*, exh. cat. (Paris: Galerie Bernheim-Jeune, 1912). This group exhibition was held February 5–24, 1912, and subsequently traveled to London and other cities in Europe. See Mattioli Rossi, "Boccioni Between Painting and Sculpture."

26 In all likelihood there were other images, which were dispersed when the album was dismantled. The group reconstructed for this essay consists of prints presently scattered in different collections. A number of photographs of the series were recently reproduced in different publications, often with erroneous attributions. To cite one example, Birolli, *Racconto critico*, fig. 23 (which is fig. 58.3 in the present volume), is misidentified as having been taken in Sprovieri's Galleria Futurista in Rome in 1913. No original print of this image has ever been found.

27 The artistic career and discography of Lucette Korsoff (1876–1955) is closely associated with that of Léon Beyle (1871–1922), her partner in her principal roles, including *Nous vivrons à Paris* (Act I), 1908 (Gramophone, Souvenirs of Rare French Opera), *Que n'avons-nous des ailes*, 1913 (Gramophone), and *Le Trouvère (Il Trovatore)* by Giuseppe Verdi. How Boccioni met Korsoff is recounted in Agnese, *Vita di Boccioni*, p. 305. Agnese also documents the singer's journey from Paris to Milan with Marinetti around mid-July 1913, when she went to see Boccioni in his studio, possibly bringing him the small photo album now dismantled. Korsoff's signature, along with the date "17 juillet 1913," are in fact inscribed in the guest book that Boccioni kept at his studio and which he called "the ghost of my friends." See Agnese, p. 308.

28 Marinetti left us a short list of some of the visitors who came to the opening of the Galeria La Boëtie exhibition: Guillaume Apollinaire, Picasso, Albert Gleizes, André Lhote, Robert Delaunay and his wife Sonia Terk Delaunay, the dealer Paul Rosenberg, the critic Felix Fénéon, the philosopher Alexandre Mercereau, the poet André Salmon, the director of the Society of Large Conventions of Moscow Tastéven, Gustave Kahn, and the writer Francis Vielé–Griffin. See Marinetti, *La grande Milano tradizionale e futurista*, p. 297.

29 A metal plaque is in the private collection possessing most of the photos of this series (as of March 2002).

30 See Boccioni's letter to Giuseppe Sprovieri, September 4, 1913. The space in question was probably the well known contemporary art gallery opened in rue Lafitte a few decades earlier by Clovis Sagot, who died in February 1913. See Guillaume Apollinaire, "Ecrits sur l'art (1): Mort de Clovis Sagot," in *L'Intransigeant*, February 13, 1913.

31 For more on *Materia*, see Flavio Fergonzi, "Umberto Boccioni: *Materia*, 1912," in Fergonzi's catalogue raisonné *The Mattioli Collection: Masterpieces of the Italian Avant-garde* (Milan: Skira, 2002), pp. 155–77.

32 The photos in this brief sequence were analyzed for the first time by Marco Rosci in his essay "La materia e lo stato d'animo plastico," in Mattioli Rossi, *Boccioni 1912 Materia*, pp. 43–64.

33 Many different accounts attest to the artist's depressive state. In 1914, Boccioni wrote from Paris to Roberto Longhi, "Believe me, dear Longhi, I'm going through a very painful period. I live in a state of absolute artistic certainty, but distressing discouragement of morale. . . . Life is a wonderful thing . . . , one suffers to feel it each day become darker and dirtier, heavier, more pointless." In Tallarico, *Boccioni. Cento anni*, pp. 236–37, 241.

34 Calvesi and Coen, no. 903, where it is dated 1913–1914; the sculpture, which is in the Peggy Guggenheim Collection, Venice, and is currently dated 1914–15.

35 The case of fig. 60.3 in the present volume is typical of the casual manner in which these photographs have been usually reproduced. The image is reproduced in full in Birolli, *Racconto critico*, fig. 30; in Mattioli Rossi, *Boccioni 1912 Materia*, p. 41 (though with sides cropped); in Fred Licht and Philip Rylands, eds., *Umberto Boccioni: Dinamismo di un cavallo in corsa + case*, exh. cat. (Venice: Peggy Guggenheim Collection, 1996) pp. 33, 51, 139, 149 (with sides cropped), 65; and in *Der Lärm der Strasse*, fig. p. 430, bottom (with sides cropped).

36 We can now ascertain that a number of paintings dating from 1914 and after were executed in other rooms in the apartment. The key compositional motif continued to be female figures seen against the light, as present also in certain snapshots. One of these paintings was *Interior with Two Female Figures* (1915; Calvesi and Coen, no. 937, which is in the collection of Civiche Raccolte d'Arte, Gabinetto dei Disegni, Milan), in which the artist's mother and his aunt Colomba Boccioni Procida are portrayed next to a window in the living room or kitchen, probably at the end of the apartment floor plan, an area never photographed. The background landscape can now be identified as that of the bastion in front of Boccioni's building. In another canvas of the period, *Two Female Friends* (1914–15; Calvesi and Coen, no. 923), we recognize the armchair and pillows, seen repeatedly in the photographs, and the two sculptures in the background. Also recurrent in these paintings of home interiors, executed in different rooms of the apartment, are the little curtains by the cast-iron railing of the balcony and the heavier curtains hanging from above. While in the same apartment, Boccioni also executed in 1914 the series of drawings for *The Street Pavers* (Calvesi and Coen, nos. 912–16) and the oil painting itself (Calvesi and Coen, no. 911): the highly realistic scene, framed from above, was probably seen by Boccioni from the windows of his studio, beneath which there was, in fact, a cobblestone pavement.

37 See *Grande esposizione Boccioni pittore e scultore futurista*, exh. cat., with writings by Boccioni and preface by Marinetti (Milan: Galleria Centrale d'Arte [Palazzo Cova], 1916). Almost all of the plasters were destroyed, perhaps by rain, but here is Marinetti's anguished testimony: "The ears drink this tragic dawn at the telephone. — Marinetti, get up, this is Azari, get up and come at once, just think, just think, last night they assassinated all of poor Boccioni's sculptural groups, I beg you, come at once, we'll save them / Inexplicably entrusted to an envious and sullen passéist sculptor they were massacred with hammers by stonemasons anxious to disencumber a useful place and now it's all over / The lugubrious courtyard is filled with the screaming massacre of the sublime plasters destroyed by angry tongues of flame that wrench sobs from me as Azari weeping pitifully gathers the pieces of a bottle and lines of force we exit with the little white corpses to sew them back together and put them back on their feet / Revived and throbbing they triumph in Boccionian vermilion." Marinetti, *La grande Milano tradizionale e futurista*, p. 148.

38 This image is published and commented on in Birolli, *Racconto critico*, pp. 16–17, fig. 26. In Birolli's fascinating fiction, the photograph is seen in conjunction with Balla's visit of April–May 1913 and the images documented to that visit, an impossible circumstance belied by an analysis of the elements present in the two series. He also misidentifies the sculpture in the middle as *Unique Forms of Continuity in Space*.

39 Calvesi and Coen, no. 899.

40 The recognizable works in figs. 60.11 and 60.12 are: at the head of the bed, *Plastic Dynamism + Horse + Block of Houses* (1913–14; Calvesi and Coen, no. 902); above, *Muscular Dynamism* (1913; Calvesi and Coen, no. 869) and *Dynamism of a Human Body* (1913; Calvesi and Coen, no. 862); behind the lamp, *Muscles in Speed* (1913; Calvesi and Coen, no. 871), followed by *Mother* (1907; Calvesi and Coen, no. 955).

41 The original print of this important snapshot of Boccioni's apartment has never been found. The available reproduction — reproduced several times in different books — is probably only a partial enlargement of the central part of the lost original print. The poor quality of the reproductions, repeatedly shot with screens, makes it difficult to read the details, to the point that the mirror has often been taken for a door. *Abstract Dimensions* (1912, cat. no. 21) is shown at the upper left.

42 "We have always rejected, with disdain and disgust, any connection, however distant, with photography, because it is outside the realm of art. Photography has value insofar as it objectively reproduces and imitates, and has managed, with its perfection, to liberate the artist from the chains of exact reproduction from life." Boccioni, "Il dinamismo futurista e la pittura francese," *Lacerba*, August 1, 1913, p. 169.

43 Boccioni, Carlo Carrà, Luigi Russolo, Giacomo Balla, and Gino Severini, "Futurist Painting: Technical Manifesto," in Umbro Apollonio, ed., *Futurist Manifestos* (New York: Viking, 1973), p. 28.

44 F. T. Marinetti and Tato [Guglielmo Sansoni], "Manifesto della fotografia futurista," signed April 11, 1930, was published as "La fotografia futurista. Manifesto," *Il Futurismo*, January 11, 1931.

Divisionism

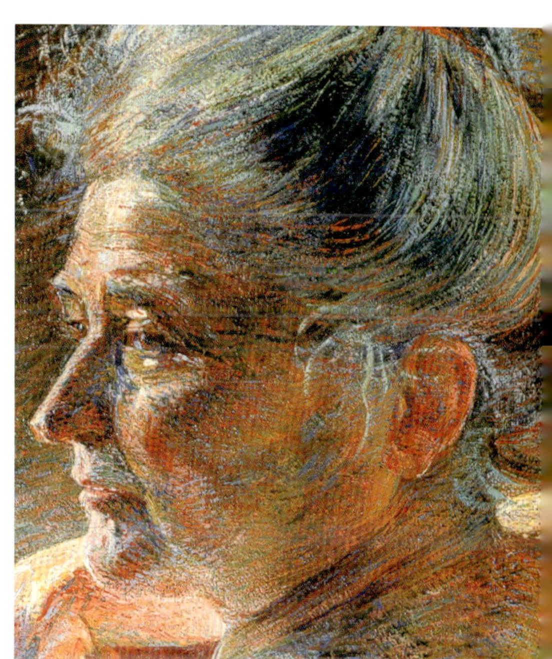

1 **Giacomo Balla** *Mother: Portrait of My Mother* (*Madre: Ritratto della madre*), 1901. Pastel and tempera on board, 46⅞ × 36⅝ inches (119 × 93 cm). Galleria Nazionale d'Arte Moderna, Rome, Courtesy of Ministero per i Beni e le Attività Culturali

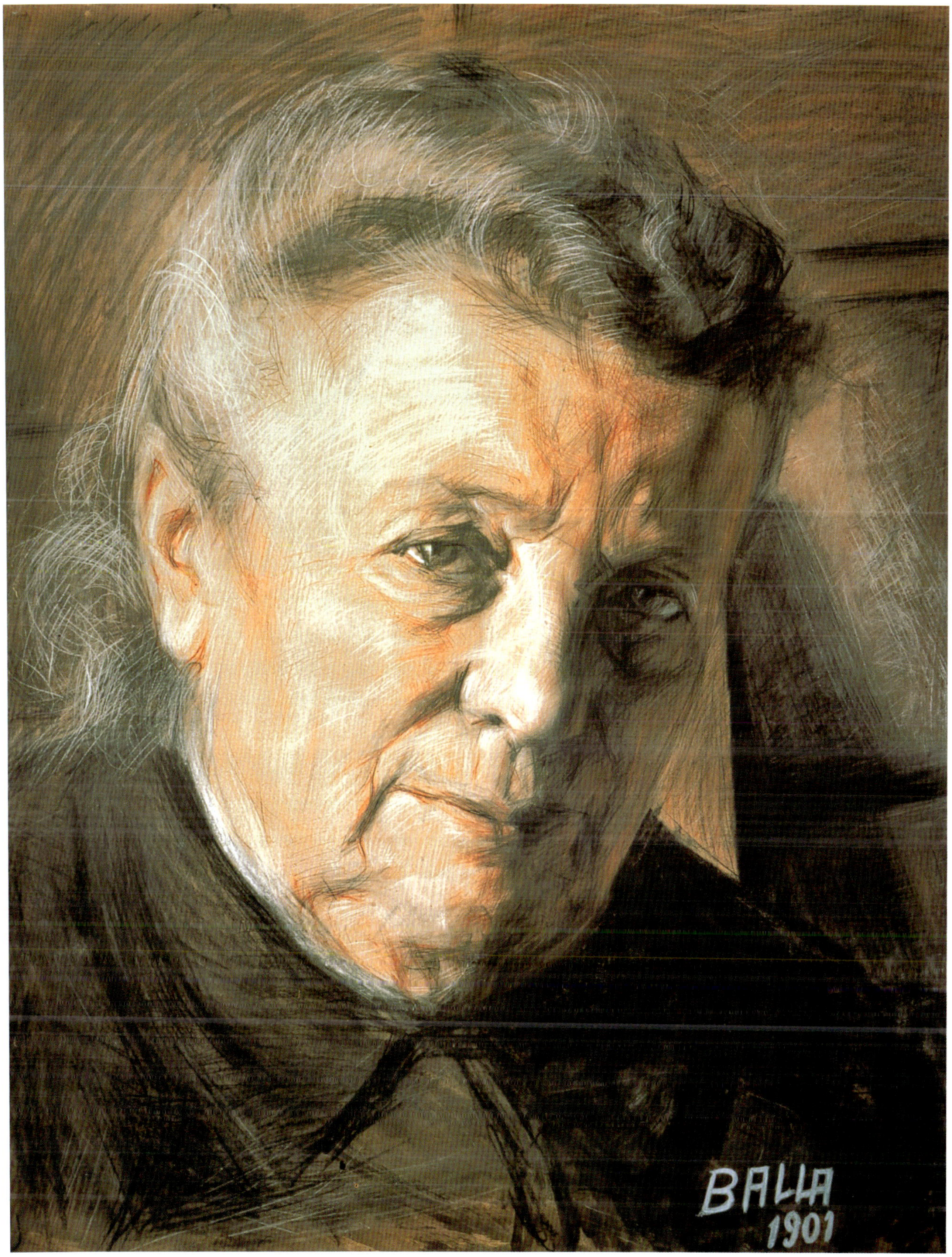

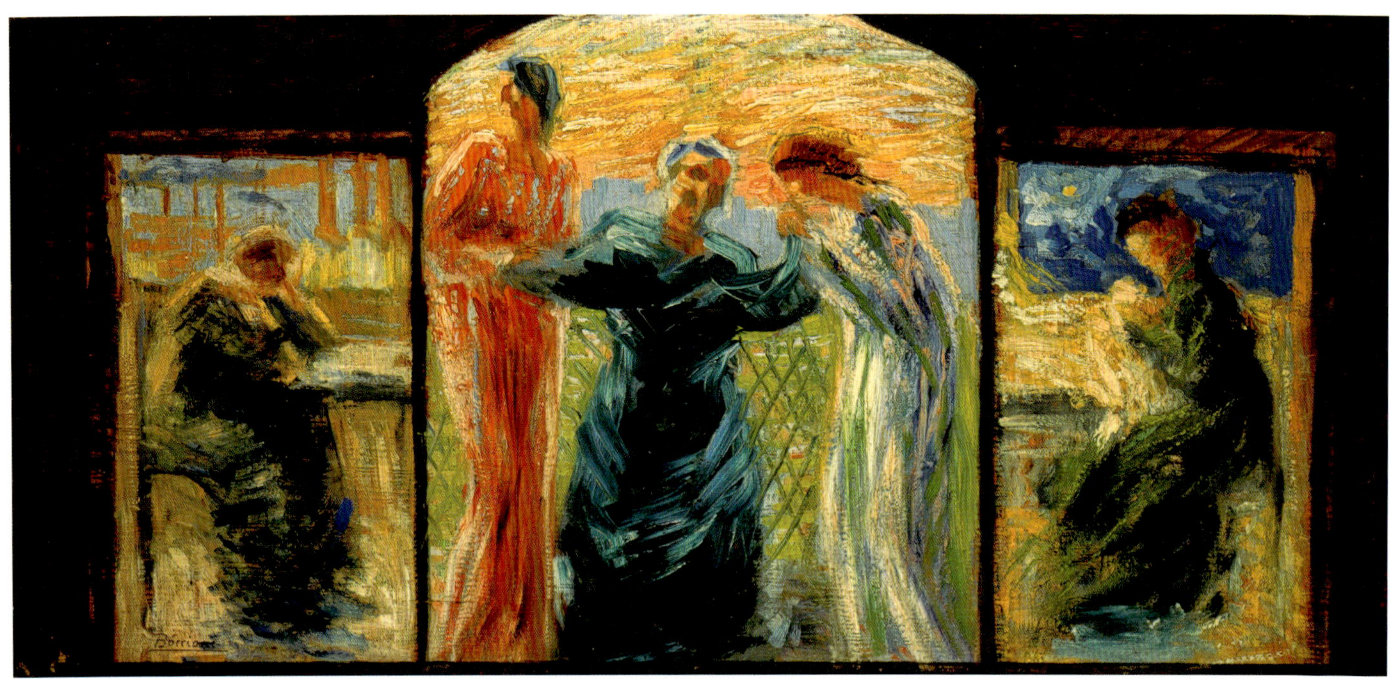

2 **Umberto Boccioni** *Triptych: We Venerate the Mother* (*Trittico: Veneriamo la madre*), 1907–08. Oil on board, 10⅝ × 22 inches (27 × 56 cm). Private collection

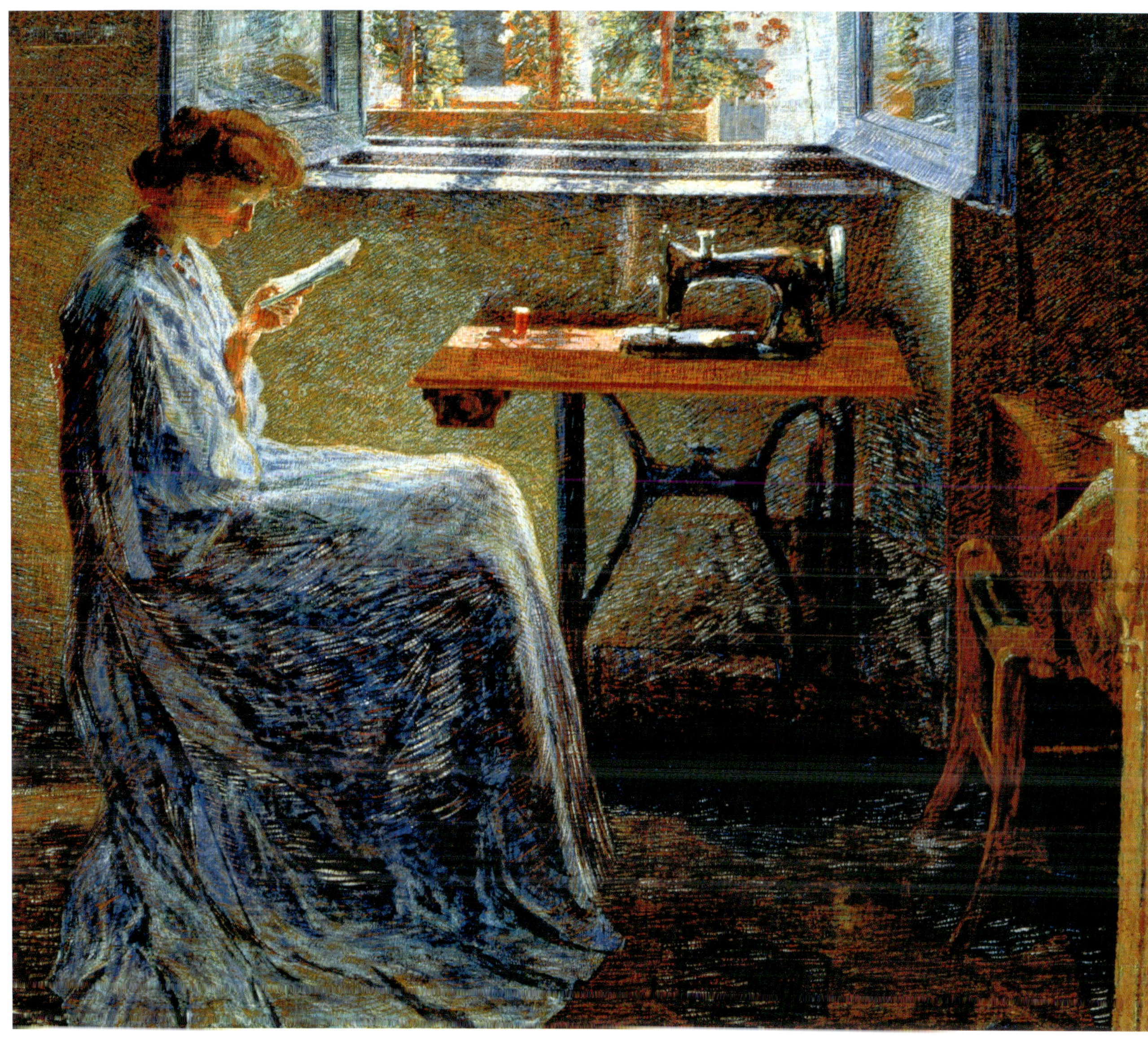

3 **Umberto Boccioni** *The Story of a Seamstress* (*Romanzo di una cucitrice*), 1908. Oil on canvas, 60⅝ × 68$^{5}/_{16}$ inches (154 × 173.5 cm). Barilla Collection of Modern Art, Parma, Italy

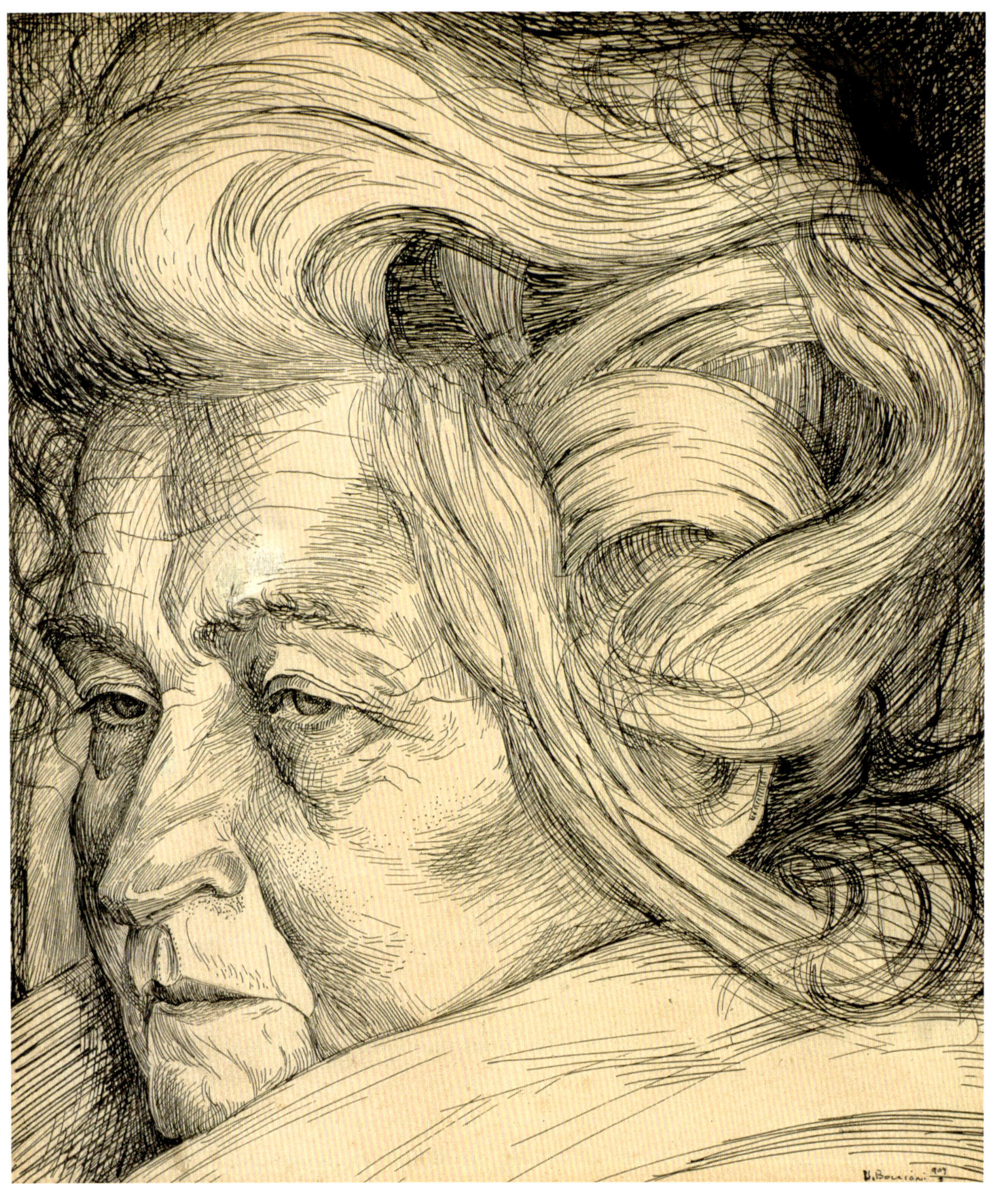

4 **Umberto Boccioni** *Mother* (*La madre*), 1909. Ink on paper, 12 15/16 × 10 15/16 inches (32.8 × 27.7 cm). Russoli Collection, Milan

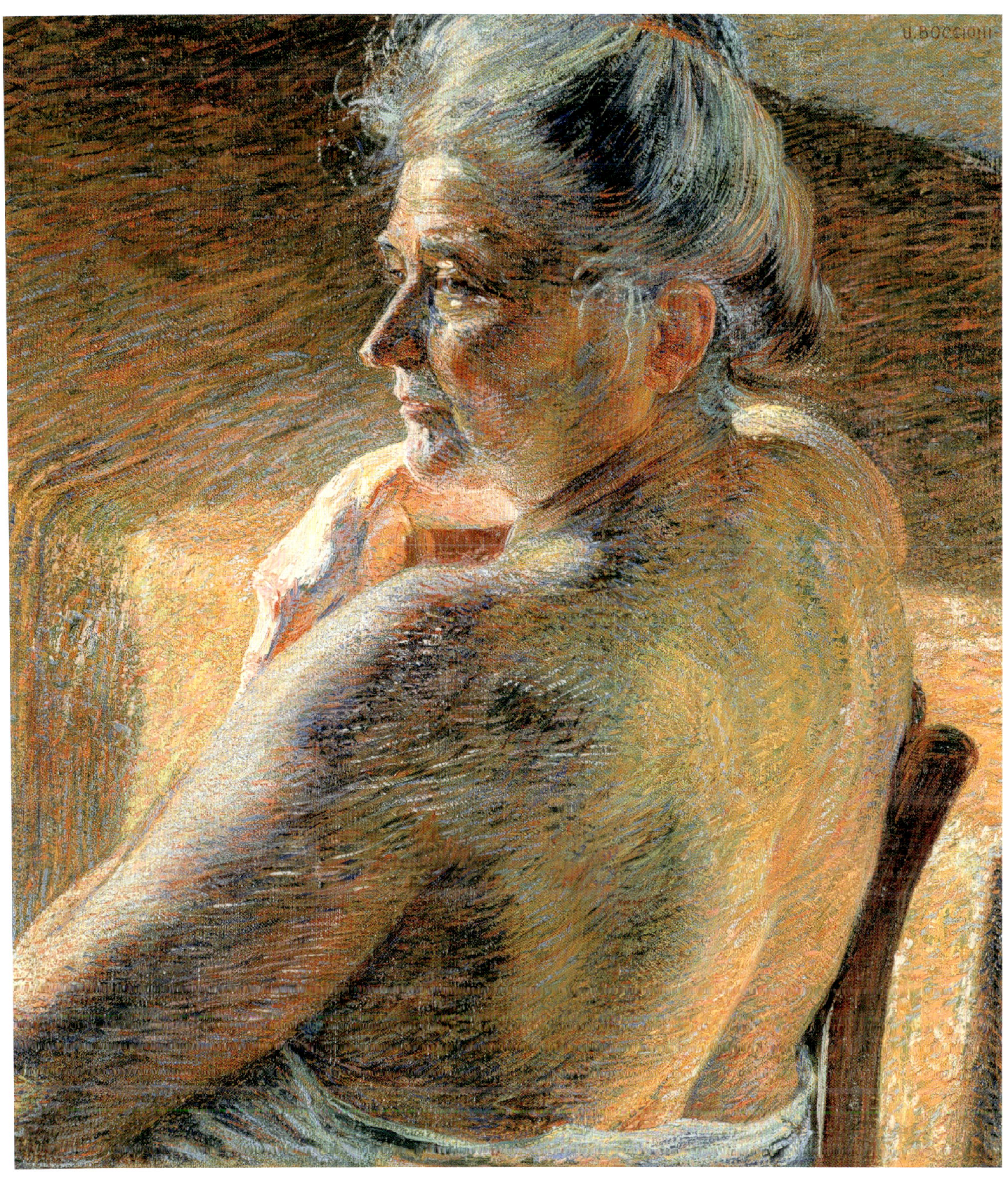

5 **Umberto Boccioni** *Controluce*, 1909. Oil on canvas, 24 7/16 × 21 5/8 inches (62 × 55 cm).
Private collection, Courtesy of Galleria dello Scudo, Verona

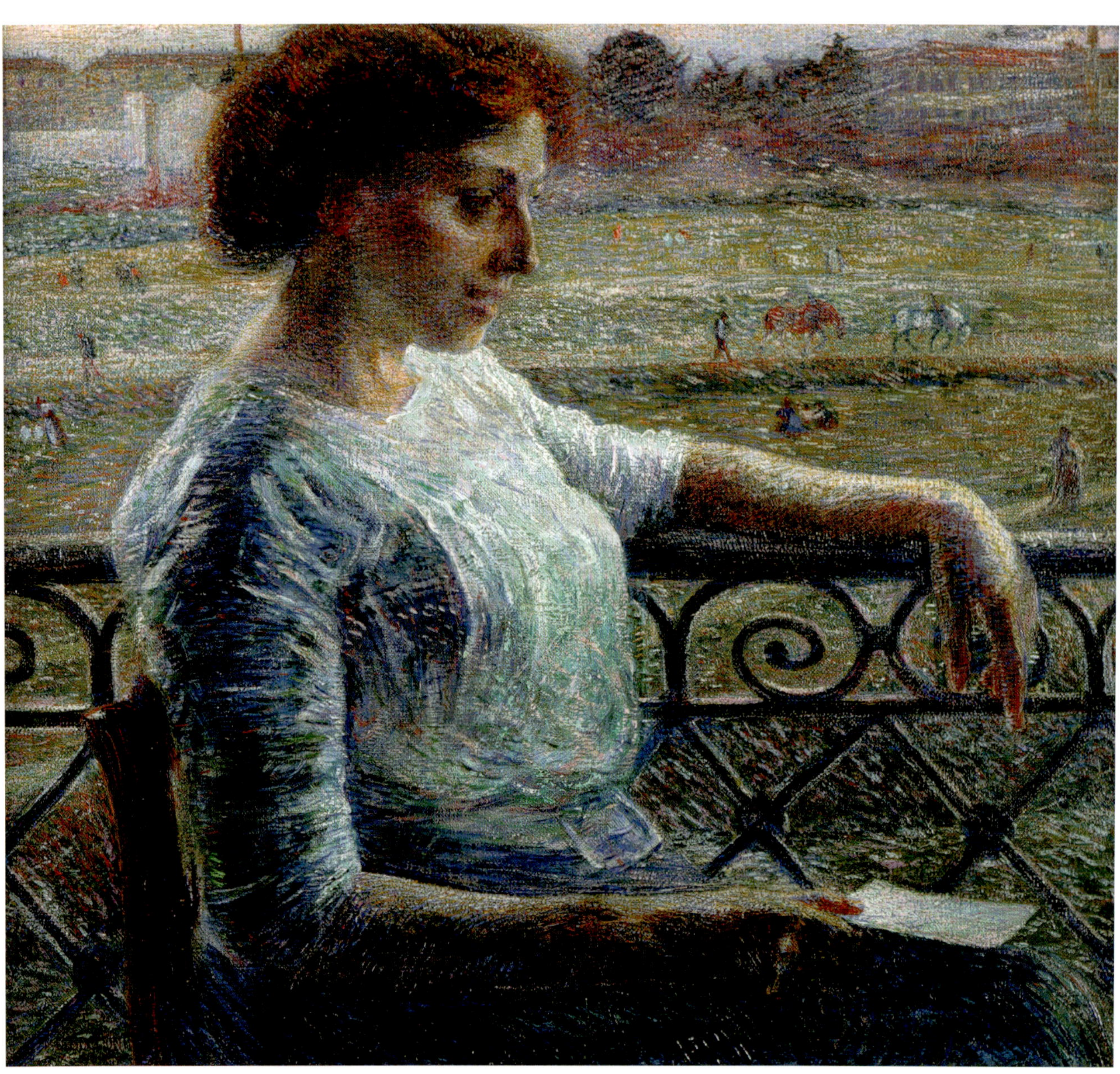

6 **Umberto Boccioni** *Sister on the Balcony* (*La sorella al balcone*), 1909. Oil on canvas, 22 1/16 × 23 5/8 inches (56 × 60 cm). Private collection, Courtesy of Galleria dello Scudo, Verona

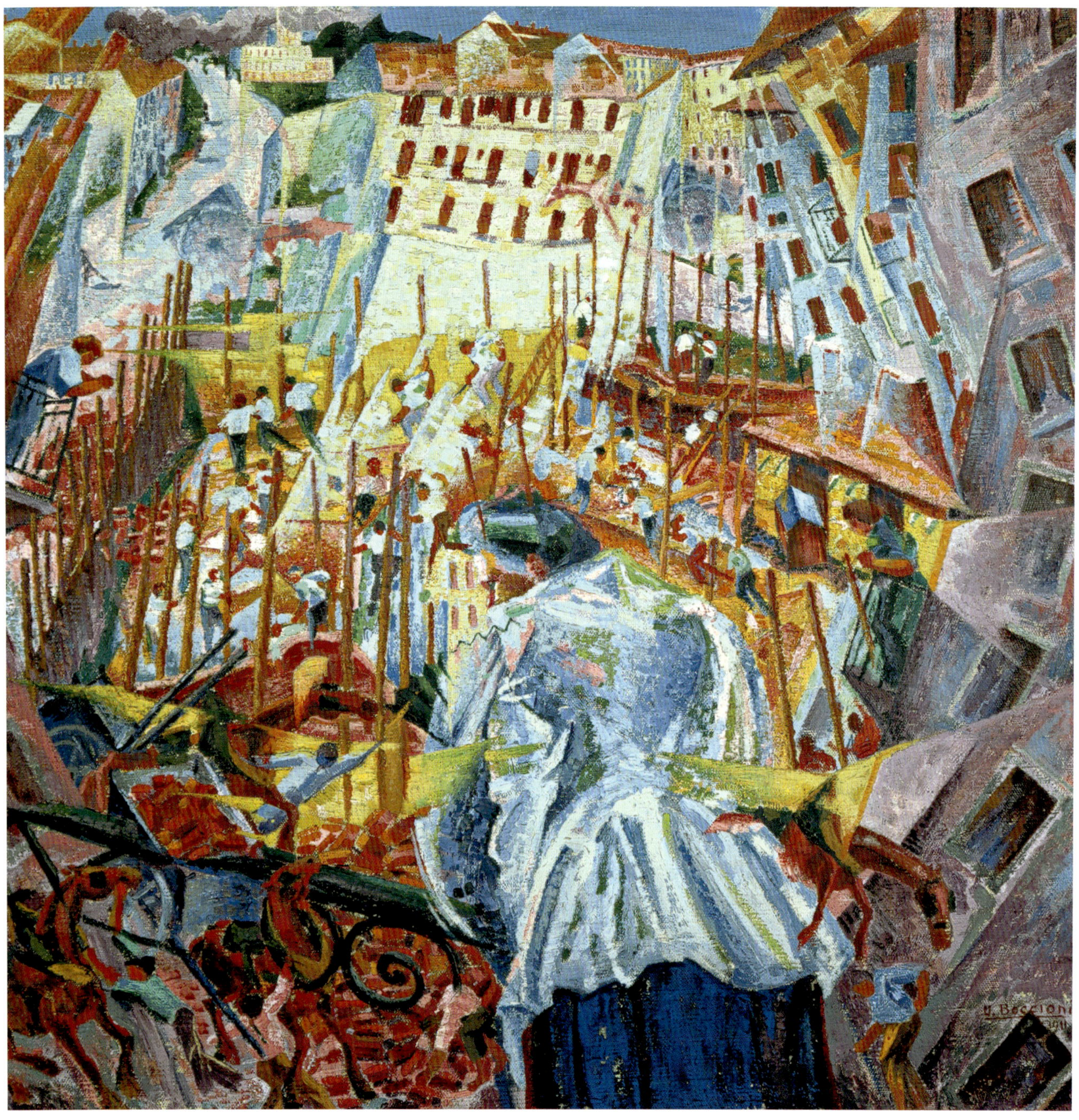

7 **Umberto Boccioni** *The Street Enters the House* (*La strada entra nella casa*), 1911. Oil on canvas, 39⅜ × 39⅜ inches (100 × 100 cm). Sprengel Museum Hannover

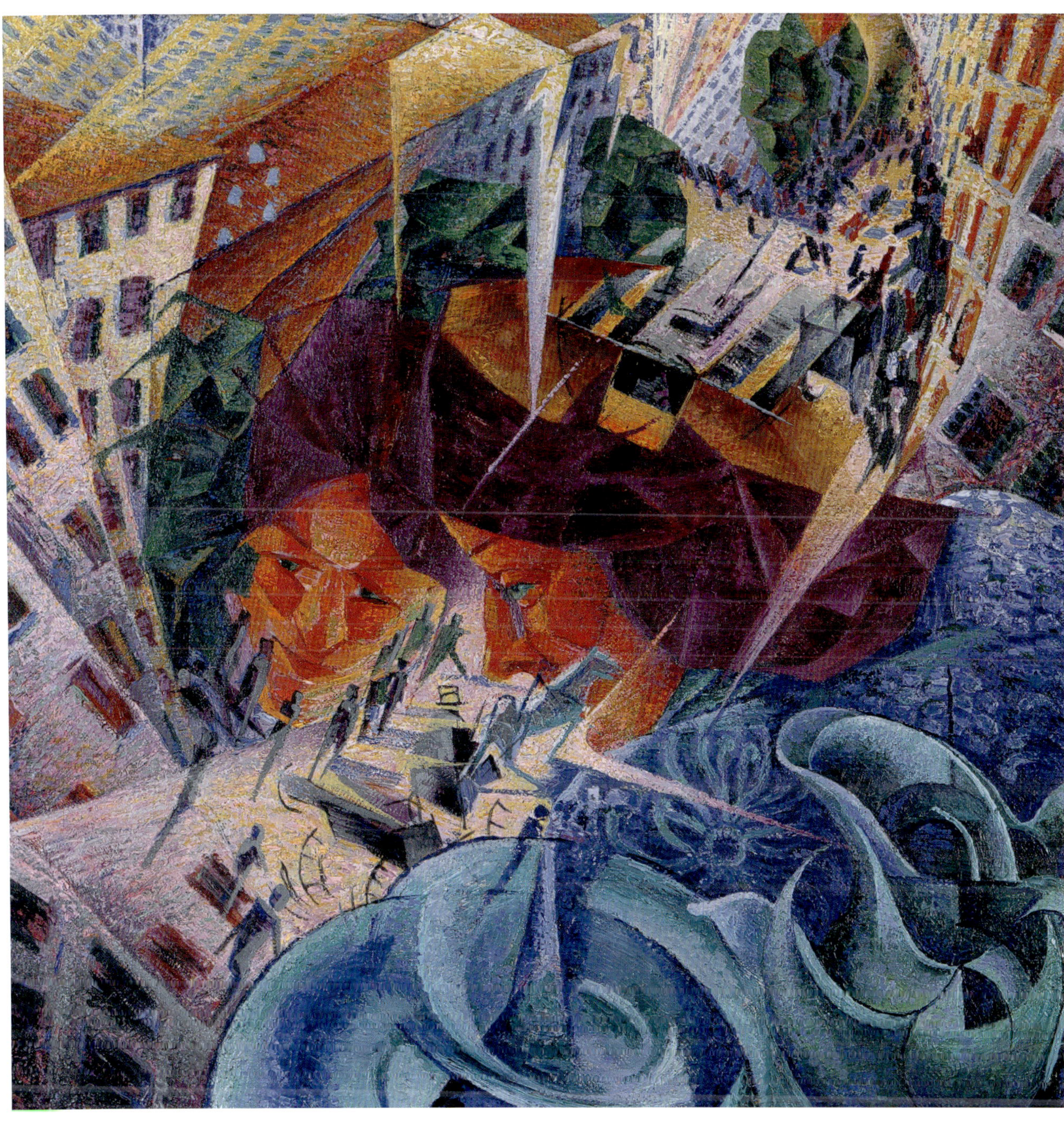

8 **Umberto Boccioni** *Simultaneous Visions* (*Visioni simultanee*), 1911. Oil on canvas, 23⅞ × 27⅜ inches (60.5 × 69.5 cm). Von der Heydt-Museum, Wuppertal, Germany

Cubism: The Figure

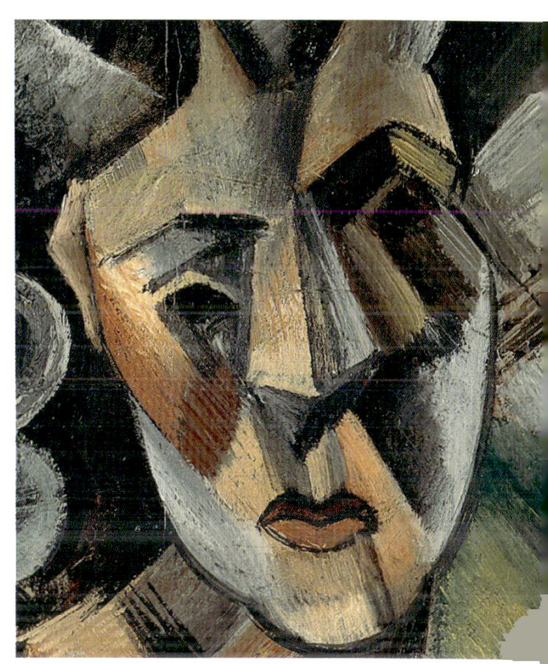

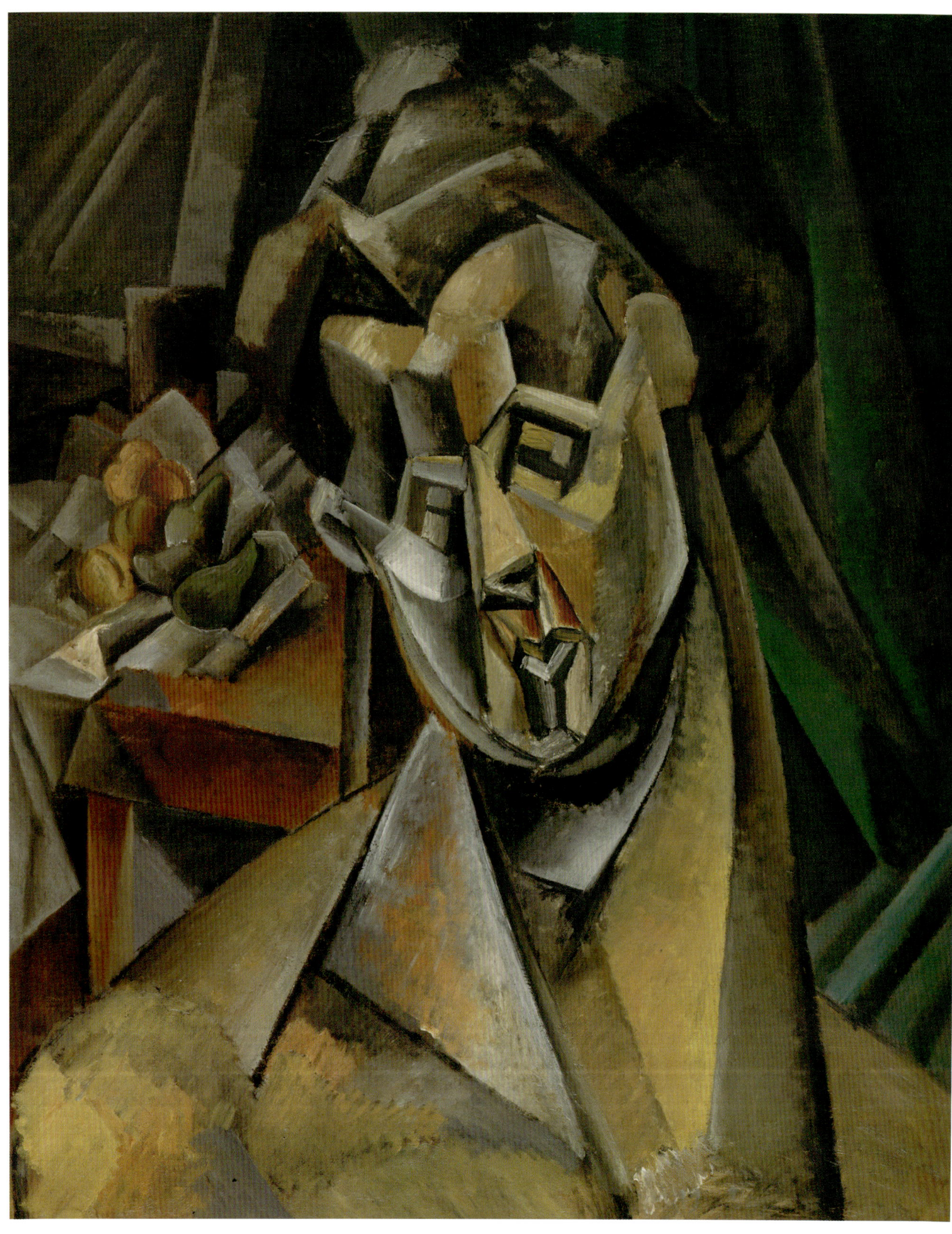

9 **Pablo Picasso** *Woman with Pears (Fernande) (Femme aux poires)*, 1909. Oil on canvas, 36¼ × 27⅞ inches (92.1 × 70.8 cm). The Museum of Modern Art, New York, Florene May Schoenborn Bequest, 1996

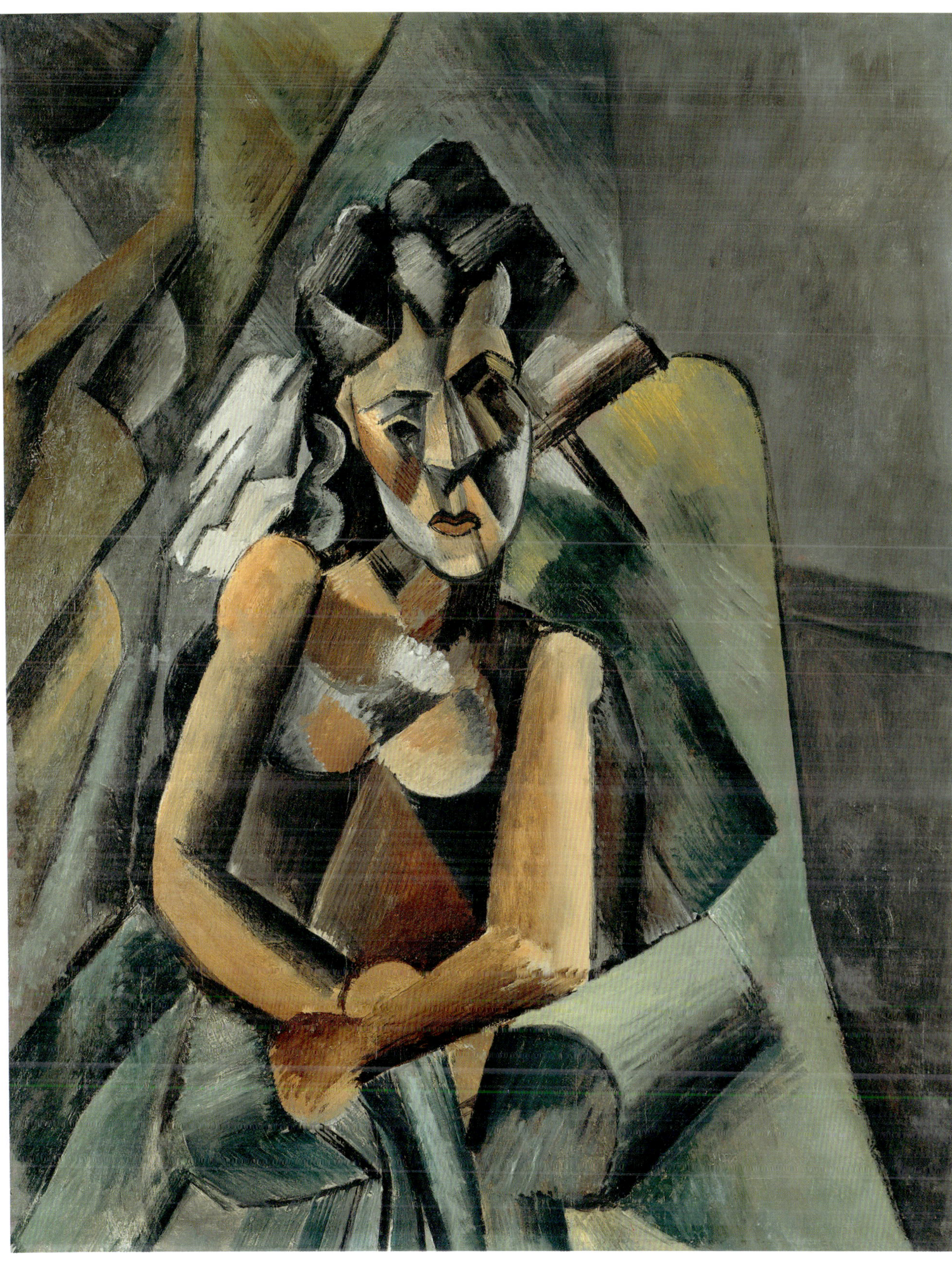

10 **Pablo Picasso** *Seated Woman* (*Femme assise*), 1909. Oil on canvas, 39⅜ × 31½ inches (100 × 80 cm). Staatliche Museen zu Berlin, Nationalgalerie

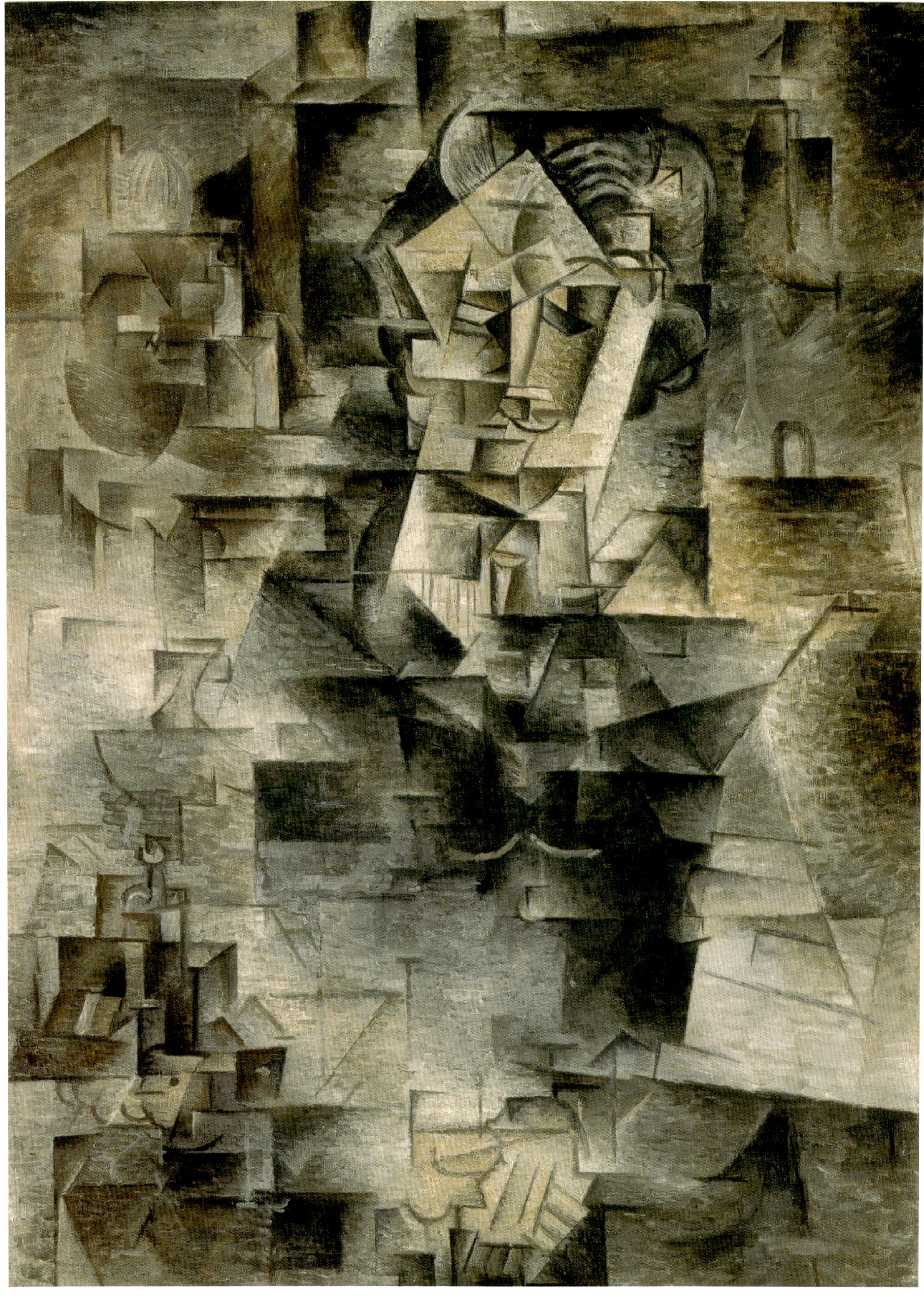

11 **Pablo Picasso** *Daniel-Henry Kahnweiler*, 1910. Oil on canvas, 39 13/16 × 28 7/8 inches (101.1 × 73.3 cm). The Art Institute of Chicago, Gift of Mrs. Gilbert W. Chapman in memory of Charles B. Goodspeed

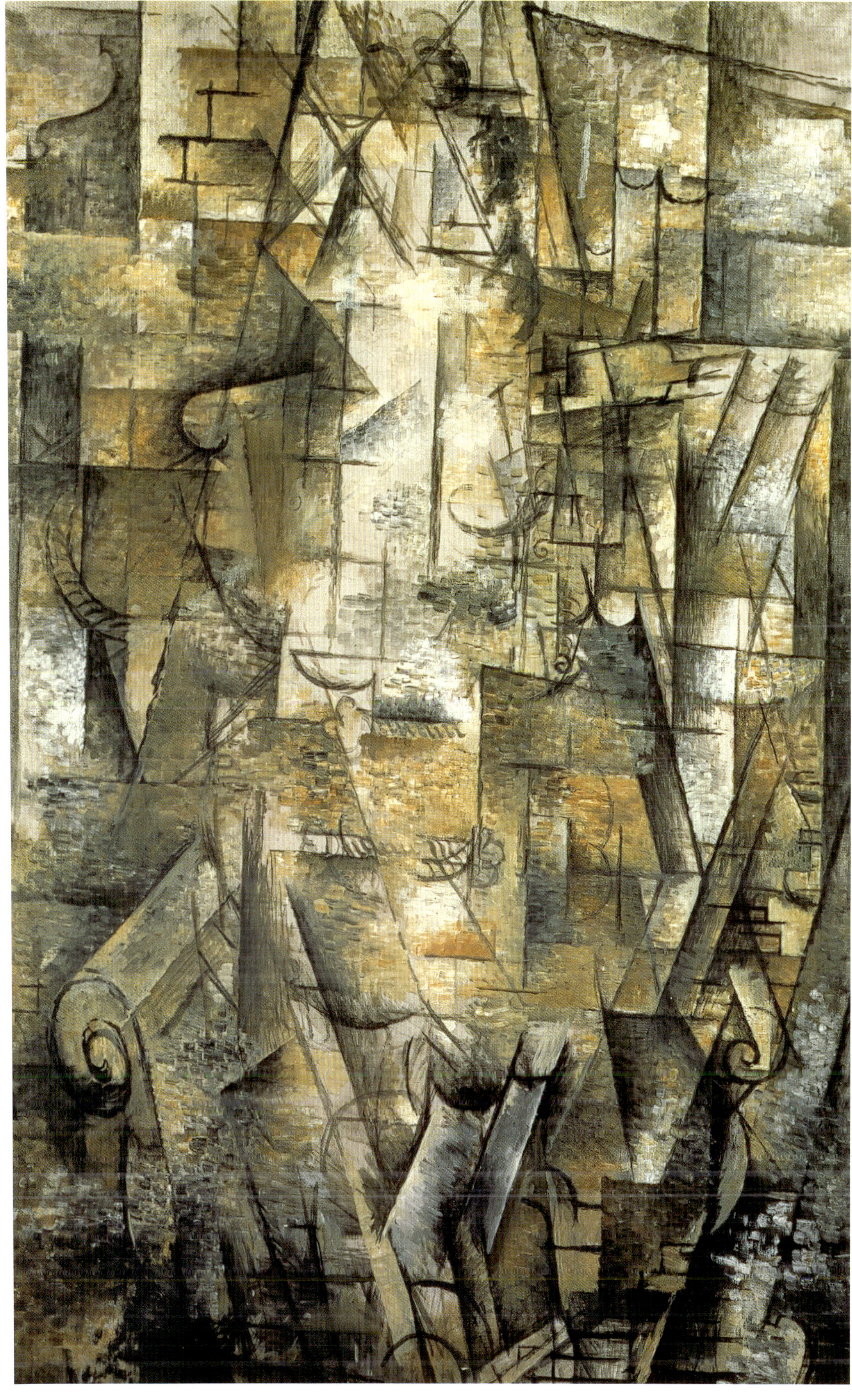

12 **Georges Braque** *Woman Reading* (*Femme lisant*), 1911. Oil on canvas, 51³⁄₁₆ × 31⁷⁄₈ inches (130 × 81 cm). Fondation Beyeler, Riehen/Basel

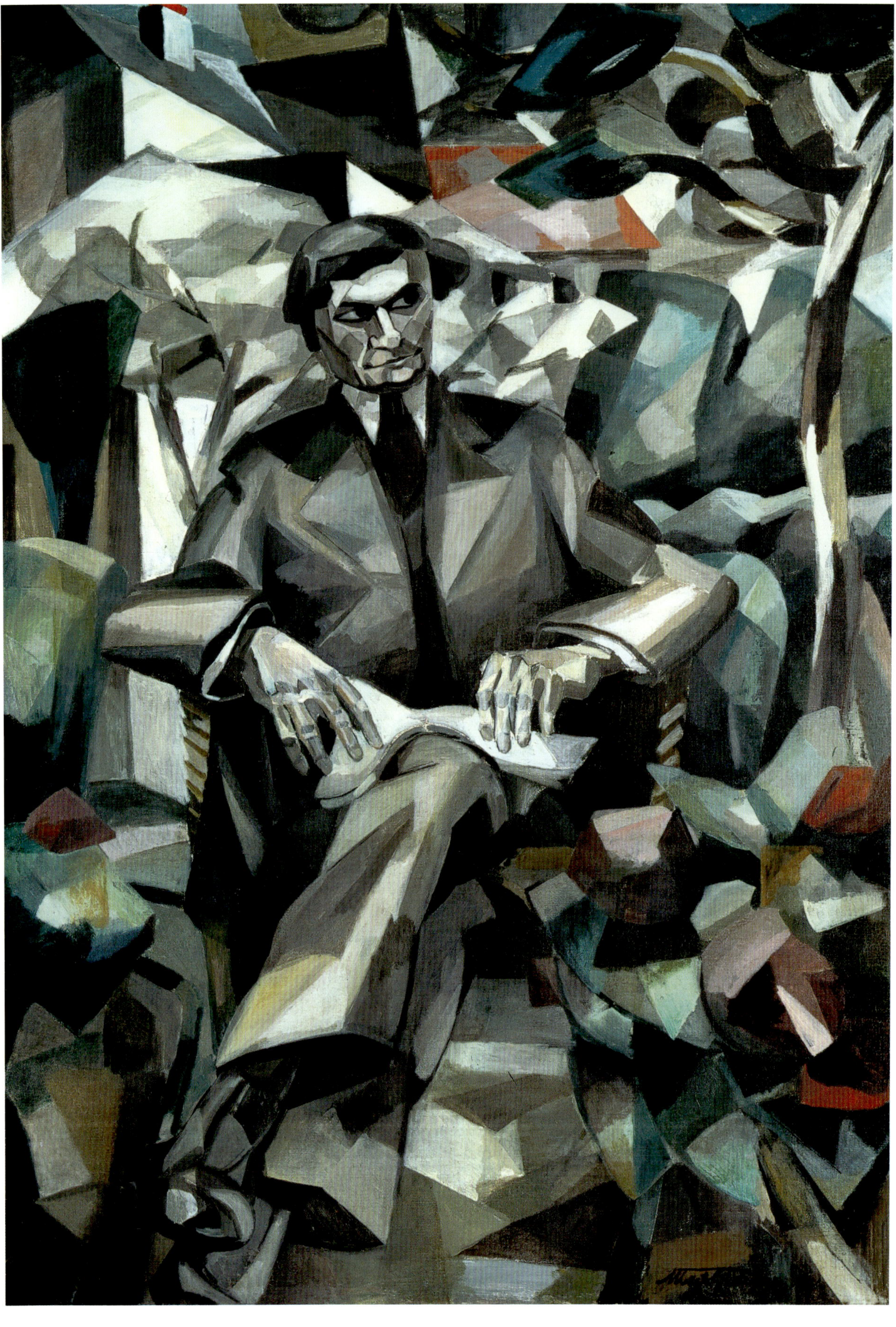

13 **Albert Gleizes** *Portrait of Jacques Nayral (Portrait de Jacques Nayral)*, 1911. Oil on canvas, 63¾ × 44⅞ inches (161.9 × 114 cm). Tate, London, Purchased 1979

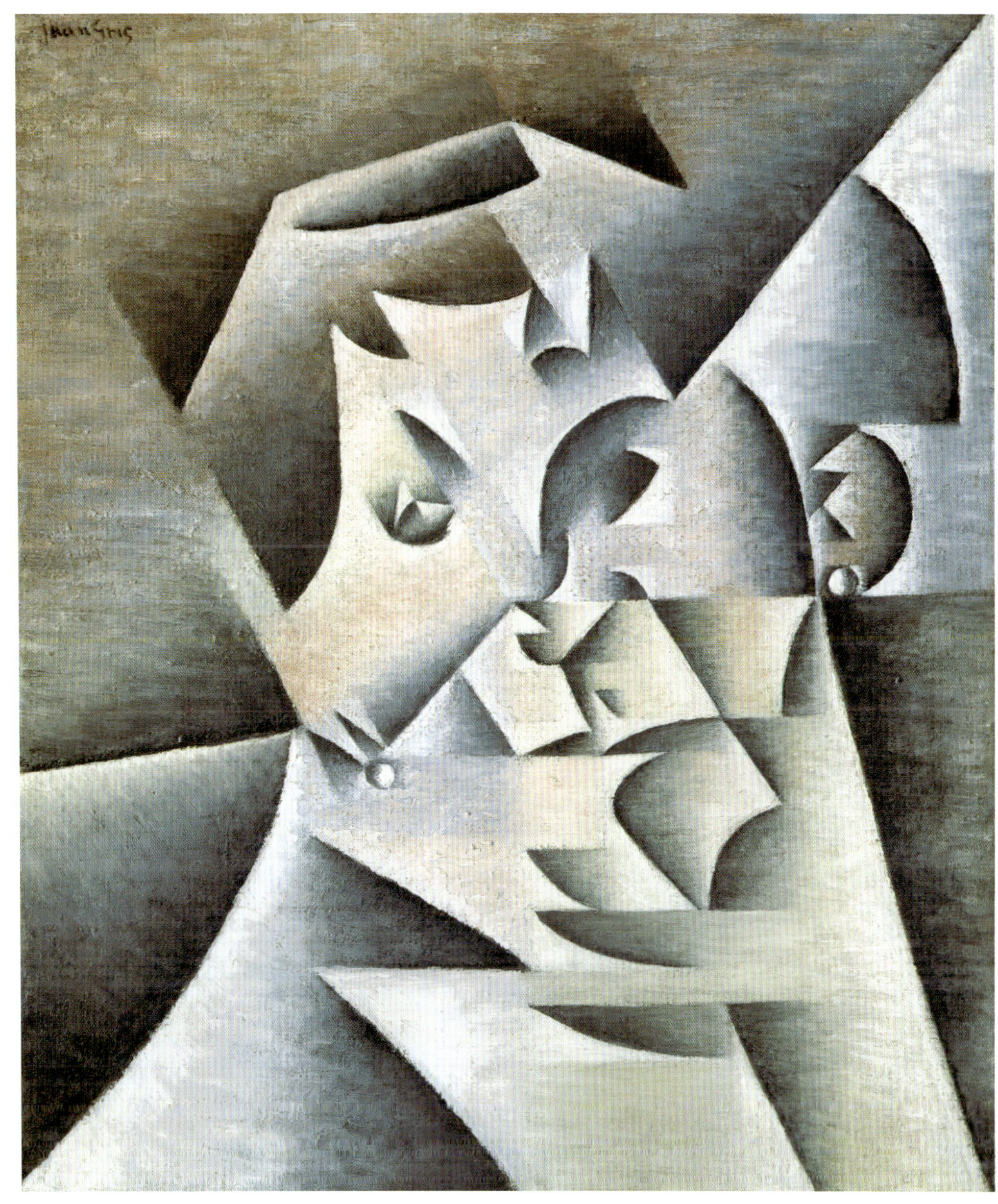

14 **Juan Gris** *Portrait of the Artist's Mother* (*Portait de la mère de l'artiste*), 1912. Oil on canvas, $21\frac{5}{8} \times 18\frac{1}{8}$ inches (55 × 46 cm). Private collection

15 **Marcel Duchamp** *Nude Descending a Staircase (No. 2)* (*Nu descendant un escalier [n° 2]*), 1912. Oil on canvas, 57⅞ × 35⅛ inches (147 × 89.2 cm). Philadelphia Museum of Art, The Louise and Walter Arensberg Collection

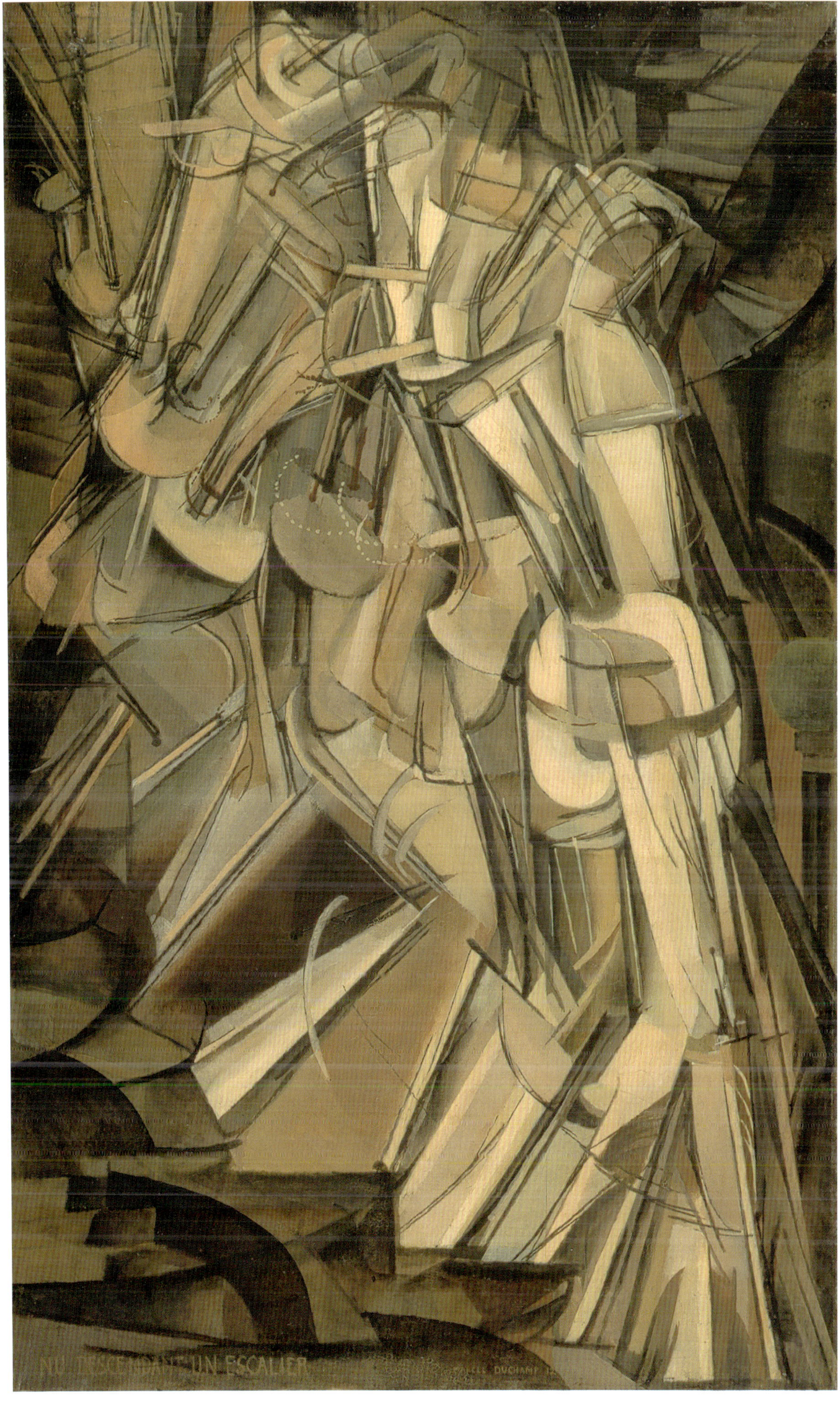
UN ESCALIER
DUCHAMP

16 **Fernand Léger** *Nude Model in the Studio* (*Nu dans l'atelier*), 1912–13. Oil on canvas, 50⅝ × 37¾ inches (128.6 × 95.9 cm). Solomon R. Guggenheim Museum, New York 49.1193

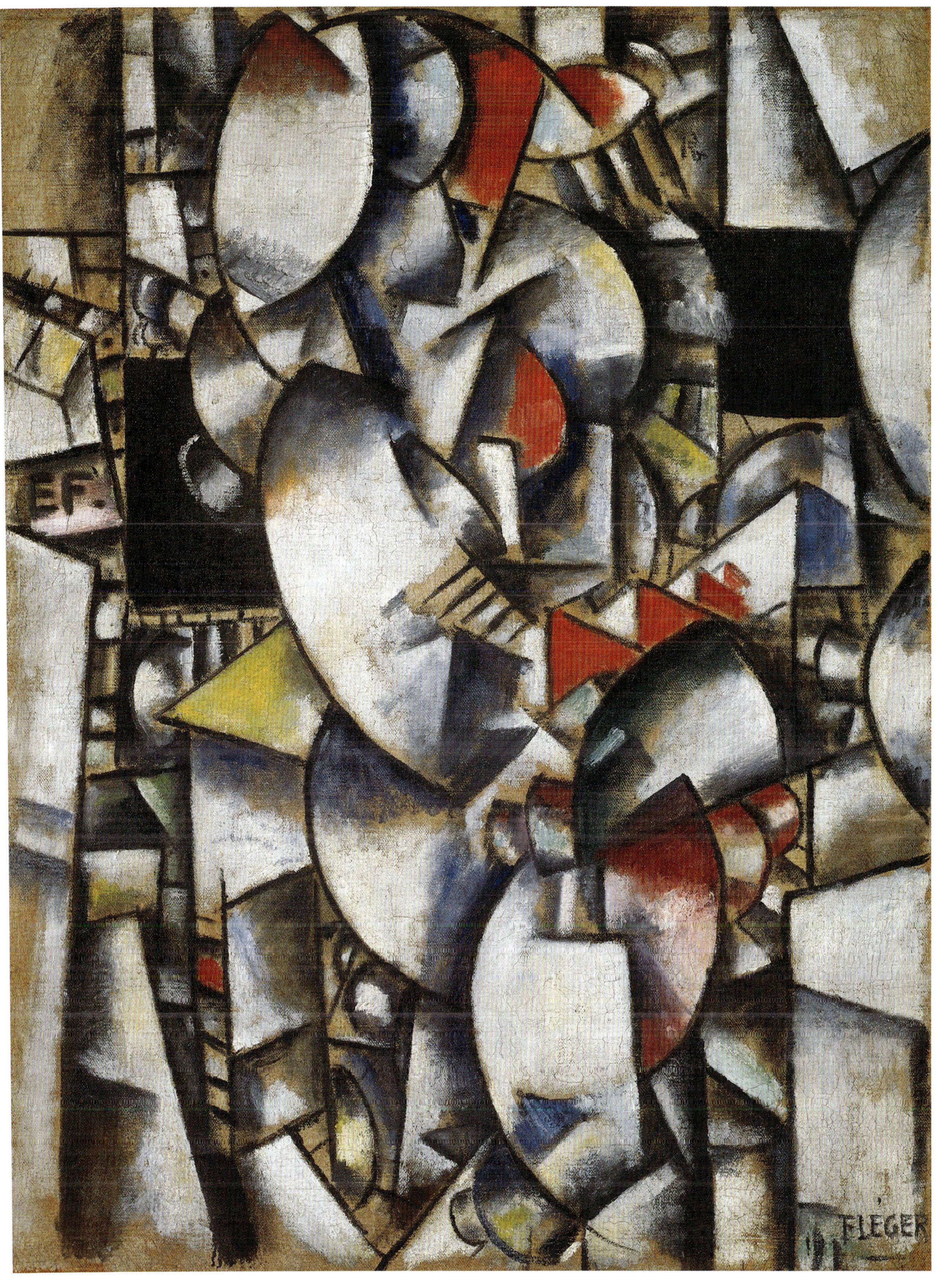
EF.
F.LEGER

Cubism: The Landscape

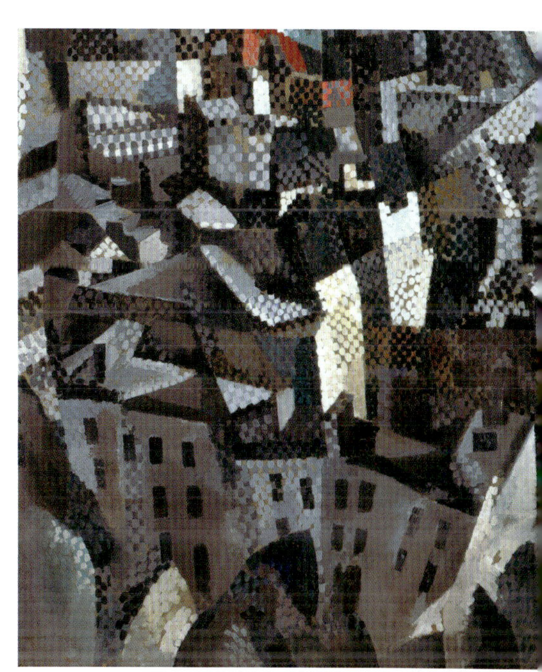

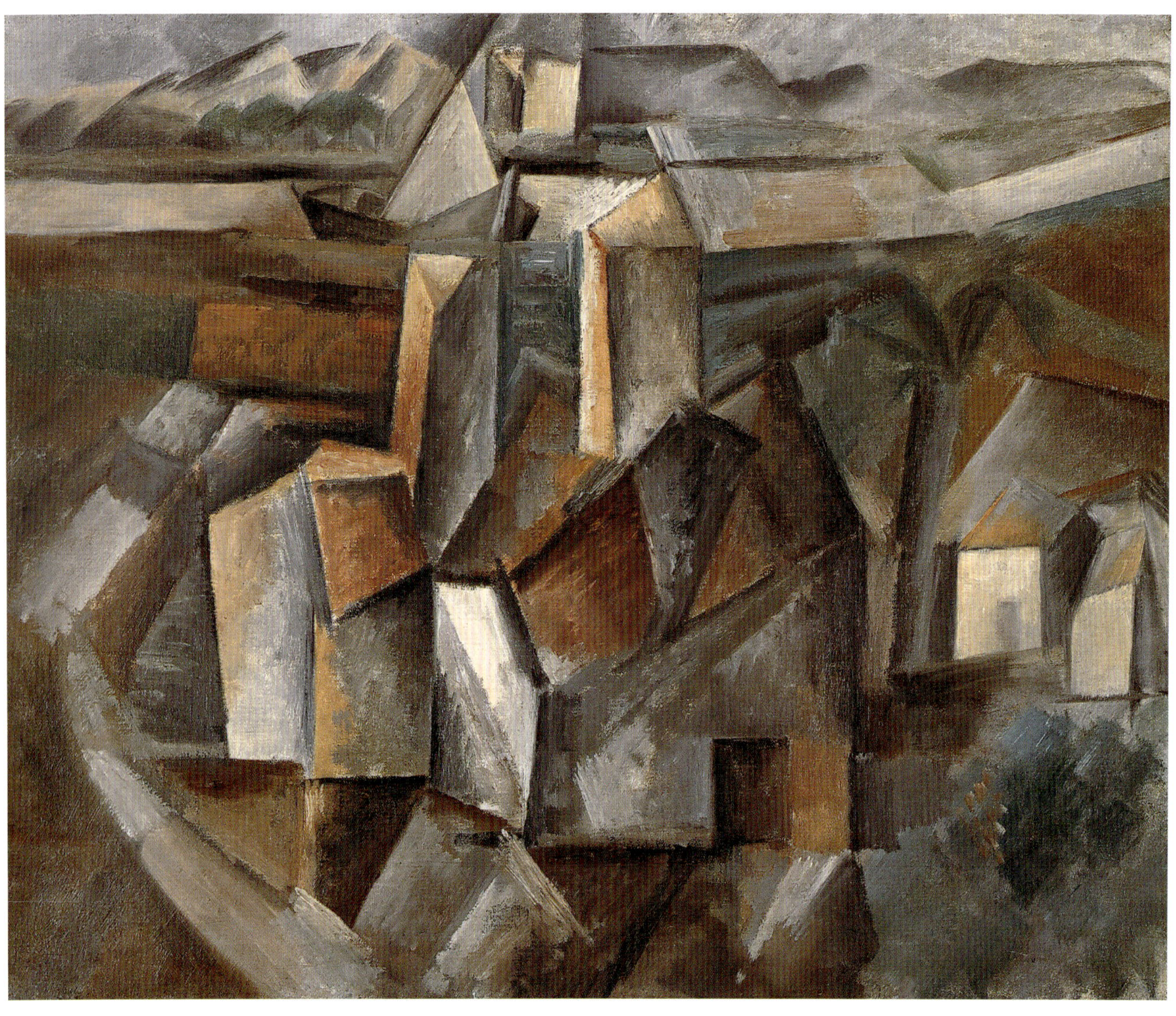

17 **Pablo Picasso** *The Oil Mill* (*Le Moulin à huile*), 1909. Oil on canvas, 15 × 18⅛ inches (38 × 46 cm).
Private collection

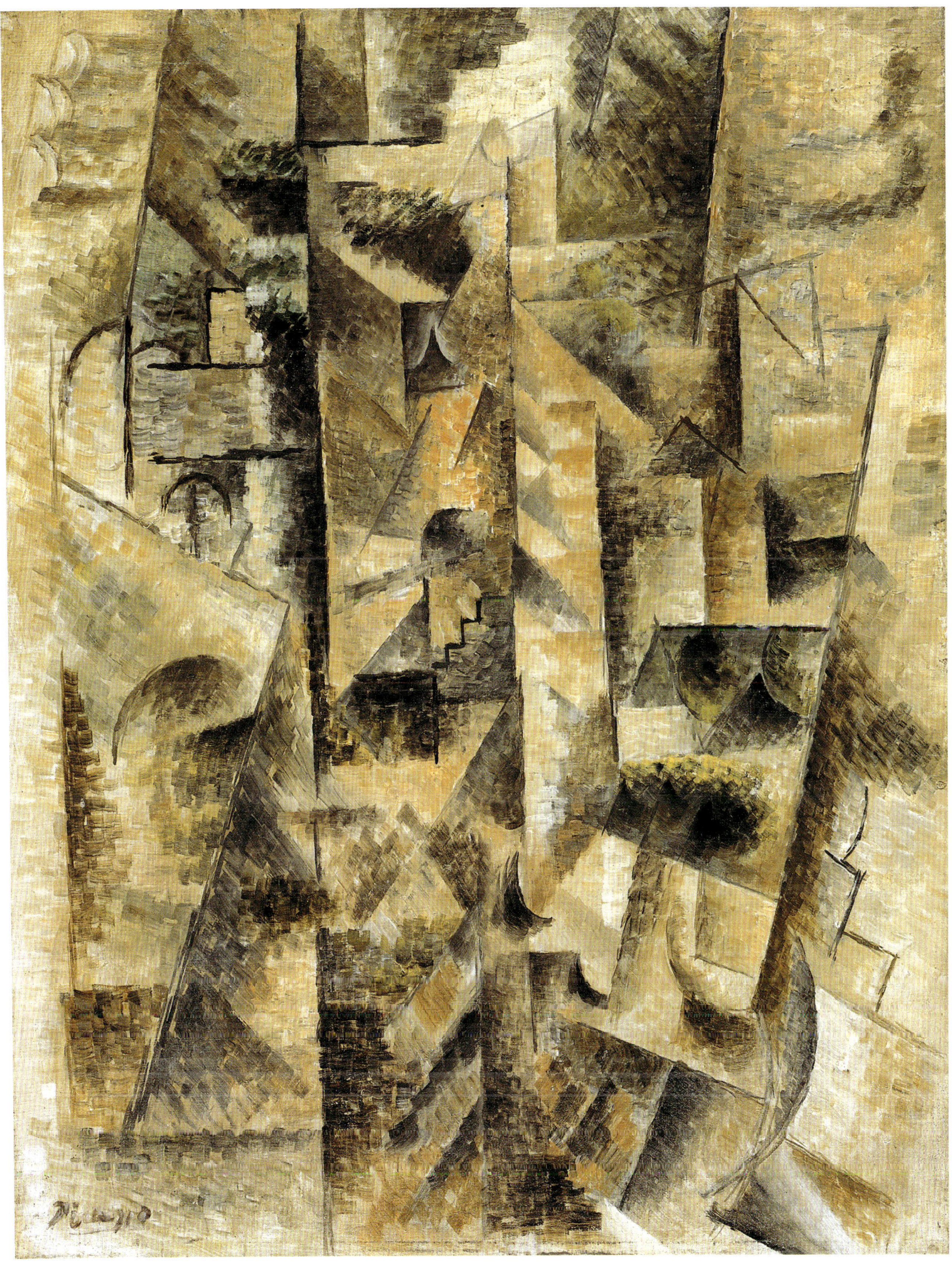

18 **Pablo Picasso** *Landscape at Céret* (*Paysage à Céret*), summer 1911. Oil on canvas, 25⅝ × 19¾ inches (65.1 × 50.3 cm). Solomon R. Guggenheim Museum, New York 37.538

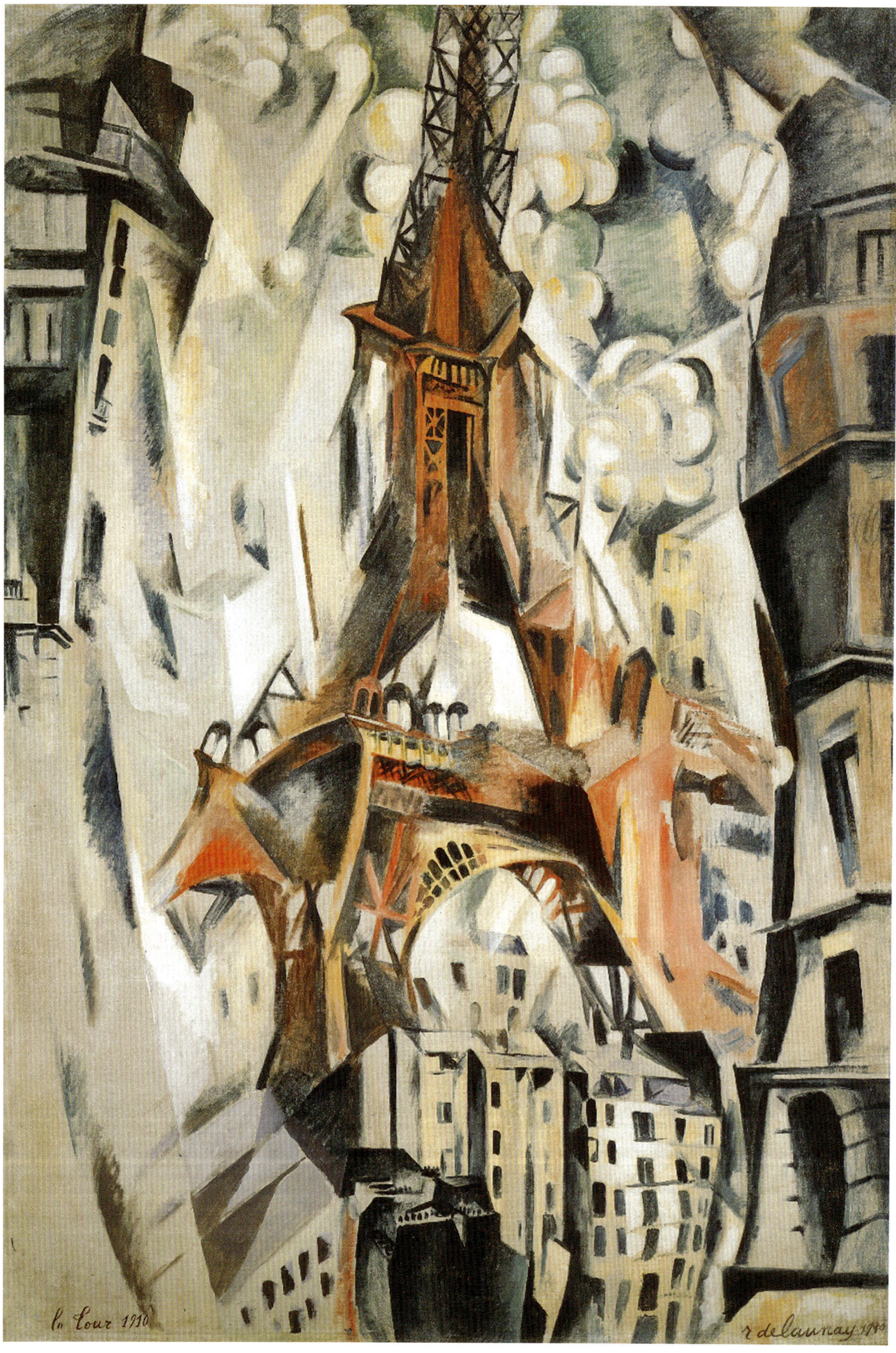

19 **Robert Delaunay** *Eiffel Tower* (*Tour Eiffel*), 1911. Oil on canvas, 79½ × 54½ inches (202 × 138.4 cm). Solomon R. Guggenheim Museum, New York, Gift, Solomon R. Guggenheim 37.463

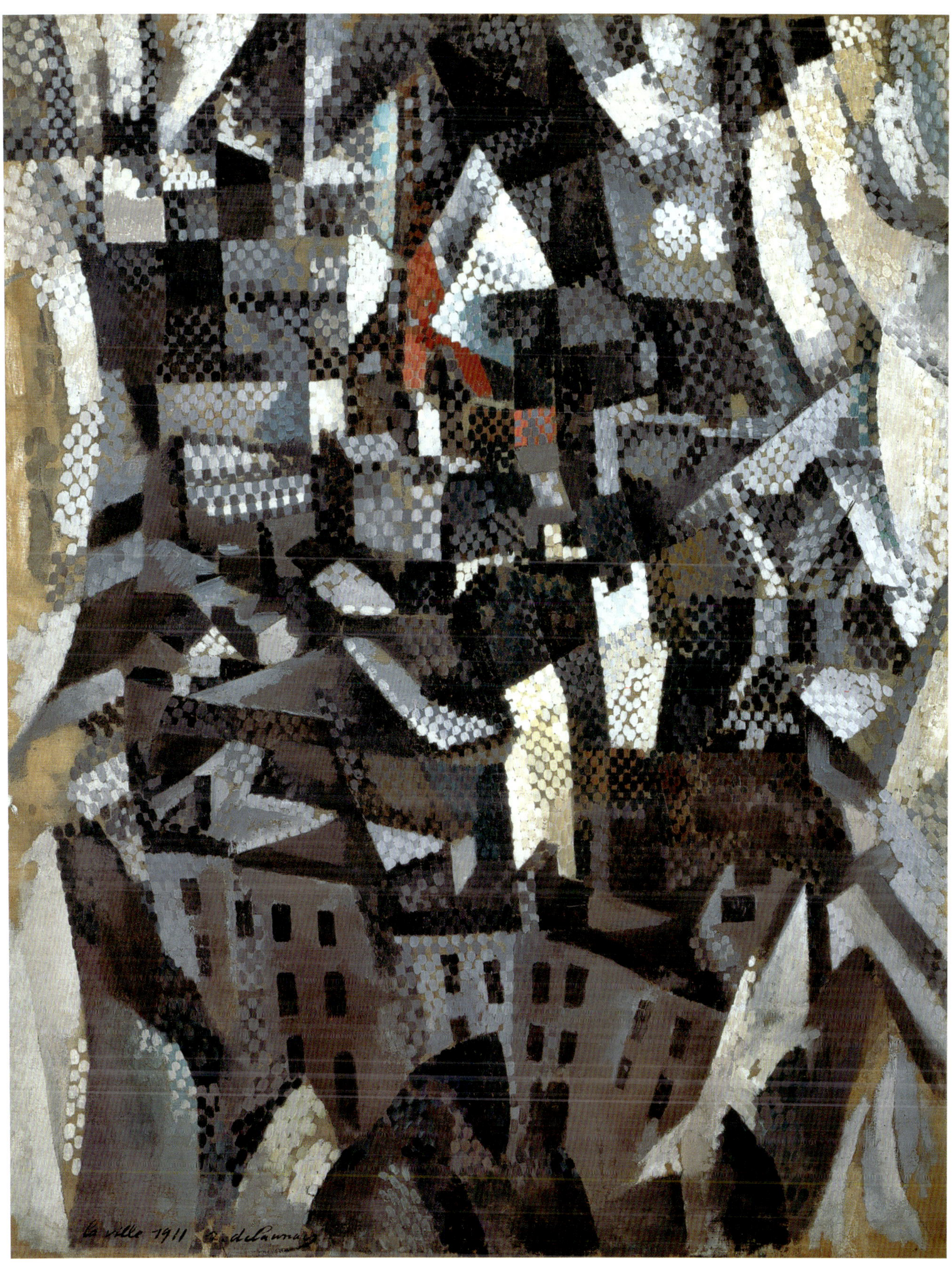

20 **Robert Delaunay** *The City* (*La Ville*), 1911. Oil on canvas, 57 1/16 × 44 1/8 inches (145 × 112 cm). Solomon R. Guggenheim Museum, New York 38.464

Boccioni: Futurism

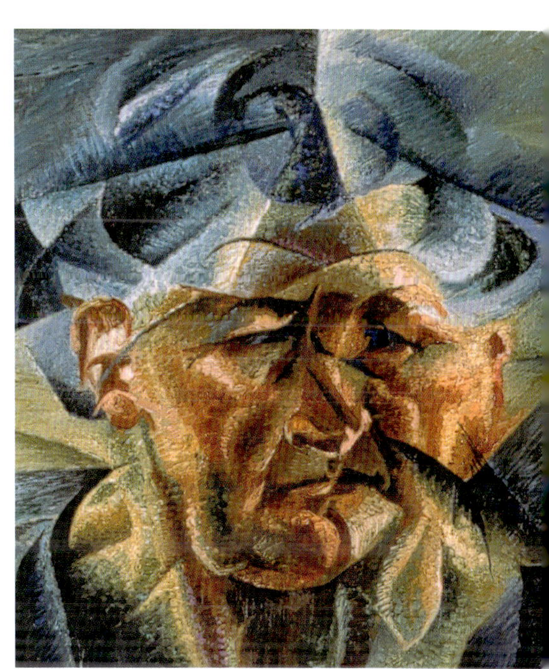

21 **Umberto Boccioni** *Abstract Dimensions* (*Dimensioni astratte*), 1912. Tempera on canvas, 23 7/16 × 23 5/8 inches (59.5 × 60 cm). Civiche Raccolte d'Arte, Museo d'Arte Contemporanea, Milan, Courtesy of Comune di Milano

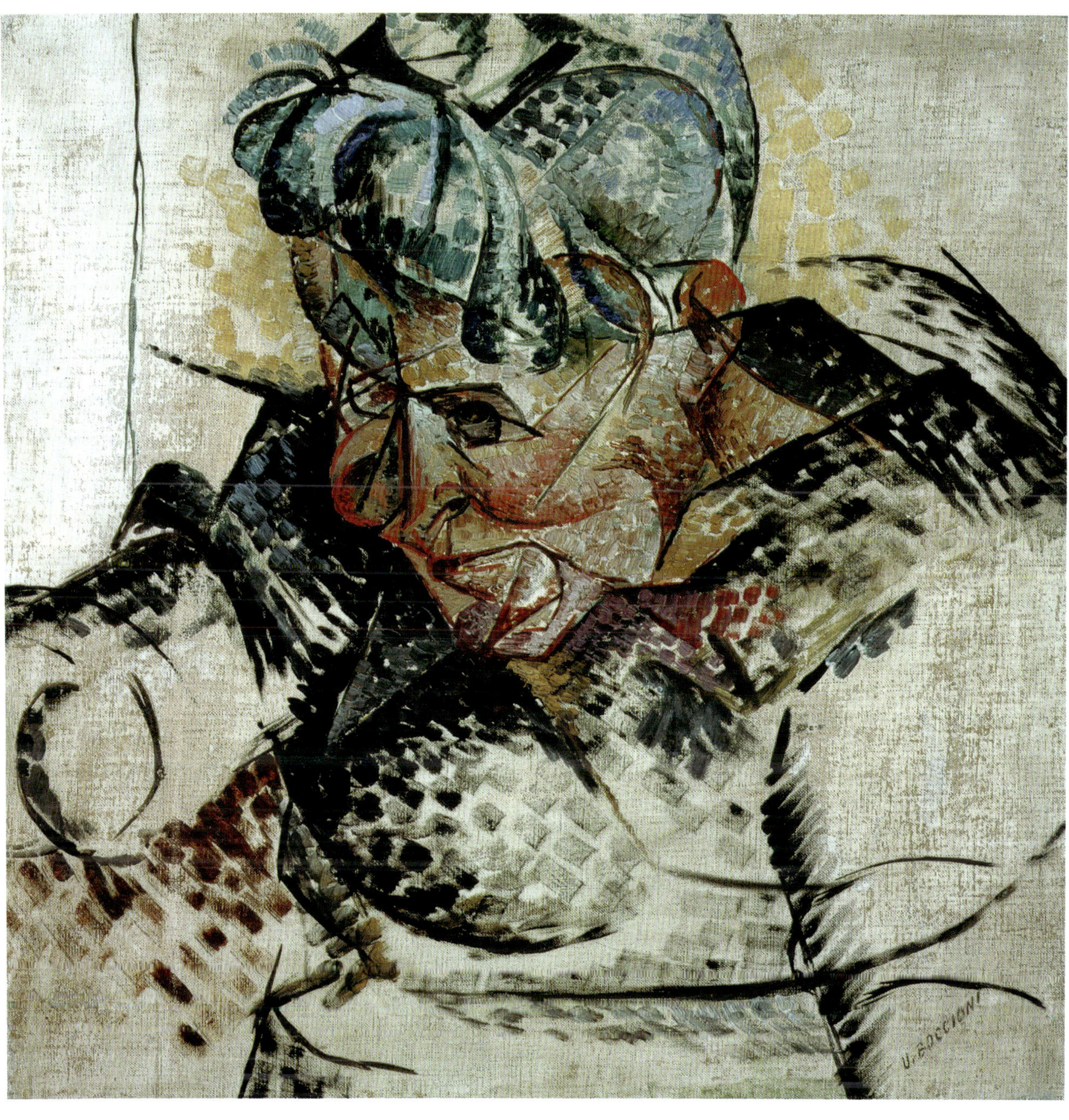
U. BOCCIONI

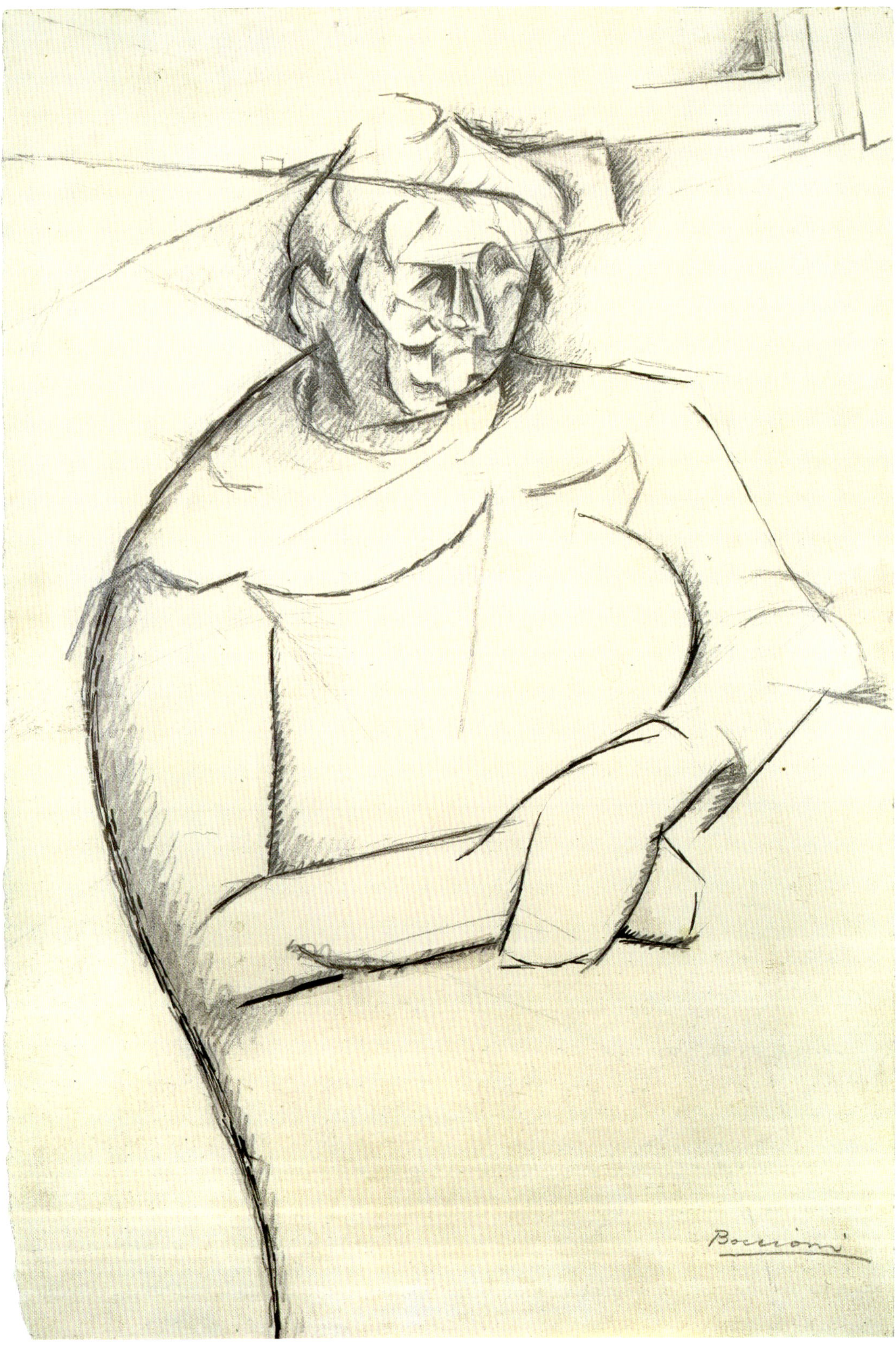

22 **Umberto Boccioni** *Seated Mother with Folded Hands (Half-Length Portrait of Mother)* (*La madre seduta con le mani incrociate [Ritratto a mezza figura della madre]*), 1911–12. Pencil and pen on paper, 12¼ × 8¼ inches (31 × 21 cm). Civiche Raccolte d'Arte, Gabinetto dei Disegni, Milan, Courtesy of Comune di Milano

116

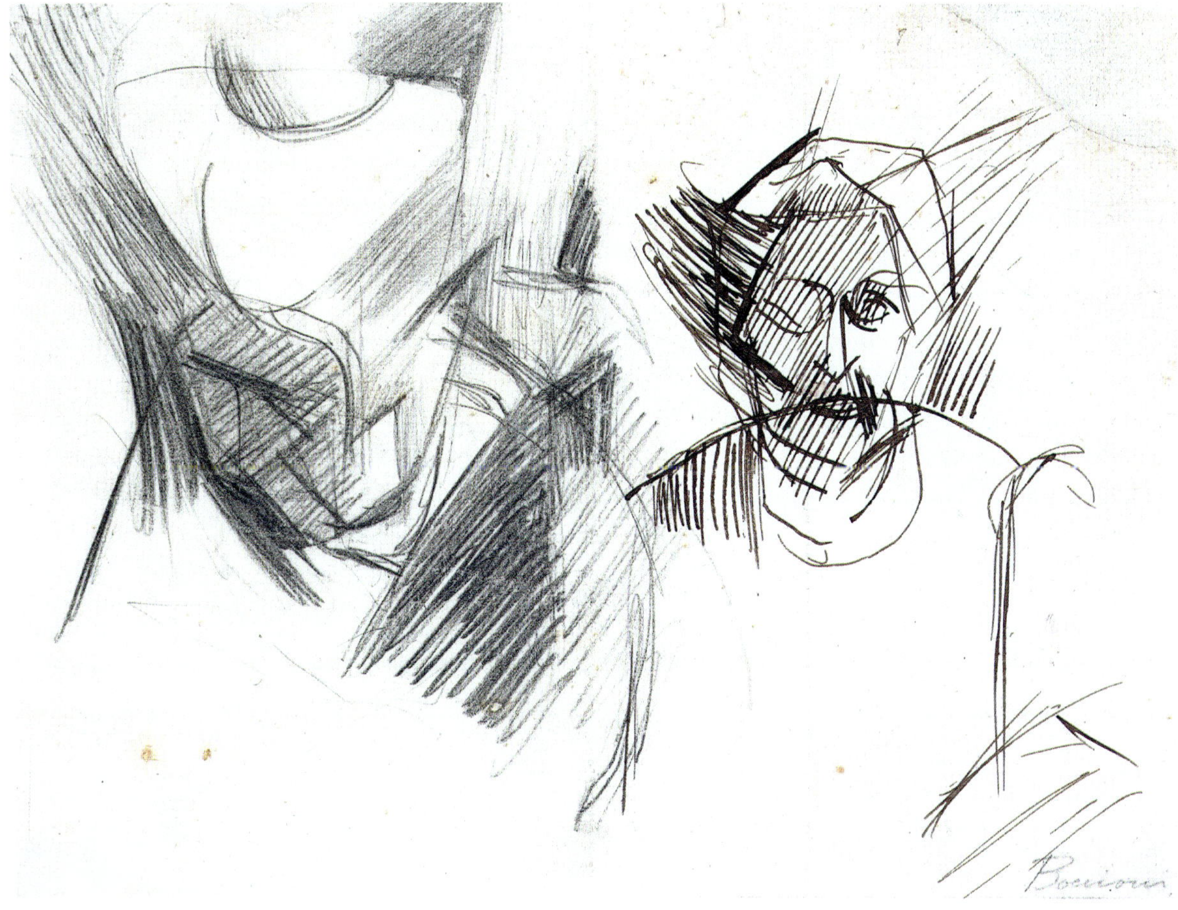

23 **Umberto Boccioni** *Studies of Head* (*Studi di testa*), 1912. Pencil and pen on paper, 6½ × 8¹¹⁄₁₆ inches (16.5 × 22 cm). Private collection

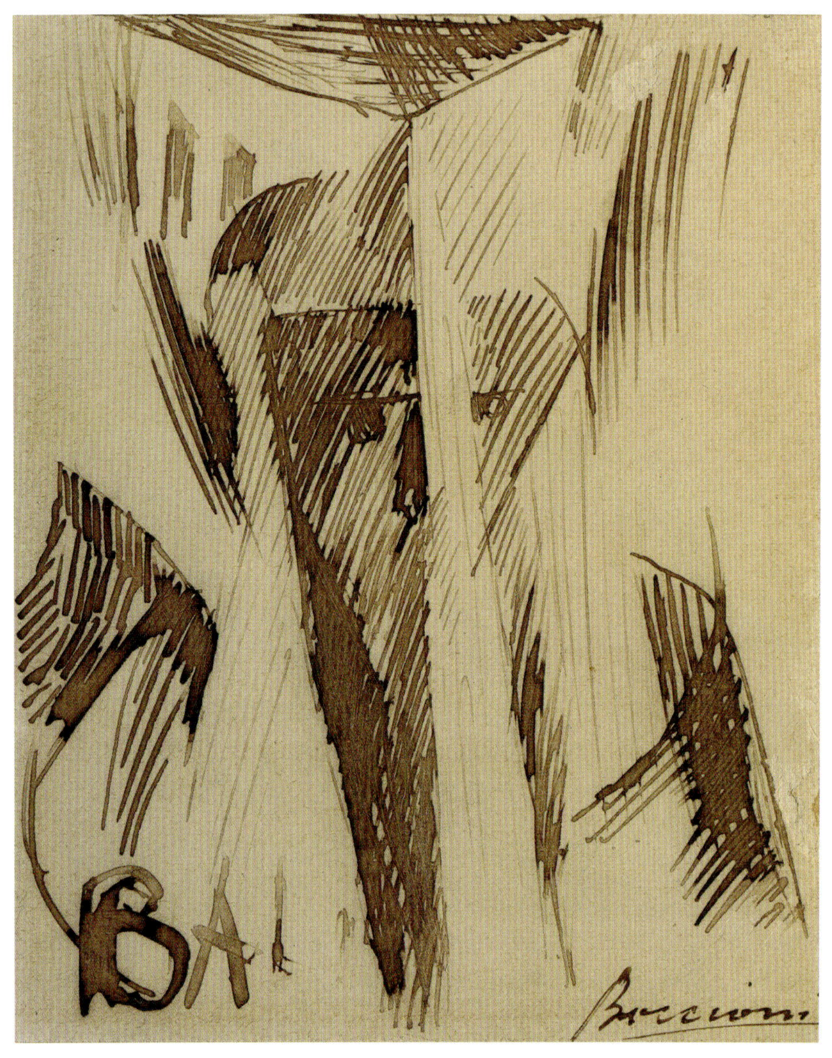

24 **Umberto Boccioni** Study for cover of Balilla Pratella's *Musica futurista*, 1912. Ink on paper, $4\frac{15}{16} \times 3\frac{15}{16}$ inches (12.5 × 10 cm). Private collection

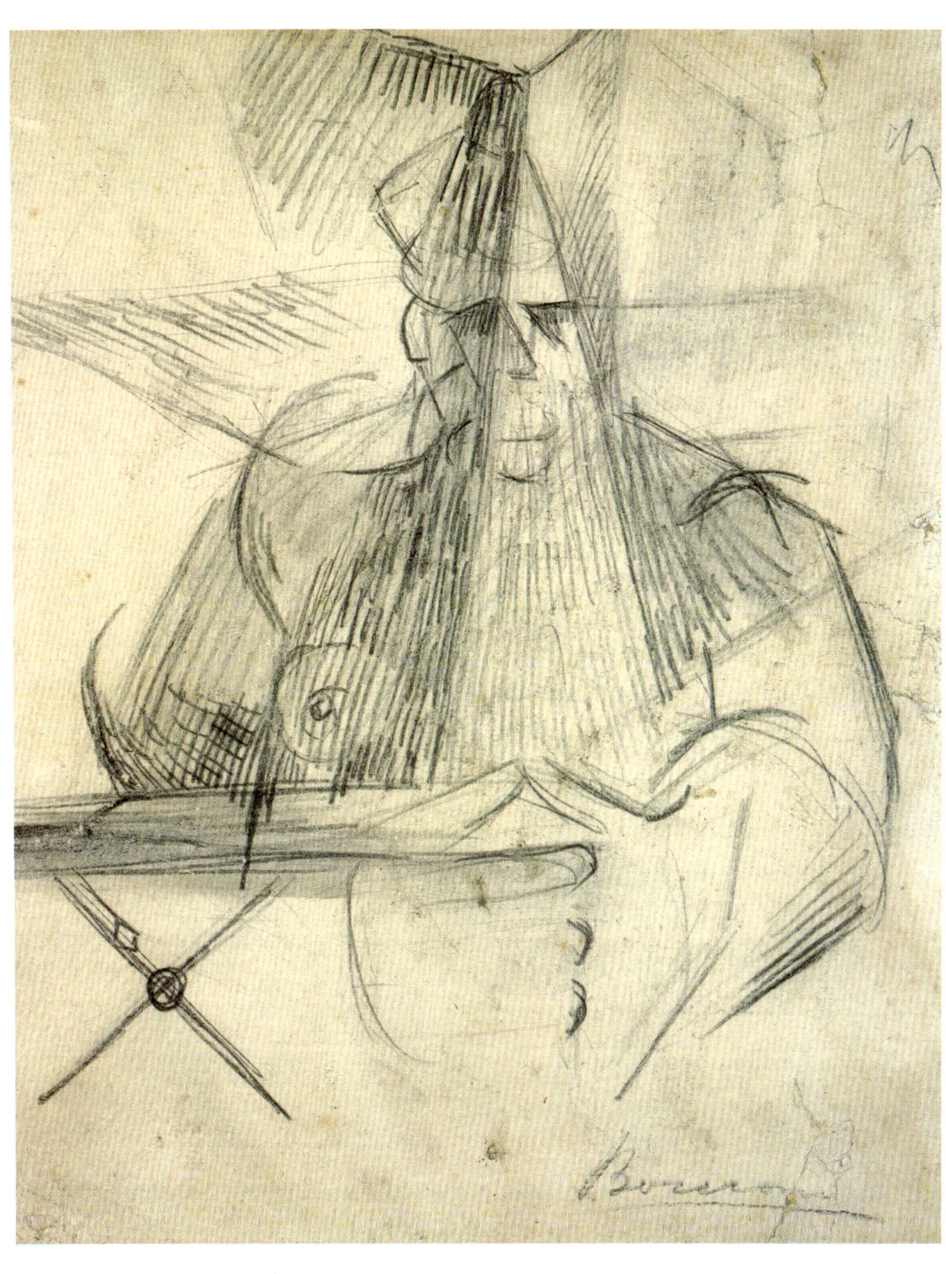

25 **Umberto Boccioni** *Mother* (*La madre*), 1912. Pencil on paper, 7 7/8 × 6 5/16 inches (20 × 16 cm). Fondazione Antonio Mazzotta, Milan

26 **Umberto Boccioni** Study for *Materia*; study for *Horizontal Construction* (*Costruzione orizzontale*), 1912. Pencil and pen on paper, 17 13/16 × 23 7/8 inches (45.3 × 60.6 cm). Civiche Raccolte d'Arte, Gabinetto dei Disegni, Milan, Courtesy of Comune di Milano

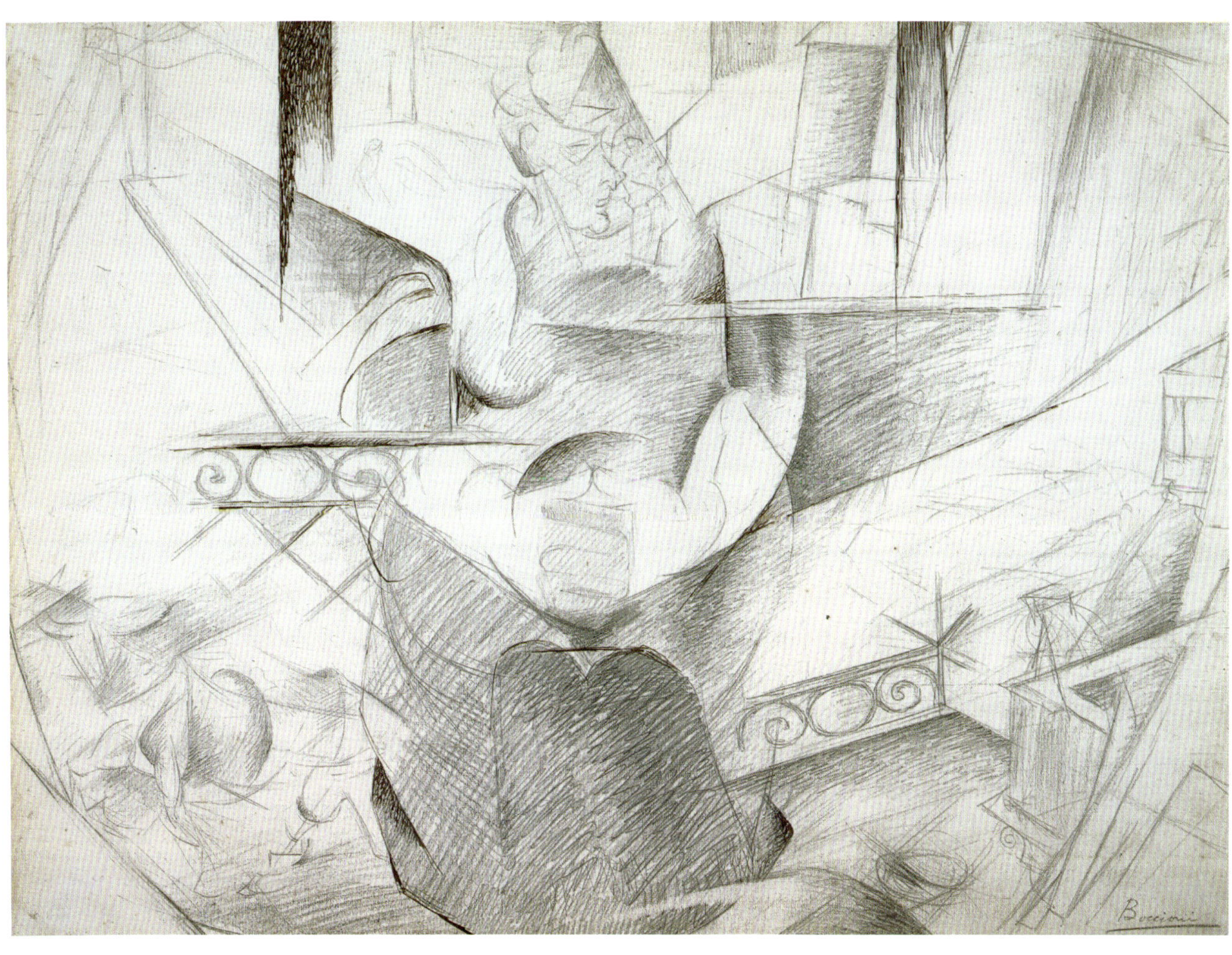
Boccioni

27 **Umberto Boccioni** *Materia*, 1912. Oil on canvas, 89 × 59 inches (226 × 150 cm).
Gianni Mattioli Collection, On long-term loan to the Peggy Guggenheim Collection, Venice

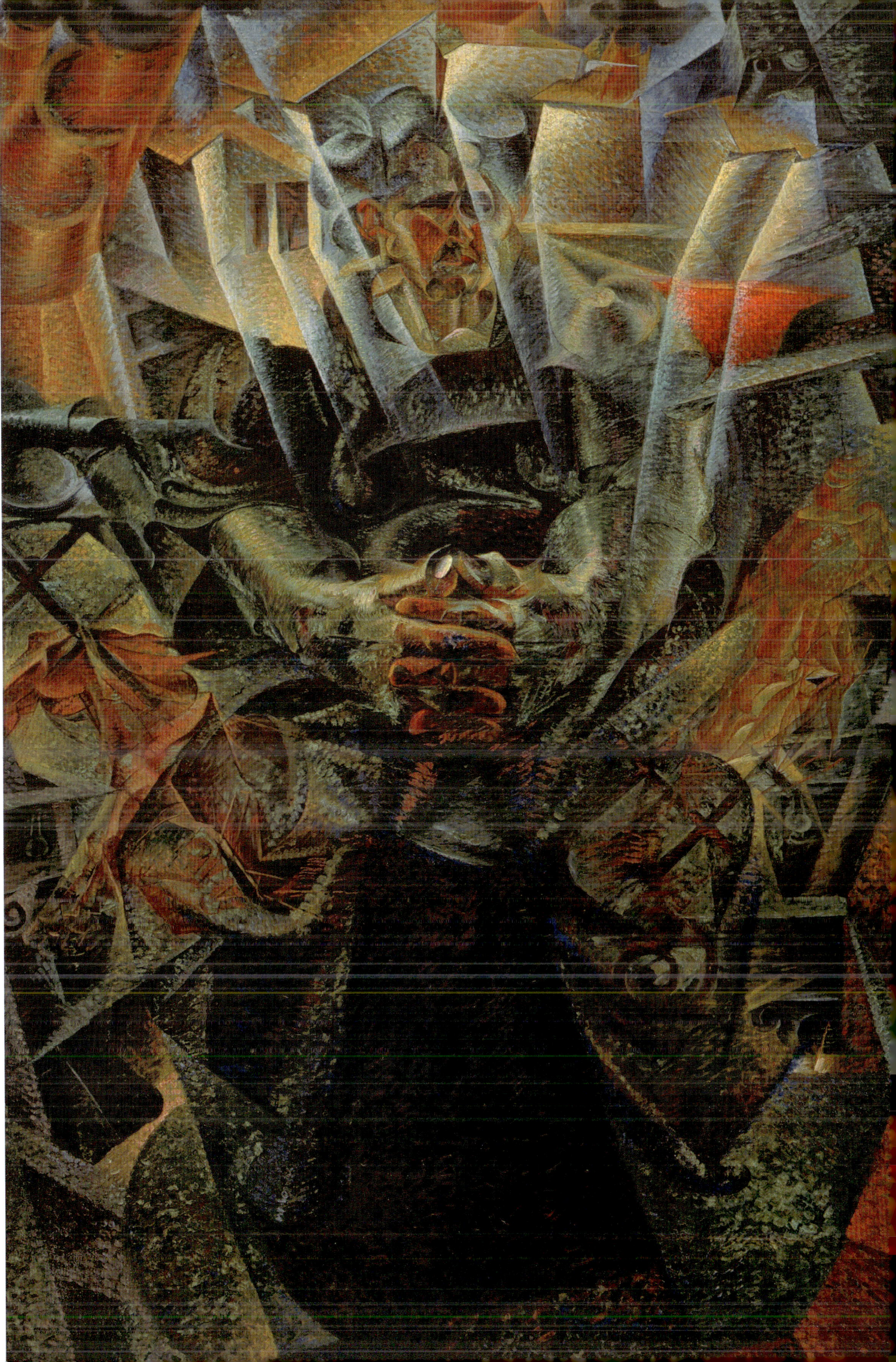

28 **Umberto Boccioni** *Horizontal Construction* (*Costruzione orizzontale)*, 1912. Oil on canvas, 37³⁄₈ × 37³⁄₈ inches (95 × 95 cm). Bayerische Staatsgemäldesammlungen, Munich

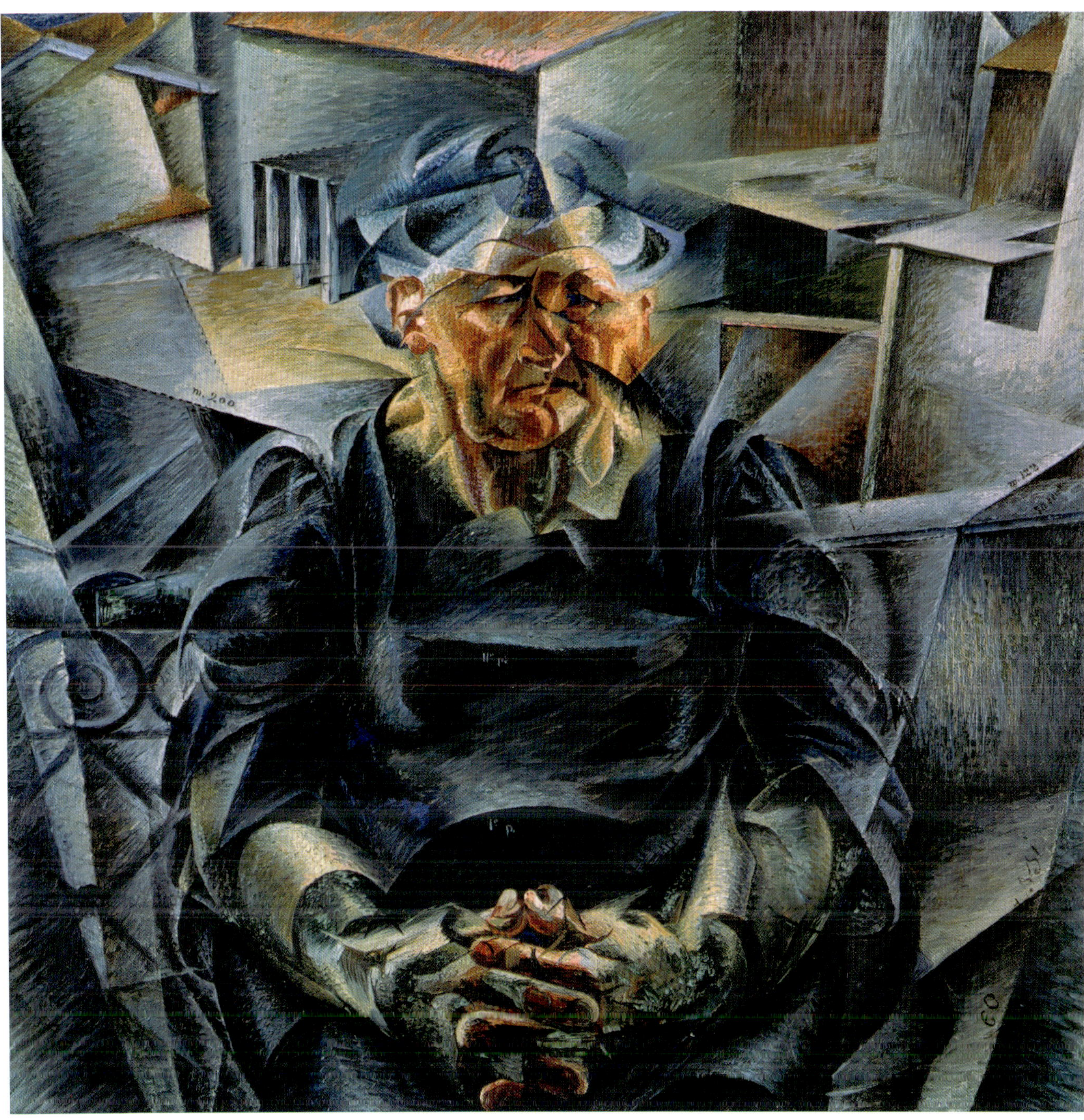

Boccioni and Sculpture

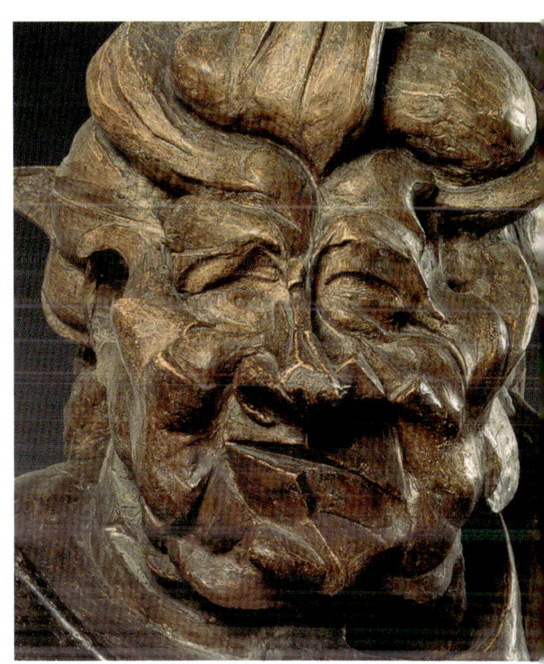

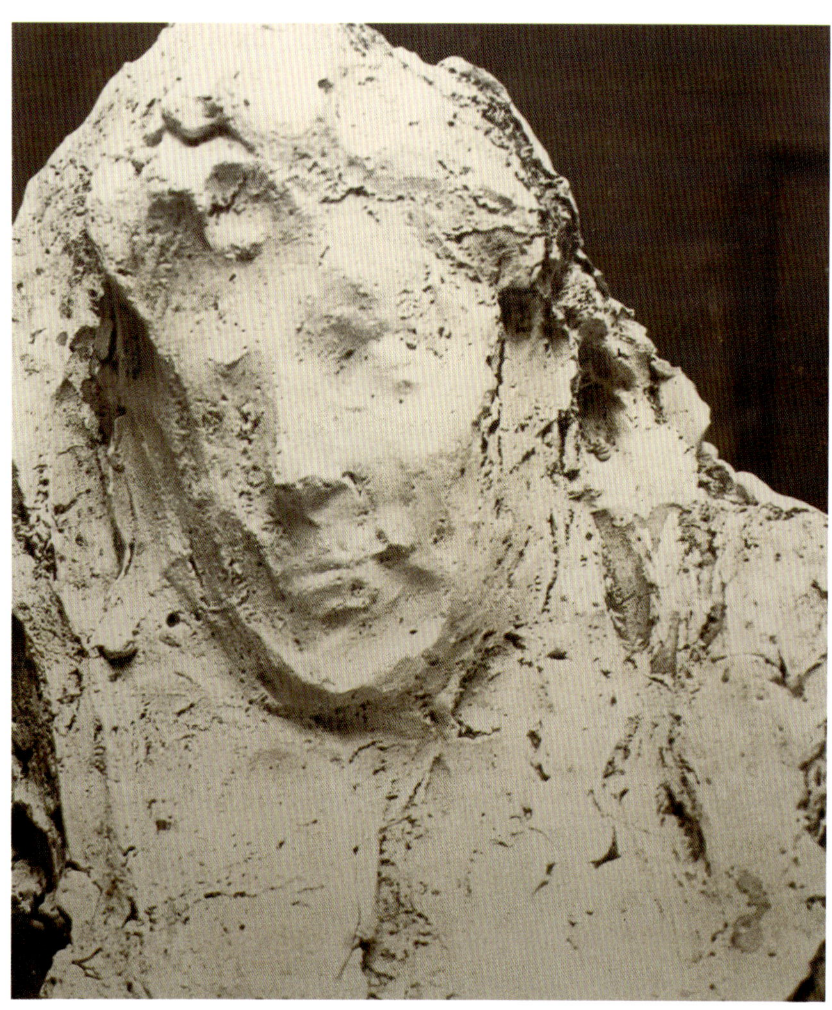

29 **Medardo Rosso** *Madame Noblet*, 1896. Plaster, 25⅜ × 20⅝ × 17⅞ inches (64.5 × 52.5 × 45.5 cm). Photograph by the artist, n.d. Museo Medardo Rosso, Barzio, Italy.

30 **Pablo Picasso** *Head (Fernande)* (*Tête de femme[Fernande]*), 1909. Plaster, 18½ × 14⅛ × 13¾ inches (47 × 35.9 × 34.9 cm). Raymond and Patsy Nasher Collection, Dallas

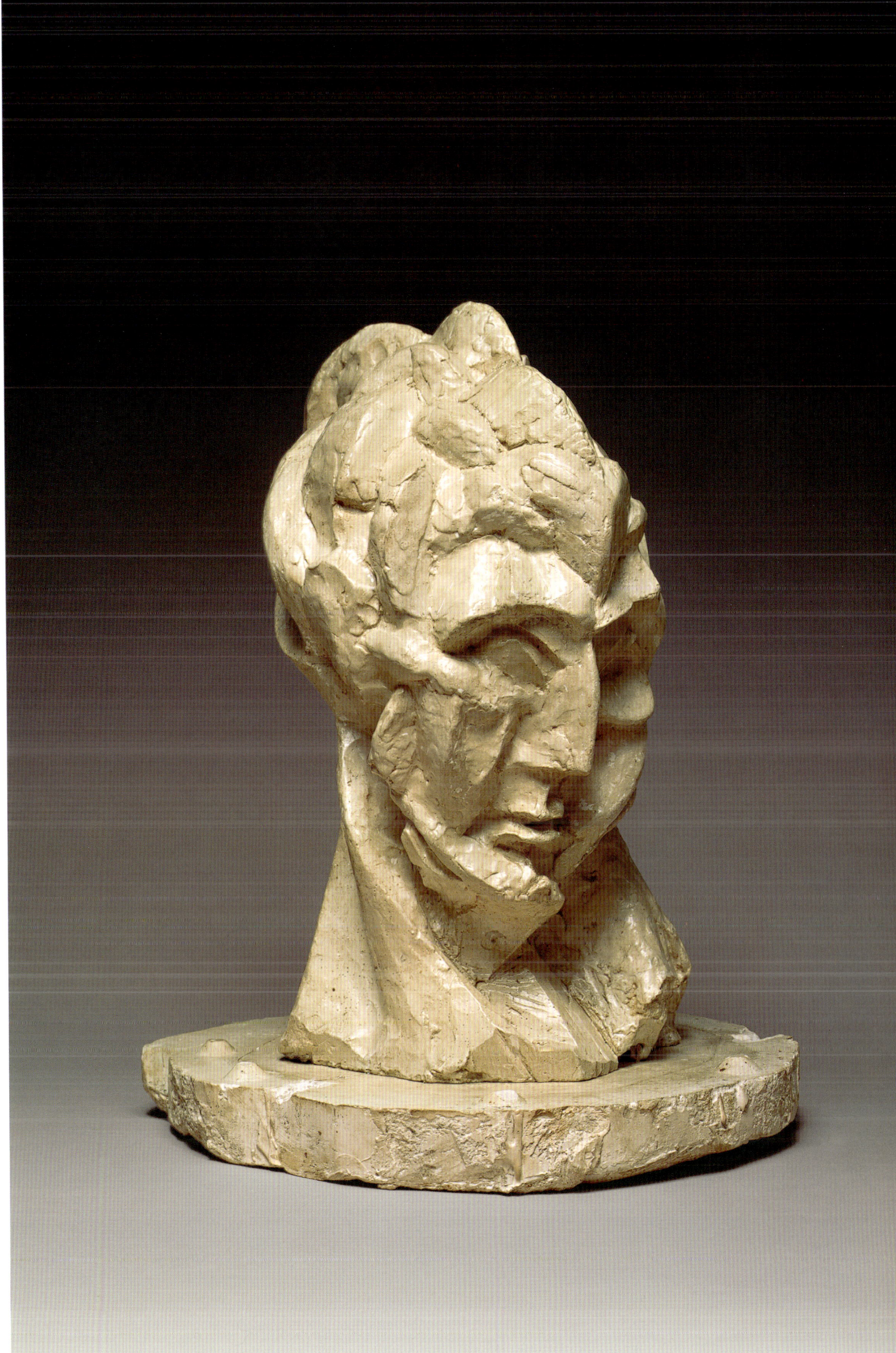

31 **Umberto Boccioni** *Antigrazioso*, 1912–13. Varnished plaster, 22 13/16 × 19 11/16 × 15 3/4 inches (58 × 50 × 40 cm). Galleria Nazionale d'Arte Moderna, Rome, Courtesy of Ministero per i Beni e le Attività Culturali

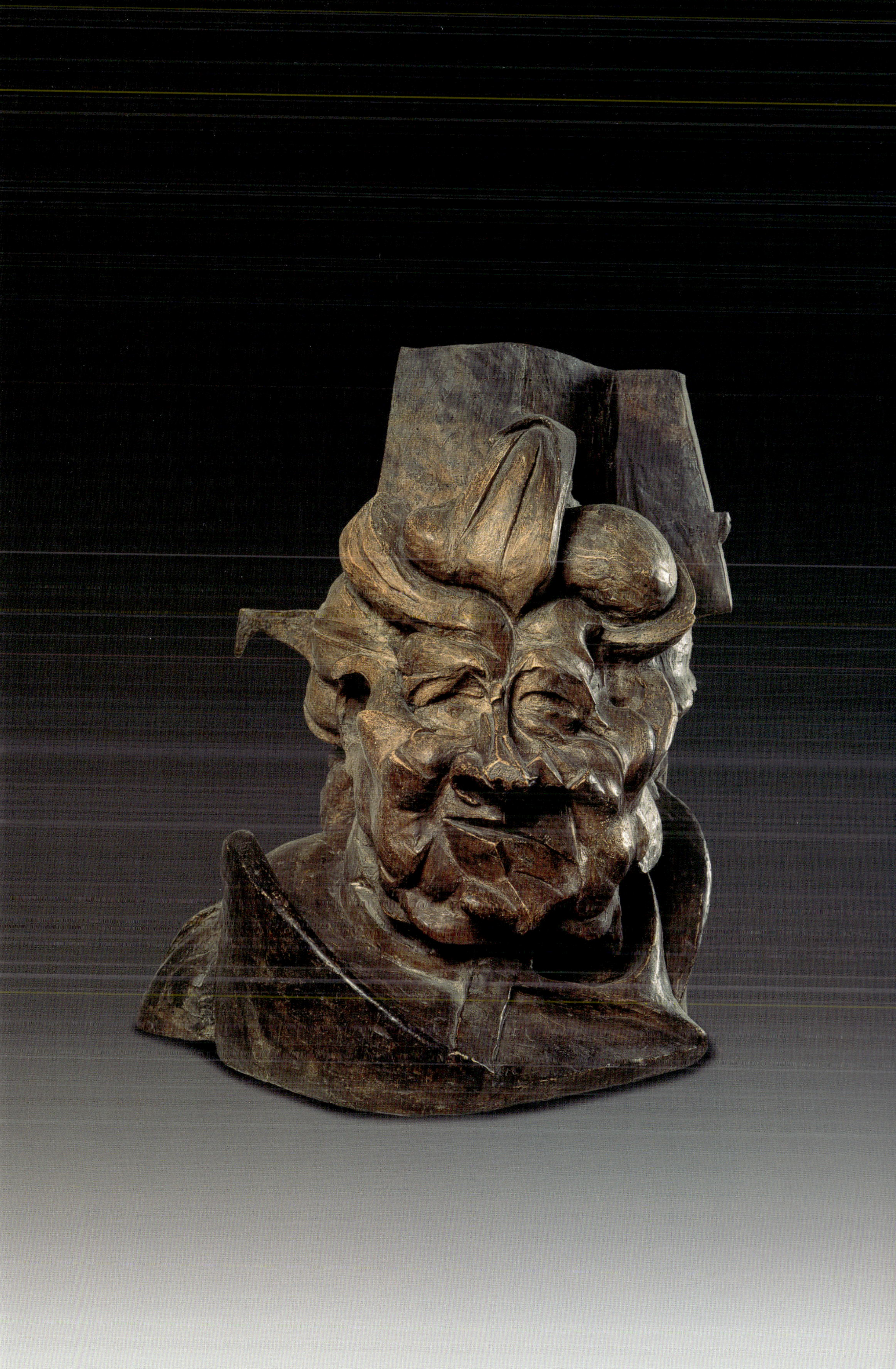

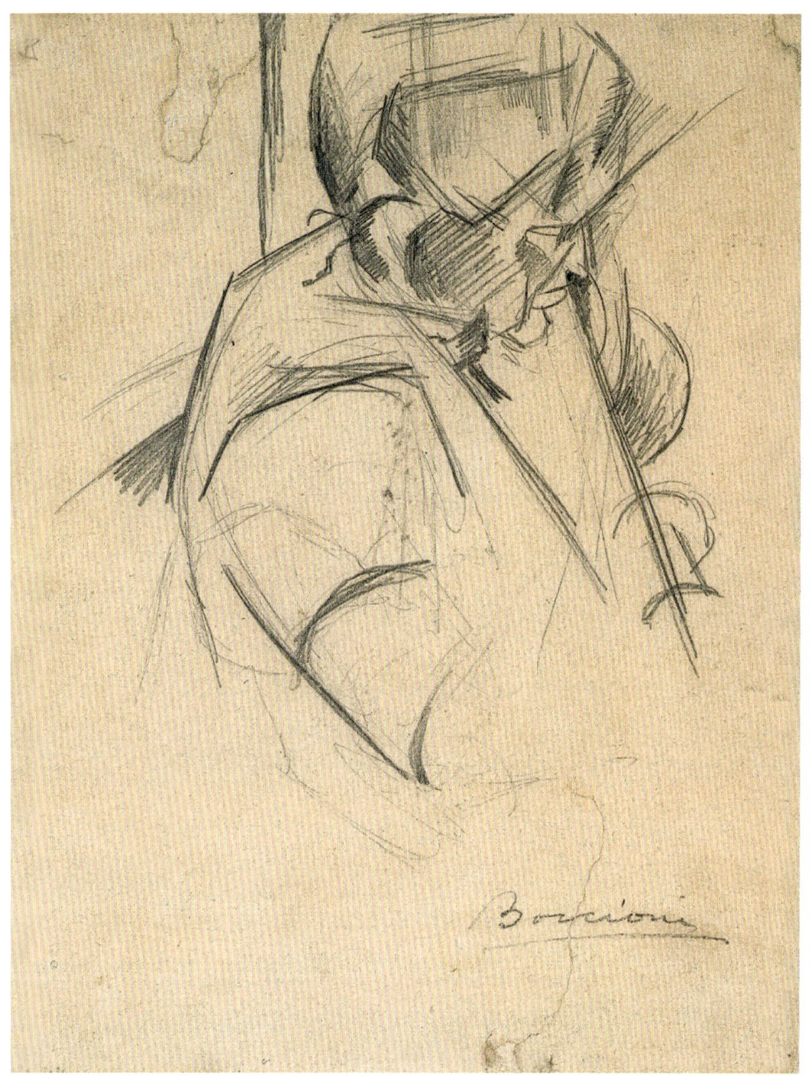

32 **Umberto Boccioni** *Bust of Mother* (*Busto della madre*), 1912. Pencil on paper, 8 11/16 × 5 7/8 inches (22 × 15 cm). Private collection

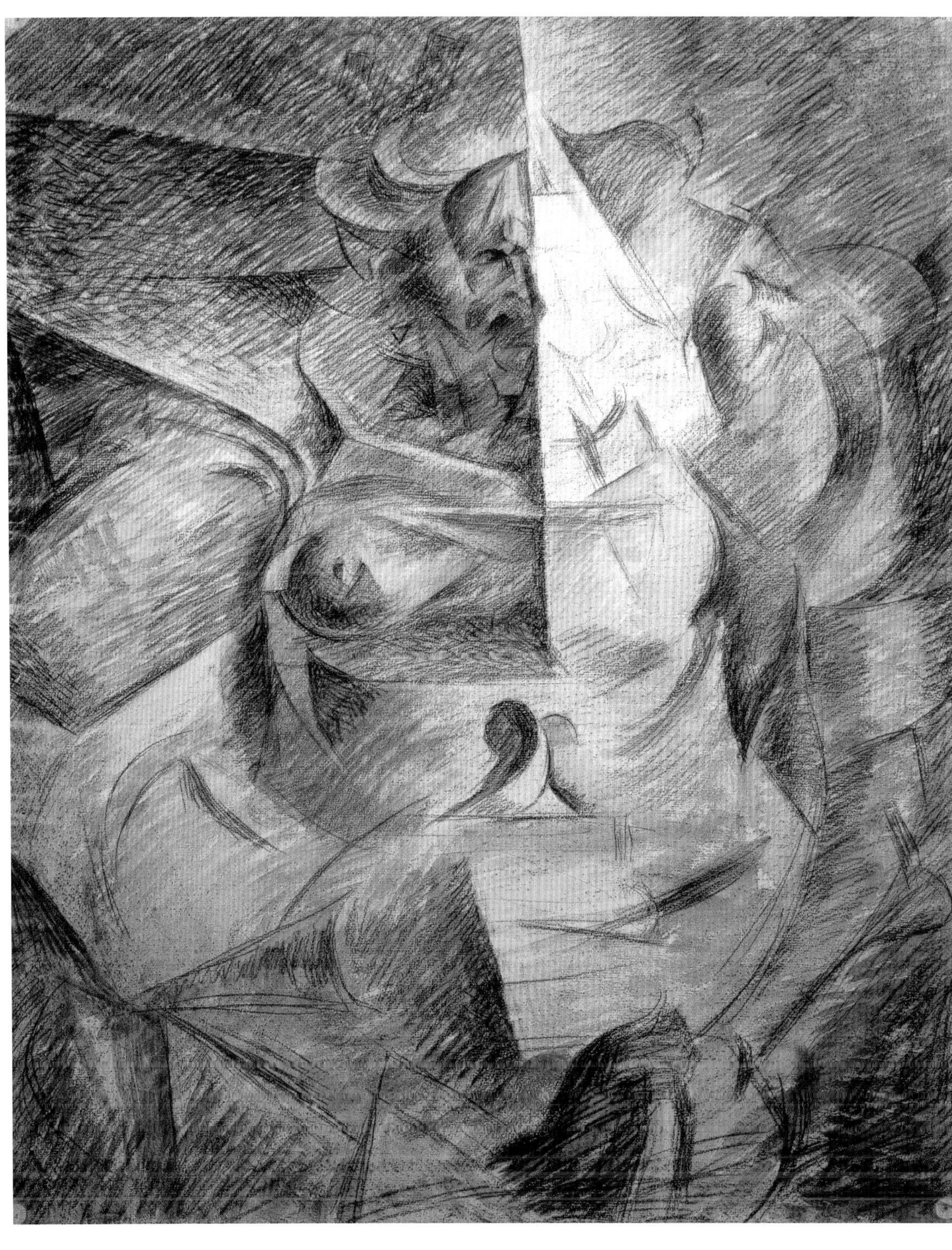

33 **Umberto Boccioni** *Head + House + Light* (*Testa + casa + luce*), 1913. Charcoal and watercolor on paper, 24 × 19³⁄₁₆ inches (61 × 48.8 cm). Civiche Raccolte d'Arte, Gabinetto dei Disegni, Milan, Courtesy of Comune di Milano

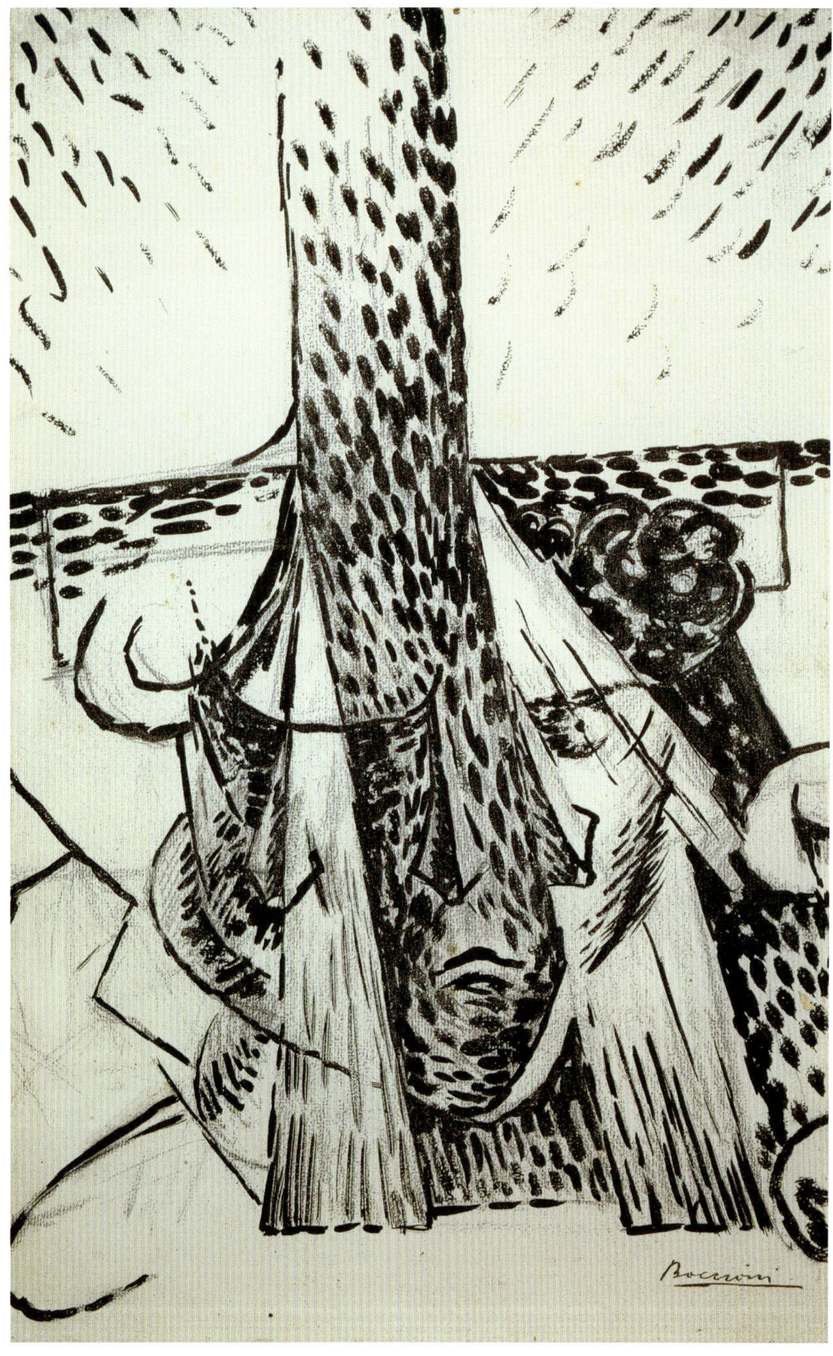

34 **Umberto Boccioni** *Fusion of a Head and a Window* (*Fusione di una testa e di una finestra*), 1912–13. Watercolor on paper, 19⁷⁄₁₆ × 12¹⁄₁₆ inches (49.3 × 30.7 cm). Civiche Raccolte d'Arte, Gabinetto dei Disegni, Milan, Courtesy of Comune di Milano

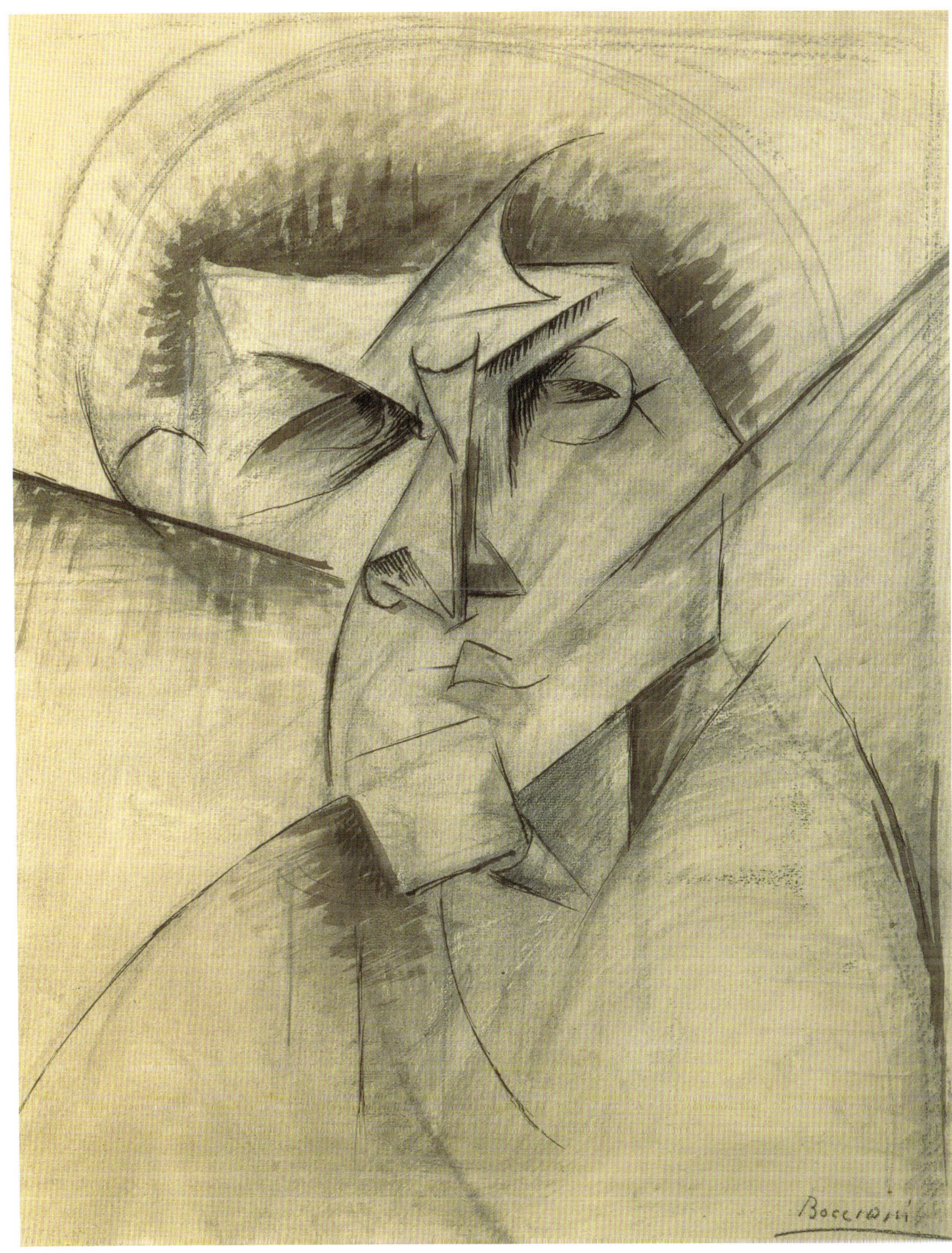

35 **Umberto Boccioni** *Empty and Full Abstracts of a Head* (*Vuoti e pieni astratti di una testa*), 1913. Ink, black wash, and pencil on paper, 22¼ × 17⅝ inches (56.5 × 44.7 cm). Estorick Collection, London

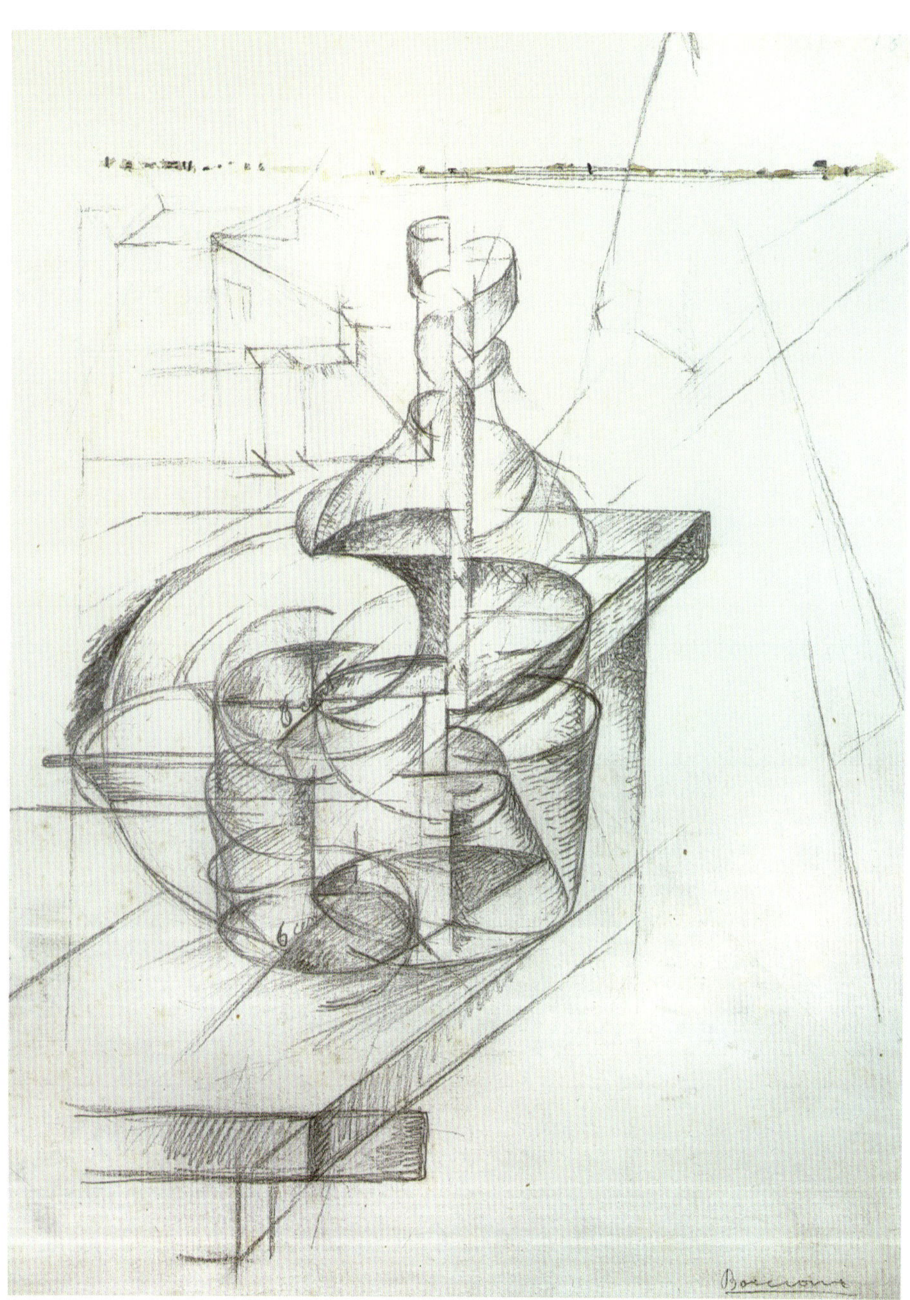

36 **Umberto Boccioni** *Table + Bottle + Block of Houses* (*Tavola + bottiglia + caseggiato*), 1912. Pencil on paper, $13\frac{1}{8} \times 9\frac{3}{8}$ inches (33.4 × 23.9 cm). Civiche Raccolte d'Arte, Gabinetto dei Disegni, Milan, Courtesy of Comune di Milano

37 **Umberto Boccioni** *Development of a Bottle in Space* (*Sviluppo di una bottiglia nello spazio*), 1912. Plaster, $15\frac{5}{8} \times 23\frac{11}{16} \times 12\frac{7}{8}$ inches (39.7 × 60.1 × 32.7 cm). Museu de Arte Contemporânea da Universidade de São Paulo

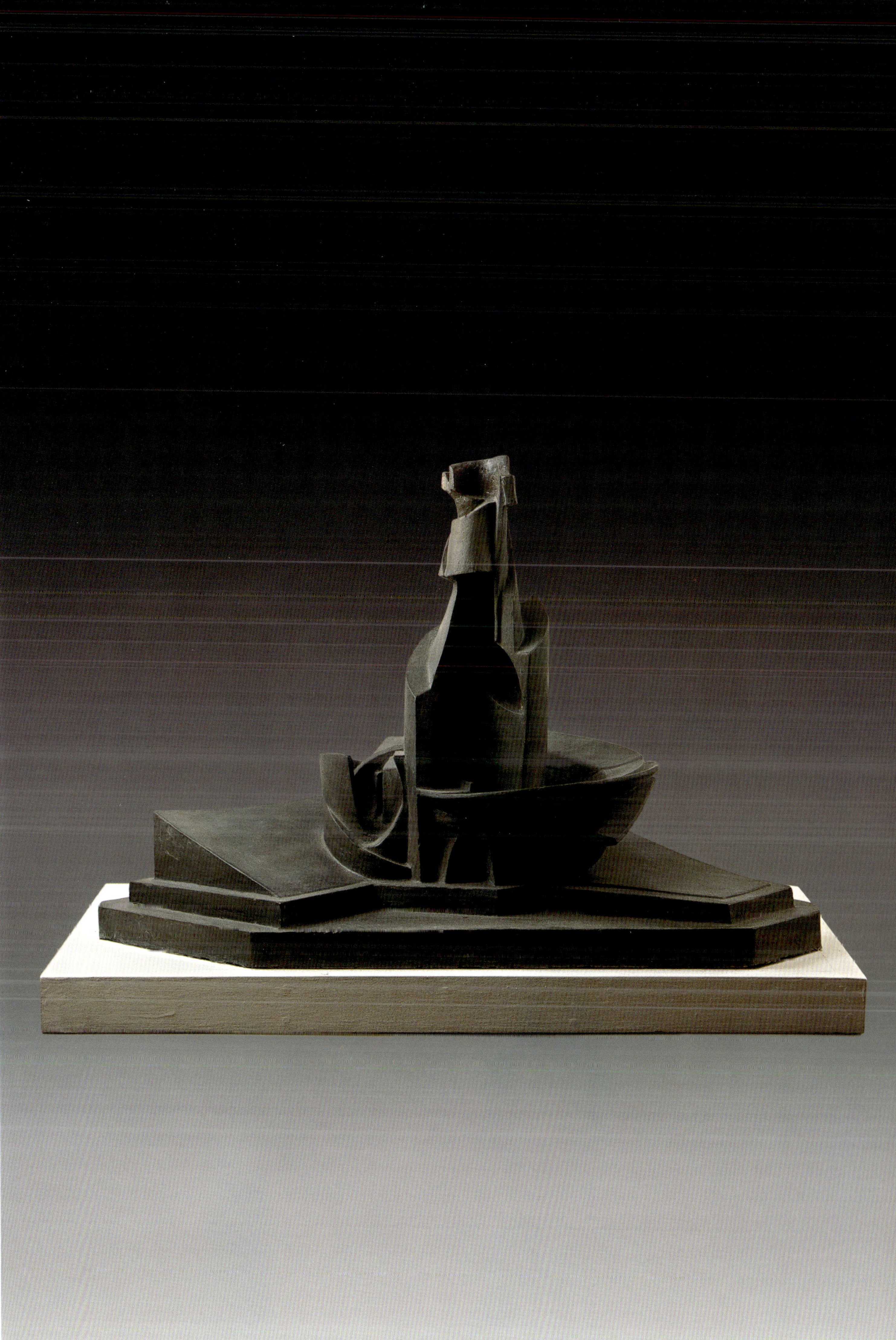

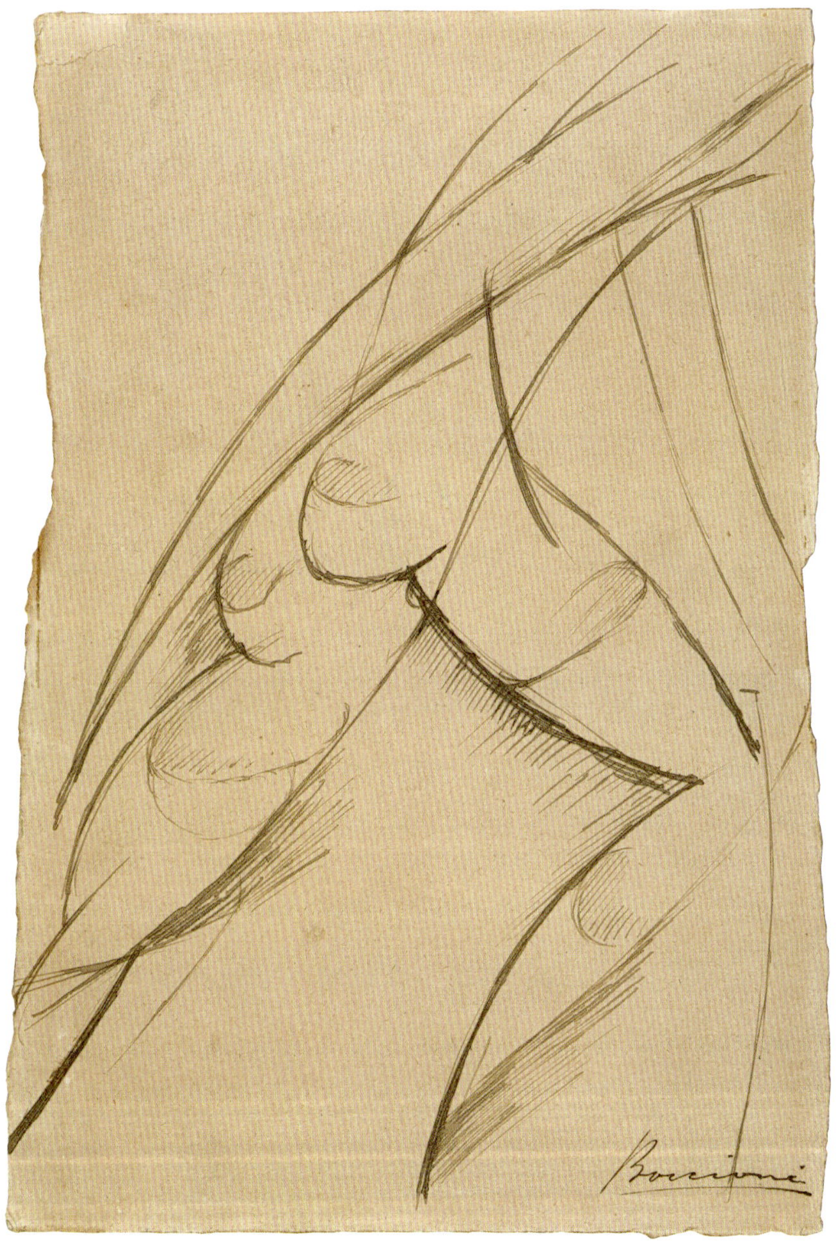

38 **Umberto Boccioni** *Figure in Motion No.1* (*Figura in movimento n.1*), 1913. Pencil on paper, 8¼ × 5¹¹⁄₁₆ inches (21 × 14.5 cm). Private collection

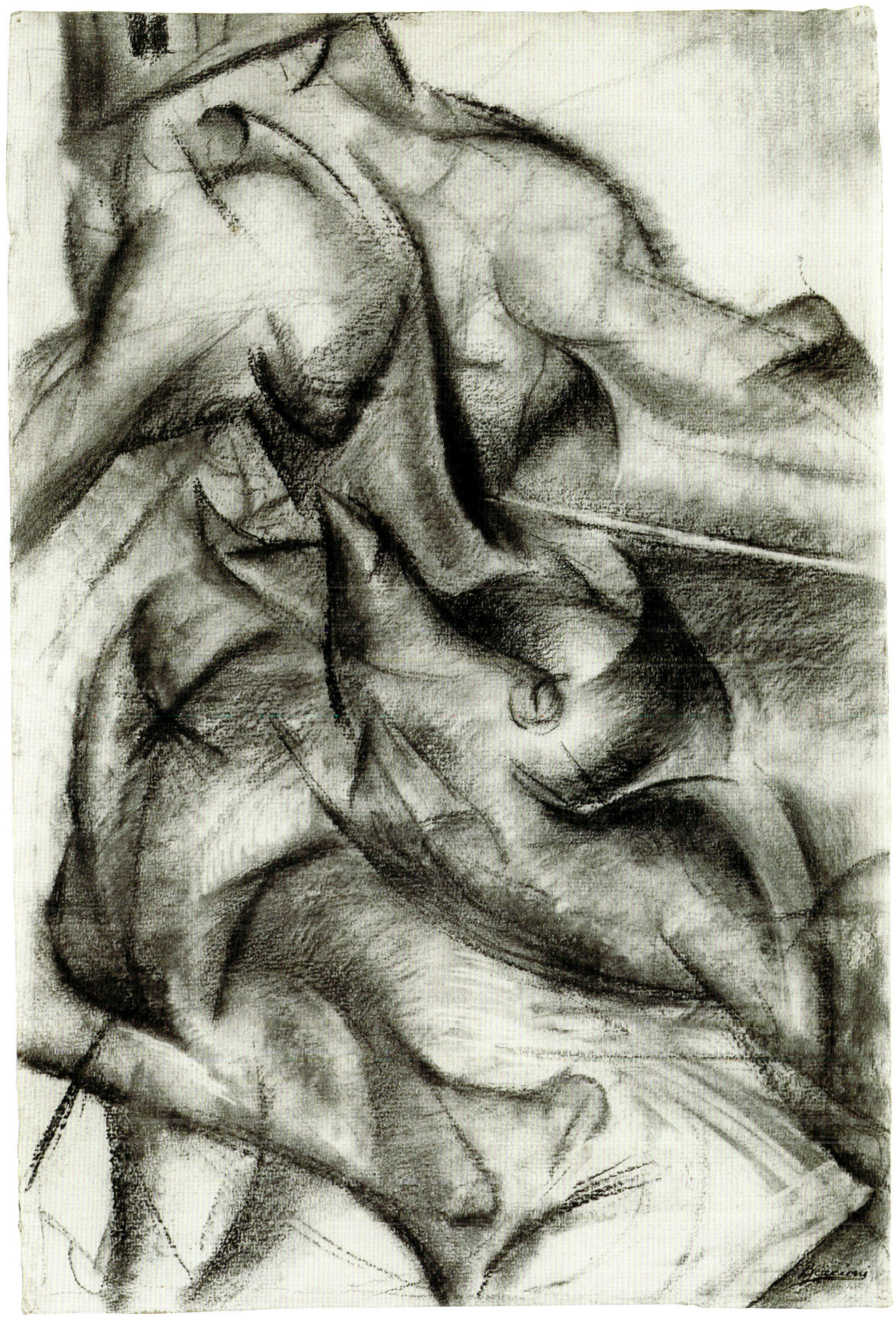

39 **Umberto Boccioni** *Muscular Dynamism* (*Dinamismo muscolare*), 1913. Pastel and charcoal on paper, 34 × 23¼ inches (86.3 × 59 cm). The Museum of Modern Art, New York, Purchase 330.1949

40 **Umberto Boccioni** *Unique Forms of Continuity in Space* (*Forme uniche nella continuità dello spazio*), 1913. Bronze, 45 13/16 × 34 1/8 × 15 11/16 inches (116.4 × 86.7 × 39.8 cm). Civiche Raccolte d'Arte, Museo d'Arte Contemporanea, Milan

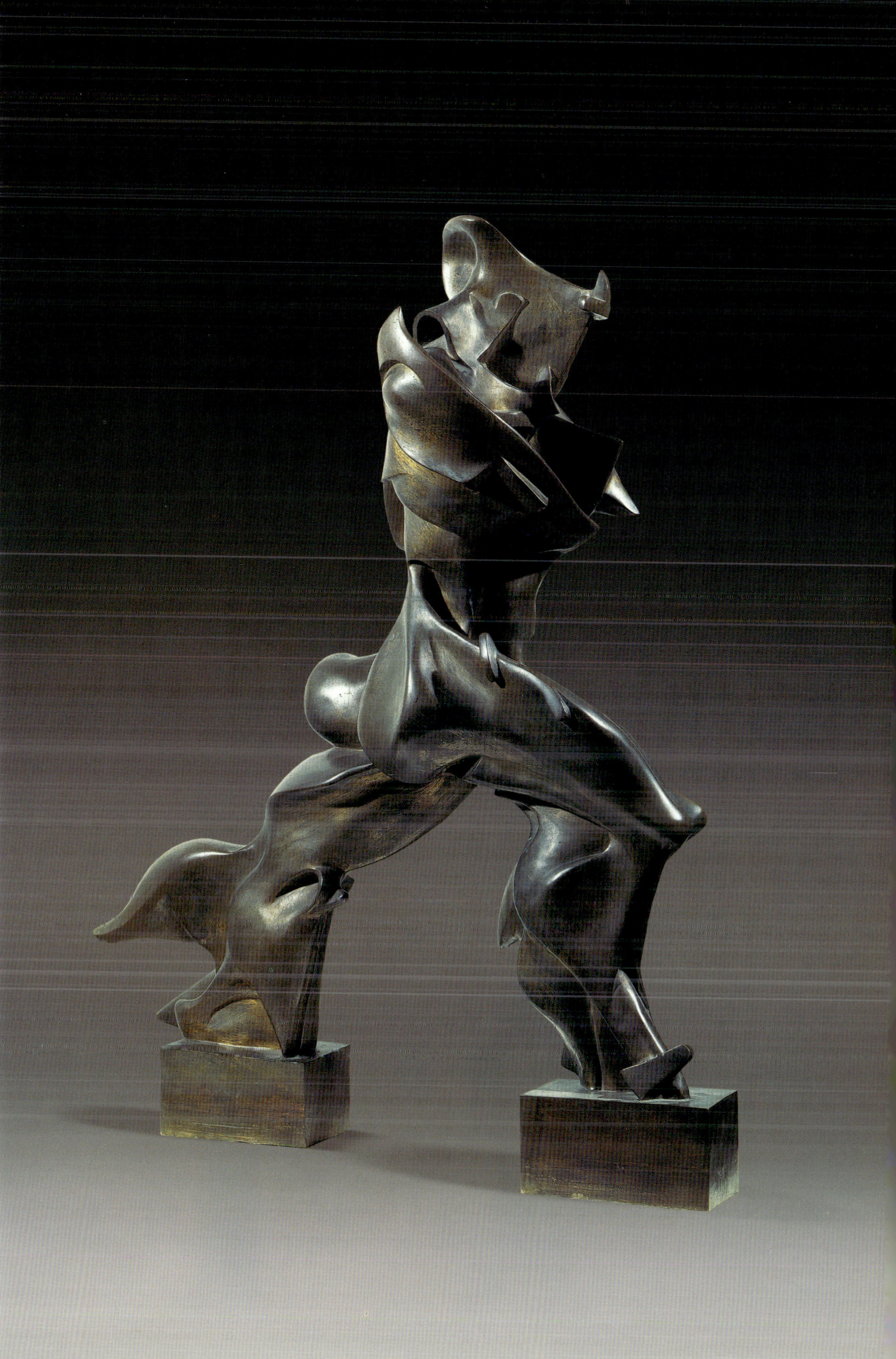

Boccioni in Milan

LAURA MATTIOLI ROSSI

There are numerous sources attesting to when and where Umberto Boccioni lived in Milan — namely, his diaries, correspondence, and paintings[1] — and these have been identified first by Leonardo Capano and Antonello Negri and now by Giovanna Ginex.[2]

The Lombard capital was home to the artist's mother Cecilia and his sister Amelia, who constitute the most stable reference point for Boccioni's affections. He stayed in Milan for some ten days in late August 1907,[3] on his way back from Venice — where he had taken up residence the previous April — and before heading on to Munich, where he hoped to plan a later trip to Russia, an idea he almost immediately abandoned.

On September 12, Boccioni wrote in his diary, "I'm in Milan and Russia is far away. . . . I'm going to begin a new life. I'm so happy to be in Milan."[4] He found lodging almost immediately in a furnished room, as he related on September 25: "I'm in my new room. Lovely and bright. I'm working on three drawings, of Mama, Amelia, and a landscape."[5] Soon thereafter, he moved into several rented rooms with the two women. On November 6, he wrote, "I'm in a new house at via Castel Morrone 7, in the home of Sig. Defeo. We'll see. I'm very close to the countryside. I want very much to work here."[6] He remained in that building — which was later destroyed — for nearly a year, amid severe and continual financial difficulties.

Probably in September 1908, Boccioni moved to the apartment on the top floor of via Adige 23 (fig. 61). In fact, he had written in his diary on August 24, "I was finally able to buy an etching press. I'm happy. In a month I'm changing residence."[7] He lived there during his last period as a Divisionist, and during his crucial years as a member of the Futurists, until early 1913.

Via Adige is on the city's southern outskirts, beyond the Spanish Walls (or Bastioni), in an area that was still predominantly agricultural when Boccioni moved there, but which was being very quickly urbanized in those very years. Blocks of low-rent apartments and industrial buildings were sprouting up in rapid succession around the thermoelectric power plant that had gone into operation in piazza Trento, at the end of via Adige, in 1905 (fig. 63). Today, via Adige 23 and the two buildings (via Adige 21 and piazza Trento 1) on either side of it remain essentially unchanged, making it possible to easily recognize many recurrent architectural details from Boccioni's works of those years. Across the street from via Adige 23 still stands the industrial building erected as the Besozzi Marzoli mill between July 1911 and March 1912, the facade of which had a triple entrance divided by two pilasters.

From his top-floor room, which featured a French window opening onto a narrow balcony, Boccioni, starting in 1909, began to paint — in close dialogue with the surrounding reality — the transformation of the landscape and the rise of the modern city. This period includes *Sister on the Balcony* (1909, cat. no. 6), where the background still shows large green spaces; *The City Rises* (1910–11, fig. 11), inspired by the major excavations that, in the summer of 1910, replaced a number of flower beds in piazza Trento with immense water tanks serving the power plant; *The Street Enters the House* (1911, cat. no. 7), which depicts the construction of the Besozzi Marzoli mill; and finally *Materia* (1912, cat. no. 27), in which one can recognize the iron railing of via Adige 23 (fig. 62), balconies of the two adjacent buildings (figs. 64 and 65), and the entrance to the mill — the features from *Materia* are visible as well in *Horizontal Construction* (1912, cat. no. 28) and the study (1912, cat. no. 26) that relates to both paintings. In the upper left of *Materia*, there are two smokestacks, which correspond to those of the piazza Trento power plant.

The two 1911 paintings *The Forces of a Street*[8]

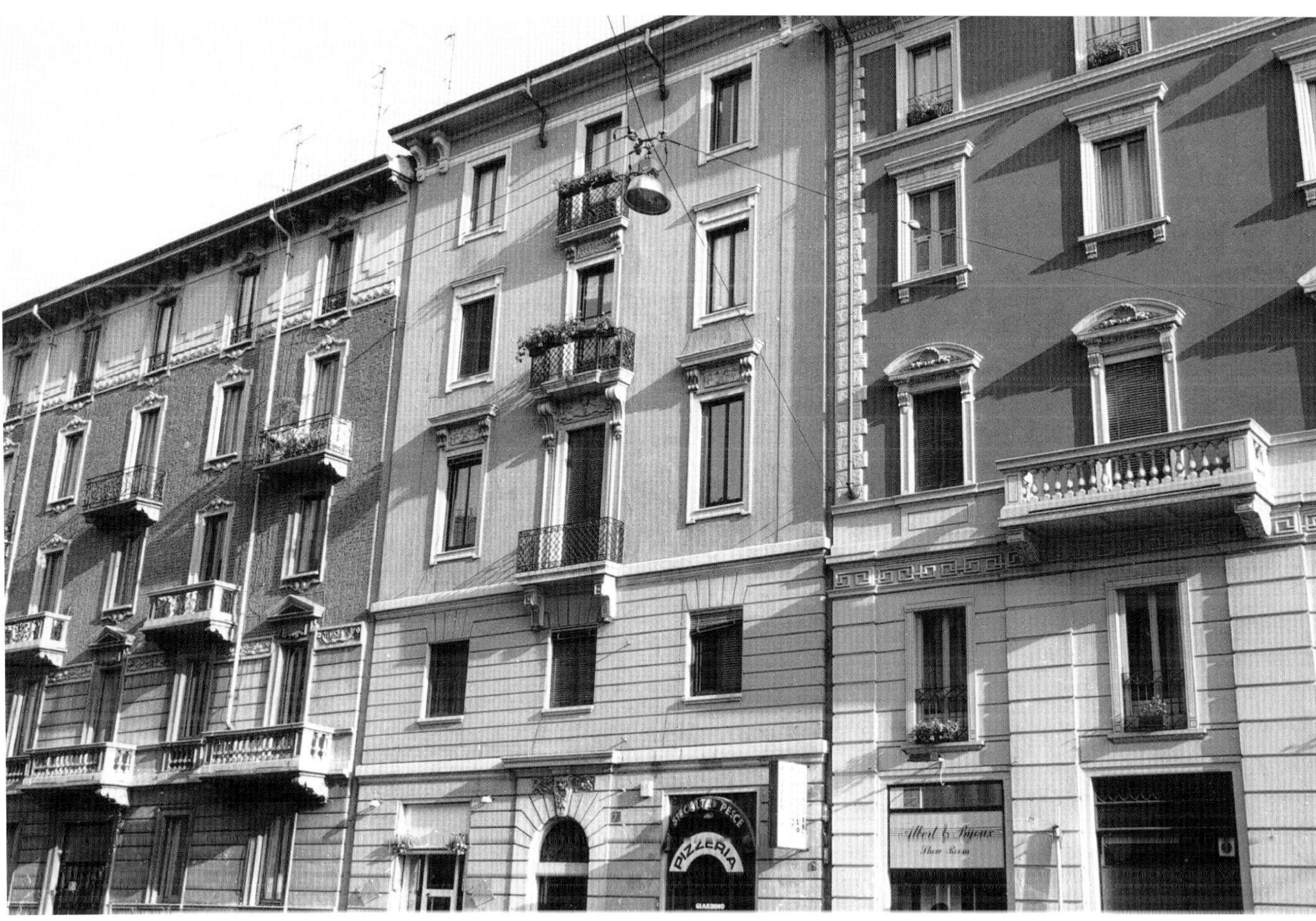

Fig. 61 Via Adige 21, via Adige 23, and piazza Trento 1, Milan, photographed by Jacopo Cima in 1991. Umberto Boccioni resided on the top floor of via Adige 23 from 1908 to 1913.

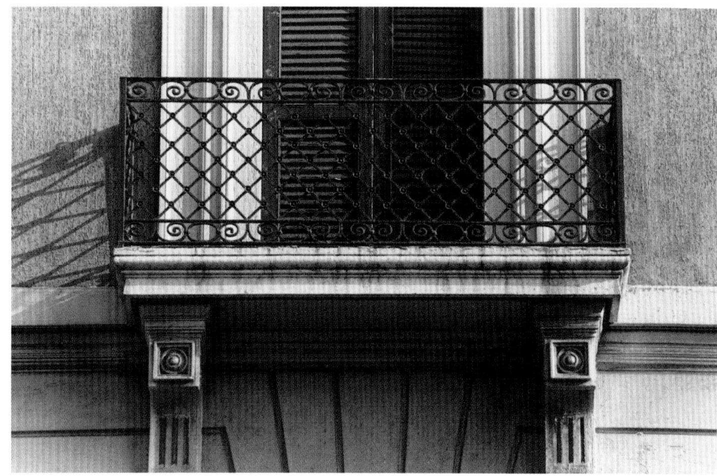

and *Simultaneous Visions* (cat. no. 8), on the other hand, may have been inspired by what one could see from the window (carriages, passersby, trams, streetlamps) of an upper story on the nearby corso Lodi, a major traffic artery that continues southward the old corso di Porta Romana. The window probably belonged to the apartment of a woman with whom Boccioni had a love affair in those years, as one may apparently gather from his second notebook: "In a month I'm moving. What will happen when I'm living near her? I'm still undecided as to whether I love her or not."[9]

Boccioni left the via Adige apartment, which was too cramped for his sculptural projects, in spring 1913 and moved into the bigger, brighter apartment-studio in Bastioni di Porta Romana 35, an address that corresponds to the present-day building at viale Regina Margherita 9. On February 19, 1913, Boccioni, from Rome, wrote to Vico Baer: "The splendid apartment I rented before leaving fills me with hope for a year of materially greater work."[10] There, in fact, he executed his first plaster sculptures and all the paintings made up to 1915; he also repainted, in the summer of 1913, various different parts of *Materia*, following the advice given by Roberto Longhi.

Translated from the Italian by Stephen Sartarelli.

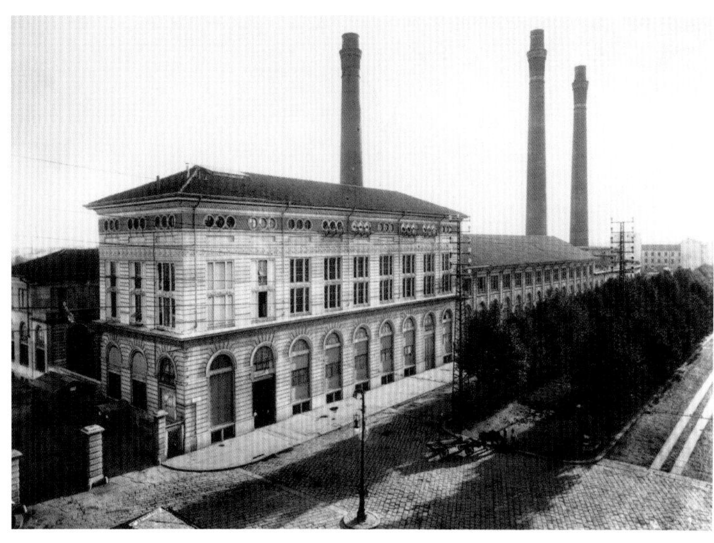

Fig. 62 Iron railing at via Adige 23, Milan, photographed by Jacopo Cima in 1991

Fig. 63 Thermoelectric power plant in piazza Trento, Milan, ca. 1905

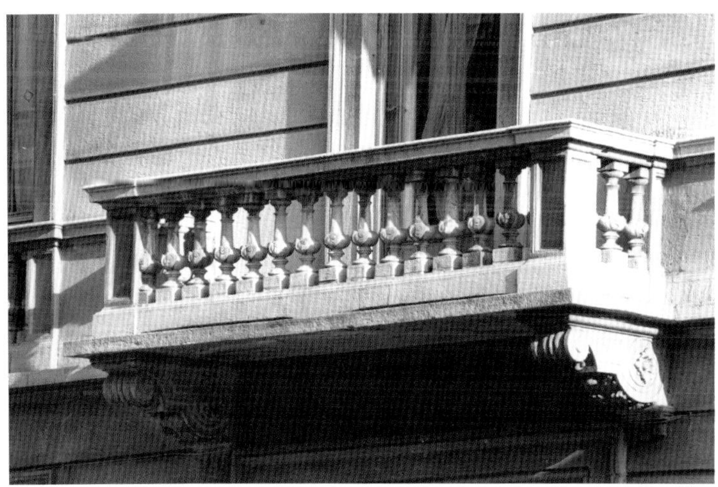

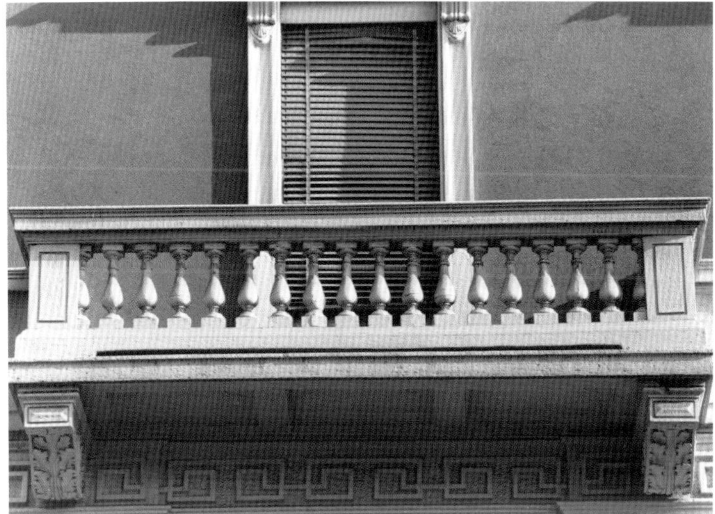

Fig. 64 Balcony at via Adige 21, Milan, photographed by Jacopo Cima in 1991

Fig. 65 Balcony at piazza Trento 1, Milan, photographed by Jacopo Cima in 1991

Notes

1 See Boccioni diaries, in Zeno Birolli, *Umberto Boccioni: Gli scritti editi e inediti*, (Milan: Feltrinelli, 1971), pp. 235–312. With regard to correspondence, see, for example, postcard from Naples addressed to Boccioni, March 1913, Calmarini Collection, Milan, published in Laura Mattioli Rossi, ed., *Boccioni 1912 Materia*, exh. cat., Fondazione Antonio Mazzotta, Milan (Milan: Mazzotta, 1995), p. 255.

2 See Leonardo Capano and Antonello Negri, "Via Adige 23," in Laura Mattioli Rossi, ed., *Boccioni 1912 Materia*, exh. cat., Galleria dello Scudo, Verona (Milan: Mazzotta, 1991), p. 253; Capano and Negri, "Ancora su Via Adige," in Mattioli Rossi, *Boccioni 1912 Materia* (1995), pp. 258–59; and Giovanna Ginex, "Snapshots from Umberto Boccioni's Studio," in the present volume, pp. 62–81.

3 In Birolli, *Gli scritti editi e inediti*, pp. 254–55.

4 Ibid., p. 258.

5 Ibid., p. 262.

6 Ibid., p. 267.

7 Ibid., p. 311.

8 Maurizio Calvesi and Ester Coen, *Boccioni: L'opera completa* (Milan: Electa, 1983), no. 747.

9 In Birolli, *Gli scritti editi e inediti*, p. 311.

10 Ibid., p. 366.

The Matter of *Materia*

GIANLUCA POLDI

I am tired of thinking and not painting . . . . Even though thinking may be my only way to evolve and forget all the horrible forms and methods I've learned and which always make me a skilled painter. There is no longer any truth but outside of the pictorial (as I understood it until yesterday); at the moment nothing interests me but matter expressed according to myself.

—UMBERTO BOCCIONI[1]

It is hardly accidental that *Materia* (1912, cat. no. 27) is itself one of Umberto Boccioni's most complex texts in its visual synthesis, elaboration, and use of pictorial technique. The care the artist devoted to the genesis and execution of this work amid those crucial, defining years for Futurist ideas about painting—from 1911, the year of the speech he gave in Rome on Futurist painting,[2] to 1913, the year of his *Pittura e scultura futuriste (Dinamismo plastico)*, in which he wrote about "a new unity that is the essential interpretation of the object, that is, the intuition of life"[3]—points to the need for detailed study of its technique of execution and for a comparison of Boccioni's practice with the statements he made in his writings. Moreover this study becomes particularly interesting when looking at the work in terms of its significant revisions, as attested by the canvas support and the paint application.

The Support

As is clear when studying the back of the work (fig. 66), the canvas of *Materia*[4] consists of four rectangular sections of similar composition having each the same width, of which the first from the top measures 26 centimeters in height, and the rest, 162, 15, and 23 centimeters, respectively, making the work's overall dimensions 226 by 150 centimeters. The tears in the sewn flaps of the canvas, caused by nails and present in the larger-sized fragment of canvas and in the flaps of the smaller, lower ones only along the bottom edge, indicate that Boccioni first began painting the larger canvas and later expanded it upward and downward at two later moments, each time mounting the canvas onto a stretcher.

The canvas has a diagonal woof, rather pronounced and clearly visible in almost every part of the painting where the color is less dense. The lower section was sewn with the woof running in the opposite direction.

On the back of the canvas one finds the signature, "U. Boccioni," painted on the upper half; stains caused by the absorption of thinning substances; and stickers from exhibitions in London (1914), Geneva (1920–21), and Milan (1933), in the central section.

To ensure better distribution of the static tensions, expansion joints were recently added to the wooden stretcher at corners.

The Painting

Only by close examination can one get a clear idea of the quantity and quality of color in *Materia* (e.g., fig. 67). Color is a fundamental part of the "plastic dynamism" that has its roots in simultaneity, that close interpenetration of sensations, space, and time forming the powerful core of Futurist thought. Indeed, among the five areas of research listed by Boccioni as necessary to simultaneity, "dynamic complementarism"—defined as the "complementary simultaneity of color + form + chiaroscuro"[5]—has a prominent place. The other four areas are: dynamism, force-lines, the solidification of impressionism, and the interpenetration of planes. Dynamic complementarism, in fact, is not unrelated to the others, contributing in an essential way toward building the "independent plastic organism that resembles itself," and is not a "realistic representation of reality."[6] In this perspective, the choice of juxtaposed complementary colors becomes fundamental:

> *As for color, fixed colors do not exist; what exists, rather, is the resultant of a color and its complement. Thus, we no longer have a yellow and a purple, but a resultant that constitutes a chromatic individuality at once variable and fixed. This complementarism will not be manifested in points,*

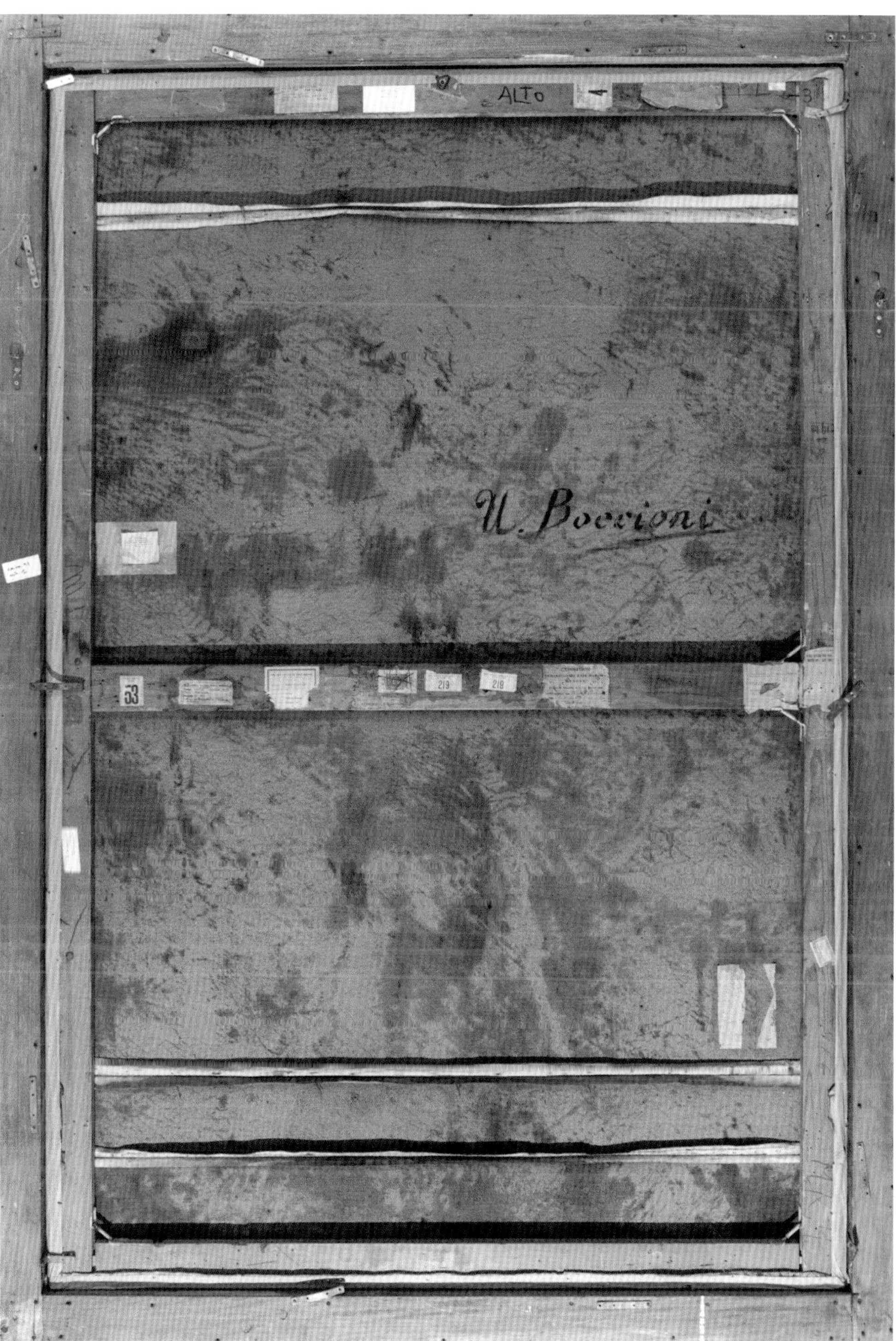

Fig. 66 Rear of *Materia* shows the canvas's three junctures of seams and is signed "U. Boccioni."

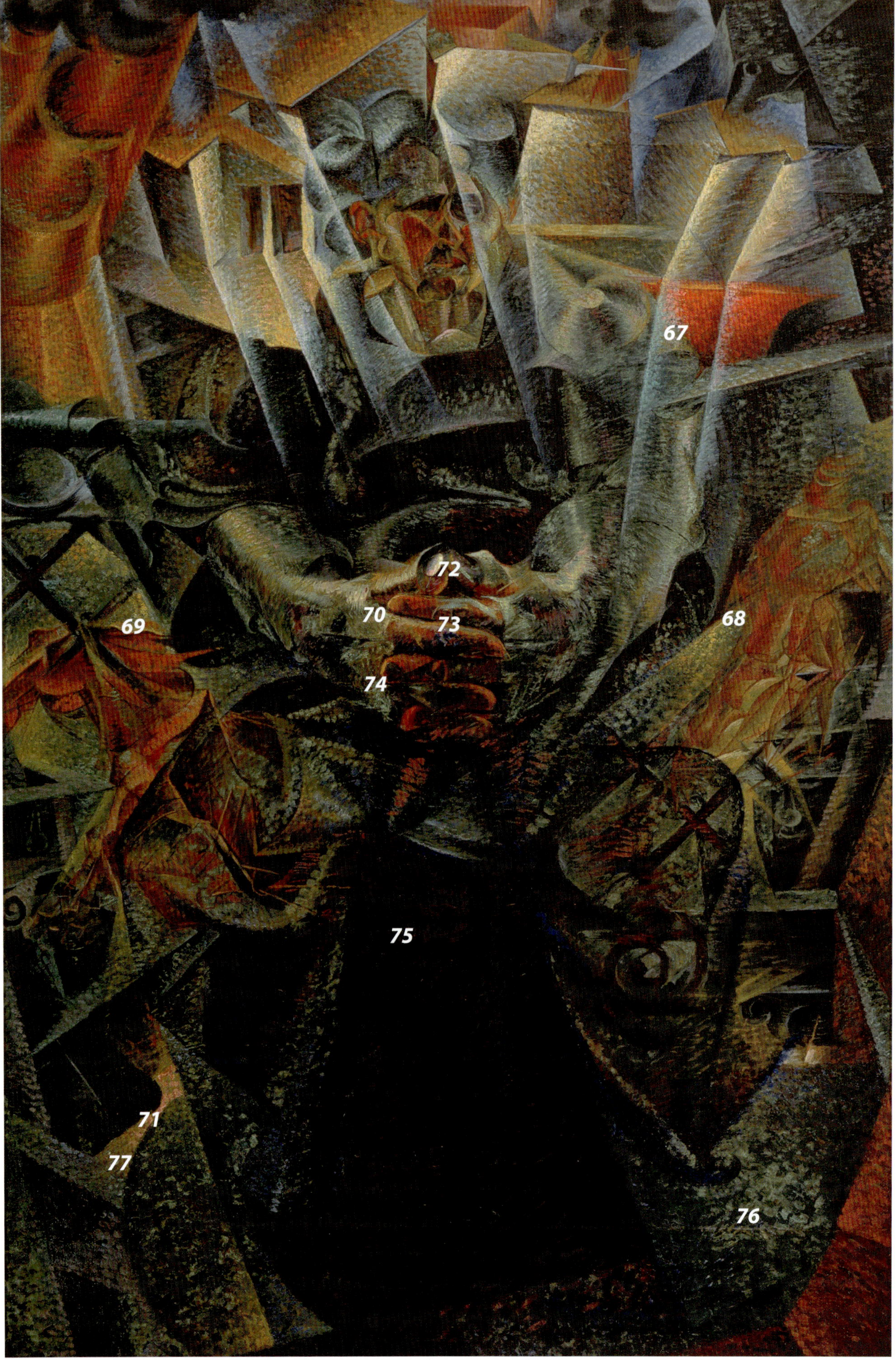
67
72
70
73
69
68
74
75
71
77
76

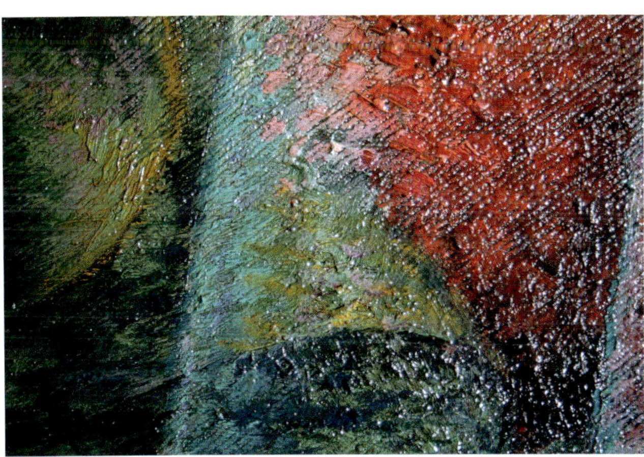

Fig. 67 Detail to right of mother's shoulder, near red roof. An example of the richness of color and of the chromatic passages in this painting.

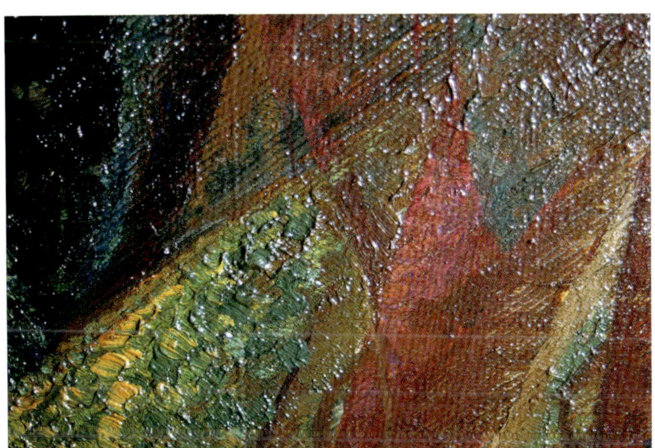

Fig. 68 Detail to left of walking man. A characteristic application of thick strokes of color, here yellow and green, in which the green is placed in counterpoint to and complemented by the more liquid orange-ocher brushstrokes that define the man.

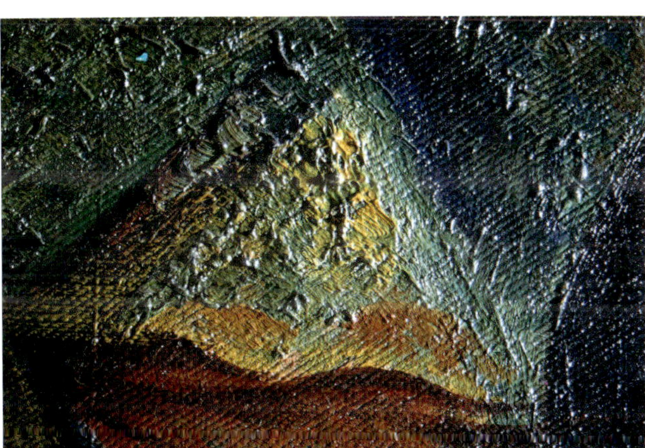

Fig. 69 Detail above horse's mane, in semiraking light. The fine, long strokes constituting the horse are in sharp contrast to the triangular form realized with daubs of yellow and blue-green clotted color.

Facing page
Umberto Boccioni, *Materia*, 1912 (cat. no. 27)
Numbers indicate locations of details shown in figs. 67–77.

> *commas, or bands—which are means conceived to achieve objective resemblance—but in complementarily colored masses, zones, and forms.*[7]

Boccioni's complementarism, however, is a method he himself used very freely, whereby juxtapositions of complementary colors in the strict sense—yellow/purple, indigo/orange, red/blue-green—are sometimes applied to juxtapositions of large shapes painted in complementary colors, and sometimes limited to small applications. Typical of the former instance are such 1911 works as *The Street Enters the House* (cat. no. 7), *Simultaneous Visions* (cat. no. 8), and *The Forces of a Street*.[8] Typical of the latter are the works that came after, including *Materia* in which greens and oranges dominate. Paintings of this second period often feature juxtapositions of complementary colors in small areas, achieving chromatic shifts by the gradual insertion of marks of pure color, not necessarily complementary, alongside and within fields created by touches of another color that eventually disappears by being translated into the other color. For example, in *Materia*, green turns into yellow (fig. 68) or orange, white turns into red, pink into green, and so on. In fact, "with the use of pure-toned colors employed simultaneously, and through contrast, affinity, and gradations, we have created the DYNAMISM OF COLOR, which had previously been made static by the continuity of chiaroscuro."[9] The mutation of color within a surface constitutes its own peculiar chiaroscuro, one unlike traditional chiaroscuro, since what effects the passage of light over a form are colors used straight out of the tube, not mixtures with browns or blacks or other tints:

> *In* Principii scientifici del divisionismo, *Gaetano Previati notes that the red and*

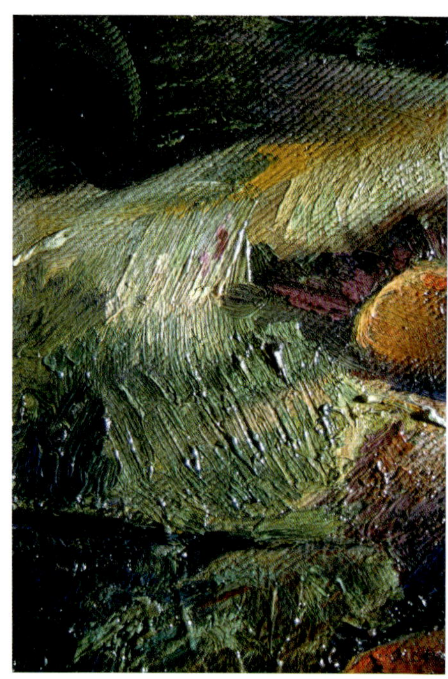
Fig. 70 Detail of hand and intersecting fingertips. Dense dashes and broken lines are superimposed over more fluid applications of a prevalently yellow-ocher tone that constitutes the background.

blue-green of the spectrum, which make white light when brought together, produce only an opaque gray when translated into colorants like cinnabar and emerald green. . . . The unbending application of scientific processes of this sort in an absolutely intuitive field such as art, produced oppressive grays and monotony, embalming objects and discouraging the artists and the public. We instead bring to the distribution of color an intuitive disorder concordant with the explanatory disorder of the universe, and we obtain results whose technical and sentimental value is utterly new! Putting mixed colors on the canvas means losing 75% of the luminosity compared with using pure colors.[10]

Materia, in many ways the summa of the artist's ideas, also shows the "intuitive disorder" with which Boccioni treats color—that is, according to his own intuition, freely, almost disdainfully, continuously modeling theory on practice, on the materials of painting.[11] In fact while, on the whole, the color in *Materia* tends to be pure, not mixed on the pallet, there are nevertheless other applications of paint (fig. 69) where the brushstroke is tainted with other tones of the same color (a darker green on a lighter green, etc.), and instances in which the brushstroke includes traces of colors belonging to different ranges of the spectrum. If sometimes it is possible that Boccioni used a poorly cleaned brush or painted over color that had not sufficiently dried, more frequently it seems as though, facing the difficulty of the work, he interpreted his theories with a certain freedom.

The entire painting is characterized by superimpositions of color layers, colors applied in marks painted with a flat brush or in disconnected or continuous strokes, and more rarely by dense, broken lines (fig. 70) applied with a round-pointed brush and perhaps with the use of the palette knife, applied mostly edgewise, as in certain works from the period from 1912 to 1914. The paint itself is generally very thick, due both to the multiple applications and to the use of a very laden brushstroke. The dense stroke also seems to have been chosen to enable the artist to conceal the parts that were changed for the last version, since what particularly stands out is the lower segment of the painting. Also of greater thickness are those passages corresponding to the lower seams of the canvas, which Boccioni tried to cover, and where one now sees two horizontal ridges in the surface of the paint (fig. 71). The brushstroke is thin essentially only for the figures of the horse, on the left, and the man, on the right, applied with a variety of ocher in rather liquid layers.

In *Materia*, the mother's hands and forearms display most of this entire range of techniques, and they also show the highest concentration of different colors, of chromatic "disorder" (figs. 72–74). The hands—whose placement at the center of the painting was only made possible by the expansion of the canvas— became for Boccioni an emblematic nucleus of the work's development. In their plastic solidity and chromatic explosion, the hands present themselves as subject matter, as an image of power—the chromatic power, of making, of shaping, sewing, gathering, or more simply of being—standing in front of the viewer.

Stretching under the hands is a broad, dark area, the skirt, in which black was used in abundance. It was the destruction of "the continuity of [traditional] chiaroscuro" that led Boccioni to reevaluate black, which naturalistic-scientific theory claims does not exist in nature but is only an expression of the absence of emitted or reflected light. Instead of using black to decrease the luminosity of other colors, he used it as a "color in

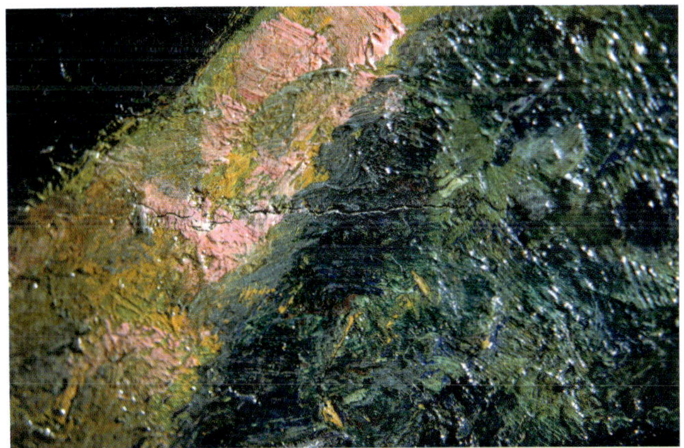

Fig. 71 Detail of upper part of semicircle on the lower left. The density of color prevents the woof of canvas to be visible, while the crackle corresponding to the seam is evident.

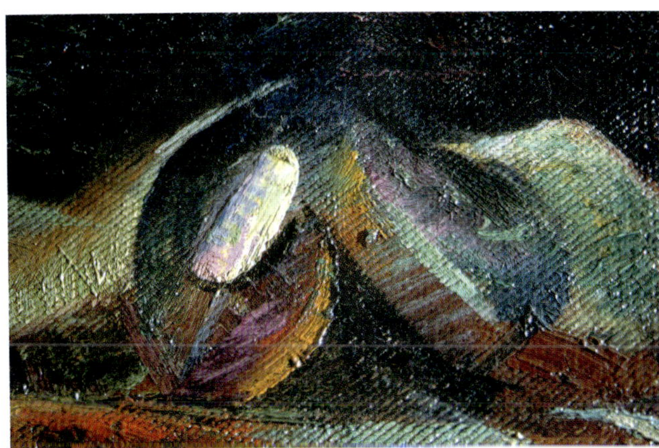

Fig. 72 Detail of thumbs shows their startling concentration of colors.

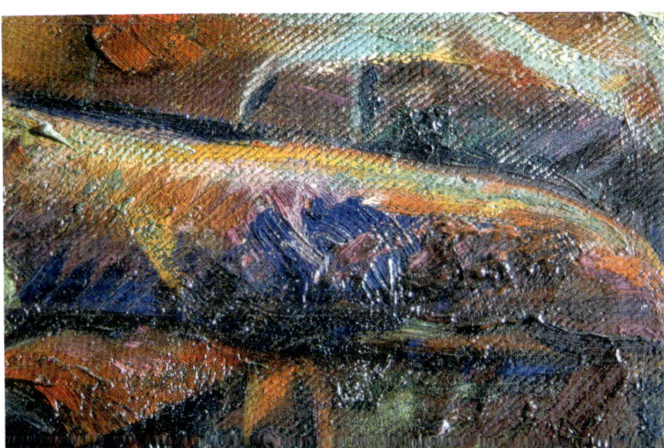

Fig. 73 Detail of fingers. The multiple layers of color are evident as is, in part, the use of black contours, then sometimes covered over, that Boccioni typically employed to delimit or put forms into relief.

itself," so that, by combining black with "the other colors vibrating on the canvas by affinity or contrast," the painting might achieve "a maximum chromatic dynamism . . . against the darkness, the grays and iciness of the Cubists, a violent, exasperated tonality obtained by pure colors."[12] The skirt's blackness is rendered vibrant by the brownish-purple strokes and blue-green hues, perhaps in a thin layer, and lightened by blue touches (fig. 75).

The fact that the skirt was not initially conceived to be so dark can be deduced not only from photographs taken before the final revisions were made (e.g., fig. 26) — in which the skirt and the lower part of the painting look generally brighter than they do today — but also from infrared images, which show the blues to be lighter and possibly painted directly onto the light-colored preparation of the canvas (fig. 76).[13] It remains to be determined whether Boccioni made any overall changes in the painting's tones together with the modifications of the lower left-hand section and of the chimneys in the upper left. Indeed, the use in some areas of the painting of an application that is quick and muddy, almost without pure colors, and similar to that employed in the semicircular form (fig. 77) added at the bottom, leaves this hypothesis open to discussion.

In terms of the pigments, it would seem, because of certain similarities with studied works,[14] that, together with zinc white, the artist used cobalt blue, chrome green or copper-based green, iron-based browns, and very few lakes. The only red that appears, the trapezoidal field to the right of the mother's head, is probably vermilion (cinnabar red), characteristically bright.

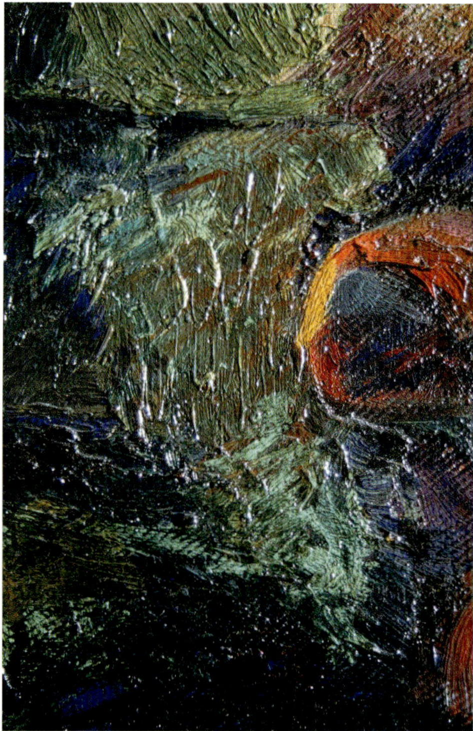

Fig. 74 Detail of hand and intersecting fingertips. An example of Boccioni's unconstrained use of color. Many, often diverse hues are grouped, and black and blue is used to diminish the tone of the back of the hand so as to obtain the shadow. The hand's colors thus look mingled, the surface watered, and the fingers, executed for the most part with superimposed, pure colors, stand out by contrast.

Fig. 75 Detail of mother's skirt. The black of the background, painted on a yellowish base, is darkened with greenish veilings and then made vibrant thanks to the use of violets, browns, and blues.

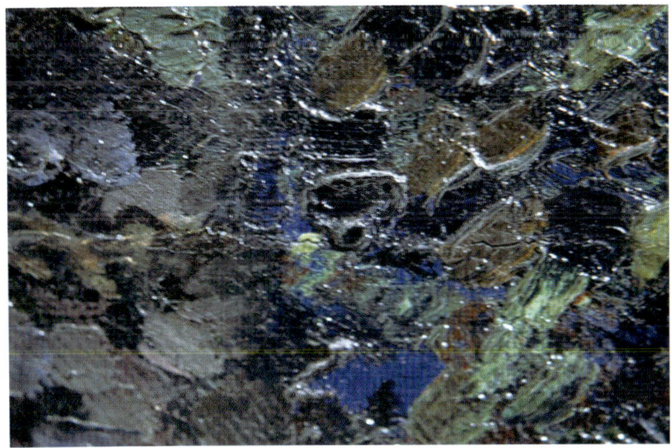

Fig. 76 Infrared detail of lower right, at the height of first seam of the canvas. The color, not always pure, is applied in abundantly superimposed daubs and without following any direction, thus probably with a fast or hurried execution.

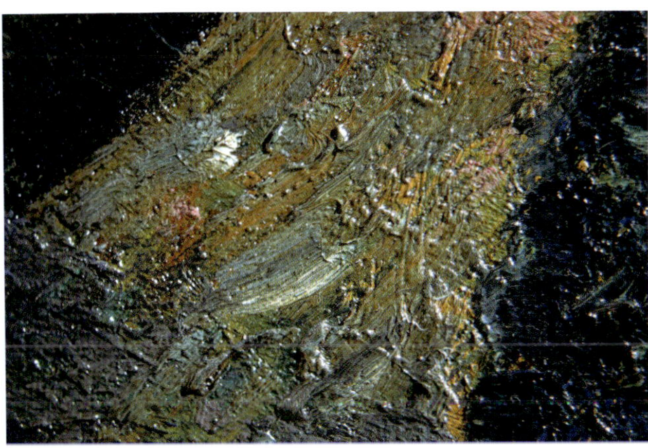

Fig. 77 Infrared detail of border of semicircle on lower left. In this zone, subject to modifications realized by Boccioni as period photographs indicate, the brushstrokes are decidedly more muddy, the color is not pure, and it is rapidly applied.

Notes

I thank Dr. Giovanni Villa of the University of Bologna for the color photographs and Dr. Nicola Ludwig of the Istituto di Fisica Generale Applicata of Milan, with whom I conducted the reflectographic analyses.

1 Boccioni to Carlo Carrà, Berlin, April 12, 1912, in Zeno Birolli, ed., *Umberto Boccioni: Gli scritti editi e inediti* (Milan: Feltrinelli, 1971), p. 353.

2 Boccioni, "La pittura futurista," in Zeno Birolli, ed., *Umberto Boccioni: Altri inediti e apparati scritti* (Milan: Feltrinelli, 1972), pp. 11–29.

3 Boccioni, *Pittura e scultura futuriste (Dinamismo plastico)* (Milan: Edizioni Futuriste di "Poesia," 1914), pp. 151–52. The book, which the artist completed working on in 1913, was published in 1914.

4 See Giovanni Rossi, "Osservazioni tecniche sull'esecuzione di *Materia*," in Laura Mattioli Rossi, ed., *Boccioni 1912 Materia*, exh. cat. (Milan: Mazzotta, 1995).

5 Boccioni, *Pittura e scultura futuriste*, p. 265.

6 Ibid., pp. 246, 245.

7 Ibid., pp. 248–49.

8 Maurizio Calvesi and Ester Coen, *Boccioni: L'opera completa* (Milan: Electa, 1983), no. 747.

9 Umberto Boccioni, "Per l'ignoranza italiana: Sillabario Pittorico," *Lacerba*, August 15, 1913, in Birolli, *Gli scritti editi e inediti*, p. 59.

10 Boccioni, "La Pittura futurista," p. 20.

11 See Boccioni, *Pittura e scultura futuriste*, p. 152: "Ours is a search for the definitive in the sequence of states of intuition."

12 Ibid., pp. 249–50.

13 For a careful reading of the infrared tests, see my essay "Reflectographic Analysis of Some Paintings in the Mattioli Collection," in Flavio Fergonzi, *The Mattioli Collection: Masterpieces of the Italian Avant-garde* (Milan: Skira, 2002), pp. 414–15.

14 A study of the colors used by Boccioni was recently conducted in Milan with non-invasive methods on three works from the years 1912–14. The results were collected in *Umberto Boccioni: Analisi tecnica di Donna al caffè, Il bevitore, Sotto la pergola a Napoli* (Milan: Civiche Raccolte d'Arte di Milano, 2001), pp. 48–58.

Monographs and Books

Antliff, Mark. *Inventing Bergson: Cultural Politics and the Parisian Avant-Garde*. Princeton: Princeton University Press, 1993.

Apollonio, Umbro, ed. *Futurist Manifestos*. Translated by Robert Brain et al. New York: Viking, 1973.

Argan, Julio Carlo, and Maurizio Calvesi. *Boccioni*. Rome: De Luca, 1953.

Ballo, Guido. *Boccioni: La vita e l'opera*. Milan: Il Saggiatore, 1964; 2d ed., 1982.

Bellini, Paolo. *Catalogo completo dell'opera grafica di Umberto Boccioni*. Milan: Salamon e Augustoni, 1972.

Berghaus, Günter. *Futurism and Politics: Between Anarchist Rebellion and Fascist Reaction 1909–1944*. Providence: Berghahn, 1996.

Birolli, Zeno, ed. *Umberto Boccioni: Gli scritti editi e inediti*. Milan: Feltrinelli, 1971.

———. *Umberto Boccioni: Altri inediti e appariti critici*. Milan: Feltrinelli, 1972.

———. *Umberto Boccioni: Racconto critico*. Turin: Einaudi, 1983.

Boccioni, Umberto. *Pittura e scultura futuriste (Dinamismo plastico)*. Milan: Edizioni Futuriste di "Poesia," 1914.

Bruno, Gianfranco. *L'opera completa di Boccioni*. Milan: Rizzoli, 1969.

Calvesi, Maurizio, and Ester Coen. *Boccioni: L'opera completa*. Milan: Electa, 1983.

Calvesi, Maurizio. *Der Futurismus*. Cologne: Taschen, 1987.

Carrà, Carlo. *Boccioni*. Milan: n.p., 1916.

Carrà, Massimo, ed. *Estetica e arte futuriste di Umberto Boccioni (1946)*. Milan: Il Balcone, 1973.

Carrieri, Raffaele. *Il futurismo*. Milan: Edizioni del Milione, 1961.

———. *Pittura scultura d'avanguardia (1890–1950) in Italia*. Milan: Edizioni della Conchiglia, 1950; 2d ed., 1960.

Crispolti, Enrico. *Il mito della macchina a altri temi del futurismo*. Trapani: Celebes, 1969.

———. *Storia e critica del futurismo*. Bari: Laterza, 1986.

De Grada, Raffaele. *Boccioni: Il mito del moderno*. Milan: Edizioni per il Club del Libro, 1962.

Drudi Gambillo, Maria, and Teresa Fiori. *Archivi del futurismo*, 2 vols. Rome: De Luca, 1958 and 1962.

Falqui, Enrico. *Bibliografia e iconografia del futurismo*. Florence: Casa Editrice le Lettere, 1988.

Fergonzi, Flavio. *The Mattioli Collection: Masterpieces of the Italian Avant-Garde*. Milan: Skira, 2003.

Gelli, Anna. *Le mostre dei pittori e scultori futuristi, 1910–1911: Dalle lezioni tenute dal prof. Marco Rosci, anno accademico 1986–1987, Facoltà di Magistero, Università di Torino*. Turin: Tirrenia, 1987.

Henderson, Linda Dalrymple. *The Fourth Dimension and Non-Euclidean Geometry in Modern Art*. Princeton: Princeton University Press, 1983.

Lista, Giovanni. *Cinema e fotografia futurista*. Milan: Skira, 2001.

———. *Futurism*. Translated by Susan Wise. Paris: Terrail, 2001.

Longhi, Roberto. *Scultura futurista: Boccioni*. Florence: Libreria de "La Voce," 1914.

Marinetti, F. T. *La grande Milano tradizionale e futurista: Una sensibilità italiana nata in Egitto*. Edited by L. De Matia. Milan: Mondadori, 1969.

———. *Let's Murder the Moonshine: Selected Writings*. Edited by R. W. Flint. Translated by R. W. Flint and Arthur A. Coppotelli. With preface by Marjorie Perloff. Los Angeles: Sun and Moon Classics, 1991.

Martin, Marianne W. *Futurist Art and Theory*. Oxford: Clarendon, 1968.

Masterpieces from the Gianni Mattioli Collection. With essays by Laura Mattioli Rossi and Emily Braun. Venice: Peggy Guggenheim Collection, 1997.

Perloff, Marjorie. *The Futurist Moment: Avant-Garde, Avant-Guerre, and the Language of Rupture*. Chicago: University of Chicago Press, 1986.

Poggi, Christine. *In Defiance of Painting: Cubism, Futurism, and the Invention of Collage*. New Haven: Yale University Press, 1992.

Salaris, Claudia. *Bibliografia del futurismo, 1909–1944*. Rome: Riuniti, 1985.

Ilaria Schiaffini, *Umberto Boccioni: Stati d'animo. Teoria e pittura*. Milan: Silvana, 2002.

Schulz-Hoffmann, Carla. *Umberto Boccioni—Volumi orizzontali*. Munich: Hirmer, 1981.

Tallarico, Luigi, ed. *Boccioni cento anni*. Rome: Volpe, 1982.

Tisdall, Caroline, and Angelo Bozzolla. *Futurism*. London: Thames and Hudson, 1977.

Exhibition Catalogues (chronological)

Mostra d'estate in Palazzo Pesaro a Venezia. Rooms 1 and 2, *Mostra collettiva di Umberto Boccioni*. With text by F. T. Marinetti. Venice: Ca' Pesaro, 1910.

Les Peintres futuristes italiens. With preface by Boccioni, Carlo Carrà, Luigi Russolo, Giacomo Balla, and Gino Severini. Paris: Galerie Bernheim-Jeune, 1912. After being shown February 5–24, 1912, in Paris, the group Futurist exhibition traveled and other editions were published: *Exhibition of Works by the Italian Futurist Painters*, Sackville Gallery, London, March; *Zweite Ausstellung: Die Futuristen*, Galerie Der Sturm, Berlin, April 12–May 15; *Les Peintres futuristes italiens*, Galerie Georges Giroux, Brussels, May 20–June 1; *I Esposizione di pittura futurista*, Teatro Costanzi, Rome, organized by Galleria Giosi, opened February 11, 1913; *Les Peintres et les sculpteurs futuristes italiens*, Rotterdamsche Kunstkring, March 18–July 15 (at which time, Ardengo Soffici first joined the other Futurists in signing the preface); *Esposizione di pittura futurista di "Lacerba,"* Galleria Gonnelli, Florence, November 30, 1913–January 15, 1914.

1re Exposition de sculpture futuriste du peintre et sculpteur futuriste Boccioni. With preface by Umberto Boccioni. Paris: Galerie La Boëtie, 1913. The exhibition was shown June 20–July 16, 1913, during an interval in itinerary of the group Futurist exhibition cited above for the catalogue *Les Peintres futuristes italiens.*

Grande esposizione Boccioni. With texts by Umberto Boccioni and F. T. Marinetti. Milan: Galleria Centrale d' Arte (Palazzo Cova), 1916. Boccioni had died on August 17, 1916, and this memorial exhibition was shown December 28, 1916–January 14, 1917.

Umberto Boccioni. Edited by F. T. Marinetti. With text by Umberto Boccioni. Milan: Bottega di Poesia, 1924.

Terza Biennale romana—Esposizione internazionale di belle arti. Room 7, *Mostra retrospettiva di Umberto Boccioni*, curated by F. T. Marinetti. Rome: 1925.

Soby, James Thrall, and Alfred H. Barr, Jr., eds. *Twentieth Century Italian Art.* New York: Museum of Modern Art, 1949.

Casou, Jean, and Paolo D'Ancona, eds. *Exposition d'art moderne italien.* Paris: Musée National d'Art Moderne, 1950. Exhibition traveled to London, where an English edition of the catalogue was published as *Modern Italian Art.* London: Tate Gallery, 1950.

Futurismo e pittura metafisica. Zurich: Kunsthaus Zurich, 1950.

XXX Esposizione biennale internazionale d'arte. Rooms 1 and 4, *Mostra storica del futurismo*, curated by Guido Ballo. Venice: 1960.

Taylor, Joshua C., ed. *Futurism.* New York: Museum of Modern Art, 1961.

______. *The Graphic Work of Umberto Boccioni.* New York: Museum of Modern Art, 1961.

XXXIII Esposizione biennale internazionale d'arte. Rooms 1–4, *Retrospettiva di Umberto Boccioni*, curated by Guido Ballo. Venice: 1966.

Ballo, Guido, et. al. *Boccioni e il suo tempo.* Milan: Palazzo Reale, 1973.

Cachin-Nora, Françoise, ed. *Le futurisme 1909–1916.* Paris: Musée National d'Art Moderne, 1973.

Futurism: A Modern Focus, The Lydia and Harry Lewis Winston Collection. New York: Solomon R. Guggenheim Museum, 1973.

Futurismus 1909–1917. Düsseldorf: Städtische Kunsthalle Düsseldorf, 1974.

Ballo, Guido, ed. *Boccioni a Milano.* Milan: Palazzo Reale, 1982.

Calvesi, Maurizio, Ester Coen, and Antonella Greco, eds. *Boccioni prefuturista.* Milan: Electa, 1983.

Hanson, Anne Coffin, ed. *The Futurist Imagination.* New Haven: Yale University Art Gallery, 1983.

Coen, Ester, Liscio Magagnato, and Guido Perocco. *Boccioni a Venezia. Dagli anni romani alla mostra d'estate a Ca' Pesaro.* Milan: Mazzotta, 1985.

Hulten, Pontus, ed. *Futurismo & Futurismi.* Venice: Palazzo Grassi, 1986.

Coen, Ester, ed. *Boccioni: A Retrospective.* New York: Metropolitan Museum of Art and Harry N. Abrams, 1988.

Braun, Emily, ed. *Italian Art in the Twentieth Century: Painting and Sculpture 1900–1988.* London: Royal Academy of Arts; Munich: Prestel, 1989.

Mattioli Rossi, Laura, ed. *Boccioni 1912 Materia.* Milan: Mazzotta, 1991 (edition for Galleria dello Scudo, Verona); and Milan: Mazzotta, 1995 (edition for Fondazione Antonio Mazzotta, Milan).

Rylands, Philip, and Fred Licht, eds. *Umberto Boccioni: Dinamismo di un cavallo in corsa + case.* Venice: Peggy Guggenheim Collection, 1996.

Crispolti, Enrico, ed. *Futurismo 1909–1944: Arte, architettura, spettacolo, grafica, letteratura . . .* Milan: Mazzotta, 2001.

Der Lärm der Strasse: Italienischer Futurismus 1909–1918. Hannover: Sprengel Museum Hannover and Milan: Mazzotta, 2001.

Lista, Giovanni, ed. *Futurism and Photography.* London: Merrell in association with the Estorick Collection of Modern Italian Art, 2001.

Il Futurismo a Milano. Anticipazioni per il nuovo museo d'Arte Moderna e Contemporanea. Padiglione d'Arte Contemporanea, Milan. Milan: Edizioni Gabriele Mazzotta, 2002.

Articles and Essays (chronological)

Cajumi, E. "Scultura futurista." *Giornale di Sicilia* (Palermo), December 10–11, 1913.

Cecchi, Emilio. "Esposizione romana—La mostra futurista." *Il Marzocco* (Florence), March 23, 1913.

Longhi, Roberto. "I pittori futuristi." *La Voce* (Florence), April 10, 1913.

Warnod, André. "Les sculptures futuristes de Boccioni, les Tableaux de Thomas Couture." *Comoedia* (Paris), June 21, 1913.

"Dynamism or Dynamite? More Futuristic Puzzles." *The Sketch* (London), April 29, 1914.

Sarfatti Grassini, Margherita. "L'opera di Umberto Boccioni." *Gli Avvenimenti* (Milan), September 24, 1916.

Marinetti, F. T. "Il pittore e scultore futurista Boccioni." *Il Primato artistico italiano* (Rome-Milan-Naples) 1 (October 1919).

Severini, Gino. "Ricordi su Boccioni." *L'Esame artistico e letterario* (Milan), no. 6 (July 1933).

"Un Demi-siècle d'art italien." Introduction by Christian Zervos. *Cahiers d'Art* (Paris), no. 1 (1950).

Petrie, Brian. "Boccioni and Bergson." *The Burlington Magazine* (London) 116 (March 1974), pp. 140–47.

Poggi, Christine. "Dreams of Metallized Flesh: Futurism and the Masculine Body." *Modernism/modernity* (Baltimore) 4, no. 3 (September 1997), pp. 19–43.

Spate, Virginia. "Mother and Son: Boccioni's Painting and Sculpture 1906–15." In Terry Smith, ed., *In Visible Touch: Modernism and Masculinity.* Chicago: University of Chicago Press, 1997.

Antliff, Mark. "The Fourth Dimension and Futurism: A Politicized Space." *The Art Bulletin* (New York) 82, no. 4 (December 2000), pp. 720–33.

Henderson, Linda Dalrymple. "Vibratory Modernism: Boccioni, Kupka, and the Ether of Space." In Bruce Clarke and Linda Dalrymple Henderson, eds., *From Energy to Information: Representations in Science and Technology, Art, and Literature.* Stanford: Stanford University Press, 2002.

Photo Credits

BY CATALOGUE NUMBER

1, 32: Giuseppe Schiavinotto; 3: Giovanni Amoretti, Parma; 4, 5: Luca Carrà, Milan; 6: Tarcisio Dal Gal, Milan; 7: Michael Herling/ Aline Gwose, Sprengel Museum Hannover; 8: Medienzentrum Wuppertal, Antje Zeis-Loi; 9, 39: digital image © 2002 The Museum of Modern Art, New York; 11: photo © The Art Institute of Chicago, All rights reserved; 12: Robert Bayer, LAC AG Basel; 13: photo © Tate, London 2002; 15: Graydon Wood, 1994; 16, 18, 20, 30: David Heald; 17: Dorothy Zeidman; 19: Sally Ritts; 21, 22, 26, 33, 34, 36, 40: Saporetti, Milan; 24: Peter Schaelcchli Fotoatelier; 25: Larissa Soffientini; 27: Sergio Martucci; 28: Joachim Blauel; 35: Estorick Collection, London/Bridgeman Art Library; 37: Romulo Fialdini; 38: Video Grafica Scilacci.

BY FIGURE NUMBER

1: Christian Baur; 2: UK/Bridgeman Art Library; 3, 18, 27, 28, 31: Saporetti, Milan; 4: Graydon Wood; 5: Laboratorio Fotoradiografico Milano, Courtesy of Ministero per i Beni e le Attività Culturali; 6: digital image © 2002 The Museum of Modern Art/ Licensed by SCALA/Art Resource, NY; 7: CNAC/MNAM/Dist.Réunion des Musées Nationaux /Art Resource, NY; 8: Photothèque des Musées de la Ville de Paris, cliché P. Joffre; 10: Gerard Blot/C. Jean, photo © Réunion des Musées Nationaux/ Art Resource, NY; 11, 20–22: digital images © 2002 The Museum of Modern Art, New York; 12: Sergio Anelli, Milan; 14, 15, 16: Urs Siegenthaler and Reto Klink, Zürich 1999; 17, 46: Nicola Eccher, Trento; 23: Tonino Binda; 24, 26, 33, 35, 45: Ellen Labenski; 25: Luca Carrà, Milan; 29, 36–41, 51, 55, 56.1–.4, 56.6–.8, 57.1, 57.2, 57.4–.14, 58.1–.13, 59.1–.3, 59.6, 59.7, 60.1–.8, 60.10–.12: Vittorio Calore, Milan; 30: G. Cigolini; 32, 34, 48: Tarcisio Dal Gal, Milan; 43: Flavio Fergonzi; 47: Larissa Soffientini; 50: Caludio Franzini, Venice; 63: Jacopo Cima; 66: Sergio Martucci, Venice; 67–75: Gianluca Poldi and Giovanni Villa; 76 and 77: Gianluca Poldi.

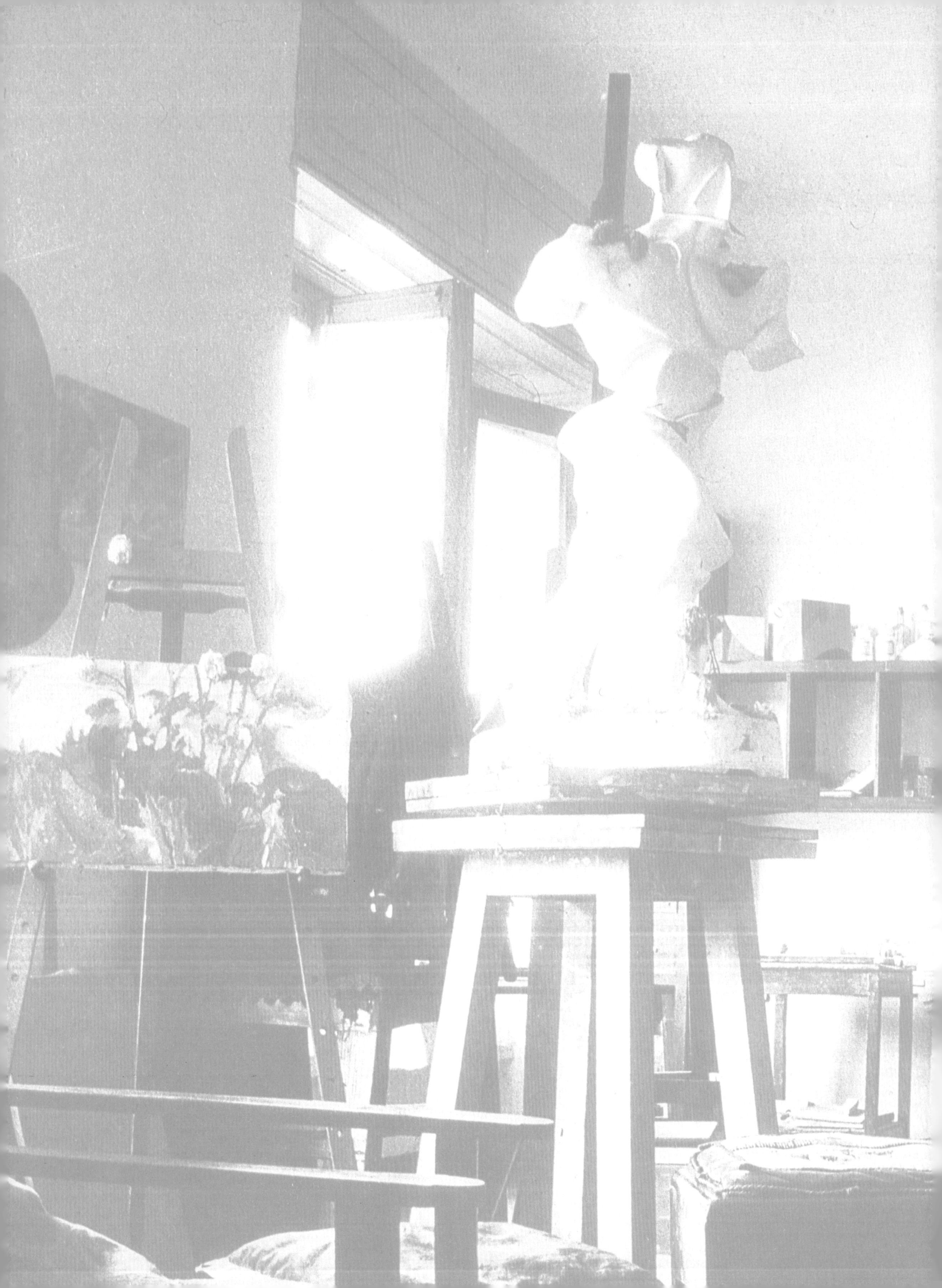